Dialect and Education:
Some European Perspectives

Multilingual Matters

MULTILINGUAL MATTERS 53
Series Editor: Derrick Sharp

Dialect and Education: Some European Perspectives

Edited by

Jenny Cheshire, Viv Edwards, Henk Münstermann and Bert Weltens

MULTILINGUAL MATTERS LTD
Clevedon · Philadelphia

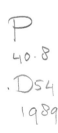

P
40.8
.D54
1989

Library of Congress Cataloging-in-Publication Data

Dialect and education
  (Multilingual matters: 53)
  Bibliography: p.
  Includes index.
  1. Language and education—Europe. 2. Dialectology.
3. Language planning—Europe. I. Cheshire, Jenny,
1946–   .II. Series.
P40.8.D54 1989   417'.2'094   88–34765

British Library Cataloguing in Publication Data

Dialect and education: Some European perspectives.
  (Multilingual matters: 53).
  1. Western Europe. Schools. Students.
Education. Implications of students' use of
dialects
I. Cheshire, Jenny
370.19'34

ISBN 1–85359–036–3
ISBN 1–85359–035–5 (pbk)

Multilingual Matters Ltd
Bank House, 8a Hill Road   &   242 Cherry Street
Clevedon, Avon BS21 7HH   Philadelphia, PA 19106–1906,
England   USA

Index compiled by Meg Davies (Society of Indexers)
Typeset by Photo·graphics, Honiton, Devon
Printed and bound in Great Britain by Short Run Press, Exeter

Contents

Preface

This collection of papers arose from the Workshop on Dialect and Education held at the Rolduc Conference Centre in Kerkrade, the Netherlands, from January 7–9, 1987. The Workshop was financed by the Economic and Social Research Council of the United Kingdom as part of a research project on British dialect grammar directed by Jenny Cheshire and Viv Edwards (ESRC project no. C-00-23-2264: 'The Survey of British Dialect Grammar'). The original aim of the workshop was to bring together researchers who had worked on similar problems in different European countries, so that we could 'pool resources', and benefit from each other's experiences; a further aim was to allow researchers in the field of dialect and education in Belgium, Denmark, West Germany and the Netherlands, whose work had not yet been widely disseminated in the English speaking world, to reach a wider audience. But when we received the responses to our invitations — early in 1985 — it became clear to us that many people were interested not just because they wanted to report their work to an English-speaking audience, but also because many of them thought it was time to revive interest in the educational problems which are posed by language variation, and which have yet to be resolved. We hope that this volume will help to revive that interest.

The chapters in this volume, then, represent a sample of the work which has been taking place in five European countries over a number of years. We are, of course, aware that there has been research in this field in other countries, besides those represented at the Workshop and in this volume, but we hope that this collection marks the beginning of a shared European perspective on the topic. Our aim has been to provide an historical perspective on this work, as well as to present more recent and previously unpublished research findings. In addition to the ten papers first presented at the Workshop, a further nine contributions have been invited to extend the scope of the volume and to give a more representative picture of research initiatives and classroom innovations in these five European countries (these nine are the two papers by Ammon; and the papers by Cheshire & Trudgill; Hagen; Jones; Rosenberg; van Calcar, van Calcar & de Jonge; Hollingworth and Williams).

One paper, 'Language in the Classroom' by Co van Calcar, Wim van Calcar and Coen de Jonge, deserves special mention here. Co van Calcar was killed in a tragic road accident in Paris in December, 1986. He was greatly missed at the Workshop three weeks later, and he will be greatly missed in the future. We feel privileged to be able to include this, his last piece of work, in the present volume.

The Editors
London/Nijmegen
March, 1988

1 Dialect and education in Europe: A general perspective

JENNY CHESHIRE, VIV EDWARDS, HENK
MÜNSTERMANN and BERT WELTENS

The issue of dialect and education is by no means a new one. It has sparked a great deal of heated debate in Europe and elsewhere for at least a century (see Hollingworth, 1977; and Hollingworth, this volume, Chapter 19), and there is little sign of any satisfactory resolution. The last 20 years has seen a rapid growth in serious study of the subject. In most cases, research has addressed local issues: linguists and educators have been slow to realise that many of the problems—and possible solutions to those problems—are common to many different situations in many different countries. This is particularly true within the United Kingdom. While researchers in Continental Europe have, to some extent, discussed ideas and pooled their experience, British researchers whose attention has been focussed more closely on developments in the English-speaking world than on the other side of the Channel and the North Sea, are only starting to discover the work of European colleagues and the potential for co-operation on a wider scale.

A quick review of the work presented in this volume makes it clear that there are a number of differences between the situation in Britain and elsewhere in Europe. The degree of mutual intelligibility between indigenous British dialects is almost certainly higher than is the case, for instance, in the Netherlands, Germany, France or Italy. The relationship with the standard is also a little different, with many European dialects enjoying greater status than British non-standard varieties. However, points of similarity are far more noteworthy and we hope to show that there is enough common ground to justify comparisons and co-operation.

An appreciation of this common ground depends, to a large extent, on an understanding of the social, political and linguistic history of the countries concerned. The aim of this introduction is therefore to provide a brief overview of the various issues which recur in discussions of dialect and schooling. Such a framework is essential if we are to be able to interpret the many disparate elements which have made up European research on language in education over the last two decades.

Linguistic Diversity in Europe

Although Europe is recognised as a linguistically diverse area, the extent of that diversity tends to be underestimated. Countries such as Belgium and Switzerland, which officially recognise more than one language within their frontiers, are the exception rather than the rule, and the picture which emerges from a rapid survey of the national languages of Europe is, at the very least, misleading. German, for instance, is spoken not only in the Federal Republic and East Germany and Austria, where it is recognised as the official language, but in Denmark, Belgium, France, Italy, Yugoslavia, Rumania, the USSR, Hungary, Czechoslovakia and Poland. Danes are normally assumed to speak Danish, but Denmark also has substantial German and Frisian speaking populations.

Nor is linguistic diversity restricted to multilingualism: there is considerable variation within the same language. In multilingual countries that share the standard language with neighbouring countries, e.g. Dutch in Belgium or German in Switzerland, the standard language has developed distinct regional standard varieties, at least in the spoken form. Thus a distinction can be made between standard Dutch as spoken in the Netherlands and 'Belgian Dutch' (cf. Van de Craen & Humblet, this volume, Chapter 2), a distinction which has much in common with that between 'British English' and 'U.S. English', except that in this case distinct national varieties have not been codified and officially sanctioned.

In other situations, where languages are spoken within a country but do not have official status, we are typically dealing with dialects of neighbouring standard languages. The fact that these situations are often the result of territorial conflict between adjacent countries does, of course, explain why these varieties have not received official recognition. A prime example is the (now) French region of Alsace where a German dialect, Alsatian, is spoken. Another well-documented case is the Hungarian-speaking rural community in Austria reported in Gal (1979). The varieties concerned are often forced into a position comparable to that normally associated with minority languages, such as Breton in France; Basque in France and Spain; Frisian in the Netherlands, Germany and Denmark; and and Welsh and Gaelic in Britain.

Dialect and Standard

Variation is also to be found within the same language in the same country. In Europe and, indeed, in other parts of the world, certain varieties have emerged over the centuries as standard languages. This process has been a lengthy one, often lasting for centuries and passing through a number of separate though often overlapping stages (see, for discussion, Haugen, 1966; Leith, 1983). In each case, one dialect came to be used as the dominant variety, particularly by the rich and powerful sections of society. There followed a period of elaboration in which the number of domains in which the new standard variety was used was greatly extended. Eventually, the standard language was codified, through the writing systems of the various countries, through dictionaries and grammars and, in some countries, through language academies.

The range of variation that exists within a single language differs from country to country, and also within different countries. Linguistic differences between dialects and the standard variety can exist at any or all linguistic levels: phonetic, phonological, prosodic, morphological, lexical, syntactic, or pragmatic. We have chosen not to discuss the various terminological and theoretical distinctions that could be made here, since they do not bear directly on the theme of this volume. For discussion of the terms 'language', 'dialect' and 'accent' we refer readers to Chambers & Trudgill (1980).

In some regions the linguistic differences between dialect and standard are relatively great, and 'bidialectal' speakers may switch from dialect to standard in different situations. Communities of this type have been termed 'divergent dialect communities' (see Trudgill, 1986). Often speakers see the varieties as distinct entities—they are, that is, 'focussed' (see Milroy, 1982; LePage & Tabouret-Keller, 1985) — so that they are able to respond to questionnaires asking which variety they use in different societal domains (see, for example, the research reported in Weltens & Sonderen, this volume, Chapter 9). In other regions there may be no awareness of 'dialect' as a distinct entity; speakers will not switch from dialect to standard in different situations, but instead will increase or decrease the relative frequencies of individual standard or non-standard linguistic features. Linguistic variation in communities of this type have been described for cities such as Norwich, in England (Trudgill, 1974) and New York (Labov,

1966); variation of this type also occurs within continental Europe; for example, in parts of Germany (see Barbour, 1987) and in the Netherlands, such as in Amsterdam and Rotterdam.

Linguists and other researchers have used different descriptive and theoretical frameworks to analyse this range of linguistic variation. The variationist framework, for example, based on the work of William Labov, is a quantitative approach which analyses the relative frequencies with which speakers use standard and non-standard variants. Chapter 11 in this volume by Williams adopts this approach. Other research traditions identify discrete varieties of standard and non-standard speech: traditional dialectology, for example, sees 'dialect' and 'standard' as distinct, though related, systems, such that there are speakers who can be considered to be speaking 'pure' dialect or 'classical' dialect. Chapters 7 and 14 by Ammon, and Chapter 3 by Jørgensen & Pedersen, show the influence of this tradition. Van de Craen & Humblet (Chapter 2), on the other hand, describe the linguistic variation that exists in Flanders as a continuum, along which they identify four major codes. Future collaborative research within Europe would doubtless benefit if we were all to use the same theoretical and descriptive framework; in the meantime, the research presented in this volume has to be seen as stemming from a number of different research traditions.

Despite differences in the nature of the linguistic relationship between dialect and standard, and differences in the way in which this relationship has been described by researchers, it is clear from the chapters presented here that there are shared educational implications for dialect speakers. For example, the elevation of one dialect to the status of a standard variety inevitably has consequences for the status of the non-standard varieties which remain. In divergent dialect communities, a kind of diglossic situation has emerged (see Ferguson, 1959; Fasold, 1985) in which the non-standard dialect is used in informal speech with family and friends, while the standard is reserved for more formal settings like school, or interactions with authority figures. While all speakers recognise the prestige of the standard variety, dialect speakers may feel that people who use non-standard speech are more sincere and trustworthy; and often consider standard speakers to be prissy and effeminate (cf. Giles & Powesland, 1975; Ammon, this volume, Chapters 7 and 14).

There is an important class dimension to this equation, since standard language speakers usually come from middle-class backgrounds and dialect speakers from working-class backgrounds. Within Europe there is, admittedly, important variation in this respect. In Britain, middle-class educated speakers, particularly in southern England, will often use only the standard variety —

or, at least, only standard grammar and vocabulary. In countries like Germany and the Netherlands, in contrast, middle-class speakers may well be bidialectal, speaking the dialect in addition to the standard. There is, often, none the less, an important correlation between language and class, particularly in urban areas, where the non-standard variety tends to be more closely associated with working-class families and the standard more closely with middle-class families. In an educational setting, dialect-speaking children are therefore subject to two conflicting forces: pressure from teachers to use the high status standard variety and pressure from peers not to abandon the variety which marks their own group identity.

Dialect and Education

A brief look at how the educational systems of Europe have dealt with the exigencies of promoting the standard variety reveals some striking similarities. The unchallenged position of the standard as the medium of education has seemed to necessitate savage and uncompromising attacks on the vernacular. Breton, Welsh and Gaelic speakers were subjected to ridicule and corporal punishment for the use of their mother tongues. Dutch teachers were led to believe that only standard speakers would be received into Heaven (Sturm, this volume, Chapter 20). Speakers of British non-standard dialects were characterised as having 'evil habits of speech' (Hollingworth, this volume, Chapter 19).

Early opposition to dialect needs to be seen in a broad historical context. The introduction of compulsory education was perceived by many as a moral crusade to educate the masses. In an atmosphere such as this, it is easy to understand how language could be equated with ignorance: the task of the educator was to eradicate the dialect in an attempt to ensure greater equality of educational opportunity. The absence of an adequate theory of language further ensured that educational policy makers and teachers would be swayed by widespread class and linguistic prejudice (Hollingworth, 1977).

However, the development of linguistics as an independent discipline during the 1940s and 1950s and the rapid growth of sociolinguistics in the 1960s and 1970s had important consequences for the stage on which the arguments about standard and non-standard speech were rehearsed. The first serious discussion about the relationship between language and educational success emerged in the work of the British sociologist, Basil Bernstein, throughout the 1960s. Bernstein postulated two polar codes—the 'elaborated' and the 'restricted' codes—and he argued that the different distribution of these codes might account for the evidence that working-class children tend to underachieve at all stages of education (see Bernstein, 1971–1975). Although Bernstein has strenuously denied that this was his intention, his work was widely interpreted in Britain, in North America and in Europe as suggesting that the standard language could be equated with the elaborated code and working-class non-standard dialects with the restricted code.

Bernstein's work has been attacked on a number of fronts. Jackson (1974), for instance, has pointed out that the theory of language codes is both untestable and unrelated to linguistic evidence. Writers such as Labov (1970), Stubbs (1976) and Trudgill (1975) have pointed to the lack of linguistic evidence and the fact that the brief examples which Bernstein uses are often invented or based on artificial test situations. Labov (1970), in particular, has suggested that Bernstein has failed to take into consideration the effect which situation can have on speech, showing how a child who appears 'non-verbal' in formal settings like school behaves as a 'normal' fluent speaker in other, less threatening situations.

A great deal of recent research has provided further evidence against the Bernsteinian stance. Writers such as Tizard & Hughes (1984) and Wells (1985, 1987) have shown that the main differences in language use occur not between middle and working-class children, but between home and school. At home, conversations are frequently longer and more equally balanced between adult and child; children ask more questions and spend more time in conversation with adults. None the less, the legacy of Bernstein lives on. The highly influential *Language for Life* (Bullock, 1975) advocates that health visitors should urge parents to 'bathe their children in language'. Tough (1985) talks in stereotypical terms of homes where children do not engage in conversation with adults and where children ask them questions only when seeking permission. Teacher attitudes in many countries reflect similar concerns (see, for instance, Dannequin, 1987, for France; and, in this volume, van Calcar *et al.*, Chapter 16, for the Netherlands, Van de Craen & Humblet, Chapter 2, for Belgium and Jørgensen & Pedersen, Chapter 3 for Denmark). The background to the development of language awareness programmes also reflects this concern (see Jones, this volume, Chapter 17).

The debate which developed as a result of the work of Bernstein signalled the drawing of the battle lines. On the one side were the supporters of the deficit hypothesis, mainly educationalists and psychologists, who considered that working-class non-standard dialects were inadequate for communication. On the other side were linguists, and others, who drew on the accumulated knowledge of several decades of descriptive language study and a growing appreciation of the complex interrelationships between language and society. They supported the difference hypothesis, which argues that all languages and dialects are perfectly regular, rule-governed systems and that while there are obvious *social* differences between language varieties, and the functions which they have traditionally fulfilled, there are no *linguistic* grounds for arguing that one variety is superior to another. This is a conflict which has periodically reared its ugly head in various forms in various countries ever since. If we are to understand why this should be the case, we need to move beyond the observable linguistic phenomena to take into account the wider political context in which the debate is situated.

It has to be acknowledged that the linguists' doctrine of equality, which holds that all varieties are, in some important sense, felt to be equal to one another, has ideological rather than scientific status (cf. Hymes, 1972; Graddol & Swann, 1988). It is very doubtful whether this position is open to empirical investigation (for discussion, see Hudson, 1983). It is, however, an observable fact that whenever the work of linguists challenges entrenched linguistic and social attitudes it provokes extremely hostile reactions. One such example is the legal case which forced the Ann Arbor Education Board to officially recognise Black English as the home and community language of many of its students (cf. Labov, 1982). Another example was the controversy surrounding the publication in the United Kingdom of John Honey's (1983) pamphlet, 'The Language Trap'. Honey's basic position was that the doctrine of equality espoused by linguists and sociolinguists has contributed to the declining moral and educational standards in British schools: attempts to encourage the use of non-standard varieties in the classroom are having the effect of denying children access to the standard language, which would allow them to be socially mobile. The pamphlet is ill-informed about linguistics and sociolinguistics; Graddol & Swann (1988) suggest that Honey's argument is best read as a contribution to the political debate, showing how his pamphlet was used by the political Right in a wide ranging political agenda.

Organisation of the Book

The research reported in this book can only be appreciated against the historical, social and political backcloth to language and education that we have sketched above. Part I contains brief national perspectives on the 'linguistic landscapes' of each of the five countries represented at the Kerkrade Workshop, and on what is known about the problems of dialect in education in those countries. Part II contains reports of research that has been carried out into various aspects of the problem, such as the underachievement of dialect speakers in school; teachers' attitudes towards dialect and standard; teachers' responses to dialect in school work and in classroom interaction. This research was carried out at different times during the period 1972–87, and the different contributions reflect the different prevailing intellectual climates during that period. Some of the early research was carried out at a time when Bernstein's ideas were at their most influential, and it attempted to put his theories to empirical test; some took place during the height of the linguistic difference/linguistic deficit debate, and it places itself clearly within the 'difference' camp. We present the research reports in chronological order, so that the historical perspective can be clearly seen. Perhaps the most striking aspect of the research is that although it was carried out at different times and within different intellectual traditions, it shares a common concern: dialect speakers continue to underachieve at school, and a realistic remedy for this has yet to be found. Part III contains papers reporting on some practical initiatives at implementing research insights in the classroom; again, these papers are presented in chronological order. Part IV contains typical examples of what happens when (socio)linguists embark on discussions on language in society. Finally, a 'Postscript' attempts to sum up what we have learned so far, and offers a view on where we should be directing our efforts now.

The focus for the present volume is, of course, *dialect* in education. On occasions, however, the discussion has broadened to include *languages* other than the standard. One such example is the inclusion of Frisian (cf. Wilts, Chapter 18; and Hagen, Chapter 4). The Frisian situation receives attention not because we feel the educational questions associated with it to be any more important than, for instance, those of Welsh in Wales or Gaelic in Scotland, but because the distribution of Frisian speakers across Dutch, Danish and German borders makes it a subject of concern for several European countries. On other occasions, discussion extends to the languages of ethnic minority communities within Europe (cf. Giesbers *et al.*, Chapter 15; Edwards, Chapter 21; Hollingworth, Chapter 19; Jones, Chapter 17; Sturm, Chapter 20). We believe that, if progress is to be made within the vitally important area of language in education, it is essential that links should be made between the position of indigenous dialect speakers and the more recently arrived linguistic minority communities.

This is, inevitably, a somewhat disparate collection of papers, representing as it does the research findings and the views of people working in different countries, at different times, and in different research traditions. We think, however, that although there are differences in their approach, their common theme provides a unity. Despite the research that has been carried out and the practical initiatives that have been devised, the problem of dialect in education still exists in schools throughout Europe. There are signs that interest in this important area of research is beginning to revive in Europe (see for example, Hagen, 1987; and Ammon & Cheshire, 1989); we hope that the publication of this volume will contribute to that revival. We also hope that there will be further collaboration between teachers, researchers and educationists within Europe on what is after all a common and vitally important concern for all our countries.

References

AMMON, U. and CHESHIRE, J. (eds) 1989 Dialect and School. *Sociolinguistica* 3.

BARBOUR, S. 1987 Dialects and the teaching of a standard language: some West German work. *Language in Society* 16, 227–43.

BERNSTEIN, B. 1971–1975 *Class, Codes and Control*. Volumes 1–3. London: Routledge & Kegan Paul.

BULLOCK, SIR A. 1975 *A Language for Life*. London: HMSO.

CHAMBERS, J.K. and TRUDGILL, P. 1980 *Dialectology*. Cambridge: Cambridge University Press.

DANNEQUIN, C. 1987 Les Enfants Baillonnés (Gagged Children): the teaching of French as mother tongue in Elementary School. *Language and Education* 1, 15–32.

FASOLD, R. 1985 *The Sociolinguistics of Society*. Oxford: Blackwell.

FERGUSON, C.A. 1959 Diglossia. *Word* 15, 325–40.

GAL, S. 1979 *Language Shift: Social Determinants of Linguistic Change in Bilingual Austria*. New York: Academic Press.

GILES, H. and POWESLAND, P.F. 1975 *Speech Style and Social Evaluation*. London: Academic Press.

GRADDOL, D. and SWANN, J. 1988 Trapping linguists: an analysis of linguists' responses to John Honey's pamphlet 'The Language Trap'. *Language and Education* 2, 95–111.

HAGEN, A.M. 1987 Dialect speaking and school education in Western Europe. *Sociolinguistica* 1, 61–79.

HAUGEN, E. 1966 Dialect, language, nation. *American Anthropologist* 68, 922–35.

HOLLINGWORTH, B. 1977 Dialect in school — an historical note. *Durham and Newcastle Research Review* 8, 15–20.

HONEY, J. 1983 *The Language Trap: Race, Class and the 'Standard English' Issue in British Schools*. London: National Council for Educational Standards.

HUDSON, D. 1983 *Linguistic Equality*. Congress of Languages in Education Working Paper No. 1. London: CLIE.

HYMES, D. 1972 Review of 'Noam Chomsky' by John Lyons. *Language* 48, 416–27.

JACKSON, L. 1974 The myth of elaborated and restricted code. *Higher Education Review* 6(2), 47, 49, 65.

LABOV, W. 1966 *The Social Stratification of English in New York City*. Washington, D.C.: Center for Applied Linguistics.

—— 1970 The logic of non-standard English. In N. KEDDIE (ed.), *Tinker, Tailor. . . The Myth of Cultural Deprivation*. Harmondsworth: Penguin. pp. 21–66.

——1982 Objectivity and commitment in linguistic science: the case of the Black English trial in Ann Arbor. *Language in Society* 11, 165–201.

LEITH, D. 1983 *A Social History of English*. London: Routledge & Kegan Paul.

LePAGE, R.B. and TABOURET-KELLER, A. 1985 *Acts of Identity*. London: Cambridge University Press.

MILROY, L. 1982 Social network and linguistic focusing. In S. ROMAINE (ed.), *Sociolinguistic Variation in Speech Communities*. London: Arnold. pp. 141–52.

STUBBS, M. 1976 *Language, Schools and Classrooms*. London: Methuen.

TIZARD, B. & HUGHES, M. 1984 *Young Children Learning*. London: Fontana.

TOUGH, J. 1985 *Talk Two*. London: Onyx Press.

TRUDGILL, P. 1974 *The Social Differentiation of English in Norwich*. Cambridge: Cambridge University Press.

——1975 *Accent, Dialect and the School*. London: Edward Arnold.

——1986 *Dialects in Contact*. Oxford: Blackwell.

WELLS, G. 1985 *Language Development in the Pre-School*. Cambridge: Cambridge University Press.

——1987 *The Meaning Makers: Children Learning Language and Using Language to Learn*. London: Hodder & Stoughton.

Part I
Dialect in education: Some national perspectives

2 Dialect and education in Belgium

PETE VAN DE CRAEN and ILSE HUMBLET

Introduction

This chapter offers a survey of the position of the dialects in Dutch-speaking classrooms in Belgian primary schools. Starting from a brief description of the language situation in the Dutch-speaking part of Belgium, often referred to as Flanders, attention is focussed on the present-day language situation in the schools and classrooms. In fact, this situation is a 'blue-print' of the linguistic landscape of the area. In Flanders, dialect forms an integrated part of daily interaction patterns and this is reflected in the way dialect is used in schools and classrooms. Moreover, this variation clearly follows regular patterns and plays a highly significant role in the relations among teachers, among pupils, and between teachers and pupils. Next, the attitudes of pupils, teachers and educational authorities toward language variation is discussed, as well as the educational implications to be drawn from this.

The Language Situation in Flanders

To avoid any misunderstanding, it is first necessary to point out the difference between standard Dutch as it is spoken in the Netherlands, and standard Dutch as it is spoken in the Dutch-speaking part of Belgium,[1] since this has proved to be quite a mystery to non-Dutch speakers, professional linguists and laypeople alike. The difference can best be compared to that between American English and British English, i.e. there are clear differences in pronunciation, certain lexical items and expressions, but within what is considered to be one and the same language. What is different, however, is the evolution of each of the two varieties. Since the

13

Revolt of the Netherlands in the sixteenth century and the subsequent separation of the north and the south from the seventeenth century onwards, the evolution of Dutch has been restricted in the south. It had almost no official status and French took over as the official language. In the north, standardisation went its natural course, mainly influenced by dialects from the province of Holland. In Flanders, the linguistic situation changed only towards the end of the nineteenth century[2] when, gradually, Dutch regained its position as an official language in matters of administration, education, etc. However, it is only from the 1960s onwards that a true natural standardisation process has been taking place.[3] Needless to say, this particular evolution has had a number of consequences on the linguistic level which, today, are still very much part of the linguistic landscape of Flanders.

Linguistic variants in Flanders can best be described as a linguistic continuum with four major codes.[4]

1. *Regional dialect (RD)*. Considered as an omnipresent code albeit with differences along lines of age, social and geographic origin, and education.

2. *Umgangssprache (U)*.[5] An intermediate variant between regional dialect and Belgian Dutch, based mainly on the structure of the dialect.

3. *Belgian Dutch (BD)*. A kind of typical Flemish variant of the standard language spoken by many Flemings in various circumstances, yet not considered as their standard (cf. Geerts Nootens & Van den Broeck, 1978). This code lacks some of the characteristics usually attributed to standard languages. There is no codification, no dictionaries or grammar, no leading group of speakers and no 'centre of gravity', although Brabant has frequently been documented as such (cf. Goossens, 1970; Deprez, 1985).

4. *Standard Dutch (SD)*. The highly prestigious national language based on the same linguistic norms as in the Netherlands, but mastered by proportionally fewer people in Belgium than in the Netherlands.

It should be stressed that this continuum is far from being a stable one and that, although the north and the south refer to the same linguistic norms, a number of differences will always be likely to occur, since both speech communities are situated in different countries and develop different linguistic contacts (cf. Jaspaert, 1986a).

Another feature of the Flemish language situation has to be stressed. While the northern norm has been held up as a model, speakers of standard

Dutch in Flanders have developed a considerable amount of linguistic insecurity. This has led to a discrepancy between what people think is good Dutch, i.e. norm consciousness, and what they actually use, i.e. pragmatic consciousness. This double standard is the key to the understanding of the language situation in the school system.

Language Variation in the Classroom

The following findings are based on observations over a five year period in a number of schools in the city of Antwerp and its greater suburban area (see Rijmenans & Verbruggen, 1983; Verbruggen *et al.*, 1985; Van de Craen, 1980, 1983, 1985). However, there is little doubt, judging by the numerous comments we have received from teachers and school authorities from all over Flanders, that the language situation described here is the same for the rest of the region.

In attempting to describe linguistic variation in the classroom, we have found it useful to make a distinction between teachers and pupils on the one hand, and types of interaction on the other hand.

For the teachers, a further distinction has been made between interaction directed towards instruction and interaction for other purposes. The former is subdivided into lessons about language itself, such as vocabulary or grammar, and other lessons, while with respect to non-instructive interaction the subdivision includes informal remarks, i.e. metastatements about various subjects and circumstances, joking and reproving. As for the pupils, the most common interaction processes to be distinguished are with the school authorities, viz. the headmaster, the teacher in informal as well as in formal contacts, and other pupils. An overview of the results is given in Tables 1 and 2.

From these observations it is clear that language variation forms an integral part of daily classroom interaction. Indeed, it is fair to say that all classroom interaction is directed by the language variants used by the teacher, who most of the time initiates the interactions. Moreover, appropriateness of the interventions is often judged by the appropriateness of the language variant used. Needless to say, in this kind of situation code switching occurs very frequently. This implies that each person's 'definition of the situation', in the classic symbolic interactionist sense of the word (see, for example, Hewitt, 1979), is carried out through an evaluation of the language variants. Let us attempt to illustrate this by means of an example. Table 3 shows the language variants used by teachers and 5th grade pupils (aged between 10 and 11) during classroom interaction in an Antwerp school.

TABLE 1   *Language Variants Used by Teachers in Different Types of Classroom Interaction*

| | Language variant | | | |
Type of interaction	RD	U	BD	SL
+*Instruction*				
+language lessons	−	−	+	+
−language lessons	+	+	+	+
−*Instruction*				
informal remarks	+	+	−	−
joking	+	−	−	−
reproving	+	−	−	−

'+' and '−' refer to the frequency of features of one or another variant.

TABLE 2   *Language Variants Used by Pupils in Different Types of Classroom Interaction*

| | Language variant | | | |
Type of interaction	RD	U	BD	SL
with school authority	−	−	+	(+)
with the teacher				
+formal	−	−	+	(+)
−formal	+	+	−	−
with other pupils	+	+	−	−

The brackets indicate that this variant is also used occasionally.

This typical example of classroom interaction shows that language variation is common, and that the variation not only shows regular but also functional patterns with respect to the relationship between teacher and pupils. This can be demonstrated further in the classroom by disregarding variation and addressing the pupils in one variant only. If, for instance, the dialect variant is used throughout, the pupils start laughing and shouting; if the standard Dutch variant is used throughout, the pupils are attentive at first but, after a while, begin to show signs of uneasiness, especially in those

TABLE 3 *Language Variants Used by Teachers and Pupils in a Typical Classroom Interaction (5th Grade), in an Antwerp School*

	Language variant	
Classroom proceedings	Teacher	Pupils
The teacher walks into the classroom. The pupils are already there. A fair amount of talking is going on.		RD
The teacher calls them to order.	U	
Some pupils continue talking.		RD
The teacher shouts at them to shut up.	RD	
The teacher now invites the children to gather around his desk.	SD	
One of the pupils gets a rebuke for being too slow.	RD	
The teacher starts explaining how to use a pencil to create special effects in a drawing.	BD	
Pupils react. Many talk at the same time.		RD
One pupil asks a question.		U
The teacher reacts.	U	
The teacher continues his explanation after he calls some of the pupils to order again.	SD	

instances where they apparently expect another variant. Most of them divert their attention, as if they were tired of listening.[6]

From this it is clear that language variation is more than just language alone. Apparently, this variation is a part of the world of both the teachers and the pupils. This state of affairs should not surprise us, since classroom variation is a perfect image of the linguistic landscape of the outside world (see Deprez, 1981; Jaspaert, 1986b; Van de Craen & Willemyns, 1988).

Attitudes towards Language Variation in the Classroom

Introduction

It is useful to distinguish once more between the parties involved. First, the pupils' attitudes are examined, next those of the teachers and, finally, those of the educational authorities, school headmasters and inspectors. Attention is also paid to aspects of awareness and terminology, since this is important with respect to research and to the interpretation of the results.

However, before doing this, let us first give some general idea of the attitudes towards the extreme poles of the continuum, viz. regional dialect and standard language. A questionnaire sent out to 128 people (73 female and 55 male), all parents of primary school children ranging from 6 to 13 years of age, gave the results to be found in Table 4.

TABLE 4   *General Results of a Questionnaire Survey of 128 Parents of Primary School Children Ranging from 6 to 13 Years of Age, All Inhabitants of the City of Antwerp*

The standard language has great prestige for educational and professional matters.

Little, if any, social distinction is felt between dialect speakers and standard language speakers.

Dialect is not forsaken because
—one should be able to speak both variants;
—both variants have the same communicative value;
—children should not be discouraged from speaking dialect;
—dialects should not be 'forbidden' and are not ugly.

These results corroborate the results of other attitude research projects carried out in Flanders (cf. Deprez, 1981) and they illustrate the double standard we referred to earlier: the prestige of the standard language does not prevent the dialect variant from being held in esteem as well. The following sections should be interpreted against this background.

Pupils' attitudes

Three kinds of evidence are presented: the results of a semi-matched guise test; a vocabulary test; and reports of conversations with the pupils.

The semi-matched guise test

Ninety-one children were presented with two identical stories recorded on tape by a female voice. One version was read in dialect, the other in standard Dutch. The pupils were told that they were going to hear a story read by two different people. Afterwards they were asked to judge the readers in terms of 'pleasantness', 'severity', 'intelligence' and 'friendliness'. In addition to this they were asked which person they would prefer as a teacher and how they would read the story themselves. The terms 'dialect' or 'standard language' were carefully avoided. Instead the experimenter asked: which person would you prefer, the one who read first, or the one who read second? In order to avoid possible order effects, one half of the participants listened to the dialect version first, and the other half listened to the standard language version first. Items like 'friendliness', 'severity', etc. were chosen because in a previous pilot survey they had been found to be relevant with respect to judging language and people by children. The results are summarised in Table 5.

Among others, the following conclusions can be drawn:

1. Standard language has an enormous prestige.
2. With respect to the situation examined, dialect is 'pleasant' when presented first until the age of 10; older children disregard the order of the stories completely and opt for the standard variant.
3. In the higher grades the vernacular is associated with the language of 'severity'.
4. The standard language is definitely the language of intelligence and friendliness or, in other words, the standard language is considered to be the language of knowledge and civilised behaviour.

The vocabulary test

In order to test whether the pupils' verbal reactions were a function of their attitudes, a simple vocabulary test was devised. Pupils were asked to name 34 common objects on pictures shown by the experimenter. It should be noted that the experimenter and the pupils were quite familiar with one another, since the former frequently visited the classroom and participated in class activities. All the items formed part of the children's conversational competence. They were selected partly on the grounds of simplicity and partly because there were clear phonological and morphological differences between the terms in the different language varieties. The test was carried out twice. The first time the experimenter simply showed the pictures and asked the pupils to name them. The experimenter spoke the vernacular and it was left to the pupils to choose the language variant. We refer to this as 'the spontaneous reaction'. A week later the pupils were asked the same questions again but now the experimenter, speaking in the vernacular, selected the language variety to be used: first the vernacular

TABLE 5   *Results of a Semi-matched Guise Test with 91 Pupils*

Age	Order	Pleasantness	Severity	Intelligence	Friendliness	Class	Self
7	D–SL	pro D**				pro SL**	
	SL–D	pro SL**			pro SL**	pro SL*	
8	D–SL	pro D*		pro SL*	pro SL**		
	SL–D						
9	D–SL	pro D**		pro SL*			
	SL–D	pro SL**		pro SL**	pro SL**	pro SL**	pro SL**
10	D–SL	pro D*	pro D*	pro SL**	pro SL**		pro SL**
	SL–D	pro SL**	pro D**	pro SL**	pro SL**	pro SL**	pro SL**
11	D–SL	pro SL**	pro D**	pro SL**	pro SL**	pro SL**	pro SL**
	SL–D	pro SL*		pro SL*	pro SL**	pro SL**	pro SL**
12	D–SL	pro SL**		pro SL**	pro SL*	pro SL**	pro SL**
	SL–D		pro D*	pro SL*		pro SL**	pro SL**

Pro: in favour of; * significant at the 0.05 level; ** significant at the 0.01 level; a blank space indicates that no significance was found; *class*: I'd like to have her as a teacher; *self*: I'd like to read it that way.

and then the standard language; or the other way round. We refer to this as 'the non-spontaneous variant'. It was felt that the results of this procedure could teach us something about language constraints associated with the use of the vernacular and the standard language in school. The results are presented in Figure 1.

It is clear that when the choice of the language variant is left open, the number of dialect variants decreases with age. When attention is explicitly drawn to the vernacular, however, an increase in the use of dialect words is seen until the age of about ten. After that, a rapid decrease occurs, despite the insistence of the experimenter. When the standard forms are explicitly asked for, a clear increase in the number of standard forms is observed.

Apparently, at the age of around ten, children become fully aware of the social values of the vernacular in particular situations. The increase in competence in the standard language, together with this development of social awareness, increases the number of standard forms that are used, while at the same time some kind of social barrier against the use of the vernacular is developed. These children had acquired, as part of their

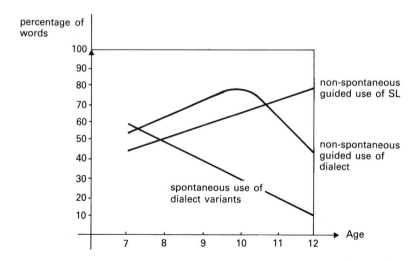

FIGURE 1 *Spontaneous and non-spontaneous reactions to the naming of common objects classified according to age of pupils*

linguistic competence, an understanding of the social values attached to the different language variants (see also Reid, 1978).

Conversations with children

The previous argument about the social awareness of the language variants seems to find additional support in the reactions of the pupils to questions about language use. However, before the age of ten we found it extremely difficult to get the pupils to talk about language differences. One reason is that terms such as 'Dutch', 'Flemish', 'dialect', etc. mean virtually nothing to them. Expressions such as 'how do people talk at school or at home' are much more comprehensible. Up to the 5th grade most pupils say there is no difference between the way people talk at home and at school. When confronted with manifest differences in labelling various objects and in pronunciations they insist that it is still the same. Apparently, they consider as most vital the meaning of the words and expressions, rather than the forms. However, from the 5th grade onwards, things change drastically. They are not only able to express the differences between codes, but they are also able to comment on various aspects of them, including their social value.

'Why do we have to speak nicely', one 12-year-old girl sighed, 'is it that important?'. A 12-year-old boy, when confronted with the question, 'Why do you have to speak nicely in class?' replied: 'Because in doing so the Turkish and the Moroccan pupils understand us better' and another boy insisted that the standard language is learned 'because we are raised to be nice people'. From ten years of age the vernacular is also considered to be the variant of 'severity' and punishment. Of course, this reflects the fact that when the teachers get angry they immediately switch to dialect. However, at this age no distinction exists between more subtle nuances, such as between dialect, *Umgangssprache* or Belgian Dutch. It is also noteworthy that, in general, pupils become very enthusiastic during lessons dealing explicitly with aspects of language variation and with different ways of speaking.

In summarizing the pupils' attitudes towards language variation one aspect should be stressed. It is clearly the school that helps to form the children's attitudes towards language variation, to a great extent. The rather ambiguous attitudes of teachers and the school system (see pp. 23–26) is, from approximately the age of ten, transposed into some kind of pragmatic attitude about the knowledge 'what language to use, how, when and to whom'.

Teachers' attitudes

Information about teachers' attitudes does not come from large surveys but mainly from conversations and observations reported in Rijmenans & Verbruggen (1983), Verbruggen *et al.* (1985), Van de Craen (1983, 1985). However, Hagen (1980) has reported the results of questionnaires, completed firstly by 65 and then by 46 Dutch-speaking primary and secondary Belgian school teachers. Let us elaborate on these studies and observations.

In conversations with and observations of primary school teachers, four aspects seem to dominate their attitudes towards language variation:

—linguistic insecurity
—reported linguistic shortcomings
—upward evaluation of their own language variants
—tolerance towards their own and their pupils' language use.

Linguistic insecurity

This can mainly be observed through the impressive amount of hypercorrection in teachers' talk as well as in their correction of the written language of the pupils. Often, these hypercorrect lexical items are introduced as correct standard Dutch and they are meant to replace the so-called incorrect dialect items.

Reported linguistic shortcomings

Although most teachers are unaware of their abundant use of hypercorrect forms, they frequently insist on the fact that their standard Dutch is not 'the real thing'. Teachers older than 45, in particular, declare that they cannot speak 'as they should', and they express feelings of guilt about this.

Upward evaluation

Confronted with the question of which kind of Dutch they speak, teachers show a remarkable tendency to upgrade their language variant. Dialect is often judged *Umgangssprache*, and *Umgangssprache* as Belgian Dutch, while Belgian Dutch is considered to be Standard Dutch.

Tolerance

In all cases, we saw a remarkable amount of tolerance on the part of the teachers toward their own and their pupils' verbal output. As a result the pupils are very seldom reproved for 'bad language'. This happens almost exclusively during language lessons and practically never during, for instance, practical activities.

The results of Hagen's surveys can easily be explained against the background of these observations. Asked to specify the norm that Dutch should follow in Flanders in matters of language education, either Dutch following the northern norm, or Dutch largely influenced by Southern variants, 72.3% answered in favour of the latter option, among them a majority of young people. Hagen also shows that as far as pronunciation is concerned, the Flemish norm is clearly singled out as the best, while syntactic differences are largely underestimated (see Hagen, 1980).

In summarising teachers' attitudes, it should be stressed that, here too, their attitudes can be seen as an image of the ongoing standardisation processes in Flanders. In recent years, sociolinguists have frequently pointed out that the spread of the standard language in Flanders will ultimately lead to some kind of 'domestic' standardisation, independent, up to a certain point, of what happens in the Netherlands. Since this attitude prevails mainly amongst younger people, it is highly probable that in future this tendency will become even more widespread. This could mean that at school the proposed continuum will be reduced to two variants instead of four. Evidence for this development can be found in the fact that regional dialect and *Umgangssprache*, on the one hand, and Belgian Dutch and Standard language, on the other hand, are not very different from one another.

Attitudes of the educational authorities

The educational authorities in Flanders have always had a keen interest in matters of language. On examination of the literature it becomes clear that this pre-occupation is directed mainly towards aspects of pronunciation (cf. Van de Craen, 1985). The general opinion is that the pupils should strive as far as possible towards the standard norm. It should be noted here that matters of pronunciation have indeed dominated the discussions about standardisation throughout the nineteenth century and a good deal of the twentieth century (see also Suffeleers, 1979). Let us examine some of the advice given in the curricula.

The official curriculum states that

the child is free to express itself. However, gradually it should learn to express itself more correctly and perfectly. This is mainly a matter of exercise, of language use. The teacher can help through his own correct language and perfect pronunciation. He has to provide for special pronunciation lessons. He has to correct childish (*sic*) expressions whenever there is no risk of shutting the children up.

Examples of bad language are:

dialect variation, incorrect words, faulty expressions and bad syntax . . . The teacher has the correct word looked up or gives it himself. It shall be used immediately. Special attention is to be paid to the correction of regional variation (Leerplan en leidraad, 1957: 35, our translation).

Another curriculum reads as follows:

The teacher uses standard language words and expressions in replacement of dialect forms. He encourages the pupils to use these new words. Without pushing, practically unnoticed, in a pleasant atmosphere, he substitutes dialect words by standard language expressions (Leerplan voor de lagere scholen 1969: 5–6, our translation).

Two assumptions seem to provide the basis for this thinking: (1) It is taken for granted that the standard language is acquired in a minimum of time; (2) no major obstacles of whatever kind are acknowledged except the fact of showing contempt for the pupils' language. Unfortunately, neither assumption applies to what really happens in a classroom, and they are therefore false.

It is interesting that this attitude has prevailed until today, despite evidence of another linguistic reality than that implied by various curricula. Recently, a high-level civil servant representing the Ministry of Education has again rephrased these arguments, but with a slightly different touch. Communication is now seen as a valuable tool for teaching the standard language. However, he insists that dialect should be banned and is totally unacceptable in the classrooms. No mention, or even hints, of language variation of any kind are made (Dambre, 1985).

Why is it that, against their better judgement, the educational authorities keep officially ignoring the existence of language variation in the classrooms? We think the answer includes two factors: ignorance and fear. More often than not the authorities are not familiar with recent research findings. As a result they lack basic insights into matters of language variation and their social implications. Typical of this ignorance is the fact that the civil servant mentioned earlier is puzzled by the good results he occasionally observes, despite what he himself describes as unsatisfactory classroom situations (Dambre, 1985: 72). He could not have shown his unfamiliarity with the standardisation processes in Flanders any better.

As a result of this unfamiliarity with both the situations themselves and analyses of them, they are afraid of everything that might disturb their preconceived ideas. It then comes as no surprise that the same Dambre with approval quotes texts referring to the language situation of Flanders of two generations ago (see Dambre, 1985: 65–66).

In summarising the attitudes of the authorities, we might say that they are highly idealistic as well as unrealistic with respect to the ongoing language processes both in and outside the schools.

Didactic Consequences and Hints for Change

In view of the previous remarks, and as a final comment, we would like to evaluate the language situation in Dutch-speaking schools in Belgium and to make some suggestions directed towards doing away with some of the more undesirable side-effects of the present-day situation.

As far as the role of the primary school is concerned, we feel it should contribute maximally to the development of all aspects of language proficiency, in a stimulating linguistic environment. Today, this goal is not achieved. A certain amount of language proficiency does develop, but usually this is in spite of, rather than as a result of the school. What we suggest is that language variation as such should be recognised and that starting from there, learning material for a better use of the available potential should be developed.

This view is supported by at least four major arguments from various disciplines: (social) psychology, education, sociology and (socio)linguistics.

(Social) psychology has made us realise that the way people think about language is as important as linguistic differences as such. We have observed that in a number of Dutch-speaking schools in Belgium, the dialect variant has a low prestige and is considered to be quite unacceptable in the classroom. However, we have also observed that dialect is an integral part of the daily language variation in the classroom. Denying this leads, at best, to some kind of schizoglossia and, at worst, towards self-hatred and frustration. It certainly does not favour either the acquisition or the use of the standard language. We should get rid of hypocritical ideas about language and open our minds to linguistic reality. In making this move education has much more to gain than to lose. We do not think that any drastic changes are needed to achieve this goal. As we have seen, in most cases the linguistic material is already available and there is a potential interest in aspects of variation. What should be done, however, is to draw explicit attention to these phenomena and convince the parties concerned of the value of the new approach.

From a pedagogical point of view the enormous gap between the curricula and reality is deplorable. However, since the curricula seem to be interested in the linguistic output of the children, why not do just that? Nobody can be criticised for following the curriculum verbatim.

From a sociological viewpoint even more important arguments can be formulated. In Flanders, regional dialects are rapidly on the way to becoming a strong social barrier. The particular language situation of the area has until now prevented this from happening (as has happened, for example, in the Netherlands, Germany, England and France). In realising the failure of the official policy towards language variation, education cannot ignore any longer the social consequences of this failure. In the near future poor mastery of the standard will virtually mean the same as being a social outcast, confined to the bottom of the social ladder. Making use of all available potential again seems the answer.

From a (socio)linguistic viewpoint the previous arguments imply that the recognition and explicit study of language variation will ultimately lead to better mastery of the standard language. Before explaining why this is so, we should distinguish between two kinds of language: language behaviour or speaking, and the study of language or the study of speech acts. Everybody is able to speak, yet few people are actually aware of how they speak, how they pronounce, etc. Cummins and his colleagues have shown that the study of language and language behaviour has positive, cognitive implications, and positive effects on language learning (see Cummins, 1984). Moreover, it has been suggested that these cognitive aspects positively influence the development of reading and writing skills as well. As a result, the study of language behaviour, which naturally includes the study of language variation, will have positive effects on the acquisition of the standard language and indeed of any other language.

Conclusion

The analysis of language behaviour in Dutch-speaking classrooms in Belgium shows language variation to be an integral part of it. Attitudes of both pupils and teachers are negatively affected by the attempts of the educational authorities to ignore this state of affairs. This leads to a number of paradoxes and negative effects on the acquisition of the standard language. There is no point in arguing, as the authorities do, that dialects or language variation should not be allowed in the classrooms, because they are already there. Therefore we are in favour of a less hypocritical, more realistic attitude in not only accepting the present state of affairs, but in using it as a tool for language teaching purposes. We expect that the acquisition and mastery of the standard language will be positively affected by this change. Arguments from (social) psychology, pedagogy, sociology and (socio)linguistics illustrate this point of view.

Notes to Chapter 2

1. Officially Belgium is a trilingual country: Dutch is spoken in the northern part by roughly 5,670,000 inhabitants, French is spoken in the southern part by roughly 3,208,000 inhabitants, and German is spoken in the eastern part by roughly 66,000 inhabitants. The capital of Brussels (980,000 inhabitants) has a bilingual status. (Official figures from the National Institute for Statistics for the year 1985.)
2. For a short time between 1814–1830 the two parts were united in the United Kingdom of the Netherlands. Although this period proved to be of psychological importance in the nineteenth century, it was too short to have a linguistic impact of lasting importance.
3. For an overview of the standardisation process in Flanders, see Van de Craen & Willemyns, forthcoming.
4. The greater Brussels area may differ from this pattern. Details are as yet unknown, but see Willemyns (1979).
5. The term *Umgangssprache* is used differently here from the way in which it is used by Ammon, this volume, Chapter 7. 'Aspects of dialect and school in the Federal Republic of Germany'.
6. This observation has frequently been made in the 4th, 5th and 6th grades. It may well be that younger pupils react differently.

References

CUMMINS, J. 1984 *Bilingualism and Special Education. Issues in Assessment and Pedagogy*. Clevedon, Avon: Multilingual Matters.
DAMBRE, J. 1985 Dialect en het aanleren van de standaardtaal in Vlaanderen. Feiten en bedenkingen. In P. VAN DE CRAEN & R. WILLEMYNS (eds)

Standaardtaal en dialect, op school, thuis en elders. Brussel: Studiereeks van de VUB. pp. 65–73.

DEPREZ, K. 1981 Naar een eigen identiteit. Doctoral dissertation, University of Leuven.

——1985 Brabant: een taaleigen centrum? In P. VAN DE CRAEN & R. WILLEMYNS (eds) *Standaardtaal en dialect, op school, thuis en elders.* Brussel: Studiereeks van de VUB. pp. 131–157.

GEERTS, G., NOOTENS, J. and VAN DEN BROECK, J. 1978 Flemish attitudes towards dialects and standard language: a public opinion poll. *International Journal of the Sociology of Language* 15, 33–40.

GOOSSENS, J. 1970 'Belgisch Beschaafd Nederlands' en Brabantse expansie. *De Nieuwe Taalgids* 63, 54–70.

HAGEN, A. 1980 Attitudes van leerkrachten tegenover het standaard-nederlands in Vlaanderen. In J. KRUIJSEN (ed.) *Liber Amicorum Weijnen.* Assen: Van Gorcum. pp. 164–75.

HEWITT, J. 1979 *Self and Society* (2nd edn). Boston: Allyn & Bacon.

JASPAERT, K. 1986a Variatie in standaadtaalstructuur in het Nederlandse taalgebied. *Gramma* 10(1), 17–40.

——1986b *Statuut en structuur van standaardtalig Vlaanderen.* Leuven: Universitaire Pers.

LEERPLAN EN LEIDRAAD 1957. Brussels: Ministry of Education.

LEERPLAN VOOR DE LAGERE SCHOLEN 1969. Brussels: Board for Catholic Education.

REID, E. 1978 Social and stylistic variation in the speech of children: some evidence from Edinburgh. In P. TRUDGILL (ed.) *Sociolinguistic Patterns in British English.* London: Arnold, pp. 158–71.

RIJMENANS, R. and VERBRUGGEN, M. 1983 Dialecttolerantie en klasinteractie. *Vonk* 13(4), 48–55.

SUFFELEERS, T. 1979 *Taalverzorging in Vlaanderen.* Brugge: Orion.

VAN DE CRAEN, P. 1980 Development communicative competence and attitudes in education. *Bulletin CILA* 31, 34–48.

——1983 Het gebruik van dialect in de klas. *Vonk* 13(4), 27–47.

——1985 De mislukking van een taalpolitiek: ABN in de klas. In P. VAN DE CRAEN & R. WILLEMYNS (eds) *Standaardtaal en dialect, op school, thuis en elders.* Brussel: Studiereeks van de VUB. pp. 45–63.

VAN DE CRAEN, P. and WILLEMYNS, R. 1988 The standardization of Dutch in Flanders. *International Journal of the Sociology of Language* 73, 45–64.

VERBRUGGEN, M., STROOBANTS, F. AND RIJMENANS, R. 1985 Dialect in de klas. Aanzet tot onderzoek in drie basisscholen uit het Antwerpse. In P. VAN DE CRAEN and R. WILLEMYNS (eds) *Standaardtaal en dialect, op school, thuis en elders.* Brussel: Studiereeks van de VUB. pp. 107–25.

WILLEMYNS, R. 1979 Bedenkingen bij het taalgedrag van Vlaamse universiteitsstudenten uit Brussel-Halle-Vilvoorde. *Taal en Sociale Integratie* 2, 141–59.

3 Dialect and education in Denmark

J. NORMANN JØRGENSEN and KAREN MARGRETHE
PEDERSEN

Introduction

The handling of dialects in Danish schools has been called 'sailing without a helm'. This refers to the fact that the school system until 1984 had no official policy as far as the classical dialects and their speakers were concerned. Consequently very little is known about the specific problems of dialect speaking pupils in our schools. The few investigations that have been undertaken, furthermore, have come to widely different results. Elsewhere it is almost axiomatic that dialect-speaking pupils are at a disadvantage compared to their standard speaking peers in school (e.g. Trudgill, 1975; Cheshire, 1982; Stijnen & Vallen, 1981; Sonderen & Weltens, 1981; Giesbers, Kroon & Liebrand, 1978; Ammon, 1978; Venås, 1979). To mention just one surprising example, Allerup et al. in 1979 found that the orthographical command of standard Danish varied significantly with how common dialect was in the area of investigation. The more common a local dialect was, the *better* the children would spell standard Danish in their written work in school (Allerup et al., 1979). There could, of course, be different reasons for this, and the aim of this chapter is to examine and compare the results of some of the investigations in this field in Denmark.

The chapter is organised as follows. First we will define some of the linguistic terms as they are commonly applied to the Danish situation. Next we will present the investigations that have been carried out in two different areas of the peninsula of Jutland. One, the most detailed investigation that has been undertaken so far, is the Hirtshals Project from Northern Jutland. The others were carried out in Southern Jutland, on the German border. The results from Northern and Southern Jutland will be compared, mainly in sociolinguistic terms, and finally we will discuss some practical conclusions concerning the school.

Terminology

In Danish dialectology the term *dialect* usually refers to the traditional dialect spoken in a geographically narrow region, often a rather small area. A dialect is defined as the combination of specific features, i.e. phonological, morphological, syntactical, or lexical. These features do not compare directly with the standard. Instead the dialects and the standard all compare historically with Old Danish. Thus, each dialect is characterised by its own combination of features. These features may cause difficulties in understanding for non-speakers of the dialect from elsewhere in the country. Defined like this, Danish dialects correspond to the classical dialects as they are found in the languages of Europe.

No barrier of understanding is found in relation to the so-called *regional varieties*. A regional variety covers a larger area which is not geographically well defined, and it is characterised by a number of features that differ from those of the national standard language, although the regional variety is a standard variety rather than a (classical) dialect. The local features of the regional variety do not enter into a fixed combination and they may differ from person to person. One person may even choose the regional form in one situation and the standard form in another situation — and still be speaking the same regional variety. The localisable features of a regional variety may derive from either the classical local dialect, or other classical dialects within the region, or they may represent a new difference from the national standard.

National standard Danish is defined as the variety without 'localisable' features, i.e. a regional variety is a variety of the standard, but one *with* local features. The national standard has its origins in the dialects in and around Copenhagen. Concurrently with the establishment of Copenhagen as the economic, political and cultural centre of Denmark — i.e. from the beginning of the 1700s — the Copenhagen dialect became the language of the administration; and standardisation began.

The cultural and linguistic influence radiating from Copenhagen is still strong, and therefore the classical dialects are primarily spoken in rural districts in the regions that are geographically most peripheral to Copenhagen. Regional varieties, on the other hand, are spoken in the dialect areas as well as in the rest of the provinces.

The school plays an important part in this standardisation. Standard Danish (be it the national variety or one of the regional varieties) is in many respects the language of the school and of the entire educational

FIGURE 1 *Danish regions where classical dialects are still spoken (hatched areas)*

system in Denmark. It is not specifically stated anywhere in the legislation covering the educational system that it must be so. Since the national standard is the spoken variety most closely related to written Danish, however, it has of course become the norm of the schools.

Contributory elements are also the status and education of the teachers. In the directives for teacher training (Dansk, 1986) a command of the standard language is not demanded, but it is certainly expected. Under the subject of 'rhetoric', for example, it is mentioned that oral diction has to be taught as standard Danish. One can nevertheless become a certified teacher without speaking standard Danish. As a pupil, one can pass the examinations for the leaving certificate after 9 or 10 years of school without speaking standard Danish.

The concepts of national standard, regional variety, and dialect, are mentioned nowhere in the general directives on the objective of the school nor in the directives concerning the subject of Danish as a mother tongue. This subject is taught (non-split) 4–6 lessons a week in the 9 grades included in compulsory education.

In the guidelines for the school subject of Danish as a mother tongue issued in 1984 (Dansk, 1984), the classical dialects appear as an object for study for the first time. Schools are not suddenly supposed to teach the classical dialects, rather *about* the classical dialects. These guidelines stress the importance of linguistic awareness — a notion that has also been generating an increasing interest in the professional literature.

Nevertheless, dialect speaking pupils are not mentioned, nor are educational difficulties connected with linguistic differences. The general attitude is that teachers should encourage children to develop linguistic confidence and articulateness in their own language. It is of course questionable whether this actually happens — or whether speaking a classical dialect can in fact cause problems for pupils, their parents and teachers.

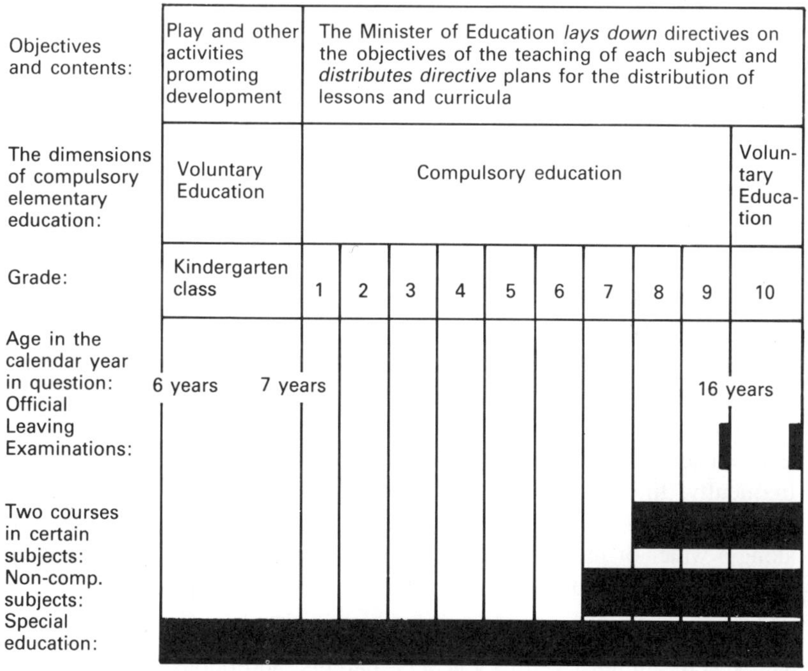

Objectives and contents:	Play and other activities promoting development	The Minister of Education *lays down* directives on the objectives of the teaching of each subject and *distributes directive* plans for the distribution of lessons and curricula									
The dimensions of compulsory elementary education:	Voluntary Education	Compulsory education									Voluntary Education
Grade:	Kindergarten class	1	2	3	4	5	6	7	8	9	10
Age in the calendar year in question: Official Leaving Examinations:	6 years 7 years									16 years	
Two courses in certain subjects: Non-comp. subjects: Special education:											

FIGURE 2 *General rules for the Danish school*
Non-comp = non-compulsory (after Skov, 1983 p. 392)

We shall now proceed with discussion of some efforts to answer that question.

The Hirtshals Project

In an attempt to describe the effect of dialect speaking on the school, a team of linguists, sociolinguists, and educationalists in 1981–83 studied several factors which were considered important in this respect in the municipality of Hirtshals, Northern Jutland (Hansen & Lund, 1983, see also Lund, 1986).

Linguistically there are three types of Danish represented in the community. First, there is the classical dialect. It was expected beforehand, and during the investigation it was confirmed, that only the very oldest people in the community spoke the most classical form of this dialect. The classical dialect had developed considerably in the speech of the younger generations, most of the changes having made the linguistic distance from the standard smaller. It was also found that no children nowadays grow beyond the age of 8–9 years without knowing a standard variety of Danish. We must note, however, that all of the children understood the classical dialect perfectly, even in a rather old version, when they were tested on that.

Secondly, there is the national standard. There are even fewer speakers of the national standard than classical dialect speakers in Hirtshals, but the national standard is well represented in the media that cover the whole nation. Thirdly, there is the regional variety (Jørgensen, 1983a).

It was obvious that the classical dialect was disappearing. That is not the same as saying that the speakers were abandoning the classical dialect. Rather, it had rapidly, within two or three generations, developed into a regional variety of wider communicative range — without losing its roots. One fact that lends probability to such an explanation is that there were few bidialectal speakers, i.e. code switching was a rare phenomenon. More frequently, the speakers adjusted their choice of forms according to the expected skills — and, granted, wishes — of the listener(s), thereby sliding along a wider or narrower continuum of features with no clear boundaries between (classical) dialect and (regional) standard (Jørgensen, 1983b).

To shed light on the sociolinguistic and pedagogical issues, question-naires were administered to teachers, parents, and pupils alike. These sub-projects had extremely high response rates, in some cases close to 100%.

The pupils were asked about their parents' use of dialect and standard respectively, as well as whether they had experienced any problems with, or because of, the dialect, educationally or socially. Frequently pupils reported the use of dialect in their home, but they all described their parents as more 'dialectal' than themselves. They had no problems with the dialect as far as the school was concerned. A few of them reported having been teased because of the use of specific linguistic forms, but this happened just as often with non-dialect as it did with dialect forms.

The pupils believed that learning a standard variety would be an asset in their future professional careers, although only one in four felt that standard speakers would be preferred over dialect speakers by employers (Nyberg & Larsen, 1983).

The majority of the teachers were born and raised in the region, although not in this specific community. They were well acquainted with the dialect, but most of them did not feel that the dialect had any special effect on everyday teaching. Roughly one-third thought that speaking a dialect may make it a little harder for a school beginner to learn to read and as many as 60% believed that spelling may be made more difficult. There is no discrepancy in this — compared to other nations Danish schools do not emphasise spelling skills very much.

The teachers believed that dialect interference should be corrected in written work and in very formal oral tasks, but that dialect forms should be permitted along with standard forms in everyday oral work. On the other hand, only 2% favoured the use of dialect as a medium of instruction (Gimbel, 1983).

In informal classroom observations it was noticed that some teachers were more tolerant in their practice than others. But the use of dialect forms was not ridiculed or stigmatised. Instead, it was pointed out that a given form was dialectal — and the pupil was asked to supply the corresponding standard form.

The parents of all children in kindergarten, grade 1 and grade 2, were asked a number of questions regarding language and school. It became obvious — as expected — that dialect use increased with lower social status and with age. Men are more often dialect speakers than women, but quite a few reported speaking the regional variety ('town language') to their children. (As we have seen earlier, this probably means that they adjust the form of certain variables according to their perception of their children's skills, rather than that they switch codes.) The parents said that they themselves had had few problems in school because of their dialect, and the parents of only 5 out of 606 children found that their children had problems caused by language. This ran contrary to everything expected, especially since it could be tempting for parents of children with any sorts of problems to ascribe these problems to language differences.

The parents believe that the school should teach the children a standard, and the teacher of Danish, especially, was expected to use standard Danish in school. Only a small minority, however, saw any reason for correcting dialect forms that were used by children in school (Hansen, 1983).

The conclusions are that the classical dialect is on the retreat, in the home as well as in the school. The gradual societal shift to the regional variety is not perceived as a problem by the speakers, however, at least not for school children. Sociolinguistically, the dialect has its place at the narrow end of a diglossic situation (see the Introduction to this volume), and this space is becoming still narrower. The standard is widely accepted as the means of wider communication, but only rarely rated any more highly or as being more valuable to the individual speaker for that reason.

Pedagogically it is important that the teachers know and appreciate the dialect. They mostly believe in letting dialect forms pass without remarks in the classroom, although certainly not in written work. There seems to be almost unanimous agreement that the school must teach the standard and accept the dialect.

As far as the actual results of the teachers' efforts are concerned, several subprojects investigated the written work of dialect speaking pupils. It was found that 4th graders and 9th graders in the community's schools (see Figure 2 for the ages of children in these grades) command the formal writing rules of the standard variety just as well as everybody else (Sandersen, 1983). From each class eight pupils were selected, half of them dialect speakers. Their writing skills were compared to those of their peers in the nationwide yearly essay test. Altogether 328 essays were compared. Dialect interference could be found, but few dialect features were found to be consistently interfering with the (standard Danish) writing of the pupils. The dialect speakers did not commit more spelling errors than the standard speakers. There were certainly spellers who had many examples of dialect interference, but they were all poor spellers in every conceivable way.

Another subproject studied the variation in content and creativity among 5th graders, applying some of Luria's concepts (Schiødt, 1983). It was found that girls vary more and are more creative than boys. Pupils with high grades in Danish as a subject score higher than those with lower grades, and standard speakers do better than dialect speakers. This was explained by Schiødt (p. 300) as being a result of the fact that the dialect speakers had not acquired the standard to the level of creativity, and therefore constantly took care to use standard forms that they knew well.

The dialect speaking 2nd graders were compared to other 2nd graders in standardised reading tests (Møller, 1983). No evidence was found that they were poorer readers of the national standard than standard speakers. This may seem less surprising in view of the fact that Danish is a language with an extremely complicated relationship between spelling and pronunciation, and that the national standard is hardly any 'closer' to the spelling in its pronunciation than is the dialect of Hirtshals.

The only possible conclusion is that dialect-speaking children in this community are *not* at a clear disadvantage with respect to education when compared to their standard speaking peers.

The South Jutland Projects

In 1974 one of the first Danish research projects on dialect and school was carried out in the public school in Gram, a small town in Southern Jutland (see Figure 1 above). The school takes some of its pupils from two nearby village schools, in grade 3 and 7 respectively. These pupils were among the 170 participants in the project, who were selected from the range kindergarten class to grade 8 (ages 6–15; see Figure 2).

The pupils were audiotaped in school in a rather formal situation with a standard-speaking interviewer, and they were expected to speak standard Danish if they were able to. Almost half of the pupils (46.9%) spoke the dialect in this situation, 30.8% spoke the regional variety, and 22.9% were judged to be national standard speakers. Dialect speakers dominate in the kindergarten class and in grade 8, together with the two classes from the village schools. It is surprising that there are so many dialect speakers in the higher grade, but the children gave an explanation during the interviews, namely that speaking (or learning to speak) the standard was only mandatory in the first grades. Either they do not care about the norm of the school any longer, having acquired their own identity, or they may have adjusted their own language in the classroom so much that it is accepted there.

The feeling of a demand for language shift is typical among the girls in grade 8, but not among the boys. This may reflect different upbringing patterns, something that may also be reflected in the distribution of language varieties between the sexes: almost twice as many boys as girls were dialect speakers.

Fifteen years later the distinction between dialect and regional variety that was used in this investigation seems rather dubious. The classification used for the pupils' language corresponded well with the judgement of their classroom language by their teachers, however. And half of the parents answering a questionnaire about their own language use identified the dialect as their only language. However, the questionnaire allowed a choice only between dialect and standard. In this investigation the term dialect must probably be taken to cover quite a wide range between the pure classical dialect of the area and a regional variety heavily loaded with local features.

The project also analysed the reading and writing of the pupils. Reading aloud (in the standard) without any self-corrections, teacher interruptions, long pauses or stops, was seen as the ideal, solely because this is the ideal of the school. In several respects the dialect speakers did not fulfil this ideal. The two village classes and the 8th grade differed particularly from the others — another indication of the wide use of dialect in these classes. The report on the project discusses the necessity of either reducing the demand for standard language in elementary reading or focussing on the pupils' linguistic background before beginning to read (aloud).

The pupils' written work was analysed with respect to deviations from standard orthography, lexicon, and syntax. In grade 1–6 the standard speaking pupils had the highest percentage of deviations, but in grade 7 and 8 most of their 'standard' errors and deviations had disappeared. In these grades the dialect-speaking pupils had the highest percentage of deviations. They appear to be caused by the dialect and seem to be difficult to get rid of. That the dialect-speaking pupils were 'better' writers up to that point may be conditional on an awareness of language problems in general. Focussing on the linguistic aspects in written language might, however, have an influence on the wording, so that the dialect-speaking pupils, in their striving for a standard language, might lose some nuances. This aspect was not analysed. According to their teachers, these children had no problems in reading, but the teachers regarded the dialect as a handicap in writing. Furthermore, all deviations from the standard were looked upon as errors. Nevertheless, the teachers say that the problems connected with dialect in school are few. The pupils, on the other hand, do not find the problems small. The conclusion of the project was that the problems were experienced by the pupils and *not* by the teachers. The result is that the pupils get the impression that their dialect is inferior — because it is always corrected or neglected. The teachers do not look upon it as something they have to take seriously. It is suggested in the project report that deviations from standard Danish should be regarded not as errors, but as expressions of the vernacular language. They have to be converted into standard language before compulsory education ends, but not from the very first day at school. It is also suggested that dialect becomes a topic in school. That is often neglected in Denmark and this will therefore be a step towards acceptance — depending of course on how it is done. Several ways of doing it positively are mentioned in the report.

The main conclusion is that the pupils should be taught a standard variety in order to gain social acceptance, but not at the expense of their dialect, nor at the expense of their feeling of identity or their feeling of security (Pedersen, 1977).

Magda Nyberg has published a study of the linguistic phenomena that may cause problems for pupils in Southern Jutland (Nyberg, 1979). The material for this study was partly drawn from the Gram investigation. Nyberg has also conducted a questionnaire project on attitudes towards classical dialects among teachers and pupils all over the country. The results (Nyberg, 1980 and 1981) were that teachers have positive attitudes towards dialects and towards a dialect speaking environment. They even stress the necessity of creating a secure atmosphere in school so that children dare to speak their dialect; but they also agree on the necessity of learning a standard language. The overwhelming majority of teachers in dialect areas find that the linguistic problems are rather small, but the psychological and social frustration of the children seems to be serious. Nyberg stresses the difference between these two types of information. Perhaps linguistic problems seem small because there are other educational problems more serious to the teacher. The pupils simply pick up the standard from mass media and teaching in general, or so the teachers think.

The pupils' own point of view was asked for a year later. 446 out of 531 answers are from areas where a classical dialect is still spoken, including Southern Jutland, which of course is not the same as saying that 446 of the pupils were actually dialect speakers themselves. Nevertheless the answers show a remarkably high percentage of dialect speakers. 54% of the pupils regard themselves as dialect speakers. 66% of them think that speaking a standard at home is 'unnatural'. The feeling of dialect having less prestige than standard language in some situations is typical of all answers, and it is a generally accepted view that command of a standard variety is necessary for self-confidence. Several pupils, also in Southern Jutland, report having been in situations where they did not utter a word — because of their dialect, fearing not to be understood, or because they felt shy. In the light of this experience, only a few report difficulties in school because of their dialect. About 1% of the answers from Southern Jutland report that dialect is a handicap in all school subjects, whereas a total of 30% do so for the subject of Danish. The difficulties are primarily connected with writing (61%), whereas oral production has only 30%, and reading a mere 7%. The same tendency was found in the teachers' answers. Pupils and teachers also agree on the advantage of knowing the pupils' dialect. Most teachers do not oppose the use of dialect forms in class, and they say that they do not comment on them. Confrontations on this point seem to be rare. Nevertheless, dialect speaking is more often described as an inconvenience than as an asset. The feeling of inferiority is the dominating psychological factor reported in the nationwide investigation. This is not due to the linguistic distance between the national standard and the classical dialects, but rather to the distance in status between them. In Southern Jutland the dialect has a comparatively high status, and 89% of the students living there do not want to stop speaking their dialect. They want to become bidialectal — and that may be where the problems arise, the report finds. The conclusion is that conflict in connection with dialect speaking in schools should not be played down or neglected.

A pilot study carried out in Tinglev, Southern Jutland (see Figure 1 above) in 1983 describes the language use of 31 children of 4–5 years of age, attending nursery schools, i.e. day care institutions for children 3–6 years old, and 34 grade school pupils of 12–13 years of age. Half of them belong to the German minority which has the local *Danish* dialect as their first language and German as the second language.

As far as the majority children are concerned, the recently published report (Pedersen, 1986) finds that the parents describe the children in nursery schools as 20% standard speakers, 30% dialect speakers, and 50% speakers of both. The school children are described as 33% standard speakers, 33% dialect speakers and 33% speakers of both. The children in the latter group also completed a questionnaire, and they report themselves to be 61% bilingual and 33% monolingual standard speakers. This disagreement between parents and children probably derives from the fact that the parents do not hear the dialect-speaking children use the standard language, or they may not perceive the standard in the same way as their children. Tape recordings of the school-children were analysed, and they show that children regarding themselves as bilingual in dialect and standard, were actually bidialectal in dialect and a regional variety, but the option of 'regional variety' was not offered in the questionnaire.

Few school children say that they speak the dialect in the school subject of Danish. More than half of them prefer the standard, and the rest both standard and dialect. School problems related to the dialect were reported as follows: 21% have experienced problems in general with their language, 11%

have had problems with reading aloud, and 32% have had problems with writing. These figures resemble the Gram results and Nyberg's conclusions. As for problems in general with language, the parents of 16% of the pupils said that their children had had difficulties, whereas 53% of the children themselves reported problems. Such a significant difference shows that 'language' and 'dialect' have been perceived very individually, and that a linguistic problem is probably a very personal experience.

The pilot study is being developed into a longitudinal project. Tape recordings are going to be made every three years with the same children in different communicative settings, with dialect-speaking and standard-speaking interlocutors respectively. Questionnaires will also be used. The aim of the project is to describe variation within the dialect, and the languages of German and Danish, so there are not too many results concerning the relationship between dialect and education. It is interesting, however, that some of the pupils have changed their attitude towards the dialect. In the pilot study they reported a comparatively high degree of bidialectism. Now they describe themselves as increasingly 'local' — perhaps realising that the 'standard' which they speak is quite a way from the national standard. Or maybe it is because they now regard the standard as an irritating necessity in school and education.

Some Sociolinguistic Implications

Lund (1983) is an attempt to measure the degree of localness in the speech of the Hirtshals school children. He concludes that all pupils used local features. None of them used a *pure* classical dialect, however. The informants were chosen to form a stratified sample of all the children attending local schools. As expected, Lund found more local forms among the boys than among the girls. His figures confirm the intuitive guess of the linguists involved in the project, and other results from this project. Jørgensen (1983b) also found that between the two theoretical extremes — the pure classical dialect and the national standard — there was a continuum of language use, with no clearcut borderlines.

Another way of expressing the relationship between dialect and standard is used by Kjeld Kristensen, who has studied the language of Vinderup, a village in Western Jutland (Kristensen, 1977, 1979; Kristensen & Thelander, 1984; see also a critical review of the Hirtshals project, with a summary in English, in Kristensen, 1984).

Kristensen (1977) uses a so-called *total index*, based on an analysis of 14 features in the speech of 100 informants, ranging from 0 (equal to pure classical dialect) to 1 (pure national standard). With the 100 informants ranked according to total index on the horizontal axis and their actual total indices on the vertical axis, one finds a curve in the shape of an S with one plateau for the near-dialect speakers, another plateau for the near-national-standard speakers, and in between a mixed language, spoken by relatively few of his informants.

This curve has the advantage of stressing that the regional language can only be demarcated from the dialect *by decision* of the linguist, and that this decision has to be based on a detailed feature analysis.

Kristensen has also carried out a co-occurrence analysis of his material, as well as an attempt at analysing the fluctuation in his informants' degree of localness during their conversations. He has found the main independent variable to be the social status of the speaker (under the conditions of his project). His basically quantitative sociolinguistic method may be well suited to explain the difference between Vendsyssel (with Hirtshals), and Southern Jutland. The S-shaped curve of Western Jutland seems to develop into almost a straight line when we move north into Vendsyssel, judging from the evidence in the Hirtshals project. Contrary to that, the curve may prove to be more of a Z-curve in Southern Jutland, although the linguistic evidence is still not described quantitatively. This region of Denmark has had a turbulent history of take-overs by Germany and Denmark, including some heavy-handed attempts at language monopolisation. Furthermore, some five to ten distinct language varieties are spoken as mother tongues by a considerable number of speakers in the larger region (i.e. Schleswig North and South of the border), namely High German, Low German, Standard Danish, the classical dialect of Danish, and a number of Frisian varieties. This all contributes to enhancing linguistic awareness and language loyalty in the region.

Consequently the borderlines between the languages when they are in use will be sharper in Southern Jutland than in Vendsyssel. This could very well affect the purely linguistic borderlines, and would account for the more or less straight line of Vendsyssel and the Z-shaped curve of Southern Jutland. This difference in turn is connected to the different experience of problems reported by school children in the two areas.

Language is an issue in Southern Jutland, in Vendsyssel on the other hand, it simply is not.

Schiødt (1986 and personal communication) was the first to suggest this description with respect to the Hirtshals project. Rasmussen & Møller (1982) also compare language use and attitudes among grade school pupils and high school pupils in the two areas. The results are somewhat different from the results of the Hirtshals project. The conclusion, however, is basically the same: in Vendsyssel the classical dialect is perceived as part of the regional identity, whereas in Southern Jutland the classical dialect is part of the personal identity of the speaker.

Another sociolinguistic description focusses on the stage of language shift in the two regions. Vendsyssel is in the process of transforming from a rural, classical dialect society into an industrialised, standard-speaking society. The language shift is *societal* in that very few individuals actually abandon one variety in favour of another. Rather, fewer and fewer new language users grow up with a command of the classical dialect. The low degree of code-switching is evidence of this, among other things. The shift is therefore uncontroversial, and the intelligibility problems non-existent (see also Jørgensen, 1984).

In Southern Jutland quite a substantial number of speakers are required to abandon one variety or code, in favour of another. The transition is therefore not smooth, and in some cases it is not only societal, but also individual. There is little doubt, however, that the classical dialect is on the retreat here, too.

As always, we have to take into consideration the possibility that the results may be different because the projects were designed differently. One point can be rejected immediately, namely that the projects yielded different results because they were designed to. All the projects, including the Hirtshals project, expected to find out something about *what* problems the dialect speakers had in school — the Vendsyssel situation came as a surprise to the project group.

Nevertheless, it is clear that the Southern Jutland projects have not distinguished between varieties as clearly as the Hirtshals project. This becomes especially clear in the cases where the classification of children into dialect speakers etc. rests on the judgements of themselves, their parents, or their teachers. These groups cannot be expected to be familiar with the linguistic terms of (classical) dialect and standard. Consequently, *problems* which the informants ascribe to dialect speaking may turn out to be something else, if linguistic attitude, meta-linguistic awareness, and meta-linguistic knowledge are taken into account. One difference still stands out, though, namely that between the Southern Jutland children's reports about problems and those of the adults in the region. This clearly must have practical implications for the schools in their everyday relationship with dialect-speaking pupils.

Practical Implications

Most teachers nowadays say they have a positive attitude towards dialect, but it seems as if they neither prevent nor solve the school problems experienced by pupils who have a dialect as their mother tongue. Therefore, 'dialect' should be a topic in teacher training and in-service teacher training.

A dialect awareness programme in teacher training currently offered at Tønder Statsseminarium, a teacher training college in Southern Jutland, is based on discussions about dialects and their linguistic, psychological, and sociological aspects. Most important, however, is an analysis of the way in which dialects are treated in educational materials, and an analysis of interaction in classes with dialect-speaking pupils. Alternative ways of dealing with dialect both as a topic and as a reality in everyday teaching, are seen as the goal.

Books used in mother tongue teaching in Denmark are often divided into, on the one hand, books designed to give training in language skills, and, on the other hand, readers containing fiction and non-fiction. This is an unfortunate distinction that prevents a general view of form and content.

In books designed to give training in language skills one finds only a few exercises dealing with dialect. A 1985 study of books for grades 8–10 (Christiansen, 1985) found that only 0.5% of the total number of books contain such exercises. These normally consist of simple sentences written in dialect, placed together with examples of misspellings or other linguistic 'errors'. The pupils are requested to note differences and they can hardly avoid getting the impression that dialect is incorrect language. In other cases dialect is seen in opposition to 'normal' language so that the pupils cannot but conclude that dialects are abnormal.

One can find whole texts written in dialect in these books, but they are rare. Often the purpose for their inclusion is for pupils to rewrite them in the standard language. This need not be bad, but again the focus is on the linguistic expression and not on the content.

An analysis in the 1960s (Jansen, 1970) of all readers for grades 1–7, found very few texts written in dialect. Furthermore, all of them were written in the same Jutland dialect, and none was written for children. Later anthologies with texts adapted for children have improved somewhat on this — at least two new collections for 13–16 year-old pupils deal with 'living in the provinces' (as opposed to Copenhagen) as their overall theme. Here we find several texts in or about dialects on equal terms with other texts. Working with such texts involves content interpretation as well as linguistic observation. By focussing on content as well as form, the teacher may deliver the message that a dialect is just as much a means of communication as the standard.

For secondary education there are even audiotapes with some of the Danish dialects and suggestions for activities in areas where dialects are found: interviews, questionnaires etc. These exercises show the dialect as a spoken language — which is to a certain degree preferable to the written dialect texts.

Unfortunately, most dialect tapes are of adults or old people. This may prevent children from identifying with the persons and may create a view of dialects as something antiquated. Furthermore, the tapes are rarely an integrated part of a theme or a topic. If the teacher does not take other aspects than the language into consideration, the dialect is in danger of being stigmatised as an extraordinary and isolated phenomenon.

There are no educational materials about dialects for 6 to 10-year-old children. This is a gap that needs to be filled. For these children as well as older children, the potentials of reading fictional literature in connection with linguistic training are often forgotten. In short stories and novels written for children one may find characters not only speaking a dialect, but also expressing their feelings and experience in connection with being a dialect speaker. The pupil with dialect-related problems (psychological, linguistic, or social) gets a chance to identify with a character with similar problems. Discussing such problems in relation to another character (than oneself) is of course a more comfortable way of getting to the core.

Dialect awareness programmes only exist at teacher training colleges in dialect speaking areas. Teachers educated elsewhere usually have very vague ideas about (classical) dialects, and no knowledge about potential problems and their solutions. This is not as serious a problem as one could expect (and certainly not as serious as in Britain (see Cheshire, 1982), since teachers are very often recruited from the local teacher training colleges — Hirtshals being an excellent example.

References

ALLERUP, P. *et al.* 1979 *Retstavning—nogle første analyser af folkeskolens afgangsprøve i 1978. I–IV.* København: Danmarks Pædagogiske Institut.

AMMON, U. 1978 *Schulschwierigkeiten von Dialektsprechern.* Weinheim und Basel: Beltz Verlag.

BEKENDTGØRELSE OM UDDAUNELSE AF LAERERE TIL FOLKESTOLEN 1986 København: Underrisningsministeriet.

CHESHIRE, J. 1982 Dialect features and linguistic conflict in schools. *Educational Review* Vol. 34, No. 1, p. 53–67.

CHRISTIANSEN, T.B. 1985 *Skriftlig dansk-bøger for 8.–10. klasse.* København: Danmarks Pædagogiske Institut.

DANSK 1984 *Undervisningsvejledning for folkeskolen (1) "Dansk 1986".* København: Undervisnings-ministeriet.

GIESBERS, H.W.M., KROON, J.W.M. and LIEBRAND, R.J.D. 1978 *Dialect en school. En empirisch sociodialectologisch onderzoek naar de invloed van dialectgebruik op schoolprestaties in het basisonderwiejs in Gennep.* Master's thesis, University of Nijmegen.

GIMBEL, J. 1983 Hirtshalslærernes meninger om dialekt og rigsmål i skolen. In E. HANSEN & J. LUND (eds) (1983), pp. 59–106.

HANSEN, E. 1983 Forældre-børn-sprog. Forældres mening om sproget i hjemmet og i skolen. In E. HANSEN & J. LUND (eds) (1983) pp. 151–96.

HANSEN, E. and J. LUND (eds) 1983 *Skolen, Samfundet og Dialekten.* 11 afhandlinger om elevers, læreres og foældres sprog og sprogsyn—belyst ud fra undersøgelser af forholdet mellem skole og dialekt i Hirtshals Kommune. Frederikshavn: Dafolo Forlag.

JANSEN, M. 1970 *Danske læsebøger 1.–7. skoleår.* 1. del. København.

JØRGENSEN, J. NORMANN 1983a De danske sprog i Hirtshals Kommune. In E. HANSEN & J. LUND (eds) (1983), pp. 13–35.

——1983b Variationsbredden hos dialekttalende. In E. HANSEN & J. LUND (eds) (1983), pp. 197–224.

——1984 *Sociolinguistic Papers.* København: Royal Danish School of Educational Studies.

KRISTENSEN, K. 1977 Variationen i vestjysk stationsbymål. En kvantitativ sociolingvistisk dialektundersøgelse i Vinderup, Ringkøbing Amt. *Dialektstudier,* 4.bind, 1.halvbind, pp. 29–109, København: Akademisk Forlag.

——1979 Kvantitative blandingssprogsstudier. *Dialektstudier* 4.bind, 2.halvbind, pp. 161–236, København: Akademisk Forlag.

——1984 Dialekten og skolen i Danmark. En kritisk præsentation af en dialektsociologisk undersøgelse. *Svenska Landsmål och Svenskt Folkliv,* pp. 60–90, Uppsala.

KRISTENSEN, K. and THELANDER, M. 1984 On dialect levelling in Denmark and Sweden. *Folia Linguistica* XVIII/1–2: 223–46.

LUND, J. 1983 Dix—et middel til måling af regional variation. En undersøgelse af dialektpræget hos elever i Hirtshals Kommune. In E. HANSEN & J. LUND (eds) (1983), pp. 37–58.

——1986 *Dialectes et langues regionales dans l'enseignement primaire au Danemark.* København: Ecole Nationale des Hautes Etudes Pedagogiques.

MØLLER, L. 1983 Udtale og læseudvikling. Læseudvikling hos skoleelever i 1.–3.klasse. In E. HANSEN & J. LUND (eds) (1983), pp. 326–64.

NYBERG, M. 1979 Dialekt og rigsmål i skolen. *Danske Folkemaal,* 22.bind, hæfte 1, p. 1–39, København: C. A. Reitzel.

——1980 Findes der dialektbarrierer i Danmark? Rapport om et rundspørge blandt 112 lærere i folkeskolen. *Danske Folkemaal,* 22.bind, hæfte 2, p. 1–28, København: C. A. Reitzel.

——1981 Findes der dialektbarrierer i Danmark? (2). Rapport om et rundspørge blandt 531 skoleelever. *Danske Folkemål,* 23.bind, pp. 69–130, København: C. A. Reitzel.

NYBERG, M. and LARSEN, M.B. 1983 Elevernes opfattelse af eget sprog. Spørgeskemaundersøgelse blandt elever 5.–10. klasse. In E. HANSEN & J. LUND (eds) (1983), pp. 107–49.

PEDERSEN, K.M. 1977 *Dialekt, regionalsprog, rigssprog—en analyse af børns skolesprog.* Aabenraa: Institut for Grænseregionsforskning.

——1986 *Mødet mellem sprogene i den dansk-tyske grænseregion. En-, to- og flersprogede børn i Sønderjylland.* Aabenraa: Institut for Grænseregionsforskning.

RASMUSSEN, J.R. and MØLLER, B.M. 1982 *Hva mener du?—en holdnings — og sprogvaneundersøgelse foretaget blandt skoleelever i Vendsyssel og Sønderjylland.* Aalborg: Aalborg Universitetscenter.

SANDERSEN, V. 1983 Skriftsprog og dialekt. Skriftsprog i 4. og 9. klasse. In E. HANSEN & J. LUND (eds) (1983), pp. 231–70.

SCHIØDT, H.J. 1983 'Jeg besøger en arbejdsplads'. En undersøgelse af 119 stile fra 5. klassetrin. In E. HANSEN & J. LUND (eds) (1983), pp. 271–301.

——1986 Aspects of Dialect Loss in North Western Denmark. Unpubl. paper, Royal Danish School of Educational Studies at Copenhagen.

SKOV, P. 1983 *Værdinormer om skolen.* København og Lund: Munksgaard.

SONDEREN, J. and WELTENS, B. 1981 *Taalvariatie en schoolsucces in een brugklas.* Masters' thesis, University of Nijmegen.

STIJNEN, S. and VALLEN, T. 1981 *Dialect als onderwiejsprobleem. Een sociolinguistisch-onderwijskundig onderzoek naar problemen van dialectsprekende kinderen in het basisonderwiejs.* 's-Gravenhage: Stichting voor Onderzoek het Onderwijs, Staatsuitgeverij 's-Gravenhage.

TRUDGILL, P. 1975 *Accent, Dialect and the School.* London: Edward Arnold.

VENÅS, K. 1979 Dialekt og riksspråk i skulen. In *Rapport fra et nordisk symposium på Lysebu, 2.–5.april 1979.* Oslo: Universitet i Oslo.

4 Dialect, Frisian and education in the Netherlands

ANTON M. HAGEN

Introduction

This chapter describes the relationship between dialect, standard Dutch and Frisian, and discusses some of the main findings of Dutch research into the role of dialects and Frisian in education. It sketches the place of Dutch dialects and Frisian in the Dutch 'linguistic landscape' and then focusses on sociolinguistic aspects of Dutch dialects and Frisian, stressing the great variety of dialect–standard situations that exist in the Netherlands, and the nature of Dutch–Frisian bilingualism. It goes on to describe some Education Acts which regulate the position of the dialects and of Frisian in the educational system, and refers to some of the main findings of the research that has carried out into the role of the dialects and of Frisian in education. The main points are summarised in the conclusion.

Language Variation

Standard Dutch and Dutch dialects

The 'linguistic landscape' of the Netherlands consists of a relatively diverse range of dialects. The most recent attempt at classifying and mapping these dialects (Daan & Blok, 1970) distinguishes as many as 28 main regional groups in the Dutch-speaking area. This grouping is based primarily on native speakers' awareness of dialect differences; but the classification is also supported by isogloss patterns.

The Dutch linguistic landscape is not equally varied in all parts of the country. Since the sixteenth and seventeenth centuries, the western part of the Netherlands (the present provinces of North and South Holland) has been the centre of the emergence and the spread of the standard Dutch variety. The eastern and southern regions, on the other hand, have been the areas into which the standard language has diffused least, and where the dialects have therefore held relatively strong positions. Daan & Blok (1970) capture this contrast aptly with the terms *Randstad* and *Landrand*. *Randstad* means, literally, 'border town' and refers to the urban agglomeration in the western part of the Netherlands, comprising the principal towns of Amsterdam, Rotterdam and The Hague; *Landrand*, on the other hand, means literally 'countryside border' and refers to the peripheral areas in the eastern and southern parts of the Netherlands. Many *Randstad* speakers do not consider themselves to be dialect speakers, even though their speech may sound as if it is dialect, when compared to standard Dutch. The general pattern is that differences from standard Dutch increase in proportion to the distance of the dialects from the centre, as shown in Map 1.

Dialect differences in the Netherlands are so great that not all dialects are mutually intelligible. This is due to deep structural isoglosses such as the *Uerdinger Linie* and the *Benrather Linie*. This latter isogloss (see Map 1) marks the High German consonant shift and gives the 'shifted' dialects of Kerkrade and the surrounding area a noticeable German-like structure. No wonder that these deep structural differences can cause serious problems in education (pp. 55–81).

There is a long tradition in the Netherlands that standard Dutch should be a regionally neutral variety, referred to as ABN — 'Algemeen Beschaafd Nederlands' (General Educated Dutch) — or, more recently, as simply 'Standaard Nederlands' (standard Dutch). This was proposed by Van Haeringen (1924), for example, following Jespersen's idea of a neutral standard. In practice, however, this idealisation often turns out to mean that standard Dutch should not contain features that can be identified as typical of a region other than the *Randstad*. This means, therefore, that standard Dutch speech is speech with a 'western' accent.

This 'Hollando-centrism' in the realisation of standard Dutch is gradually giving way to a greater degree of regional pluralism. Apart from national and ethnolectal varieties such as 'Belgian Dutch' and 'Surinam Dutch', several regional forms of the standard — that is, standard varieties spoken with a regional accent — are increasingly heard in the Dutch-

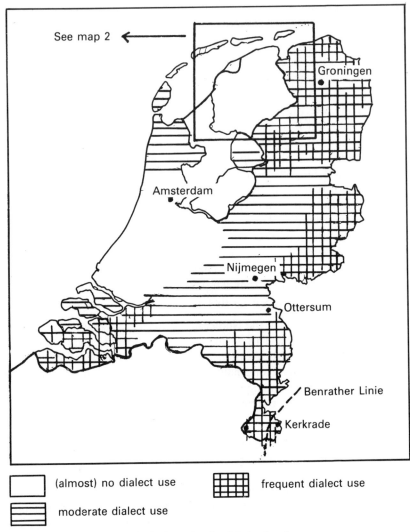

See map 2 ←

Groningen

Amsterdam

Nijmegen

Ottersum

Benrather Linie

Kerkrade

	(almost) no dialect use		frequent dialect use
	moderate dialect use		

MAP 1 *Use of traditional dialects in the Netherlands*

speaking area nowadays, including on radio and television. However, these changes provoke very negative evaluative comments and stereotyping in terms, for example, of 'eastern' and 'southern' speech.

Dutch and Frisian

The province of Friesland is a bilingual area with two recognised languages, Dutch and Frisian. Frisian has to be considered as a separate language for several reasons: its linguistic structure (it belongs to the Anglo-Frisian branch of West Germanic); its history (written documents exist in Old Frisian which are even older than Dutch texts); its functions (it is a language 'with an army and a navy' — see Haugen (1966) — in that it has a long tradition of writing and a codified spelling and grammar); furthermore, the Frisian standard language was developed by the so-called *Fryske Akademy*.

For some time now, the functions of Frisian have been its weak point. Standard Dutch has been used as the official language of administration, religion and education from the sixteenth century onwards in Friesland, and even the romantic 'Frisian Movement' in the first half of the nineteenth century was unable to bring about any substantial restoration of the use of written Frisian. For centuries, therefore, Frisian has had the status of a weak, regional language. Not until the middle of this century did pressure groups and an actual riot (*Kneppelfreed* or 'Cudgel Friday') manage to enforce proper recognition of the right to use Frisian in formal domains.

As can be seen in Map 2 (from *De Friese Taal*, 1987), Frisian is only spoken in part of the province of Friesland. Note that from the sixteenth century a distinctive linguistic variety has been spoken in the towns shown on the map (Leeuwarden, Sneek, etc.), which is known as *Stadsfries* or 'City Frisian', as opposed to *Landfries* or 'Rural Frisian'. Over the centuries the number of Hollandic elements in this urban variety has increased (elements, that is, which originate from the provinces of North and South Holland) and this has been at the cost of Frisian features. Het Bildt is a polder area with a mixed Frisian-Dutch variety. In Stellingwerven a Saxonian Dutch dialect is spoken.

Sociology of Language

Dialect and standard situations

In the description of dialect situations it is very useful to distinguish between urban and rural dialects. Since the Dutch standard language originated in the urban areas of Holland, it is here that we find the earliest records of dialects being stigmatised. To this day the urban dialects of the *Randstad* are the most heavily stigmatised, since it is here that the social distribution of dialect and standard is most evident (see Münstermann, this volume, Chapter 10). A similar pattern of evaluation is spreading, very quickly, to the cities and towns of the *Landrand*. Research in Nijmegen, near to the Dutch-German border, for example, shows that more than 80% of the population associate speaking the urban dialect with lower social

MAP 2 *Friesland and the Frisian language area* (from *De Friese Taal* 1987: 11)

status, and the majority of the population have very negative attitudes towards the local dialect (Van Hout, 1980). But this is not the whole picture. In some places, and in particular in the province of Limburg, the dialect is not seen as characteristic of lower social status, but is a positive marker of local or regional identity. The very high prestige of the urban dialect of Maastricht, the capital of Limburg, is particularly noteworthy (see Münstermann & Hagen, 1986; Weltens & Sonderen, this volume, Chapter 9).

Dialect has traditionally been spoken more extensively in the country and in smaller towns; here it has always been a marker of 'regionality' rather than of 'lower social class'. However, research in Ottersum, in Northern Limburg, a typical, originally agrarian, rural community, shows that the association between speaking a dialect and lower social status is becoming increasingly evident; and this also holds for 'rural' dialects (for further details, see Hagen & Giesbers, 1988).

A clear indication of changing attitudes towards dialect and standard language is the growing preference for the use of the standard language as the language used in the family. Table 1 shows that in a number of rural communities in the eastern part of the Netherlands, parents use dialect considerably less often with their children than they do with each other. When the figures given in Table 1 are broken down into different age groups, it can be seen that 50% of the younger parents speak dialect with their spouse and standard Dutch with their children, but that only 10% of the older parents do so (see Daan et al., 1985: 92).

TABLE 1 *Dialect Use by Parents in a Number of Communities in the Countryside (adapted from Daan et al. 1985: 91)*

	Zwolle (Gld)	Sauwerd	Bredevoort	Gennep
with spouse	93%	62%	84%	67%
with children	35%	35%	57%	33%

Data of this kind indicate that it is becoming increasingly problematic to see the distribution of dialect and standard language in terms of a simple continuum of formal domains (= standard language) and informal domains (= dialect). Instead, there seems to be a tripartite division into (1) 'instrumental public' domains (for example, school, official institutions, speaking to strangers) where standard Dutch is used; (2) 'solidarity' domains (for example, speaking to friends, neighbours, or partner) where the dialect is used; and (3) a separate domain ('family'), where the standard language is gaining in importance (see Münstermann & Hagen, 1986; Van Hout & Münstermann, 1988). The consequences for education of the relative instability of this third domain are obvious.

Frisian-Dutch bilingualism

A recent survey, 'Taal yn Fryslân' (Gorter et al., 1984), gives general information on language attitudes and language choice in Friesland. A representative sample of the Frisian population gave self-reports of their linguistic competence in Frisian as shown in Table 2. It should be noted

TABLE 2   *Self Reports of Linguistic Competence in Frisian (from Gorter* et al., *1984)*

comprehension	94%
speaking	73%
reading	65%
writing	10%

that for most people who have productive skills in Frisian, the choice of using Frisian is restricted to the informal domains of family, friends, neighbourhood and certain types of work and public service. Compared with the figures that resulted from a previous language survey (Pietersen, 1969), competence in writing has decreased fairly sharply (from 31% to 10%). In fact, however, it is not the elaboration of Frisian for use in formal and public domains that is proving to be difficult, but the acceptance of its use in these domains. The paradox for Frisian is, apparently, that the spectacular success of Frisian language policy in past decades (see p. 55) has coincided with a public reluctance to accept Frisian in formal domains, and with the stabilisation of, or decline in, the use of Frisian in the speech community (see Daan *et al.*, 1985; Van der Plank, 1985; Gorter, 1987).

Educational Language Policy

Policy towards dialects

Compulsory universal education was introduced into Dutch society in 1901. After a bitter struggle for freedom in education, the first comprehensive Elementary Education Act in the Netherlands was introduced in 1920. Pressure from Friesland brought about a change to section 2, part 1, of this Act in 1937, which permitted the teaching of 'regional dialect in active use' as an optional subject in primary education. In fact, the possibility of teaching dialect was probably introduced into the Act unintentionally; we know of no schools where the possibilities that this legislation offered for dialects have been systematically exploited.

The 1980 Education Act put an end to the educational status of regional dialects as optional subjects. Section 10, part 5, of the 1980 Act restricts dialects in education to use only as a 'medium of instruction', additional to standard Dutch. This 'pedagogical' use of dialect in education is exactly what was advocated by Dutch sociolinguists during the 1970s on the basis of their research findings (see pp. 55–8).

There is no legislation concerning the position of dialects in Dutch secondary education.

Policy towards Frisian

In 1907 the Provincial Council of Friesland was already supporting the idea of public lessons in Frisian, though not during school hours. As mentioned earlier, in 1937 pressure from Friesland brought about an amendment of the 1920 law on primary education; Frisian was not named, however, and it was in fact referred to as a dialect. It was not until 1955 that the phrase 'a regional dialect in active use' was changed to 'the Frisian language or a regional dialect in active use'.

In 1955 Frisian was allowed for the first time the status of a 'language of instruction' in grades 1–3 in primary schools in Friesland. This decision was taken after a successful experiment in bilingual education had taken place in 9 schools in Friesland. Soon afterwards a special Bureau for Bilingual Education was founded, and the number of bilingual schools increased until it reached a peak in 1965, with 84 bilingual schools.

A new change in the Education Act in 1974 allowed Frisian to be the medium of instruction in all grades, and — a major change — made the teaching of Frisian a compulsory subject in all primary schools in Friesland. Exemption from this was given only in special cases (such as the non-Frisian speaking area of Stellingwerven, shown on Map 2).

In 1977 the Provincial Council of Friesland asked permission from the Dutch government to introduce Frisian as a compulsory subject in secondary education also; but this was refused 'for financial reasons'. Only if at least 20 pupils in a school ask for lessons in Frisian is the school obliged to offer facilities for this (further details are given in Wijnstra, 1976; *De Friese Taal*, 1987).

Educational Practice

Dutch dialects and the school

It will be clear from what has been said so far that from 1937 the Netherlands has had a very liberal official language policy towards dialects in education. However, there is a discrepancy between policy and practice. The research that has been carried out into the use of dialects and standard Dutch in school shows that the school is a straightforward standard language domain (for an overview, see Hagen & Sturm, 1982). Even in regions of the country where the position of the dialect is strong, such as in Kerkrade and Maastricht (see p. 52), it has been found that contrary to teachers' self-reports of their language behaviour, the dialect is rarely used in the classroom (see Stijnen & Vallen, this volume, Chapter 8; Weltens & Sonderen, this volume, Chapter 9).

Since the 1970s, a good deal of research has been carried out on the topic of dialect and school in the Netherlands. One official government investigation was reported in a brochure entitled *Schooltaal—Thuistaal* (ACLO-M, 1978). This reports on teachers' attitudes to the problem of dialect in education. In addition to the Kerkrade project (again, see Stijnen & Vallen, this volume, Chapter 8), a parallel project that was carried out in Gennep should be mentioned (see Giesbers *et al.*, 1978; forthcoming). Smaller scale projects have also been carried out in Maastricht (see Sonderen & Weltens, 1981; Weltens & Sonderen, this volume, Chapter 9), in Groningen, in the northern part of the Netherlands (see Oosterhof *et al.*, 1984; Van Oosterhout, 1986), and in several other places (see Hagen & Sturm, 1982).

From this research a general picture emerges of dialect-related problems in the following areas:

Dutch language skills

Details of some of the problems that were found to exist in Maastricht and in Kerkrade are given in the papers by Weltens & Sonderen and Stijnen & Vallen, in this volume. Further details on the relationship that was found between dialect and spelling in Kerkrade can be found in Hagen (1985); on spelling and reading in Groningen, in Van Oosterhout (1986); and on problems with grammatical gender in spoken Dutch in Groningen, in Oosterhof *et al.* (1984). Some indirect manifestations of language problems were found in the research carried out in Kerkrade (see Hagen, 1981; Stijnen & Vallen, 1981). These included avoidance phenomena, linguistic insecurity, self-repairs and code-switching.

Other subjects and general achievement

Different research projects have found different results in these areas. A general tendency, however, is that the problems experienced by dialect speakers are most evident in Dutch language skills and in other subjects where language plays an important role. If one looks at general educational achievement in a broad sense — including, for example, the results of school tests, evaluation and other forms of assessment — then it is clear that dialect speakers are at a disadvantage (see Stijnen & Vallen, this volume, Chapter 8). Furthermore, the Kerkrade research showed that the problems experienced by dialect speakers are not confined to the early years of school; the effects tend to accumulate in the higher grades of school, and they continue even into secondary school (see ACLO-M, 1978; Weltens & Sonderen, this volume, Chapter 9).

Language attitudes

All the research that has been carried out has found that teachers' attitudes play a crucial role in the relationship between dialect and education (see Münstermann, this volume, Chapter 10; Van den Hoogen & Kuijper, this volume, Chapter 13). As mentioned earlier, a striking result of the Kerkrade research was that although teachers may appear to have a positive attitude towards dialect, from the answers that they may give in a survey of their views, this does not necessarily reflect the way that they behave in the classroom. This suggests that teachers are subject to heteronomous norms in their classrooms, which results in dialect either being explicitly forbidden in class, or simply not used.

Classroom interaction

Research carried out in Kerkrade and elsewhere has found that dialect is rarely used in classroom interaction. In this respect there is a clear difference from the situation that exists in Dutch-speaking Belgium (see Van de Craen & Humblet, this volume, Chapter 2). Furthermore, the research that has been carried out in the Netherlands shows that dialect speakers tend to be under-represented in verbal interaction in the classroom.

A unique aspect of the Kerkrade project is that, using an RDD (Research-Development-Diffusion) model, the *research component* was followed by a *development component* and by a *diffusion component*. The development phase of the project concentrated on

—the role of dialect in verbal interaction in school;
—the attitudes of teachers and pupils towards the use of dialect in teaching situations;
—writing skills, especially grammatical correctness in written Dutch.

The Gennep research project also made some useful practical contributions. The research team developed a series of lessons on various aspects of language variation, which was designed to be used by teachers in Dutch secondary schools (see Giesbers *et al.*, this volume, Chapter 15). Other practically-oriented approaches, which make dialect the focus of thinking about language, can be found in Hagen & Sturm (1982), Van Calcar *et al.*, (this volume, Chapter 16), and in the publications on the development phase of the Kerkrade project (Hos *et al.*, 1982; Swachten & Vaessen, 1982; Van den Hoogen and Kuijper, this volume, Chapter 13). Copies of Hos *et al.* (1982) were sent to all primary schools and teacher information centres in the Netherlands; copies of Swachten & Vaessen (1982) were sent to all primary schools in the Kerkrade area.

Frisian and the school

The successful incorporation of the Frisian language into educational policy has been underlined by educational research, particularly research into the effects of bilingual education. The most prestigious research project to date — comparable in its scope to the Kerkrade project and, like the Kerkrade project, subsidised by the Foundation for Educational Research — is the 'Friesland project' (see Wijnstra, 1976). The aim of the project was to 'investigate school success, including reading and writing in Dutch . . . in relation to the oral command of Dutch/Frisian, under different schooling conditions' (Wijnstra, 1976: 277). Central to this research was a comparison of different types of schooling and, in particular, a comparison between bilingual schools and monolingual (Dutch) schools, in order to obtain valid information about the advantages and disadvantages of bilingual education. It was concluded that a bilingual education had no influence on school achievement of any kind — in other words, that it had neither a negative effect nor a positive effect. This result was interpreted in Friesland as constituting an argument in favour of bilingual education, on the grounds that if bilingual education is not detrimental to children's educational achievement, then those children who have had a bilingual education have the added advantage of being enriched by the possession of a second language, whilst at the same time supporting the Frisian language.

Friesland has its own *Fryske Akademy* (Frisian Academy), a *Provinsjale Underwiisried* (Provincial Educational Board) and other institutional facilities, so that a good infrastructure for the teaching of Frisian is available. One of the most successful teaching aids has proved to be the 'Teleboard' (TV-blackboard), a special form of educational television (see Gorter, 1984).

However, bilingual education has not proliferated in Friesland, despite the ideological advancement of Frisian, the results of Wijnstra's 1976 research, and the good supporting infrastructure. After the 1965 peak, when there were 84 bilingual schools, the number has now stabilised at about 70 of the 500 or so primary schools in Friesland. As for the teaching of Frisian as a compulsory subject, research has shown that most schools spend 30–45 minutes per week on the subject, and this time is spent on a number of diverse activities, from singing Frisian songs to the teaching of oral Frisian as part of the curriculum. About 70 schools have been given special permission not to teach Frisian (see *De Friese Taal*, 1987).

Conclusion

The situation concerning Dutch dialects can be summarised as follows. The Dutch linguistic landscape has some areas where the dialects differ very greatly from each other. Where dialects resemble standard Dutch more closely, the dialects and accents tend to elicit negative attitudes. The general pattern — though there are some exceptions — is that the traditional, divergent dialects are also beginning to elicit negative connotations; this is accompanied by a clear language shift, particularly in the family domain. The official Dutch language policy is very liberal and tolerant towards dialects, but this policy is not put into practice in the schools. Research in Kerkrade and elsewhere has shown that dialect speakers experience problems in education with respect to language skills, and also in other school subjects, as well as in their general level of achievement. Language attitudes and verbal interaction are also affected. Some interesting practical suggestions designed to overcome these problems have been suggested.

Frisian functions as a separate language, and this is supported by official language policy. During the last few decades the official position of Frisian has been considerably strengthened. However, the sociolinguistic situation of Frisian in terms of its use in the speech community tends not to reflect its political status. Recent legislation has been very favourable towards the use of Frisian in school: it can be used as a medium of instruction, and it is a compulsory subject in primary schools. In education, however, as in the speech community generally, the possibilities that have been offered by legislation have not been fully exploited.

References

ACLO-M 1978 *Schooltaal—Thuistaal*. The Hague: Staatsuitgeverij.
DAAN J. and BLOK, D.P. 1970 *Van Randstad tot landrand. Toelichting bij de kaart:*

dialecten en naamkunde. Amsterdam: Noord-Hollandsche Uitgeversmaatschappij.

DAAN, J., DEPREZ, K., VAN HOUT, R. and STROOP, J. 1985 *Onze veranderende taal*. Utrecht/Antwerpen: Spectrum.

De Friese Taal 1987 Leeuwarden: Provinciaal Bestuur van Friesland.

GIESBERS, H., KROON, S. and LIEBRAND, R. 1978 *Dialect en school. Een empirisch-sociodialectologisch onderzoek naar de invloed van dialectgebruik op schoolprestaties in het basisonderwijs in Gennep*. Master's thesis, Department of Dialectology, University of Nijmegen.

—— forthcoming, Bidialectalism and primary school achievement in a Dutch dialect area. *Language and Education*.

GORTER, D. 1984 The use of the Teleboard for language education in Friesland. *International Journal of the Sociology of Language* 48, 99–113.

—— (ed.) 1987 The sociology of Frisian. Special issue of the *International Journal of the Sociology of Language*.

GORTER, D., JELSMA, G.H., VAN DER PLANK, P.H. and DE VOS, K. 1984 *Taal yn Fryslân*. Leeuwarden: Fryske Akademy.

HAGEN, A.M. 1981 *Standaardtaal en dialectsprekende kinderen. Een studie over monitoring van taalgebruik*. Muiderberg: Coutinho.

——1985 De relatie tussen spelvaardigheid en dialect. In E. ASSINK & G. VERHOEVEN (eds), *Visies op spelling*. Groningen: Wolters-Noordhoff. pp. 164–73.

HAGEN, A.M. and GIESBERS, H. 1988 Dutch sociolinguistic dialect studies. In F. COULMAS & J. STALPERS (eds), *The Sociolinguistics of Dutch* (Special issue of the *International Journal of the Sociology of Language* 73, 29–44).

HAGEN, A.M. and STURM, J. 1982 *Dialekt en school*. Groningen: Wolters-Noordhoff.

HAUGEN, E. 1966 Dialect, language, nation. *American Anthropologist* 68, 922–35.

HOS, H., KUIJPER, H. and VAN TUIJL, H. 1982 *Dialect op de basisschool. Het Kerkrade-project van theorie naar onderwijspraktijk*. Enschede: Foundation for Curriculum Development (SLO).

MÜNSTERMANN, H. and HAGEN, A.M. 1986 Functional and structural aspects of dialect loss: a research plan and some first results. In B. WELTENS, K. DE BOT & T. VAN ELS (eds), *Language Attrition in Progress*. Dordrecht/Providence: Foris. pp. 75–96.

OOSTERHOF, F., WIERANGA, A. and VAN ZANTWIJK, A. 1984 *Regiolectische varianten in de beheersing van het genus*. Master's thesis, Department of Dutch, State University of Groningen.

PIETERSEN, L. 1969 *De Friezen en hun taal*. Drachten: Laverman.

SONDEREN, J. and WELTENS, B. 1981 *Taalvariatie en schoolsucces in een brugklas*. Master's thesis, Department of General Linguistics, Univeristy of Nijmegen.

STIJNEN, S. and VALLEN, T. 1981 *Dialect als onderwijsprobleem*. Den Haag: Staatsuitgeverij.

SWACHTEN, L. and VAESSEN, M. 1982 *Werken met dialect in de klas. Het Kerkraads voorbeeldenboek*. Nijmegen: University of Nijmegen.

VAN HAERINGEN, C.B. 1924 Eenheid en nuance in beschaafd Nederlandse uitspraak. In C.B. VAN HAERINGEN *Nederlandica. Verspreide opstellen*. Den Haag (1962): 9–29.

VAN HOUT, R. 1980 De studie van stadsdialekt: van dialectologie, empirische linguistiek en sociolinguistiek. *Toegepaste Taalwetenschap in Artikelen* 8, 143–62.

VAN HOUT, R. and MÜNSTERMANN, H. 1988 The multidimensionality of domain configurations. *International Journal of the Sociology of Language* 74, 107–24.

VAN OOSTERHOUT, E. 1986 *Wat staat daar nog maar? Een toepassingsgericht sociolinguistisch onderzoek nar de verwerving van lees—en schrijfvaardigheid bij kinderen met een varieteit van het Gronings als thuistaal.* Groningen: typescript.

VAN DER PLANK, P.H. 1985 *Taalsociologie.* Muiderberg: Coutinho.

WIJNSTRA, J.M. 1976 *Het onderwijs aan van huis uit friestalige kinderen.* Den Haag: Staatsuitgeverij.

5 Dialect and education in West Germany

PETER ROSENBERG

Research on Dialect in School: An Historical Perspective

Dialect speakers have experienced problems in German schools ever since the time that German replaced Latin as the official language of education. Dialect has always been seen as lacking in refinement and, even for those who were well-disposed towards the pupils, the use of dialect, much like picking your nose, was considered to be a bad habit to be cured as quickly as possible (Bausinger, 1983: 75). The existence of specific educational difficulties experienced by dialect-speaking children is thus by no means a recent discovery. Two hundred years ago teachers were criticised for speaking 'a language unfamiliar to the people' (von Cölln, 1784). One hundred years ago Standard High German was referred to as the new 'Latin' of the village school teachers (Hildebrand, 1867; see also Gutbier, 1854; Winteler, 1878; Meyer-Markau, 1907; Karstädt, 1925; von Greyerz, 1913; Beckmann, 1920; Brechenmacher, 1925; Kürsten & Kramer, 1935; Niebaum, 1979b: 109).

Although German dialectologists were aware of the educational implications of the relationship between dialect and standard (see Wegener, 1879; Kretschmer, 1918; Naumann, 1925; Maurer, 1933), they paid no attention to the position of the dialect speaker in school. Until relatively recently, their interest was firmly focussed on the description of German dialects and their geographical distribution. Systematic empirical research on the social distribution of language varieties and the implications for education only began to emerge in the late 1960s.

There are several reasons why this should be the case. Most important is that the development of sociolinguistics as an autonomous area within linguistics coincided with changing political demands in the field of education.

Economic and technological advances created a demand for labour. There was a call for better qualifications and greater social mobility, often discussed in terms of 'equal opportunity' and 'permeability' of the education system. At this time, linguistics assumed a new and socially important function. There was widespread discussion of the 'language barrier' which impeded equal opportunities both in schools and in the workplace. This marked change in thinking was largely triggered by the dissemination in West Germany of the controversial work of Bernstein on elaborated and restricted codes, though Bernstein's theories soon began to meet with criticism.

During the early 1970s the discussion moved into the field of dialectology. Answers to the question: 'Is dialect a language barrier?' vary greatly. 'Language barrier' has been interpreted variously as a 'communication barrier', a 'cognitive barrier', 'an impediment to social success' and 'difficulty in transposition from language system 1 to language system 2' (see Mattheier, 1974). It is therefore not surprising that the research on this question has been undertaken from a number of different perspectives.

Ammon (1972, 1978a, this volume, Chapters 7 and 14), for instance, advances the widely accepted thesis that dialects produce a communication barrier. He argues that dialect and standard are correlated with working class and middle class speakers respectively, and that they are regionally restricted; they are also non-standardised and lexically unelaborated. Seen from this perspective dialect speech is deficient. Ammon therefore advocates 'standard German for all' in place of 'hypocritical' norm tolerance. In contrast, writers like Hasselberg (1972, 1976) Jäger (1970) and Besch & Löffler (1973, 1977) argue that dialect is different rather than deficient and point to the widespread interference and linguistic insecurity of dialect-speaking children in learning and using High German. Besch & Löffler, for instance, conclude that, if these children are to become bidialectal, they need greater and more directed assistance from teachers sensitive to dialect problems. Their series of contrastive booklets (*Dialekt/Hochsprache-Kontrastiv*) is the most important practical result of the 'language barrier' debate. (See Ammon, this volume, Chapter 14.)

The most important theoretical contribution of this debate was the focussing of attention on the social context of dialect use. Although traditional German dialectology had always dealt with the heterogeneity of the linguistic community, it usually took a purely diatonic (regional) perspective, in which the geographical distribution of dialects was used to interpret subsequent stages in the historical development of German. When, in the early 1970s, sociological methodology was introduced into dialectology, the implicit assumption that dialects are homogeneous and only vary from region to region, was empirically refuted. This was a break with the mono-dimensional view of traditional dialectology and was the real achievement for the new social dialectology.

For some time, however, sociolinguistic dialectology was constrained to some extent by traditional approaches to the subject, for recognition of social as well as regional heterogeneity did not necessarily involve recognition of the social functions of the variability of speech (see Goossens, 1986: 257). The assumption, for instance, of a socially determined distribution of language varieties, differing from class to class, but being used in a self-contained and monolithic manner, still has a great deal in common with the old premise of invariant language behaviour. Yet the analysis of the speech of dialect speaking children soon made it clear that speakers exploit variation for a range of communicative purposes. Sometimes children's ability to vary their language appeared to be more important for educational achievement than their social class background. Language has been found to vary both with situational factors and according to the linguistic value systems of the speaker and more recent research has paid increasing attention to factors such as these.

For this reason, researchers in the field of dialect and school have paid considerable attention to ways of measuring 'dialect distance', or the extent to which different children should be considered 'dialect speakers'. This has raised a number of problems which have yet to be solved. Some of these problems concern methodology, but for the most part they are a reflection of the general dialect situation in West Germany and of the inadequacy of the available descriptive models to account for the West German situation. Before proceeding with an account of the research that has taken place in West Germany into dialect and the school, it will be useful to discuss the different approaches that have been taken in describing the West German dialects, and to outline the changes that are occurring in the dialects today.

In the past, German dialects were usually thought of in one of three ways: in terms of clusters of isoglosses; in terms of primary and secondary dialect features, which were determined intuitively (and which were sometimes described in terms of deep structure versus surface structure features); or in terms of a number of transition rules relating the dialect to the standard (see Schirmunski, 1930; Goossens, 1977).

Recent empirical research which attempts to measure the 'dialect distance' of speakers (or the extent to which they can be considered to speak dialect) continues this tradition to some extent. Stellmacher (1977), for example, measures 'dialect distance' in terms of the frequency with which variable dialect features occur, using a type-token ratio. Intermediate stages cannot be measured using this method. Ammon (1973; 1978a; 1985; and this volume) makes an interesting attempt at establishing dialect levels. He sets up a dialect ladder which is gradated according to the range of usage, in terms of standard German features and regional, dialect, features. Some of the individual dialect levels, however, are chosen arbitrarily, as Ammon (1985) acknowledges; moreover, it seems inadequate to define dialect distance as a smooth linear approximation to the standard language, along an axis which takes account merely of regional usage. Ammon's method expresses the dialect distance of speakers as an average rate (e.g. 3.67), but the individual intervals are not of equal importance and it certainly cannot be assumed that each step in the ladder implies a wider regional radius of acceptability. This approach does not take into account the prestige of different language varieties. A further attempt at establishing dialect distance is that of Reitmajer (1979), who combines Gfirtner's (1972) syllable-reduction method with the diphthong method; however, unreduced and reduced syllables are measures mainly of colloquialness, rather than of dialect. The evaluation of Bavarian diphthong realisation shares the same limitations noted for Stellmacher (see above). The 'Erp' project, on the other hand (see Mattheier, 1980; Besch, 1982/1983), measured the relationship between standard and non-standard pronunciation in terms of both dialect features and regional colloquial features.

More recent work sees the relationship between dialect and standard in terms of a continuum, such that there are no discrete divisions on the continuum and no clearcut dichotomy between speaking a dialect and speaking the standard. It is assumed that dialect distance is governed by an interrelated set of rules, stemming from the two poles of dialect and standard (Hasselberg, 1981, 1982; Wegera, 1983; see also Niebaum, 1983). Herrgen & Schmidt's (1984, 1985) research in Mainz leads them to argue for what they term 'a listener based dialectality' rather than 'a system contrastive dialectality'. Their methodology involved inserting a single dialect feature into a 'constructed linguistic variety', and asking 47 students to judge whether the stretch of speech was 'dialect' or not. Listeners' assessments were found to be independent of phonetic criteria, independent of systematicity and independent of the regional distribution of dialect features. Herrgen & Schmidt stress, however, that their method is only suitable for use with listeners who have an active competence in standard German, which clearly limits the validity of their conclusions with respect to other types of listeners.

Each of these conceptualisations of dialect — whether in terms of distinct social or regional varieties, or in terms of a continuum between dialect and standard — is limited in its application to the West German situation. Each of these two approaches was borrowed, in turn, from research traditions that developed in Britain and the USA, and that seemed better suited to analysing linguistic variation within the socially heterogeneous community of the Federal Republic than traditional methods of dialectology, based as they were merely on regional variation. This, however, has resulted in a number of problems, since the sociolinguistic situation in West Germany has a different history from that of the social and ethnic differences in Britain or the USA.

The German standard language is relatively young. A long period of national fragmentation, the unsynchronised pattern of economic development and late transition to bourgeois society all prevented the smooth, continuous development of standard High German; a development which was mostly unsupported by the national élites. For this reason, the geographical distribution of German dialects is relatively firmly established. In addition, the use of dialect is less stigmatised in West Germany than it is in, say, England.

On the other hand, signs of the disintegration and destabilisation of the old dialect areas have been clear for some time. The growth of cities, the development of industry and the popularity of the urban lifestyle have played a dominant role in this, and the use of dialect in rural areas as well as in urban areas has been affected. Various factors have contributed to the growth of a geographically and socially highly mobile society: factors which include population movement and social and psychological loss of roots, as a consequence of the rise of National Socialism and defeat in World War II, the modernisation of education since the 1960s; and the decline of the manufacturing industry and the growth of the service sector of the economy. The expansion of regional colloquial languages is an unmistakable consequence of developments such as these. Today, then, linguistic variation can be thought of as a complex of features whose use is governed by overlapping social, situational and social psychological factors but which, none the less, can be seen to have regionally distributed traits (see Löffler, 1986: 235).

The research that has been carried out on dialect and education mirrors general developments within the field of dialectology in West Germany. The emphasis on social stratification in language on the non-standard nature of dialects and on the social consequences of their use can be interpreted as the beginning of a new era of dialectology, just as was the case a hundred years ago when it became the 'credo' of the Neogrammarians to let the 'fresh air' of the 'living languages' into the study rooms of Indo-European research (Osthoff & Brugmann, 1878). The logical continuity of this process is to be seen in the focus on linguistic variability within the standard–dialect continuum as dependent on situation, communicative intent and linguistic value systems. Thus, the sociolinguistics of the 1970s has developed into the variationist linguistics of the 1980s. Parallel trends can inevitably be observed in the research on dialect in education (see, for instance, Mattheier, 1980, 1986; Löffler, 1986).

West German Dialect Research from 1970: The Problems of Dialect Speaking Pupils

Besch (1974: 153) describes the ways in which dialect-speaking children were treated in traditional dialectology as a 'history of negligence'. One aspect of this negligence was the recurrent prediction that dialects would die out in the near future, in which case the problem would no longer exist. In fact, 25% of school children in both West and East Germany still use dialect and an even greater proportion is influenced indirectly either by a dialect or a colloquial language closely related to dialect (Mattheier, 1980: 109).

However, regional variation needs to be taken into account (see Schmid, 1973; Ammon, 1983: 1499). The linguistic distance from the standard, for instance, is greater in the north, while dialect tolerance, and therefore the importance of dialect variation, is greater in the south. The main problems can be summarised thus:

1. *Direct dialect influence* on school achievement because of interference from the dialect in the use of Standard High German. It should be remembered, however, that it is not necessarily the case, as was once widely assumed, that the greater the contrast between two systems, the greater the risk of interference. On the contrary, increased interference is often a function of the proximity of the systems (see James, 1972: 32ff; Nickel, 1972: 10; Kielhöfer, 1975: 115ff; Reitmajer, 1979: 145).

2. *Indirect dialect influence* as a result of a combination of the dialect and intermediate forms of a regional or super-regional colloquial language (*Umgangssprache*)[1] which diverges from the standard in fewer respects than the dialect, or even in a different way. Not every divergence from standard German can be traced directly to dialect. There are, for instance, difficulties in transposing spoken German into written German. However, dialect tends to increase the general problem areas with the written language (see Wegera, 1977: 254; Rosenberg, 1986).

3. *Social problems* experienced by dialect speakers in the form, for
    instance, of social prejudice against dialect and users of dialect,
    who are often assumed to be on a socially lower level and to be
    less competent. Löffler (1979: 348ff) argues that a dialect problem
    begins when the teacher's language differs from that of the pupils.
    Teacher attitudes to dialect play a critical role in understanding
    this problem.

The first empirical study of the problems of dialect speaking pupils
was carried out in 1968 by Hasselberg in Giessen grammar schools
(*Gymnasium*). The results were published in 1972. (Data dealing with the
corpus, the methodology and results for all the studies reported in this
section are given in the Appendix, pp. 81–3.) His results, which take into
account the form of language used, scholastic achievement and regional
origin of pupils, offer a number of interesting insights. Hasselberg's study
shows that 17% of the pupils speak dialect alone, 16% dialect and standard
German and 67% standard German. The correlation with data on social
background and scholastic achievements shows that the dialect-only speakers
are predominantly of rural origin and come from working class backgrounds
(especially labourers, farmers and employees with primary schooling only).
In the middle years of secondary school, these dialect-speaking children
show a definite tendency to underachieve (particularly in mathematics).
Social and/or linguistic background would thus appear to have an effect on
more than the 'language subjects'. This study is, however, based on pupils'
self-reports which are frequently unreliable; nor were linguistic and social
variables investigated separately. In addition, the 'Gymnasium' is a selective
school, not representative of the population as a whole.

Another pioneering study was conducted by Jäger (1970) in Mannheim.
Jäger analyses the problems of dialect and colloquial language use in spelling,
grammar and lexical usage and argues that a 'dialect-based language barrier'
exists and that the greatest source of error is in the choice of grammatical
case. According to Jäger, rigorous norms, especially in spelling, are the
central problem. He understands them as middle class norms which
disadvantage lower class children and which therefore ought to be reformed.
Jäger (1970: 172) postulates a strong correlation between dialect and working
class membership on the basis of the social composition of the catchment
areas for the schools in the research sample. He emphasises, however, that
the links between social disadvantage and dialect interference are of an
indirect nature.

The work of Besch & Löffler (1977) provides practical resources for
teachers of dialect-speaking children in the *Dialekt/Hochsprache—Kontrastiv*

series (see Ammon, this volume, Chapter 14). However, these writers also offer interesting theoretical insights on the question of dialect and education. The assumption that the differences between dialects and the standard are similar to the differences between separate languages is the linch-pin for their research. On the basis of structural discrepancies between the two systems, they postulate various forms of interference and hypercorrection which they estimate as making up 8–20% of the errors in school writing in the central Alemannic area. They advocate that teachers should take these difficulties in transposing speech to writing into account, since error prognoses based on contrastive analysis can provide important information about how to teach the standard without forcing children to give up their dialect. A frequent criticism of this concept is that a given dialect and the standard language are not like separate languages, as the source variety and the target variety are neither completely separated nor self-contained homogeneous systems, but are rather poles of a variation continuum which, depending on the speaker's stylistic repertoire, includes a greater or lesser quantity of transitional forms. Since other sources of error must also be taken into account, error prognoses made on this basis are not reliable (see Mattheier, 1980: 132ff; Rosenberg, 1986: 12ff).

A further contribution to the language barrier debate has been made by the extensive research of Ammon. The importance of Ammon's work lies in the fact that he has observed the influence of dialect in very different spheres over a four year period, correlating non-linguistic variables with the dialect levels (see Ammon, this volume, Chapter 7) of the pupils. The results are of interest: there is no significant correlation between the language variety used and social class (although this was one of Ammon's presuppositions). In using the standard language, local dialect users made no more dialect-related mistakes than did standard-speaking children newly arrived from other areas. Broad dialect users, however, performed less well throughout. They made more dialect based errors, participated orally less frequently, wrote shorter essays with a smaller vocabulary, read aloud less fluently and had lower marks in all subjects, including maths. Moderate users of dialect, however, often perform even better than standard language users (Ammon, 1978a: 143, 242). Using the matched guise technique, Ammon showed that dialect speakers are considered more likeable by local people but that they are generally judged to be less intelligent, worse at school, more likely to belong to the lower classes and less trustworthy, even by dialect speakers themselves. Ammon (1978a: 172) describes this as an 'alarming finding'. It should be mentioned, however, that the method for classifying the degree of dialect usage in this study is not particularly sophisticated (see above); nor is the method for assigning speakers to different social categories. The method of attitude measurement is also problematic; pupils are expressly asked to judge *speakers* on the basis of their *language*, so that it is not surprising that they make their judgements in accordance with social stereotypes.

In another wide-ranging research project, Hasselberg (1976) investigated dialect speakers in Hessian comprehensive schools. He found that 24% of the pupils used dialect, 20% standard and an intermediate group of 56% used both standard and dialect. This grouping was based on the subjective assessment of class teachers. 70% of the dialect speakers were felt to come from working class backgrounds, and 60% of the standard speakers from middle class backgrounds. Teacher ratings of pupil performance as well as actual test results showed that dialect speakers, irrespective of social class background, are clearly disadvantaged; even middle class dialect speakers do worse than working class standard speakers.

Between 1972 and 1975, Reitmajer investigated the influence of dialect on achievement in Bavarian pre-schools, primary and secondary schools (Reitmajer, 1979). According to parents' ratings, 53% of the sample spoke only dialect, 11% only the standard and 36% were 'bilingual'. Pupils' language levels were arrived at using a combination of Gfirtner's 'syllable-reduction method' (developed in 1972) and the total of diphthongs characteristic of Bavarian dialects (see above). The results show that pre-school dialect-speaking children have significantly fewer standard language encoding skills than do others. Up to the fourth year these differences decrease, no doubt as a result of school attendance. Achievements in German at the *Gymnasium* (grammar school), however, show no relation to the language group to which the pupils belong. A comparison of the performance of pupils from Bavaria and the control group from Hannover on story re-telling tasks, indicates that this is not a straightforward matter. It emerges that certain errors assumed to be related to dialect are in fact general characteristics of colloquial speech often found in the Hannoverian control group. Interestingly, typical Bavarian diphthongs do not interfere with written work, no doubt because pupils are only too aware of their difference from the standard.

Wegera (1977) undertakes a contrastive analysis of dialect-related problems in East Hessen. Problems in children's writing were found to be related to the unrounding of front vowels, the nature of diphthongs, vowel quality, lenition of plosives, consonant gemination and noun apocope (omission of final sound or sounds). The distinction which Wegera makes between dialect-based and other errors is, however, problematic. He generally assumes that all errors between the two poles of the dialect–

standard continuum may be defined as mere gradations of a possible maximum contrast. The particular version of the dialect spoken by the pupils, their stylistic range and the possible influence of colloquial speech are thus considered irrelevant (Wegera, 1977: 18ff).

Henn (1978a) also draws on a contrastive analysis to examine dialect interference in the northwestern Palatinate region. Using a system of error classification which differentiates between contrast levelling, contrast shifting and contrast exaggeration, 80% of syntax, 84% of lexical and 28% of orthographic errors are considered to be dialect related. These findings seem extremely high, no doubt because colloquialisms have been subsumed under the heading of dialect.

Kettner (1978) offers a study of schools in two towns in Niedersachsen with very different sized dialect speaking populations. He determines a large proportion of dialect related errors (64–79%) in essays, mainly due to syntax and especially to case choice. Since such mistakes occur with similar frequency in both places, among dialect as well as standard speakers, Kettner (1978: 302) presumes that they are the result of North German colloquial language rather than of the Low German dialect. The linguistic difference between dialect and standard in the north is more evident than in the south and, consequently, there appear to be fewer transitional levels. So, he concludes, all pupils are fluent in a dialect-influenced super-regional North German colloquial language which, none the less, is associated with problems in an educational context.

Kraemer (1978) deals with dialect-related problems in phonology in the Moselle-Franconian area. Particular problems are documented for consonants, especially plosives. Direct transfer is more common than hypercorrection. Interestingly, certain kinds of essay (narratives describing personal experience and imaginative stories) are associated with a greater number of dialect errors. Once more, there are problems of definition: dialect errors are interpreted quite broadly which makes interpretation of the findings difficult. Pupils who make no dialect related errors are found to come predominantly from middle class backgrounds and to have better marks. Pupils who show considerable influence of dialect in their writing usually come from working class backgrounds and tend to underachieve. Pupils between these two extremes are difficult to characterise and in some subjects, including English, tend to perform better than children in the other groups, possibly because of their experience in adapting to 'other' language systems (1978: 186f).

Kalau (1984) investigates dialect-related problems in morphology for Nürnberg children. She finds that 75% of the errors in the sample examined are dialect-based, which again seems extremely high. Special problems are noted with respect to case markers and the use of the preterite where as many as 90% of the errors can be traced to dialect.

Rosenberg (1986) examines school problems experienced by dialect speaking children and young people in Berlin. On the basis of the variable spoken dialect of the pupils, contrastive analysis is used to identify errors as obviously dialect-based, indirectly dialect influenced and colloquially-based. Mistakes caused or influenced by dialects make up approximately 18% of the sample. In standardised text dictations, significant differences are noted between the Berlin and the Hannoverian control groups. The problem of case (dative and accusative) is at the head of a hierarchy of errors. The kind of written work also influences the error structures: in essays incorrect case and missing endings are prevalent, while in dictations hypercorrections increase. In comparisons between children of various ages, errors in transposing speech to writing are more common in the work of younger children and hypercorrections in the work of older children. The main problems are experienced by broad dialect speakers. In the case of children from abroad (especially Turkish pupils) who frequently use dialect, high rates of dialect-related mistakes are noted, while hypercorrections play a less important role. A recent Berlin project shows that stylistic variation is extremely important (see Rosenberg, 1989). Individual case studies show that academic achievement depends less on whether the pupils are dialect users than on whether they use dialect exclusively or nearly exclusively. Using a newly developed model based on socio-situational markedness, it is possible to demonstrate clear connections between the ability to style shift, scholastic achievement and the pupil's 'social world'.

Dialect and Education: Progress and Prospects in the German Speaking Area

Although various problems remain, certain clear trends emerge from the research on dialect and education.

Problems of dialect speakers

The problems of dialect speakers are obvious; the explanations for this phenomenon, however, are by no means clear cut. On the one hand, difficulties faced by dialect speakers are explained in terms of structural differences between dialect and standard. On the other hand, these difficulties are related to social class membership and social and linguistic stereotyping. The role of intolerance and ignorance on the part of teachers in questions of this kind cannot be overlooked.

Social class and dialect use

There is very little evidence which suggests a direct correlation between social class and dialect use. However, when speakers have access to the dialect alone, the links become much clearer. Dialect *per se* is not a sociolect of the working classes. Ammon (1978b: 55) concludes that this correlation is 'accidental'. Hasselberg (1983) sees the correlation as a multifactorial complex including subjective social and linguistic prestige norms and value systems. Thus while social class and language use overlap, the fit between the two is by no means perfect. Rein (1983) sees language choice as depending on factors such as speaker, audience, goal and situation. Frequently, however, the most important criterion is speaker intention rather than linguistic output. Steinig (1980), for instance, argues that linguistic markers of social background and of dialect should be treated separately in attitude research, even if these markers are identical in form.

Mattheier (1980) considers that the need to reflect social trends in social categories as well as subjective findings is critical (see also Hasselberg, 1983). There is clearly a case for multidimensional models which combine social and situational information and which take speakers' attitudes into account. Concepts such as 'social network' or 'social worlds' (see Kallmeyer *et al.*, 1981) have seldom been applied in research into dialect and education. Recent results of work in this area suggest new perspectives (see Rosenberg, 1989). Mattheier (1980) emphasises the influence of the parents, and the importance attached to their value judgements on speech. As the study of ethnic minority speakers of dialect bears out (Rosenberg, 1989), the peer group plays a further important role in the social world of children.

'Dialect-only' speakers

'Dialect-only' speakers experience obvious disadvantages — in writing, oral work and lowered teacher expectations — throughout their school careers. Ammon explains this phenomenon in terms of an objective deficit in the dialect, on the grounds of regional limitation in its use and lack of elaboration. Other writers do not necessarily consider dialect to be deficient, but pragmatically different. They argue that limits associated with regionality are often secondary to the prestige factor (see Mattheier, 1980; Kemper, 1974) and that lexical shortfalls are associated more with the need for a technological terminology than with any standard–dialect differences. Very often differences attributed to dialect are more properly explained in terms of differences between speech and writing, each of which operates with its own particular rule system (Knoop, 1978; see also Williams, this volume, Chapter 11). Wegera (1977) identifies the dialect as not simply of equivalent value to the standard, but, in some areas such as the reduction of inflection, better equipped and more progressive in terms of language development. As Steinig (1980) points out, the standard derives its prestige from normative considerations rather than from its inherent linguistic merits.

Language problems experienced by dialect speakers using the standard can result from interference from a dialect learned under very different conditions and with very different motivation. This language, however, is not acceptable in school, where the standard language is the only acceptable medium of communication. Language problems thus permeate every area of the curriculum. Dialect related problems are even to be found in foreign language learning, especially in phonology (see, for instance, Viereck, 1983). However, most obviously affected are German lessons, in which Standard High German is not only the language of instruction, but simultaneously the object and the learning goal. Frequently, German is considered to be the most important subject studied in school.

Spelling

Correct spelling is used as a measure of general intelligence. Spelling has always had an aura of objective measurement. However, it is precisely in this connection that dialect speakers are confronted with a double obstacle. In addition to transforming spoken language into written language, they have to contend with the numerous forms of interference which arise from the differences between the dialect and Standard High German. Major difficulties are to be found in the area of grapheme-phoneme relationships, including rounding and unrounding, the confusion of *ä* and *e*, quantity marking with respect to vowels, plosives (lenition or spirantisation), *r*-vocalising and 'sharpening' of consonant sounds. Löffler (1980) calls attention to typical 'northern zones' (e.g. *r*-vocalising, spirantisation of stops) and 'southern zones' (e.g. unrounding). According to him, the highest error susceptibility is to be found in 'mixed areas', where dialect and colloquial speech are in close contact.

Grammar

The greatest frequency of grammatical mistakes is to be found in the area of case confusion and generally in noun inflection as well as in the use of the preterite. This occurs disproportionately more often in essays than in dictations. Categories of error clearly depend on the kind of written work and whether this is being undertaken independently by the pupils or with the teachers' guidance.

Vocabulary

Dialect vocabulary can lead to incorrect or inappropriate lexical choice. More frequently, however, problems arise from general insecurity and self-imposed limitations in vocabulary.

Identifying errors

The research findings reported above differ widely on the question of the proportion of dialect-related errors. This discrepancy is almost certainly a function of the difficulty in identifying such errors (Mattheier, 1980). Various studies do not distinguish, for instance, between the influence of dialect and colloquial speech. Further, they do not take into account the general problems of transposing the spoken language into written form. Very often, no attempt is made to establish a hierarchy of errors which might be useful for teaching purposes. In some cases, no control groups were used. Frequently, statistically significant differences were not established. None the less, it seems important to establish the relative importance of different influences, especially in view of the fact that pupils' success hinges on their ability to vary their speech.

Oral participation

There are marked differences in rates of oral participation. Even when teachers show greater tolerance to dialect, there is a strong expectation that dialect-speaking children should approximate to the standard. Pressure from standard-speaking peers and teachers often results in timid withdrawal and silence.

Problems at text level

Dialect-related problems at discourse level have not yet been investigated in any detail. Muhr's (1984) analysis of the language of schoolchildren in Styria, Austria, however, concludes that text generating produces the most serious educational problem. Jäger (1981) recognises the difficulties experienced by rural dialect speakers in producing formal texts. He examined regional and social factors in the speech of 55 pupils at a *Gymnasium* (grammar school) near Freiburg, in a number of different situations. His conclusion was that whether or not pupils spoke dialect was a decisive factor in the extent to which they conformed to the norms of formal language use: dialect speakers tended to use frequent repetition, anacoluthon, word fragmentation, and fewer well-formed sentences. In contrast, dialect did not affect content. It should be noted, however, that the pupils were grouped according to their self-assessment of whether or not they were dialect speakers, and on their regional background (urban or rural), rather than on the basis of their actual speech. Klein (1978) emphasises the importance of analysing the role of topic in text cohesion in children's written and oral texts. Similarly, Kraemer (1978) finds that, in certain types of written work, topics which allow free expression and which are emotive (such as personal narratives or fantasies) can influence the proportion of dialect-based errors that occur in a text.

Dialect in other German speaking regions

Officially, dialect is unacceptable in school, which is a public domain calling for the standard language (see Mattheier, 1980). Dialect-speaking children are frequently assumed to have lower academic potential than their standard-speaking peers; and the same stereotypical views seem to be held by both teachers and pupils (Ammon, 1978a). The position is different in various other German speaking settings. In Switzerland, for instance, there would appear to be greater tolerance of dialect usage in certain situations (see Kropf, 1986). In Austria, Köb (1981) found that student teachers in Voralberg held relatively strong views against the use of dialect in school, influenced by a timid respect for the educational authorities. In the Italian South Tyrol, dialect has much wider social acceptance and a dialect-oriented school text book has been funded by the government. None the less, there are reports of language problems in this society, too (Saxalber-Tetter, 1985). Dialects also appear to be more acceptable in the German Democratic Republic. This is especially apparent in Berlin (see Hartung, 1981). In education, however, dialect plays as negligible a role as it does in the Federal Republic. Spangenberg & Wiese (1974) report on various difficulties in the use of standard German which can be attributed to dialect-influenced regional colloquial language. These writers investigated 5,077 errors in 1,501 written texts from 203 pupils aged between 11 and 14, from schools in Jena, Potsdam and Berlin. The proportion of errors in the texts varied from approximately 10% in Potsdam and Berlin to 17% in Jena. One of the most serious problems, even for older pupils, was choice of grammatical case. Interestingly, it was found that both in nursery school and in the later years of school, pupils tended to use a dialect-influenced colloquial language which was independent of the children's home dialect. This is a marked difference from the situation in West Germany, where the role of the school is to counteract the use of dialect.

Dialect usage

Even though it is not officially accepted, dialect is spoken in West German schools. Research has recently begun on the communicative-pragmatic functions of dialect in school. Mattheier (1980) points to the 'breaktime communication situation', emphasising that research needs to be carried out which examines the language used in the playground as well as the language used in teacher–pupil and teacher–teacher interaction. In general, teachers are 'representatives of the standard language' and if they use dialect they stand to lose face. Ehlich & Rehbein (1983) distinguish between 'primary' and 'secondary' communication in school (without, however, specifically mentioning dialect). Kropf (1986) investigated the communicative function of dialect in the classroom in the special circumstances that prevail in German-speaking Switzerland, where dialect is the main variety that is used and standard German remains for the most part a language used in school (see also Ammon, this volume, Chapter 7). His analyses of classroom recordings indicated dialect 'sub-areas' (*Dialektreviere*) within the standard German domain. Linguistic variation results in a highly differentiated system of language use which is used to direct the processes of interaction and to communicate sociolinguistic information. Thus the primary function of dialect usage was to 'create symmetry': it was used by the teacher, for instance, to ensure understanding, to illustrate or to 'play down' the importance of a topic. In contrast, it was used by the pupils to show solidarity with another pupil, to 'cry for help' or to cause disruption. Sitta (1979) describes dialect as the language of leisure and standard German as the language of work, although dialect is commonly used in Swiss schools in certain types of situation and even in certain school subjects. In an earlier publication, Ramge (1978) discussed the issue of 'dialect-oriented' teacher speech in the Saar. He concluded that teachers often made use of functional variation, especially when speaking with pupils on a one-to-one basis. Standard-speaking teachers usually used dialect forms with a specifically didactic intention, whereas dialect-speaking teachers used them to lessen the effect of institutional demands in teacher–pupil interaction. The primary functions of dialect usage, therefore, are attention, mitigation, activation and illustration. Finally, Rosenberg (1989) found that dialect was used by pupils both in the classroom and in less formal situations. Dialect usage was found to depend on the choice of topic and on the interlocutor; it was used particularly frequently in the recounting of emotive events (such as fights) and in altercations.

Dialect-related school difficulties

The most serious dialect-related school difficulties seem to be experienced by pupils who have a strong orientation towards the use of dialect and whose linguistic repertoire encompasses a relatively narrow range of stylistic variation. In contrast, bidialectal pupils have fewer problems and it seems that they may even be at an advantage. The fact that children speak a dialect is unrelated to their level of educational achievement; instead, the ability to exploit linguistic variation and to code switch may be a determining factor of educational success (see Hasselberg, 1981; Wegera, 1983). In order to evaluate this, however, it would be necessary to determine the nature of a speaker's linguistic repertoire, including the command of different registers of speech. Furthermore, there are a number of as yet unsolved problems in measuring the extent to which speakers are 'dialect' speakers. Some of these problems are methodological; to a greater extent, however, they are related to the dialect situation in Germany and to the adequacy of the currently available descriptive models (as we saw on pp. 65–6).

One attempt at measuring the linguistic repertoire of school children and which takes account of the criticisms that can be made of existing models of variation is reported in Rosenberg (1986: 64ff; 1989). A model for measuring the degree of dialect spoken by pupils is developed in these publications, based on a modification of markedness theory (see Chomsky & Halle, 1968). The model distinguishes between variation which is free and variation which is marked for a particular social context and also includes 'subjective' assessment by the pupils. For example, the typical features of the 'colloquial language' of Berlin (such as centralisation and moderate opening in the short vowel system) are classed as unmarked, free variation, whereas certain features of the dialect and the corresponding standard features are classed as examples of marked variation, albeit marked in different directions. They normally carry social or situational information and they therefore affect speaker attitudes. This research has drawn up typologies of different types of linguistic repertoire, which can be correlated with social and situational features as well as with educational achievement.

Conclusions

There have been very few practical innovations resulting from the research that has been carried out. Even the *Dialekt/Hochsprache—Kontrastiv* series of booklets has not been used as much as had been anticipated, possibly because of difficulties in use in applied contexts. From the research literature four themes emerge as suggested targets in education (see Mattheier, 1980: 127ff; Niebaum, 1983: 112ff):

   a)   the substitution of standard German for the dialect. This is the

      traditional, though unspoken, goal of the school;
b)   bidialectal education, with the aim of pupils learning both dialect and standard at school (see Schuppenhauer, 1980: 102ff);
c)   a relaxing of the norms governing the use of the standard (see Jäger, 1970);
d)   encouraging 'functional bidialectalism', with dialect and standard being used in those situations that are appropriate for their use (see Besch & Löffler, 1973).

Various criticisms have been made of these goals. Ammon, for example, who in earlier writings likens dialect to 'ballast', weighing down children from the lower socioeconomic classes (1978a: 270), warns against 'glorifying' dialect. He points out that since the school offers pupils their only opportunity of learning standard German, to relax the norms governing the use of the standard would simply reproduce in a different form the social problems that are faced by children from the lower socioeconomic classes (Ammon, 1982: 97). Mumm (1978), on the other hand, stresses the consequences of paying insufficient attention to dialect in school: if standard German is seen as the only goal in education, children risk losing an awareness of themselves and of the world in which they live; and the social identity of dialect-speaking pupils is put in jeopardy, since their earliest learning experiences have been connected with the use of dialect as their primary means of communication.

The suggestion of teaching 'functional bidialectalism' is not without problems. In order to achieve this goal, teachers would have to make a realistic appraisal of the local dialect, including the linguistic variation in their pupils' speech. It, however, would have to be borne in mind that young children do not seem to have a conscious awareness of the nature of linguistic variation; experiments carried out by Kohler & Ramge (1978) with children aged between 7 and 10 found that dialect features were not perceived as dialect but simply as 'different', 'louder' or 'faster' (1978: 10; see also Löffler, 1979: 354).

Above all, schools need to be made aware of the nature of dialect and of the problems that can be caused by the coexistence of dialect and standard. Heidtmann (1985: 91), for example, shows that the language assessment methods that are commonly used in schools are not capable even of distinguishing dialect features from speech impediments; and this is sometimes true for dyslexia also (see also Milroy & Milroy, 1985, for discussion of a similar situation in the United Kingdom).

In West German schools dialect still rarely features in the curriculum, and even when it does, it is only in the later years of school (Niebaum,

1983: 105), and usually for comic effect in dialect stories (Neuland, 1979). Recently, however, there have been some attempts to include dialect in a more constructive way in the curriculum: teaching materials have been developed that include dialect as a part of language study in the higher years of school (Bausinger, 1983; Schlobinski & Blank, 1985); dialect has been included as part of the subject-matter of in-service training courses (Reitmajer, 1980); and testing materials and exercises have been developed for use in German lessons and also in remedial lessons in primary schools (Rosenberg, 1989).

Löffler (1979: 354) points out that in fact the main burden of coping with the coexistence of dialect and standard falls not on the researcher but on the teacher. Nevertheless, there is an important goal that should be borne in mind by those who carry out socially-engaged research and who hope that their research will have practical implications. In the best sociolinguistic tradition, researchers should aim not only at obtaining a linguistic corpus from their object of study — the pupils — but they should endeavour to give something to the pupils in return — practical assistance and an enlightened awareness in schools of the nature of dialect and of the relationship between dialect and standard language.

Appendix

Important studies concerning 'Dialect and School' in the Federal Republic of Germany

Author	Year	Region	Corpus	Schools	Analysis/Methods	Most important findings
Hasselberg	1972 (1968)	Giessen	322 pupils	Gymnasium	scholastic achievements (various subjects) language groups questionnaires (language, social data)	problems of 'dialect-only'-speakers (especially middle forms; mathematics) social correlation
Jäger	1970	Mannheim	450 pupils	primary school, 'Hauptschule' (15 classes: 10–15 year olds)	scholastic achievements (orthography, grammar, vocabulary) social makeup of school districts	linguistic problems (especially case choice) social correlation rigorous norms ('middle class norms')
Besch/Löffler	1973	Middle Alemannic area	2,700 texts	'Hauptschule' (13 classes: 14–15 year olds)	Contrastive Analysis (phonology, morphology, syntax, vocabulary): dialect-based mistakes	widespread interference and hypercorrection (8–20%)
Hasselberg	1976	Hessen	7,004 pupils	26 comprehensive schools (11–12 year olds)	scholastic achievements (achievement tests and prognoses) social data language groups (teacher-assessed)	lower performance rates for dialect speakers in tests and prognoses (independent of social class)
Wegera	1977	Fulda region (Eastern Hessen)	7,000 texts (1,000 in detail)	primary school, 'Hauptschule', Gymnasium (9–11 year olds)	Contrastive Analysis: dialect-based and colloquial mistakes	dialect systematically reinforces general risk areas

cont'd

Important studies concerning 'Dialect and School' in the Federal Republic of Germany (continued)

Author	Year	Region	Corpus	Schools	Analysis/Methods	Most important findings
Ammon	1978 (et al.)	Swabia (Reutlingen district)	473 pupils 14 classes (from 104 classes of 9–10 year olds) observation in: 13 classes (6–10 year olds) 106 teachers	primary school	scholastic achievements (written works, oral participation, reading, marks) language groups (dialect levels) questionnaires (social data, origin), attitudes teacher interviews	widespread problems of noticeable dialect users, advantages for moderate dialect users low self-image among dialect speakers
Henn	1978	Northwest Palatinate area	50 pupils 165 written works	primary school, 'Hauptschule' (9–11 year olds)	Contrastive Analysis: dialect-based mistakes (contrast-levelling, shifting, exaggeration)	high proportion of dialect mistakes (orthography: 28%, syntax: 80%, vocabulary: 84%)
Kettner	1978	East Friesland and Niedersachsen (2 towns)	280 pupils 3,911 mistakes	2 'Hauptschulen' 1 'Realschule' (9 classes: 12–14 year olds)	dialect mistakes in essays (without orthography) comparison: 2 towns with high and low dialect speaking proportion	problems resulting from North German colloquial language (mistake proportions: 64–79%; especially syntax)
Kraemer	1978	Bad Ems/ Lahn (Moselle-Franconian area)	195 pupils 3,625 written works	primary school, 'Hauptschule' (10–14 year olds)	Contrastive Analysis scholastic achievements (dialect mistakes, marks, various subjects) social data achievement groups (according to number of dialect mistakes)	dialect mistakes (especially consonants; transfer; specific essay types: fantasy stories, personal narrative correlations (social, marks): with respect to extreme groups

Author	Year	Region	Corpus	Schools	Analysis/Methods	Most important findings
Reitmajer	1979	Middle Bavarian area (5 places)	114 pupils re-narration test: 91 Bavarian pupils, 88 Hanoverian pupils	pre-school, primary school, Gymnasium	scholastic achievements (dialect mistakes, marks) language groups (parental intuition, linguistic levels) social data control group (Hanover)	noticeable dialect users: pre-school, lesser competency in Standard High German; primary school, less pronounced (with limitations); Gymnasium, no difference (marks) social correlation typical dialect sounds: few difficulties (diphthongs)
Kalau	1984	Nuremberg (and surroundings)	259 pupils (1,041 mistakes exemplified)	primary school, 'Hauptschule' (11 classes: 8–11 year olds)	Contrastive Analysis (morphology)	75% of mistakes due to dialect (especially case-choice, preterite usage: each ca. 90%)
Rosenberg	1986	Berlin	257 pupils 2,000 written works 20,000 mistakes dictation test (156 Berlin, 83 Hanover)	2 primary schools (7–12 year olds), vocational school	Contrastive Analysis: dialect-based, dialect-influenced, colloquial mistakes language groups, age-groups, foreign pupils mistake hierarchies (dictations, essays) comparison groups (Hanover)	significant differences Berlin–Hanover 18% dialect-based or influenced mistakes (especially case-choice) age: youngest predominantly transfer mistakes foreign pupils: high proportion of dialect mistakes, fewer hypercorrections noticeable dialect speakers: most serious problems

Note to Chapter 5

1. The term *Umgangssprache* is used differently here and in Ammon's chapter from the way in which it is used by Van de Craen & Humblet, in Chapter 2 of this volume.

Bibliography

AHRENS, I. 1977 Plattdeutsch in Hamburger Schulen. *Niederdeutsche Tage in Hamburg 1977.* Hamburg: Arbeitsgemeinschaft Niederdeutsche Tage in Hamburg. pp. 57–69.

AMMON, U. 1972 *Dialekt, soziale Ungleichheit und Schule.* Weinheim: Beltz.

——1973 *Probleme der Soziolinguistik.* Tübingen: Niemeyer.

——1978a *Schulschwierigkeiten von Dialektsprechern. Empirische Untersuchungen sprachabhängiger Schulleistungen und des Schüler- und Lehrerbewuβtseins— mit sprachdidaktischen Hinweisen.* Weinheim und Basel: Beltz.

——1978b Begriffsbestimmung und soziale Verteilung des Dialekts. In U. AMMON, U. KNOOP & I. RADTKE (eds), *Grundlagen einer dialektorientierten Sprachdidaktik. Theoretische und empirische Beiträge zu einem vernachlässigten Schulproblem.* Weinheim und Basel: Beltz. pp. 49–72.

——1979 Regionaldialekte und Einheitssprache in der Bundesrepublik Deutschland. *International Journal of the Sociology of Language* 21, 25–40.

——1982 Sprachnormen als notwendige Lehrziele im Primärsprachunterricht. *Der öffentliche Sprachgebrauch*, 3, bearb. von B. Mogge und I. Radtke. Stuttgart: Klett-Cotta. pp. 91–102.

——1983 Soziale Bewertung des Dialektsprechers: Vor- und Nachteile in Schule, Beruf und Gesellschaft. In W. BESCH *et al.* (eds), *Dialektologie. Ein Handbuch zur deutschen und allgemeinen Dialektforschung.* 2. Halbband. Berlin, New York: de Gruyter. pp. 1499–1509.

——1985 Möglichkeiten der Messung von Dialektalität. In W. BESCH & K.J. MATTHEIER (eds), *Ortssprachenforschung. Beiträge zu einem Bonner Kolloquium.* Berlin: Schmidt. pp. 259–82.

——1986 Die Begriffe 'Dialekt' und 'Soziolekt'. In A. SCHÖNE (ed.), *Kontroversen, alte und neue. Akten des VII. Internationalen Germanisten-Kongresses Göttingen 1985*, 4. Tübingen: Niemeyer. pp. 223–31.

AMMON, U., KNOOP, U. and RADTKE, I. (eds) 1978 *Grundlagen einer dialektorientierten Sprachdidaktik. Theoretische und empirische Beiträge zu einem vernachlässigten Schulproblem.* Weinheim und Basel: Beltz.

AMMON, U. and LOEWER, U. 1977 *Dialekt/Hochsprache — Kontrastiv. Schwäbisch.* Düsseldorf: Schwann.

BARTSCH, R. 1985 *Sprachnormen: Theorie und Praxis.* Tübingen: Niemeyer.

BAURMANN, J., GIER, E.-M. and MEYER, M. 1987 Schreibprozesse bei kindern — eine einzelfallstudie und einige folgerungen. *OBST* 36, 81–109.

BAUSINGER, H. 1972 *Deutsch für Deutsche. Dialekte — Sprachbarrieren — Sondersprachen.* Frankfurt/M: Fischer.

——1983 Dialekt als Unterrichtsgegenstand. *Der Deutschunterricht* 35, 2, 75–85.

BAUSINGER, H. *et al.* (eds) 1973 *Dialekt als Sprachbarriere? Ergebnisbericht einer*

Tagung zur alemannischen Dialektforschung. Tübingen: Vereinigung für Volkskunde.

BECKMANN, K. 1920 *Die Pflege der Mundart im deutschen Unterricht*. Köln.

BERNSTEIN, B. 1971 *Class, Codes and Control*. Vol. I. London: Routledge.

BESCH, W. 1974 Dialekt als Barriere bei der Erlernung der Standardsprache. *Sprachwissenschaft und Sprachdidaktik*, Jahrbuch des Instituts für Deutsche Sprache 1974. Düsseldorf: Schwann. pp. 150–65.

—— (ed.) 1982/83 *Sprachverhalten in ländlichen Gemeinden. Forschungsbericht Erp-Projekt*. 2 Bde. Berlin: Schmidt.

BESCH, W. and LÖFFLER, H. 1973 Sprachhefte: Hochsprache/Mundart—Kontrastiv. In H. BAUSINGER *et al.* (eds), *Dialekt als Sprachbarriere? Ergebnisbericht einer Tagung zur alemannischen Dialektforschung*. Tübingen: Vereinigung für Volkskunde. pp. 89–110.

——1977 *Dialekt/Hochsprache—Kontrastiv. Alemannisch*. Düsseldorf: Schwann.

BESCH, W. and MATTHEIER, K.J. (eds) 1985 *Ortssprachenforschung. Beiträge zu einem Bonner Kolloquium*. Berlin: Schmidt.

BESCH, W. *et al.* (eds) 1982/83 *Dialektologie. Ein Handbuch zur deutschen und allgemeinen Dialektforschung*. 2 Bde. Berlin, New York: de Gruyter.

BICHEL, U. 1973 *Problem und Begriff der Umgangssprache in der germanistischen Forschung*. Tübingen: Niemeyer.

BIERE, B.U. 1980 Forschungsbericht. Kindersprache, kindliche Kommunikation und Spracherwerb. *Zeitschrift für Germanistische Linguistik* 8.2, 236–51.

BLUME, H. 1987 Niederdeutsch und Zweisprachigkeit. Bericht über ein Bremer Symposion (28. bis 31. Oktober 1986). *Zeitschrift für germanistische Linguistik* 15, 104–109.

BRAUN, A. 1986 Ein Modell zur Analyse von Rechtschreibfehlern bei Kindern ausländischer Arbeitnehmer. In A. BURKHARDT & K.-H. KÖRNER (eds), *Pragmantax. Akten des 20. Linguistischen Kolloquiums Braunschweig 1985*. Tübingen: Niemeyer. pp. 321–31.

BRECHENMACHER, J.K. 1925 *Schwäbische Sprachkunde in ausgeführten Lehrbeispielen. Versuch einer bodenständigen Grundlegung des schaffenden Deutschunterrichts*. Stuttgart: Bonz.

CHOMSKY, N. and HALLE, M. 1968 *The Sound Pattern of English*. New York, Evanston, London: Harper & Row.

VON CÖLLN 1784 Beytrag zur Charakteristik des Lippischen, Ritbergischen und Paderbornischen Bauern. *Westphälisches Magazin* 1: 2, 105–16.

DITTMAR, N. 1982 Soziolinguistik. Teil I: Theorie, Methodik und Empirie ihrer Forschungsrichtungen. *Studium Linguistik* 12, 20–52. Teil II: Soziolinguistik in der Bundesrepublik Deutschland. *Studium Linguistik* 14, 20–57.

DITTMAR, N. and RIECK, B.-O, (eds) 1980 *William Labov: Sprache im sozialen Kontext*. Königstein/Ts. Athenäum.

EGLI, H.R. 1975 Mundart und Schriftsprache in den Volksschulen der deutschsprachigen Schweiz. In E. WOLFRUM (ed.), *Taschenbuch des Deutschunterrichts*. Baltmannsweiler: Schneider. pp. 769–82.

EHLICH, K. and REHBEIN, J. (eds) 1983 *Kommunikation in Schule und Hochschule. Linguistische und ethnomethodologische Analysen* (= Kommunikation und Institution, 2). Tübingen: Narr.

ERMERT, K. (ed.) 1979 *Gibt es die 'Sprachbarriere' noch?* Düsseldorf: Schwann.

EßER, P. 1983 *Dialekt und Identität. Diglottale Sozialisation und Identitätsbildung*. Europäische Hochschulschriften, Reihe 11, Bd. 1387. Frankfurt/M., Bern: Lang.

GFIRTNER, F.X. 1972 *Experimentelle Studie über den schriftlichen und mündlichen Sprachgebrauch von Kindern unterschiedlicher sozialer Herkunft.* München: unveröff. (ms).

GLOY, K. 1978 Ökologische Aspekte der Dialekt-Verwendung. Ein Beitrag zur neuen Dialektwelle. In U. AMMON, U. KNOOP & I. RADTKE (eds), *Grundlagen einer dialektorientierten Sprachdidaktik. Theoretische und empirische Beiträge zu einem vernachlässigten Schulproblem.* Weinheim und Basel: Beltz. pp. 73–92.

GOOSSENS, J. 1977 *Deutsche Dialektologie.* Berlin, New York: de Gruyter.

——1986 Über die Einseitigkeit des punktuellen Standpunkts in der korrelativen Soziolinguistik und die Vernachlässigung der Variation in der Dialektologie. In A. SCHÖNE (ed.), *Kontroversen, alte und neue. Akten des VII. Internationalen Germanisten-Kongresses Göttingen 1985,* 4. Tübingen: Niemeyer. pp. 257–62.

GÖSCHEL, J. *et al.* (eds) 1976 *Zur Theorie des Dialekts.* Wiesbaden: Steiner.

VON GREYERZ, O. 1913 *Die Mundart als Grundlage des Deutschunterrichts.* 2. Aufl. Aarau.

GUMPERZ, J.J. 1975 *Sprache, lokale Kultur und soziale Identität.* Düsseldorf: Schwann.

GUTBIER, A. 1854 Ideen über den Vergleich der Mundart mit der Schriftsprache in der Volksschule. *Die deutschen Mundarten* 1, 24–33.

HÄFNER, K. 1949 Mundartbedingter Sprachunterricht. *Die Schulwarte* 2, 94–105; 614–27.

——1955/56 Dorfsprache und Schulsprache. *Die neuere Landschule* 6, 220–25.

HAIN, U. 1980 Hochsprache im Deutschunterricht. Einige Bemerkungen zur Diskussion um einen demokratischen Deutschunterricht. *Linguistische Berichte* 65, 37–50.

HANNAPPEL, H. and HEROLD, TH. 1985 Sprache und Stilnormen in der Schule. *Sprache und Literatur in Wissenschaft und Unterricht* 16:1, 54–66.

HARTIG, M. 1985 *Soziolinguistik. Angewandte Linguistik des Deutschen,* 1. Bern, Frankfurt/M., New York: Lang.

HARTUNG, W. 1981 Differenziertheit der Sprache als Ausdruck ihrer Gesellschaftlichkeit. In *Kommunikation und Sprachvariation.* Von einem Autorenkollectiv unter Leitung von W. Hartung und H. Schönfeld. Berlin (DDR): Akademie-Verlag. pp. 26–72.

HASSELBERG, J. 1972 Die Abhängigkeit des Schulerfolgs vom Einfluß des Dialekts. *Muttersprache* 82, 201–23.

——1976 *Dialekt und Bildungschancen. Eine empirische Untersuchung an hessischen Gesamtschulen.* Weinheim und Basel: Beltz.

——1981 Mundart als Schulproblem. *Hessische Blätter für Volks- und Kulturforschung.* Neue Folge 11/12, 29–55.

——1982 Kommunikationsbehinderungen nicht ausschließlich hochsprachlich geprägter Sprecher in der Schule. *Der öffentliche Sprachgebrauch,* Bd. 3, bearb. von B. Mogge und I. Radtke. Stuttgart: Klett-Cotta. pp. 243–48.

——1983 Die soziolinguistische Problematik der Schichtzuordnung von Dialektsprechern. In W. BESCH *et al.* (eds), *Dialektologie. Ein Handbuch zur deutschen und allgemeinen Dialektforschung.* Berlin, New York: de Gruyter. pp. 1468–74.

HASSELBERG, J. and WEGERA, K.-P. 1976 *Dialekt/Hochsprache—Kontrastiv. Hessisch.* Düsseldorf: Schwann.

HEGER, K. 1969 'Sprache' und 'Dialekt' als linguistisches und soziolinguistisches Problem. *Folia Linguistica* 3, 46–67.

HEIDTMANN, H. 1985 Die Berücksichtigung des Dialektproblems in ausgewählten sprachdiagnostischen Verfahren. *Germanistische Linguistik* 81, 81–95.
HELMERS, H. 1976 *Didaktik der deutschen Sprache. Einführung in die Theorie der muttersprachlichen und literarischen Bildung.* 9. Aufl. Stuttgart: Klett.
——1984 Die Pflege der niederdeutschen Sprache und Literatur im Deutschunterricht. *Quickborn* 74, 3–12.
HELMIG, G. 1972 Gesprochene und geschriebene Sprache und ihre Übergänge. Beobachtungen zur Syntax und zum Aufbau von Erzählungen zehnjähriger Schüler. *Der Deutschunterricht* 24: 3, 5–25.
HENN, B. 1978a Mundartinterferenzen. *Am Beispiel des Nordwestpfälzischen.* Wiesbaden: Steiner.
——1978b Kontrastive Syntax: Pfälzisch-Einheitssprache. In U. AMMON, U. KNOOP & I. RADTKE (eds), *Grundlagen einer dialektorientierten Sprachdidaktik. Theoretische und empirische Beiträge zu einem vernachlässigten Schulproblem.* Weinheim und Basel: Beltz. pp. 333–48.
HENZEN, W. 1954 *Schriftsprache und Mundarten. Ein Überblick über ihr Verhältnis und ihre Zwischenstufen im Deutschen.* 2. Aufl. Bern: Francke.
HERRGEN, J. and SCHMIDT, J.E. 1984 Zum Dialektalitätsbegriff der Angewandten Linguistik. In: W. KÜHLWEIN (ed.), *Sprache, Kultur und Gesellschaft. Kongreßberichte der 14. Jahrestagung der Gesellschaft für Angewandte Linguistik.* Tübingen: Narr. pp. 56–8.
——1985 Systemkontrast und Hörerurteil. Zwei Dialektalitätsbegriffe und die ihnen entsprechenden Meßverfahren. *Zeitschrift für Dialektologie und Linguistik* 52:1, 20–42.
HILDEBRAND, R. 1867 *Vom deutschen Sprachunterricht in der Schule.* Leipzig: Klinkhardt.
HOFMANN, E. 1963 Sprachsoziologische Untersuchungen über den Einfluß der Stadtsprache auf mundartsprechende Arbeiter. *Marburger Universitätsbund, Jahrbuch 1963.* Marburg: Elwert. pp. 201–81.
HYMES, D. 1962 The ethnography of speaking. In T. GLADWIN & W. STURTEVANT (eds), *Anthropology and Human Behavior.* Washington D.C.: Anthropological Society. pp. 13–53.
JACKWIRTH, H.-J. 1979 Plattdeutsch in der Schule. *Niederdeutsche Tage in Hamburg 1979,* 99–100. Hamburg: Arbeitsgemeinschaft Niederdeutsche Tage in Hamburg.
JÄGER, K.-H. 1981 *Sprachbeschreibung und Sprachdiagnose. Empirische Untersuchungen zur Beschreibung und Diagnose des mündlichen sprachlichen Handelns von Schülern der Orientierungsstufe.* Tübingen: Niemeyer.
——1982 Sprachliches Handeln von Schülern. Untersuchungen zur Pragmatik der gesprochenen Sprache von Schülern im alemannischen Sprachraum. *Deutsche Sprache* 10, 156–92.
JÄGER, S. 1970 Sprachnorm und Schülersprache. *Sprache und Gesellschaft. Jahrbuch 1970 des Instituts für Deutsche Sprache.* Düsseldorf: Schwann. pp. 166–233.
——1971 'Sprachbarrieren'? 21 Thesen zur Diskussion. *Linguistische Berichte* 15, 61–62.
——1972 'Sprachbarrieren' und kompensatorische Erziehung. Ein bürgerliches Trauerspiel. *Linguistische Berichte* 19, 80–99.
——1984 (W)Ende der Soziolinguistik? *OBST* 29, 156–81.
JAMES, C. 1972 Zur Rechtfertigung der kontrastiven Linguistik. In G. NICKEL (ed.), *Reader zur kontrastiven Linguistik.* Frankfurt/M.: Athenäum. pp. 21–38.

88DIALECT AND EDUCATION

JAMES, A.R. 1974 Dialekt, Fremdsprache und phonischer Transfer. Eine Kontrastive Analyse Schwäbisch-Englisch. *Linguistische Berichte* 32, 93–110.
JANSSEN, A. 1974 *Phonetisch-phonemische Analyse als Teil einer kontrastiven Untersuchung Mundart/Hochsprache im Raum Kleve*. (Unveröff., ms.) Bonn.
JOSS, H. 1974 *Sprechverhalten in Mundart und Hochsprache. Ein Vergleich zwischen siebenjährigen Kindern und Erwachsenen*. (Diss., unveröff.) Bern.
KALAU, G. 1984 *Die Morphologie der Nürnberger Mundart. Eine kontrastive und fehleranalytische Untersuchung*. Erlangen: Palm und Enke.
KALLMEYER, W., KEIM, I. and NIKITOPOULOS, P. 1981 Zum Projekt 'Kommunikation in der Stadt'. In K.H. BAUSCH (ed.), *Mehrsprachigkeit in der Stadtregion. Jahrbuch 1981 des Instituts für Deutsche Sprache*. Düsseldorf: Schwann.
KARSTÄDT, O. 1925 *Mundart und Schule*. 4. erw. Aufl. Langensalza: Beyer und Mann (1st edn 1908).
KEMPER, H.G. 1974 Sprachbarrieren/Dialekt. In H.G. KEMPER (ed.), *Angewandte Germanistik*. München: Fink. pp. 194–361.
KESELING, G. 1973 Bemerkungen zur Mundart und zum sogenannten restringierten Kode. *Niederdeutsches Jahrbuch* 96, 127–38.
KETTEMANN, B. and VIERECK, W. 1978 Muttersprachiger Dialekt und Fremdsprachenerwerb. Dialekttransfer und Interferenz: Steirisch-Englisch. In U. AMMON, U. KNOOP & I. RADTKE (eds), *Grundlagen einer dialektorientierten Sprachdidaktik. Theoretische und empirische Beiträge zu einem vernachlässigten Schulproblem*. Weinheim und Basel: Beltz. pp. 349–76.
KETTNER, B.U. 1978 Niederdeutsche Dialekte, norddeutsche Umgangssprache und die Reaktion der Schule. In U. AMMON, U. KNOOP & I. RADTKE (eds), *Grundlagen einer dialektorientierten Sprachdidaktik. Theoretische und empirische Beiträge zu einem vernachlässigten Schulproblem*. Weinheim und Basel: Beltz. pp. 285–312.
KIEFFER, G. 1974 *Analyse einer Kommunikationsbarriere. Ein diagnostisch-therapeutischer Beitrag der Psychologie zur Sprachbarrierenproblematik in der Orientierungsstufe*. Tübingen: Narr.
KIELHÖFER, B. 1975 *Fehlerlinguistik des Fremdsprachenerwerbs. Linguistische, lernpsychologische und didaktische Analyse von Französischfehlern*. (Skripten Linguistik und Kommunikationswissenschaften 14). Kronberg/Ts: Scriptor.
KLEIN, E., MATTHEIER, K.J. and MICKARTZ, H. 1978 *Dialekt/Hochsprache-Kontrastiv. Rheinisch*. Düsseldorf: Schwann.
KLEIN, W. 1978 *Linguistik und Didaktik der Kindersprache im Grundschulalter. Untersuchungen zu Konstitution und Kohäsion von Schülertexten*. Paderborn: Schöningh.
——1984 *Zweitspracherwerb. Eine Einführung*. Königstein/Ts: Athenäum.
KNOOP, U. 1976 Die Differenz von Dialekt und Schriftlichkeit — ein vorläufiger Überblick. *Germanistische Linguistik* 3/4, 21–54.
——1978 Dialekt und schriftsprachliches Gestalten. In U. AMMON, U. KNOOP & I. RADTKE (eds), *Grundlagen einer dialektorientierten Sprachdidaktik. Theoretische und empirische Beiträge zu einem vernachlässigten Schulproblem*. Weinheim und Basel: Beltz. pp. 157–74.
KÖB, F. 1981 Wofür der Lehrer keine Einser hat. . . Dialekt, Schulbürokratie und Lehrerausbildung in Vorarlberg. *Allmende* 1981: 3, 75–86.
KOHLER, M. and RAMGE, H. 1978 Wie Grundschüler den Gebrauch von Dialekt und Standardsprache einschätzen. *Praxis Deutsch* 27, 9–11.
KOSS, G. 1972 Angewandte Dialektologie im Deutschunterricht. *Blätter für den Deutschlehrer* 16, 92–102.

KRAEMER, W. 1978 Umsetzungsschwierigkeiten von Dialektsprechern bei dem Gebrauch der Schriftsprache. Am Beispiel einer phonologischen Fehleranalyse in Bad Ems/Lahn (Grund- und Hauptschulklassen). *Laut und Schrift in Dialekt und Standardsprache. Beiträge von R. Müller, E. Gabriel, W. Kraemer.* (Zeitschrift für Dialektologie und Linguistik, Beihefte, Neue Folge 27, hrsgg. von J. Göschel und W.H. Veith). Wiesbaden: Steiner. pp. 93–219.

KRETSCHMER, P. 1969 *Wortgeographie der hochdeutschen Umgangssprache.* 2. Aufl. (1. Aufl. 1918). Göttingen: Vandenhoeck und Ruprecht.

KROPF, TH. 1986 *Kommunikative Funktionen des Dialekts im Unterricht. Theorie und Praxis in der deutschen Schweiz.* Tübingen: Niemeyer.

KÜRSTEN, O. and KRAMER, W. 1935 *Von der Mundart zur Hochsprache. Sprachkunde und Sprachlehre für Thüringer und Sachsen.* Erfurt.

LEVY, P. 1913 *Die Verwertung der Mundarten im Deutschunterrichte höherer Lehranstalten unter besonderer Berücksichtigung des Elsässischen.* Leipzig, Berlin: Teubner.

LÖFFLER, H. 1972 Mundart als Sprachbarriere. *Wirkendes Wort* 22: 1, 23–39.

——1974a Deutsch für Dialektsprecher: Ein Sonderfall des Fremdsprachenunterrichts? Zur Theorie einer kontrastiven Grammatik Dialekt/Hochsprache. *Deutsche Sprache* 2, 105–22.

——1974b *Probleme der Dialektologie. Eine Einführung.* Darmstadt: Wissenschaftliche Buchgesellschaft.

——1978a Dialekt als Schulproblem: Chance oder Hindernis. *Mundart und Mundartdichtung im alemannischen Sprachraum. Situationsberichte.* Hrsgg. von A. Finck, R. Matzen, M. Philipp. Strasbourg: Institut de dialectologie alsacienne. pp. 42–70.

——1978b Orthographieprobleme der Dialektsprecher am Beispiel des Alemannischen. In U. AMMON, U. KNOOP & I. RADTKE (eds), *Grundlagen einer dialektorientierten Sprachdidaktik. Theoretische und empirische Beiträge zu einem vernachlässigten Schulproblem.* Weinheim und Basel: Beltz. pp. 267–84.

——1979 Mundart als Problem und Möglichkeit im Unterricht. *Rheinische Vierteljahresblätter* 43, 344–55.

——1980 Dialektfehler. Ansätze zu einer deutschen 'Fehlergeographie'. In D. CHERUBIM (ed.), *Fehlerlinguistik. Beiträge zum Problem der sprachlichen Abweichung.* Tübingen: Niemeyer. pp. 94–105.

——1985 *Germanistische Soziolinguistik.* Berlin: Schmidt.

——1986 Sind Soziolekte neue Dialekte? Zum Aufgabenfeld einer nachsoziolinguistischen Dialektologie. In A. SCHÖNE (ed.), *Kontroversen, alte und neue. Akten des VII. Internationalen Germanisten-Kongresses Göttingen 1985,* 4. Tübingen: Niemeyer. pp. 232–39.

MAAS, U. 1985 Schrift–Schreiben–Rechtschreiben. *Diskussion Deutsch* 16, 4–25.

MACHA, J. 1986 Die Bedeutung individueller Variation. Zur Umwertung eines traditionellen Störfaktors. In A. SCHÖNE (ed.), *Kontroversen, alte und neue. Akten des VII. Internationalen Germanisten-Kongresses Göttingen 1985,* 4. Tübingen: Niemeyer. pp. 300–304.

MATTHEIER, K.J. 1974 Sprache als Barriere. *Deutsche Sprache* 2, 213–32.

——1980 *Pragmatik und Soziologie der Dialekte.* Heidelberg: Quelle und Meyer (UTB).

—— (ed.) 1983 *Aspekte der Dialekttheorie.* Tübingen: Niemeyer.

——1984 Dialektologische und dialektdidaktische Aspekte des Koexistenzmodells und des Variabilitätsmodells. *Germanistische Mitteilungen* 19, 5–17.

——1985 Dialektologie der Dialektsprecher. Überlegungen zu einem interpretativen Ansatz in der Dialektologie. *Germanistische Mitteilungen* 21, 47–67.

——1986 Die Dialektologie zwischen Dialektgeographie und Soziolinguistik. In A. SCHÖNE (ed.), *Kontroversen, alte und neue*. *Akten des VII. Internationalen Germanisten-Kongresses Göttingen 1985*. Tübingen: Niemeyer. pp. 251–56.

MAURER, F. 1933 *Volkssprache*. *Abhandlungen über Mundarten und Volkskunde*. Erlangen.

MEYER-MARKAU, W. 1907 *Sprachliche Heimatkunde für Duisburger Schulen*. Duisburg.

MILROY, J. and MILROY, L. 1985 *Authority in Language*. London: Routledge.

MÖHN, D. 1978 Zur Tradition der kontrastiven Methode im Niederdeutschen. *Korrespondenzblatt des Vereins für Niederdeutsche Sprachforschung* 85, 26–27.

MUHR, R. 1984 Sprachförderung dialektsprechender steirischer Kinder—Bericht über ein Unterrichtsprojekt. In P. WIESINGER (ed.), *Beiträge zur bairischen und ostfränkischen Dialektologie*. *Ergebnisse der Zweiten Bayerisch-Österreichischen Dialektologentagung Wien, 27. bis 30. September 1983*. Göppingen: Kümmerle. pp. 219–34.

MUMM, S. 1978 Das Problem des Selbstverständnisses beim Übergang vom Dialekt zur Hochsprache. In U. AMMON, U. KNOOP & I. RADTKE (eds), *Grundlagen einer dialektorientierten Sprachdidaktik*. *Theoretische und empirische Beiträge zu einem vernachlässigten Schulproblem*. Weinheim und Basel: Beltz. pp. 117–56.

NAUMANN, H. 1925 Über das sprachliche Verhältnis von Ober- zu Unterschicht. *Jahrbuch für Philologie* I, 55–69.

NEULAND, E. 1975 *Sprachbarrieren oder Klassensprachen? Untersuchungen zum Sprachverhalten im Vorschulalter*. Frankfurt/M.: Fischer.

——1979 Dialekt in sprachbüchern. Ergebnisse einer exemplarischen auslese und kritischen analyse von neueren sprachbüchern der primarstufe und der sekundarstufe I. *Wirkendes Wort* 29, 73–93.

NICKEL, G. (ed.) 1972 *Reader zur kontrastiven Linguistik*. Frankfurt/M.: Athenäum.

NIEBAUM, H. 1977 *Dialekt/Hochsprache—Kontrastiv*. *Westfälisch*. Düsseldorf: Schwann.

——1979a *Niederdeutsch und Sprachunterricht*. (Schriften des Instituts für Niederdeutsche Sprache. Reibe: Vorträge No. 2) Bremen: Institut für Niederdeutsche Sprache.

——1979b Ein frühes Konzept zur Überwindung der dialektalen Sprachbarriere in Westfalen. *Korrespondenzblatt des Vereins für Niederdeutsche Sprachforschung* 86, 73–77.

——1983 *Dialektologie*. Tübingen: Niemeyer.

OSTHOFF, H. and BRUGMANN, K. 1878 *Morphologische Untersuchungen auf dem Gebiete der indogermanischen Sprachen*. (Neudruck 1974). Hildesheim/New York: Olms.

RADTKE, I. 1973 Die Umgangssprache. Ein weiterhin ungelöstes Problem der Sprachwissenschaft. *Muttersprache* 83, 161–71.

——1976 Bibliographie zur Sozialdialektologie. *Germanistische Linguistik* 3/4, 161–204.

——1978 Drei Aspekte der Dialektdiskussion. (Einführende Bemerkungen zum vorliegenden Band). In U. AMMON, U. KNOOP & I. RADTKE (eds), *Grundlagen einer dialektorientierten Sprachdidaktik*. *Theoretische und empirische Beiträge zu einem vernachlässigten Schulproblem*. Weinheim und Basel: Beltz. pp. 13–32.

RAMGE, H. 1978 Kommunikative Funktionen des Dialekts im Sprachgebrauch von Lehrern während des Unterrichts. In U. AMMON, U. KNOOP & I. RADTKE (eds), *Grundlagen einer dialektorientierten Sprachdidaktik. Theoretische und empirische Beiträge zu einem vernachlässigten Schulproblem.* Weinheim und Basel: Beltz. pp. 198–228.

REIFFENSTEIN, I. 1976 Primäre und sekundäre Unterschiede zwischen Hochsprache und Mundart. *Festschrift für A. Issatschenko.* Klagenfurt, 337–47.

REIN, K. 1977 Diglossie von Mundart und Hochsprache als linguistische und didaktische Aufgabe. *Germanistische Linguistik* 5/6, 207–20.

——1983 Bestimmende Faktoren für den variierenden Sprachgebrauch des Dialektsprechers. In W. BESCH *et al.* (eds), *Dialektologie. Ein Handbuch zur deutschen und allgemeinen Dialektforschung.* Berlin/New York: de Gruyter. pp. 1443–55.

——1986 Wer spricht Mundart, wann und zu wem? Empirische Verfahren zur Dialektalitätsmessung. In A. SCHÖNE (ed.), *Kontroversen, alte und neue. Akten des VII. Internationalen Germanisten-Kongresses Göttingen 1985.* Tübingen: Niemeyer. pp. 273–78.

REITMAJER, V. 1979 *Der Einfluß des Dialekts auf die standardsprachlichen Leistungen von bayerischen Schülern in Vorschule, Grundschule und Gymnasium — eine empirische Untersuchung.* Marburg: Elwert.

——1980 Die Bedeutung des Dialekts im schulischen Kommunikationsprozeß. *Linguistische Berichte* 67, 68–81.

RESCHKA, W., SCHNEIDER, W. and SCHNORRENBERG, J.E. 1976 *Abschlußbericht zum Projekt: Eine soziophonetische Untersuchung zum Problem schichtenspezifischer 'Sprachbarrieren'.* Köln: Institut für Phonetik der Universität zu Köln.

ROSENBERG, K.-P. 1986 *Der Berliner Dialekt — und seine Folgen für die Schüler. Geschichte und Gegenwart der Stadtsprache Berlins sowie eine empirische Untersuchung der Schulprobleme dialektsprechender Berliner Schüler.* Tübingen: Niemeyer.

——1989 *Berliner Dialekt in der Schule: Studien zur sprachlichen Variationsfähigkeit von Berliner Schülern.* Berlin: Berlin-Verlag.

RUPP, H. 1972 Sprachbarrieren: Thesen und Tatsachen. Linguistische Bemerkungen zum Problem 'soziale Herkunft und Sprachkompetenz'. *Baseler Nationalzeitung* 6. Februar 1972.

SAXALBER-TETTER, A. (ed.) 1985 *Dialekt—Hochsprache als Unterrichtsthema. Anregungen für den Deutschlehrer.* Bozen: Südtiroler Kulturinstitut, Arbeitskreis Südtiroler Mittelschullehrer.

SCHENKER, W. 1973 Ansätze zu einer kontrastiven Mundartgrammatik. *Deutsche Sprache* 1: 2, 58–80.

SCHEUTZ, H. 1980 Sprachvariation als methodologisches Problem einer soziolinguistisch orientierten Dialektologie. In P.K. STEIN *et al.* (eds), *Sprache — Text — Geschichte.* Göppingen: Kümmerle.

SCHILD, K.-W. 1981 Man spricht woanders anders: 'study abroad' und die Barriere lokaler Mundarten. *Die Unterrichtspraxis* 14, 44–52.

SCHIRMUNSKI, V. 1930 Sprachgeschichte und Siedelungsmundarten. *Germanisch-Romanische Monatsschrift* 18, 113–22, 171–88.

SCHLOBINSKI, P. and BLANK, U. 1985 *Sprachbetrachtung: Berlinisch. Arbeitsbuch für den Deutschunterricht ab der 10. Klasse.* Lehrerband und Übungsheft. Berlin: Marhold.

SCHLOSSER, H.D. 1985 *Dialektgebrauch in der Schule. Informationen —*

Bedingungen — Möglichkeiten. Alsbach/Bergstr.: Leuchtturm.

SCHMID, R. 1973 Dialekt und Vorurteil. Zur Beurteilung von Dialektsprechern. *Papiere zur Linguistik* 5, 116–35.

SCHÖNE, A. (ed.) 1986 *Kontroversen, alte und neue. Akten des VII. Internationalen Germanisten-Kongresses Göttingen 1985.* Bd. 1—11. Tübingen: Niemeyer.

SCHOOF, W. 1955 Die Behandlung der Mundart in der Schule. Ein Beitrag zum deutschen Sprachunterricht. *Muttersprache* 65, 390–93.

SCHUCHARDT, H. 1885 Über die Lautgesetze. Gegen die Junggrammatiker. In TH. VENNEMANN, T.H. WILBUR (eds) (1972), *Schuchardt, the Neogrammarians and the Transformational Theory of Phonological Change,* 1–37. Frankfurt/ M.: Athenäum.

SCHUPPENHAUER, C. 1980 Platt im Deutschunterricht—nicht Luxus, sondern Notwendigkeit. *Quickborn* 70, 101–103.

SCHWARZENBACH, R. 1974 Schweizerdeutsch in der Mittelschule. *Schweizer Monatshefte* 54, 669–74.

SIEBER, P. and SITTA, H. 1986 *Mundart und Standardsprache als Problem der Schule.* Aarau, Frankfurt/M., Salzburg: Sauerländer.

SITTA, H. 1979 Spracherwerbstheoretische Aspekte des Verhältnisses von Mundart und Hochsprache in der Schule. *Standard und Dialekt. Studien zur gesprochenen und geschriebenen Gegenwartssprache. Festschrift für Heinz Rupp zum 60. Geburtstag,* hrsgg. von H. Löffler u.a. Bern, München: Francke. pp. 165–75.

SPANGENBERG, K. and WIESE, J. 1974 Sprachwirklichkeit und Sprachverhalten sowie deren Auswirkungen auf Leistungen im muttersprachlichen Unterricht der Allgemeinbildenden Polytechnischen Oberschule. In G. ISING (ed.), *Aktuelle Probleme der sprachlichen Kommunikation. Soziolinguistische Studien zur sprachlichen Situation in der Deutschen Demokratischen Republik.* Berlin: Akademie-Verlag. pp. 285–337.

STEINIG, W. 1980 Zur sozialen Bewertung sprachlicher Variation. In D. CHERUBIM (ed.), *Fehlerlinguistik. Beiträge zum Problem der sprachlichen Abweichung.* Tübingen: Niemeyer. pp. 106–23.

STELLMACHER, D. 1977 *Studien zur gesprochenen Sprache in Niedersachsen. Eine soziolinguistische Untersuchung.* Marburg: Elwert.

——1981 *Dialekt/Hochsprache — Kontrastiv. Niedersächsisch.* Düsseldorf: Schwann.

THOMKE, H. 1978 Mundart und Hochsprache in unseren Schulen. *Schweizer Monatshefte für Politik, Wirtschaft, Kultur* 58, 875–83.

TRUDGILL, P. 1975 *Accent, Dialect, and School. Explorations in Language Study.* London: Arnold.

VIERECK, W. 1983 Probleme des Dialektsprechers beim Fremdsprachenerwerb. In W. BESCH et al. (eds), *Dialektologie. Ein Handbuch zur deutschen und allgemeinen Dialektforschung.* Berlin/New York: de Gruyter. pp. 1493–98.

WEGENER, PH. 1879 Über deutsche dialectforschung. *Zeitschrift für deutsche Philologie* 11 (1880), 450–80.

WEGERA, K.-P. 1977 *Kontrastive Grammatik: Osthessisch—Standardsprache. Eine Untersuchung zu mundartbedingten Sprachschwierigkeiten von Schülern am Beispiel das 'Fuldaer Landes'.* Marburg: Elwert.

——1983 Probleme des Dialektsprechers beim Erwerb der deutschen Standardsprache. In W. BESCH et al. (eds), *Dialektologie. Ein Handbuch zur deutschen und allgemeinen Dialektforschung.* Berlin/New York: de Gruyter. pp. 1474–92.

WEGMANN-HEINZ, G. 1974 *Phonologisch-kontrastive Analyse Mundart/Hochsprache im Bereich des Moselfränkischen*. Staatsarbeit (ms., unveröff.). Bonn.

WEINREICH, U. 1954 Is a Structural Dialectology possible? *Word* 10, 338–402.

WEISS, A. 1978 Kontrastive Untersuchungen zum Sprachgebrauch zwischen Dialekt und Hochsprache. Methodische Probleme und Entscheidungen vor einer empirischen Untersuchung. *Klagenfurter Beiträge zur Sprachwissenschaft* 4 (1978): 1/2, 97–119.

——1984 Die Rolle der Syntax für die Differenzierung von regionalen, sozialen und situativen Sprachvarietäten. In P. WIESINGER (ed.), *Beiträge zur bairischen und ostfränkischen Dialektologie. Ergebnisse der Zweiten Bayerisch-Österreichischen Dialektologentagung Wien, 27. bis 30. September 1983*. Göppingen: Kümmerle. pp. 109–21.

WERLEN, E. 1984 *Studien zur Datenerhebung in der Dialektologie*. (= Zeitschrift für Dialektologie und Linguistik, Beihefte 46). Wiesbaden: Steiner.

WERLEN, I. 1986 Dialektsprechen in mehrdialektalen Gesellschaften am Beispiel des südlichen Deutschland und der deutschen Schweiz. In A. SCHÖNE (ed.), *Kontroversen, alte und neue. Akten des VII. Internationalen Germanisten-Kongresses Göttingen 1985*. 4. Tübingen: Niemeyer. pp. 279–99.

WIESINGER, P. 1985 Gesellschaftliche und sprachliche Probleme bei der Erforschung örtlicher Sprachgemeinschaften. Schwerpunkte der Forschungsgeschichte. In W. BESCH & K.J. MATTHEIER (eds), *Ortssprachenforschung. Beiträge zu einem Bonner Kolloquium*. Berlin: Schmidt. pp. 24–48.

WILKE, E. 1921 Deutschunterricht und Mundart. *Die Deutsche Schule* 25, 302–11.

WINTELER, J. 1878 *Über die Begründung des deutschen Sprachunterrichts auf die Mundart des Schülers*. Bern.

ZEHETNER, L.G. 1977 *Dialekt/Hochsprache — Kontrastiv. Bairisch*. Düsseldorf: Schwann.

6 Dialect and education in the United Kingdom[1]

JENNY CHESHIRE and PETER TRUDGILL

In Great Britain and Northern Ireland, as in many other countries, the relationship between social and regional language varieties is such that the greatest degree of regional differentiation is found among lower working-class speakers and the smallest degree at the other end of the social scale, among speakers from the upper middle class.

Speakers who would generally be regarded as 'educated' typically use the vocabulary and grammatical features that are widely known as 'standard English'. These features are normally used in the writing of English throughout the English-speaking world. It is possible to regard this form of English as a single dialect even though it is subject to a certain amount of regional differentiation. It is well-known that there are a number of grammatical and, in particular, lexical differences between American and British standard English. Within the United Kingdom there are similar differences. To take a single example, educated speakers from the south of England tend to use such forms as

I won't do it
I haven't done it

while speakers from elsewhere in the country are more likely to say:

I'll not do it
I've not done it

Generally speaking, however, these differences are few in number and linguistically rather slight.

Accent and dialect normally go together, to the extent that we have usually to consider an accent as an integral part of a particular dialect. Most speakers of the (more or less regionless) standard English dialect, however,

94

speak with a (usually not too localised) regional accent, so that most educated people betray their geographical origins much more in their pronunciation than in their grammar or lexis. There are also a number of standard English speakers who employ the highest status British English accent, RP (Received Pronunciation), which is, at least within England, genuinely regionless. These speakers tend to have been educated at the large Public Schools or to have acquired the accent as the result of a conscious effort or training. RP speakers form a very small percentage of the British population. A random sample of the population of the city of Norwich in southern England (Trudgill, 1974) produced one RP speaker out of a total of 60 participants (figures for northern England, Scotland and Northern Ireland would be likely to be even smaller than this). The accent is nevertheless very familiar to most people as a result of its use by radio and television announcers and other public figures.

A much larger number of educated speakers have what might be termed near-RP accents: accents which have many of the features of RP but incorporate also a number of non-RP features, such as northern /a/ rather than /ɑ:/ in items such as *bath, dance*, or southern /i:/ rather than /ɪ/ in items such as *money, ready*.

The further one goes 'down' the social scale, the larger become the grammatical and lexical differences from standard English, and the phonetic and phonological differences from RP. The largest degree of regional variation is found at the level of rural dialects, particularly as spoken by elderly people of little education. Trudgill (1981) attempts to represent this situation by means of the diagram shown here as Figure 1. This emphasises the continuum-like nature of linguistic variation in Britain: it is usually even less possible to talk of discrete social dialects than it is of discrete regional dialects, since varieties merge into one another and are often a matter of the frequency of occurrence of particular forms rather than of their presence or absence. (An exception is the standard English dialect. Since this dialect is to a considerable extent codified, it requires only one deviation from this norm for a stretch of speech or writing to be perceived as non-standard.)

As an example of the way in which the frequency of occurrence of particular linguistic forms varies, we can consider the non-standard present tense verb forms that occur in the English spoken in the town of Norwich. In this variety of English, third person singular forms can occur without the -*s* suffix, as in the phrase *she go to the city on Fridays*. Table 1 shows the frequency of occurrence of non-standard verb forms of this type in the speech of people from different socio-economic classes (from Trudgill, 1974).

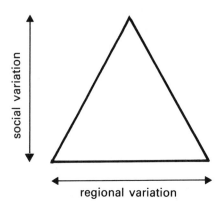

FIGURE 1 *Dialect variation in the United Kingdom*

TABLE 1   *Relative Frequency of Occurrence of Non-standard Present Tense Forms in Norwich*

Socio-economic status	% forms without -s
upper middle class	0
lower middle class	29
upper working class	75
middle working class	81
lower working class	97

Sociolinguistic studies in Norwich and in other parts of the United Kingdom have shown that the frequency with which many non-standard linguistic features occur in people's speech correlates not only with their socio-economic status, but also with other, interrelated social factors, including sex, age and — importantly — the nature of their social networks (see, for example, Petyt, 1985; Macaulay, 1977; Milroy, 1980; Trudgill, 1974).

Regional and social variation in English, then, is interrelated. Nevertheless, the diagram presented in Figure 1 is in some ways a distortion of the facts. The degree of linguistic distance between the standard dialect and regional varieties in fact varies quite considerably in different parts of the country. Standard English — to simplify somewhat — is descended from dialects of English originally spoken in the south-east of England (Strang, 1970). One result of this is that differences between standard English and non-standard dialects in the south of England, while socially very significant, tend to be relatively few in number. It is possible in most cases to list more or less exhaustively, and at not very great length, the differences involved. The following list, for instance, cites most of the forms which distinguish the working-class dialect of the town of Reading from standard English (Cheshire, 1982a). Most of the forms listed occur variably.

1. Present tense verb forms: *I wants it*
2. Irregular preterites: *He give it me yesterday*
3. Preterite auxiliary and main verb DO distinct: *You done it, did you?*
4. Preterite of BE: *We was playing. I weren't*
5. Negative present of BE *It ain't that big*
6. Negative of HAVE: *We ain't got one*
7. Negative preterite *never: She did yesterday, but she never today*
8. Multiple negation: *I don't eat none of that*
9. Reflexive pronouns: *He done it hisself*
10. Plural *that: Over by them bus stops*
11. Relative pronouns: *Are you the one what said it?*
12. Comparatives: *She gets more rougher*
13. Post-numeral plurality: *Thirteen mile*
14. Adverbs: *He done it nice*
15. Prepositions of place: *It was at London*

There are also a small number of lexical features such as:

They don't learn you nothing

Can I lend your bike?

It can be seen that the differences involved are neither very numerous nor (with the exception of 3 and, perhaps, 7) very great.

In the south of England, generally speaking, social accent differentiation is much more noticeable than grammatical or lexical variation. Even so, the differences between, say, a working-class London accent and the high-status RP accent are nearly all phonetic rather than phonological. And most of the phonological differences are either variable, such as the merger of /f/ and /θ/, and the loss of /h/, or are found fairly high up the social scale, such as the merger of the vowels of *cot* and *coat* before /l/, as in *doll* and *dole*.

The further one travels away from the south-east of England, the greater become the differences between standard English and RP, on the one hand, and broad regional dialects, on the other. These differences are greatest in the more isolated parts of rural northern England and, in particular, in the Lowlands of Scotland and those areas of Northern Ireland where the local dialects are Scottish in origin (Gregg, 1972). (In the Highlands of Scotland and in most of Wales, English was originally, and still is in many cases, learned as a second language in schools. For this reason, the English dialects of these areas tend not to be so radically different from standard English.)

It is difficult to illustrate the nature of these differences except at length, but the following brief (and mainly phonological and phonetic) examples may give some impression:

(a) *goose*   [gɪəs]
    loaf   [lɪəf]
    coal   [kʊəl]
    ground [gɹʊnd]
    blind   [blɪnd]
    wrong   [ɹaŋ]

(Conservative rural dialect forms from northernmost England; from Wakelin, 1972)

(b) [ðə tičɛr wɪz afa gwid tʌlz]
    The teacher was awful good till's
    = *The teacher was very good to me*

(Rural Aberdeenshire dialect, Scotland; from Mather, 1975)

(c) *die*	[diː]	*open*	[ɑːpən]
high	[hiç]	*any*	[ɔːne]
haven't	[hɪne]	*where*	[ʍɔːr]
above	[əbɨn]	*pound*	[pʌn]
shoes	[šɨn]	*not*	[noː]
blind	[blæn]	*cow*	[kʉː]
bridge	[bræg]	*suck*	[sʉk]
move	[meːv]	*nothing*	[nɪθən]
grass	[grɛːs]	*with*	[weː]
dinner	[dɛːnər]	*make*	[mɑːk]

(Glenoe, rural Northern Ireland; from Gregg, 1964)

Further examples of the linguistic differences that exist in regional varieties of English in the United Kingdom are given in Hughes & Trudgill (1987) and in Wells (1982). Hughes & Trudgill (1987) include details of grammatical differences as well as phonetic and phonological differences (see also Milroy & Milroy, in press).

One consequence of this differentiation is illustrated in Figure 2. This is an attempt to illustrate the fact that, while social dialect continua ranging from local dialect to standard English are found in much of England, in Lowland Scotland and in parts of the rural north of England there is discontinuity because of the greater linguistic differences involved. Southern English speakers will often command a range of the social dialect continuum and, as it were, slide up and down it according to social context. Many Lowland Scots, on the other hand, will indulge in genuine dialect switching: they will jump rather than slide.

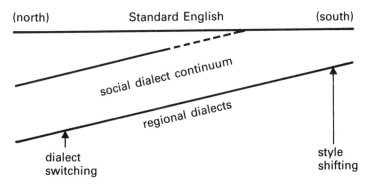

FIGURE 2 *Contextual variation in UK English*

The difference is also apparent in schools. Children in the south of England will not normally adapt their spoken language very greatly between home, play and school; and much of the adaptation, moreover, will be of a quantitative nature. Table 2 provides an example; it shows the percentage frequency of occurrence of some of the non-standard features used in the town of Reading, by a group of children who were recorded both in school and outside school (Cheshire, 1982a). The extent to which dialect-speaking children such as these adjust their spoken language towards standard English when they are at school appears to depend on several different factors, including the strength of their peer group ties and their relationship with individual teachers (again, see Cheshire, 1982a). This type of adaptation is likely to be subconscious and to go unrecognised by both children and teachers. Many Scottish children, on the other hand, are well aware that

TABLE 2   *Relative Frequency of Occurrence of Non-standard Features*

	Outside school	*In school*
Non-standard present tense verb forms	57.03	31.49
Multiple negation	90.70	66.67
Negative preterite *never*	49.21	15.38
Plural *that*	90.00	62.50

they have one dialect for school and another for other situations, and this may be true of other parts of the United Kingdom where a local variety is 'focussed' — where, in other words, speakers perceive the variety in some sense as a distinct entity (see LePage, 1978; Milroy, 1982).

Whether or not children are consciously aware of the adjustments that they make to their speech when they are at school, they are very often keenly aware of peer group pressures to use regional forms of grammar or of pronunciation (see Cheshire, in press). The frequency of use of non-standard linguistic forms increases dramatically (and often temporarily) during early adolescence, for children of all socio-economic classes (for discussion, see Cheshire, 1987). The linguistic conflict that can result is clearly illustrated in the words of a child from Birmingham (see Romaine, 1984):

> You always try to be the same as everyone else. You don't sort of want to be made fun of. . .sort of posher than everyone else. Then you get sort of picked on. But then if you use a lot of slang and that, people don't think much of you.

Conservative rural dialects of the type illustrated on page 98 (see further Orton & Wright, 1975) are almost certainly gradually dying out. (The vast majority of the population of the UK, it is safe to say, have never heard most of the forms cited in (a), (b) and (c) on page 98.) They survive for the most part only in rural districts, and England, in particular, is a very heavily urbanised country. Increasing geographical mobility, education, centralisation and urbanisation are undoubtedly factors in this decline, as is the fact that Britain has very few areas that are remote or difficult of access. The decline has been noted by a number of writers (Orton, 1933) and seems bound to continue. For example, work carried out with small-town junior-school children in Cumbria, north-eastern England in the 1970s, suggests that they are now much more ignorant of regional vocabulary items such as *yat* (gate); *lake* (play); *loup* (jump) than were children in the 1950s.[2]

Much of the traditional regional variation in language currently to be found in the country is, then, being lost. On the other hand, it appears to be the case that urban dialects are still undergoing developments of a divergent type (Wells, 1970; Trudgill, 1974, 1978, 1986) and that phonological differences between urban varieties in particular may be on the increase (see Harris, 1985).

Movements for the preservation of conservative rural dialects are not particularly strong, and the amount of regional dialect literature produced in England is very limited. There are, however, a large number of dialect societies, such as the Yorkshire Dialect Society, the Lakeland Dialect Society, the Lancashire Dialect Society and the Devon Dialect Society. In Scotland, where Scots was used as the normal written language until the eighteenth century, the tradition of writing in Scottish varieties (either regional dialects or generalised varieties — somewhat artificially — descended from earlier literary Scots, such as Lallans) has survived much more strongly. It has, moreover, been undergoing a revival (McClure, 1975) and is beginning to find its way back into schools. The Language Awareness movement (see Jones, this volume, Chapter 17) is also giving dialect a place within the school curriculum; and the forthcoming Directory of Dialect Resources (see Edwards & Cheshire, this volume, Chapter 12) is likely to further encourage an interest in dialect within schools.

There is also another important group of English speakers in Britain: those members of the population who are of Afro-Caribbean origin. Research has shown that a range of varieties of English is spoken by the Afro-Caribbean community in the United Kingdom, stretching from broad creole, or Patois, to British standard English. Many speakers, too, are bidialectal in Patois and a variety of British English, and many younger people speak non-standard British dialects with varying degrees of Patois admixture, depending on background and situation (see Wells, 1973; Sutcliffe, 1982, 1984; Sebba, 1984; Edwards, 1984, 1986; Sutcliffe & Wong, 1986). There is also evidence of white adolescents using Patois features (Hewitt, 1982), and it seems that both Patois and non-standard dialect features are used by school-children as what Halliday (1978) terms an 'anti-language' (Hewitt, 1982; Cheshire, 1982a; Edwards, 1986).

This social and regional dialect and accent variation in the United Kingdom, although obviously slight when compared to that found in many other countries, brings with it a number of problems. The most salient of these is educational. It has often been noted that working-class children do not perform so well educationally as might be expected, and it has been suggested that language may play an important role in this under-achievement (see, for example, Barnes *et al.*, 1969; Hawkins, 1984). One component of this language problem is widely felt to be connected with dialect (Trudgill, 1975). Standard English is the dialect of education; it is spoken by most teachers; it is the dialect normally employed in writing; and it is rewarded in examinations. A majority of children, on the other hand, are not native speakers of this particular dialect. (The survey of the — not very industrial — city of Norwich showed that only about 12% of the population used no non-standard grammatical forms.) Most children, then, and in particular those from the working-class and lower middle class, have to learn to handle a new dialect on entering school.

There has been very little research in the United Kingdom into the specific linguistic problems that may or may not be encountered by dialect-speaking children at school (see, however, Williams, this volume, Chapter 11). The issue is discussed at length in Trudgill (1975) and in Trudgill (1983a); and the problems in learning to read and write that certain pedagogical practices may cause for children who speak a non-standard dialect are discussed in Cheshire (1982b) and Edwards (1984). Some practical suggestions for teachers concerning the ways in which standard English grammar can best be added to children's linguistic repertoires are given in Edwards (1984) and Richmond (1982).

In educational circles as well as amongst the general public, there is still a considerable amount of confusion, misunderstanding and social and linguistic prejudice surrounding discussion of the issue. As can be imagined, the question of the teaching of standard English is often couched in terms of 'correctness', although the efforts of linguists and educationalists to bring a more informed point of view to notions of this type appear to be bearing fruit among teachers, if not with the general public. Recently Graddol & Swann (1988) have explained the continuing discrepancy between the views of the general public and those of linguists as an example of cross-cultural miscommunication (see Gumperz, 1982), occurring because academic linguists and the general public share different assumptions and background knowledge about language.

A particular problem with dialect and 'correctness' is an inadequate, if unsurprising, appreciation of the nature of dialectal forms. The rubric to an important British examination in oral English states that children will not be penalised for the use of local dialect forms. An examiners' report, however, criticises the use by London examinees of forms such as *I done it* and *I ain't got none*, which are an integral part of working-class London dialect, as 'mistakes'. There is, in fact, a widespread tendency to regard rural dialect forms as acceptable (if somewhat quaint) but to treat urban dialect forms simply as 'errors'.

A further problem that can be attributed to 'miscommunication' between academic linguists and lay people is the failure of many to distinguish between dialect, on the one hand, and style and use of language, on the other. A correspondent to the Scottish Times Educational Supplement wrote:

> There are, we are told, no correct forms in language: the child who tells a teacher to f. . . off (*sic*) is not being incorrect or impertinent, he is merely using the language of his sub-culture and should not be asked to. . .use the dialect of his teacher.

Swearing at the teacher, of course, has no connection whatever with dialect and, although sub-cultural differences in the use of and attitudes to language are a subject of considerable importance, confusions of this type are not at all helpful.

Further confusion exists in claims that standard English is more logical and/or expressive and/or adequate for the treatment of many topics than any other dialect. The point about logic has been very convincingly argued against by Labov (1972), and the adequacy argument, while not entirely straightforward (Hymes, 1975) is not one that linguists would feel to be especially convincing (see Trudgill, 1983b). It is, in fact, extremely difficult to see how minimal grammatical differences of the type cited above between Reading dialect and standard English, or of the type given in Hughes & Trudgill (1987), could possibly cause any differences in expressive power. It is more likely that these claims reflect perceived differences in discourse structure, unrelated to grammatical differences. There is research evidence which suggests that speakers from different subcultural backgrounds use different principles to relate topics to each other in discourse (see, for example, Heath, 1983; Michaels, 1981); and this can lead to difficulties where the organisation of discourse does not coincide with that which is expected in school (see Romaine, 1984). The distinction between listener-oriented and message-oriented speech (Brown, 1982) is also relevant here, as is the distinction between planned and unplanned discourse (Ochs, 1979; Givón, 1979). Clearly, distinctions of this kind are of a different nature from distinctions between standard and non-standard dialects; though they are, of course, of crucial importance in education.

Further confusion surrounds the question of the comprehension of standard English and of non-standard dialects of English. It is often said that if children do not modify their speech at least in the direction of standard English (and RP) they will be at a serious disadvantage, since people in other parts of the country will be unable to understand them. This kind of argument is obviously of some potency in some countries, although it has to be noted that claims for lack of mutual intelligibility are often unsupported by research data and fail to acknowledge that it is normally much simpler and quicker to learn to understand a new variety than to learn to speak one. In the UK, although again we do not have any data to support this, this argument is almost certainly not worthy of attention. The fact is that linguistic differences between at least a majority of English dialects are not serious enough to cause permanent comprehension problems. Some difficulties do occur, it is true (see, for example, Milroy, 1984), but they are normally temporary and fairly readily overcome. Individuals moving from one area to another may initially have some difficulties in making themselves understood, but they usually adjust their speech fairly rapidly and automatically. Some of the strategies that are used in order to do this are discussed in Trudgill (1982).

Similarly, unfamiliar accents may initially give rise to problems in understanding and in being understood, but there is evidence that people can, and do, adjust their pronunciation, both on a short-term basis (Thakerar, Giles & Cheshire, 1982) and on a long-term basis (Trudgill, 1986). The crucial factor affecting speech accommodation of this kind is the attitudes that speakers have towards each other (see Giles, 1973). Claims about comprehension difficulties, in fact, are most often rationalisations for unfavourable attitudes to low-status varieties of English.

Attitudes towards non-standard dialects (and low-prestige accents) are, in fact, very unfavourable in many sections of the community, and speakers of these varieties may often be discriminated against in employment and other situations. Macaulay (1977), for example, found that some employers in Glasgow claimed they would not employ anybody with a strong Glaswegian accent; and those employers who were reasonably tolerant towards regional accents placed strong emphasis on the use of standard grammar.

Trudgill (1983b) discusses the social evaluation of non-standard dialects and low-prestige accents. An experimental investigation into the evaluation of the aesthetic qualities of different regional accents of English found that evaluations were not based on any inherent aesthetic qualities of the accents (since there was no overall agreement between American and Canadian listeners, who, on the whole, could not recognise the regional origins of the accents, and English and Scots listeners, who could), but that instead the evaluations of English and Scots listeners appeared to reflect the social connotations of the accents. These listeners rated as least pleasant the accents spoken in heavily urbanised areas of the United Kingdom (London, West Midlands, Liverpool and Glasgow).

As informal discussion, views of this type have no particularly serious consequences. In education, however, these views can be of considerable importance, since even if teachers are persuaded that all varieties of English are equally 'correct', they may nevertheless feel obliged to try to change children's accents (see, for example, Millar, 1987). As Trudgill (1983b) points out, people tend to argue that although there may be nothing 'wrong' with the accent, and although it may be perfectly comprehensible, it is very 'ugly'; it is therefore only fair to the children to give them the chance to speak in a 'more aesthetically satisfying manner'. The grave danger here is that, whether views of this sort are accompanied by ridicule or by kindness, they lead speakers to disparage their own language, and they lead children, in particular, to develop feelings of linguistic insecurity and even of what has been called 'linguistic self-hatred' (see Van de Craen & Humblet, this volume, Chapter 2). The result is, often, individuals who become, in certain circumstances, inarticulate and reluctant to express themselves (Trudgill, 1983b: 209). For example, one of the Glaswegians who took part in the research reported in Macaulay (1977) commented on his own speech as follows:

> I mean I'm not a speaker as you can see. I don't. . .I'm just a common sort of, you know I'm not. . .I've often wished I'd gone to some sort of elocution lessons because I meet so many people in my job and I feel as if I'm lower when it comes to speaking, you know.

Not surprisingly, perhaps, the experiment reported in Trudgill (1983b) found that the high-status RP accent was evaluated as having the most aesthetic merit. Furthermore, Giles (1971a) has demonstrated that speakers with RP accents are more favourably evaluated than speakers with different regional accents, on a number of different parameters. They are almost universally evaluated as more intelligent, more reliable and more educated than other speakers (Giles, 1971b) — though they may also be seen as less friendly and sociable (Giles & Powesland, 1975; Trudgill, 1983b). Findings such as these are very relevant to education. Teachers are not immune to social attitudes of this type, and there is evidence to suggest that they may evaluate children with RP accents as having more academic potential than others (see V. Edwards, 1978; J. Edwards, 1979).

There are indications that attitudes towards regional accents are beginning to change in the United Kingdom; some news readers and programme presenters from the BBC, for example, have (usually relatively slight) regional accents, particularly on local stations. At present, however, only a select few regional accents are heard from BBC presenters on 'serious' programmes—notably mild Scottish accents.

The greatest dialect-related problems in the United Kingdom, then, continue to be the attitudes and prejudices that many people hold towards non-standard dialects and accents of English, combined with a lack of understanding about the nature of dialect differences and of their social significance. The importance of these matters in education is increasing, with the introduction in 1988 of public examinations that include a substantial oracy component (the GCSE English examinations for 16-year-old pupils). Recent government policy stresses the importance of the standard English dialect, stating that 'there can be no doubt that ease and familiarity in using and responding to it must be central to the work of all English teachers' (DES, 1986: 36). It is encouraging that the DES policy document points out that this is not to say that non-standard forms are inherently inferior, and that for many pupils 'the most effective route toward a grasp of standard forms may well be through the non-standard'. Against these fine words, however, needs to be set the reminder of Milroy & Milroy (1985: 175–76) that public discussion of the 'standard English' issue in schools continues to be less reflective and less well-informed about language than it should be, and that as yet the narrow approach to language that is still current even amongst professionals directly concerned with language is ill-fitted to achieve the aim of making the standard language available as a resource to all.

Notes to Chapter 6

1. This paper is derived from an earlier paper by Peter Trudgill, published as 'Standard and non-standard dialects and accents of English in the United Kingdom' in *International Journal of the Sociology of Language* 21, 1979.
2. The work was carried out by Alison White, a student in the Linguistics Department of Reading University, in Brampton, Cumberland.

References

BARNES, D., BRITTON, J. and ROSEN, H. 1969 *Language, the Learner and the School.* Harmondsworth: Penguin Books.

BROWN, G. 1982 The spoken language. In R.A. CARTER (ed.), *Linguistics and the Teacher*. London: Routledge & Kegan Paul.

CHESHIRE, J. 1982a *Variation in an English Dialect: A Sociolinguistic Study*. Cambridge: Cambridge University Press.

——1982b Dialect features and linguistic conflict in schools. *Educational Review* 34:1, 53–67.

——1987 Age and generation — specific use of language. In U. AMMON, N. DITTMAR & K.J. MATTHEIER (eds), *Sociolinguistics: An Introductory Handbook to the Science of Language and Society*. Berlin: de Gruyter. pp. 760–67.

—— in press, Regional variation in English syntax: Introductory matters. In J. MILROY & L. MILROY (eds), *Regional Variation in English Syntax*. London: Economic and Social Research Council.

DES (Department of Education and Science) 1986 *English from 5 to 16*. London: HMSO. 2nd edition.

EDWARDS, J. 1979 *Language and Disadvantage*. London: Edward Arnold.

EDWARDS, V.K. 1978 Language attitudes and underperformance in West Indian children. *Educational Review* 30:1, 51–58.

——1984 *Language in Multicultural Classrooms*. London: Batsford.

——1986 *Language in a Black Community*. Clevedon: Multilingual Matters.

GILES, H. 1971a Patterns of evaluation in reactions to R.P., South Welsh and Somerset accented speech. *British Journal of Social and Clinical Psychology* 10, 280–81.

——1971b Teacher's attitudes towards accent usage and change. *Educational Review* 24, 11–25.

——1973 Accent mobility: a model and some data. *Anthropological Linguistics* 15, 87–105.

GILES, H. and POWESLAND, P.F. 1975 *Speech Style and Social Evaluation*. London: Academic Press.

GIVÓN, T. 1979 From discourse to syntax: grammar as a processing strategy. *Syntax and Semantics* 12, 81–112.

GRADDOL, D. and SWANN, J. 1988 Trapping linguists: an analysis of linguists' responses to John Honey's pamphlet 'The Language Trap'. *Language and Education* 2, 95–111.

GREGG, R.J. 1964 Scotch-Irish urban speech in Ulster. *Ulster Dialects: An Introductory Symposium*. Holywood: Ulster Folk Museum.

——1972 The Scotch-Irish dialect boundaries in Ulster. In M.F. WAKELIN (ed.), *Patterns in the Folk Speech of the British Isles*. London: Athlone Press.

GUMPERZ, J. (ed.) 1982 *Discourse Strategies*. Cambridge: Cambridge University Press.

HALLIDAY, M.A.K. 1978 *Language as a Social Semiotic*. London: Edward Arnold.

HARRIS, J. 1985 *Phonological Variation and Change: Studies in Hiberno-English*. Cambridge: Cambridge University Press.

HAWKINS, H. 1984 *Awareness of Language: An Introduction*. Cambridge: Cambridge University Press.

HEATH, S.B. 1983 *Ways with Words: Language, Life and Work in Communities and Classrooms*. Cambridge: Cambridge University Press.

HEWITT, R. 1982 White adolescent Creole users and the politics of friendship. *Journal of Multilingual and Multicultural Development* 3, 217–32.

HUGHES, G.A. and TRUDGILL, P.J. 1987 *English Accents and Dialects: An Introduction to Social and Regional Varieties of British English*. London: Edward Arnold. 2nd edition.

HYMES, D. 1975 Speech and language: on the origins and foundations of inequality among speakers. In E. HAUGEN & M. BLOOMFIELD (eds), *Language as a Human Problem*. London: Lutterworth Press.

LABOV, W. 1972 The logic of non-standard English. In W. LABOV *Language in the Inner City*. Philadelphia: University of Pennsylvania Press.

LABOV, W., YAEGER, M. and STEINER, R. 1972 *A Quantitative Study of Sound Change in Progress*. Philadelphia: U.S. Regional Survey.

LePAGE, R.B. 1978 Projecting, focussing, diffusion. *Society for Caribbean Linguistics Occasional Paper* 9. Reprinted in *York Papers in Linguistics* 9.

MACAULAY, R.K.S. 1977 *Language, Social Class and Education: A Glasgow Study*. Edinburgh: Edinburgh University Press.

MATHER, J. 1975 Social variation in present-day Scots. In J.D. McCLURE (ed.), *The Scots Language in Education*. Aberdeen: Aberdeen College of Education.

McCLURE, J.D. 1975 Modern Scots prose-writing. In J.D. McCLURE (ed.), *The Scots Language in Education*. Aberdeen: Aberdeen College of Education.

MICHAELS, S. 1981 'Sharing time': children's narrative styles and differential access to literacy. *Language in Society* 10: 423–43.

MILLAR, S. 1987 Accent in the classroom: sociolinguistic perspectives on the teaching of elocution in some Belfast secondary-level schools. Unpublished Ph.D. thesis, Queens University, Belfast.

MILROY, L. 1980 *Language and Social Networks*. Oxford: Blackwell.

——1982 Social network and linguistic focusing. In S. ROMAINE (ed.), *Sociolinguistic Variation in Speech Communities*. London: Edward Arnold.

——1984 Comprehension and context: successful communication and communication breakdown. In P. TRUDGILL (ed.), *Applied Sociolinguistics*. London: Academic Press.

MILROY, J. and MILROY, L. 1985 *Authority in Language: Investigating Language Prescription and Standardisation*. London: Routledge & Kegan Paul.

—— (eds) (in press) *Regional Variation in English Syntax*. London: Economic and Social Research Council.

OCHS, E. 1979 Planned and unplanned discourse. *Syntax and Semantics* 12, 51–80.

ORTON, H. 1933 *The Phonology of a South Durham Dialect*. London: Kegan, Paul, Trench, Trubner.

ORTON, H. and WRIGHT, N. 1975 *A Word Geography of England*. London: Seminar Press.

PETYT, K.M. 1985 *Dialect and Accent in Industrial West Yorkshire*. Amsterdam: John Benjamins.

RICHMOND, J. 1982 *The Resources of Classroom Language*. London: Edward Arnold.

ROMAINE, S. 1984 *The Language of Children and Adolescents: The Acquisition of Communicative Competence*. Oxford: Blackwell.

SEBBA, M. 1984 Language change among Afro-Caribbeans in London. *Amsterdam Creole Studies* 7, 1–11.

STRANG, B. 1970 *A History of English*. London: Methuen.

SUTCLIFFE, D. 1982 *British Black English*. Oxford: Blackwell.

——1984 British Black English and West Indian Creoles. In P. TRUDGILL (ed.), *Language in the British Isles*. Cambridge: Cambridge University Press.

SUTCLIFFE, D. and WONG, I. (eds) 1986 *Language and the Black Experience*. Oxford: Blackwell.

THAKERAR, J., GILES, H. and CHESHIRE, J. 1982 Psychological and linguistic parameters of speech accommodation theory. In H. GILES & R. ST. CLAIR (eds), *Advances in the Social Psychology of Language*. Cambridge: Cambridge University Press.

TRUDGILL, P. 1974 *The Social Differentiation of English in Norwich*. Cambridge: Cambridge University Press.

——1975 *Accent, Dialect and the School*. London: Edward Arnold.

——1978 (ed.) *Sociolinguistic Patterns in British English*. London: Edward Arnold.

——1981 *Sociolinguistics*. Harmondsworth: Penguin. 2nd edition.

——1982 On the limits of passive 'competence': sociolinguistics and the polylectal grammar controversy. In D. CRYSTAL (ed.), *Linguistic Controversies*. London: Edward Arnold.

——1983a Standard and non-standard dialects of English in the United Kingdom: attitudes and policies. In P. TRUDGILL *On Dialect: Social and Geographical Perspectives*. Oxford: Blackwell.

——1983b Sociolinguistics and linguistic value judgements: correctness, adequacy and aesthetics. In P. TRUDGILL. *On Dialect: Social and Geographical Perspectives*. Oxford: Blackwell.

——1986 *Dialects in Contact*. Oxford: Blackwell.

WAKELIN, M.F. 1972 *English Dialects: An Introduction*. London: Athlone Press.

WELLS, J. 1970 Local accents in England and Wales. *Journal of Linguistics* 6, 231–52.

——1973 *Jamaican Pronunciation in London*. Oxford: Blackwell.

——1982 *Accents of English. Volume 1: The British Isles*. Cambridge: Cambridge University Press.

Part II
Research 1970–1987

7 Aspects of dialect and school in the Federal Republic of Germany[1]

ULRICH AMMON

The History of the Problem

A glimpse back into previous times

It seems that there have been dialect-related problems in German schools for as long as a standard language has been used as the medium of instruction, or taught as a subject in its own right (see also Rosenberg, this volume, Chapter 5). At first, the different regional standards were used; now, of course, it is the national standard that is used. The problems were more severe towards the south and the north of the German language area, since the dialects there differ more from standard German than in the central areas. Standard German is mainly derived from east Middle German dialects, though there have been massive incorporations from other areas, particularly from the southeast, which was the imperial centre for centuries. The Low German areas in the north suffered particularly from having to acquire and use a standard variety which was about as different from their own varieties as present day varieties of Dutch are from standard German (Möhn, 1981). The extent of their linguistic distance from standard German has led to the Low German dialects being characterised as 'pseudodialectalised' into German (i.e. High German) (Kloss, 1978), the point being that from a purely linguistic point of view they should be considered as belonging to a distinct set of language varieties.

Because of the enormous difficulties that standard German poses for speakers of Low German, there have been particularly radical suggestions for the solution of the problem. For example, the language policy of the

French Revolutionaries influenced Ludolf Wienbarg (1834) to propose the eradication of all Low German dialects, in order to enable the underprivileged classes of the population to actively participate in political life. Though Wienbarg's suggestions are often ridiculed, they have, in fact, become a reality insofar as the Low German dialects have receded to such an extent that they now cause fewer school problems than the High German dialects. The High German dialects are still very much alive, especially in the south of the German language area.

Wienbarg's objectives, like those of the French revolutionaries, were radicalisations of earlier pedagogical views, which need to be seen within the prevailing intellectual climate of the time, that of philosophical enlightenment. Language cultivation was favoured, of which standardisation was one aspect; so, too, was the teaching of the 'cultivated' variety to the population as a whole. A very crude but useful dichotomy can be made between views such as these, and the views of the Romantics, who admired 'original' (i.e. 'uncultivated') varieties or languages (see Hollingworth, this volume, Chapter 19). One finds the Romantic view, for example, in Jacob Grimm's writings. Rudolf Hildebrand (1869), who was one of Grimm's pupils, tried to combine both viewpoints, stressing that the teaching of the standard variety should be based on the child's dialect, without attempting to eradicate it.

This idea would certainly be shared by many language teachers today. Formulated so vaguely, however, it allows a wide range of variation in practice, particularly with regard to which language skills are taught to which pupils. In the German-speaking countries, as elsewhere, the lower classes were often taught only rudimentary skills in the standard language (oral comprehension and reading skills), whereas the upper classes acquired, in addition, a more active competence in the standard variety, including speaking and writing, as well as a passive understanding of a larger portion of the standard vocabulary.

The educational problems faced by dialect speakers were discussed in numerous publications up to and including the 1930s, with the main—and often the only—emphasis being on spelling (see, for example, Karstädt, 1908). In Nazi-Germany, however, these problems were no longer mentioned in educational publications, presumably because social differentiation, of which inevitably they are a part, was a taboo subject (see, for a more detailed analysis, Ammon, 1972b, 1973a: 131–42).

Rediscovery of the problem

A general awareness of social discrimination re-emerged during the students' revolt of the late 1960s, and this led to a rediscovery of the educational problems encountered by dialect speakers. Bernstein's theory of elaborated and restricted codes (see Bernstein, 1971–75) was very influential at that time, and this further stimulated an interest in the problems. A restricted code is, of course, quite different in nature from a regional dialect, one reason being that it can be used both by dialect speakers and by speakers of the standard; nevertheless, parallels were drawn between them. It was felt that both regional dialects and restricted codes placed limitations on the range of verbal activities of the lower class, albeit in different ways. This perspective, which was based on an essentially Marxist view of society, also made people aware of the verbal handicaps that the lower classes might have outside school. They were barred, it seemed, from effective political action in public life because they lacked the necessary verbal skills in the standard variety. Some controversial solutions were suggested: for example, that the lower classes should make their own varieties the medium of public political discourse and that they should endeavour to have them accepted as valid varieties in the schools. Another, equally controversial suggestion was that the lower classes should be taught the standard variety and an elaborated code, in order to be able to militate for their interests more effectively: it was thought that their regional dialects would not allow efficient transregional communication and that their restricted codes would prevent them from being sufficiently explicit in the presentation of their ideas. Marx' own elaborate writings in the standard variety were given as an example of what was required. There were, of course, numerous other opinions that can be seen as falling between the two poles of this crude dichotomy (see, for various controversial views, Der Hessische Kultusminister, 1972; Helmers, 1973; Merkelbach, 1973; Broweleit, 1978).

Various attempts were made to refine these views. Amongst these attempts were some empirical investigations of the extent to which dialect speakers might be disadvantaged in important domains of society, particularly in school. Other domains have not yet been studied in any detail. For some decades there had been virtually no publications on this topic; but suddenly several appeared in the same year (Ammon, 1972a,b; Hasselberg, 1972; Löffler, 1972). Another study (Jäger, 1971) had been published a year earlier, but had passed largely unnoticed — perhaps because of its unassuming title (*Sprachnorm und Schülersprache*: speech norm and pupils' speech). These publications triggered, in their turn, further theoretical and empirical studies on the educational problems of dialect speakers, as well as a number of practical suggestions and educational programmes designed to overcome the problems (see Ammon, this volume, Chapter 14). It might have been helpful if some of these studies had taken into account earlier views of the problems, or if they had looked at similar studies that had been carried out in countries other than the Anglo-Saxon ones. For example, a considerable amount of research on the school problems of dialect speakers had taken place in Italy (see, for instance, Grassi, 1987).

This chapter describes the investigations carried out by the present author in Swabia during the 1970s (see also Ammon, 1972a,b, 1978). It will first consider the problems of definition that arise in any study of dialect and standard language, and the social characteristics of dialect speakers; it will then examine the main findings of the investigations, relating them to a range of educationally important issues.

Some Definitions, and Preliminaries

Dialect and standard

It is notoriously difficult to define unambiguously the concept of a standard variety and a non-standard variety. A definition in terms of the people who speak the varieties is problematic, one reason being that there are certain non-standard forms that may be used by all speakers in colloquial speech (German *Umgangssprache*[2]). Ammon (1986) distinguishes standard and non-standard varieties in terms of the different normative relationships that exist *vis à vis* each of these within a community. The standard forms, roughly speaking, are validly prescribed by certain authorities (for example, teachers) to certain subjects (for example, pupils) in certain situations (in this case, schools), whereas the non-standard forms are not — though the non-standard forms may be used by both sets of individuals in other situations (for a fuller discussion, see Ammon, 1986).

Despite the general difficulties of defining particular varieties or dialects of a language in terms of the people who use them, the term 'regional dialect' can be used here without difficulty, to refer to a variety that is characteristic of a subset of all the speakers of a language. In what follows, the term 'dialect' will be used with the sense of regional dialect.

Further problems arise with other terms that are frequently used, such as 'moderate dialect' or 'broad dialect'. These terms refer to the continuum between dialect and standard, whose extremes are sometimes referred to as

'pure dialect' or 'pure standard'. There is no doubt that adjectives such as
'broad' or 'moderate' involve implicit value judgements, a fact which becomes
clear when one tries to apply them in a similar way to standard speech — for
one does not speak of 'moderate standard' or 'broad standard'. Neutral
substitutes, however, cannot easily be found. A further problem is that the
vagueness of the terms makes them inadequate when precision is needed. It
is possible, however, to make the terms more precise, defining specific points
in the continuum between pure dialect and pure standard speech. We call such
points *dialect–standard levels* (DS levels).

We can sketch only roughly here the method that has been developed
to measure the DS level of utterances. The method is described in detail in
Ammon (1973a and 1985). Briefly, the method consists of analysing the infinite
number of gradations that could be made on the continuum between pure
dialect and pure standard speech into a finite number of minimal gradations
within single linguistic units (for example, the occurrence of a phoneme,
morpheme, word or idiom, the word order in a phrase, and so on). In order
to measure the DS level of an utterance it is necessary to identify all those
minimal distinctions that occur within a given dialect area — excluding, of
course, performance errors — and to describe them clearly and comprehens-
ively, as in a descriptive linguistic grammar (see Ammon, 1973a). In most
cases there will be a large number of phonetic distinctions (i.e. differences in
the lexical incidence of phonemes), a smaller number of morphological, and
lexical and idiomatic differences, and a still smaller number of syntactic
differences (such as differences in word order). Examples of each kind of
distinction are given in Table 1. Some items can be classed in different
categories, depending on the grammatical framework that one chooses to use.

TABLE 1   *Some Differences Between Swabian and Standard German*

	Swabian	Standard German	
phonetic:	[guət]	[gu:t]	'good'
morphological:	*drecket*	*dreckig*	'dirty'
lexical:	*Zibebe*	*Rosine*	'raisin'
idiomatic:	*dreiviertel (drei)*	*Viertel vor (drei)*	'a quarter to (three)'
syntactic:	*(das habe ich nicht) können machen*	*machen können*	'(I) could (not) do (that)'

For example, where the gender of the noun is indicated by the definite article, this may be categorised either as a lexical difference or as a syntactic difference (e.g. *der Butter* in Swabian is *die Butter* in standard German: 'the butter').

In order to limit the number of features that would need to be classed as examples of phonetic differences, it is useful to include only those alternant forms that differ by at least one feature that is phonemic, either in the dialect system or in the standard system (for example, only [e] (Swabian) versus [œ] (standard German) in *möcht* ('would'), without any phonetic variants in between). Even with this restriction, however, it is still possible to find variation which one would wish to consider as including more than two alternant forms. For example, in the Swabian area where our research was carried out the word *böse* occurs with the vowels [aɪ], [e:] and [ɸ:]; or the word *fünf* occurs with the vowels [aɪ], [e], [ɪ] and [y].

Full details of our method of analysis can be found in the references given above. In brief, we call a complete set of alternants between dialect and standard, such as those described above, a *dialect–standard ladder* or a *DS ladder* (in German: *dialektale Stufenleiter*). Any of the alternant forms within such a DS ladder we call a *DS step*.

In some cases it is difficult to distinguish the standard form of a linguistic feature from its non-standard form or forms. In German, however, this is not usually too difficult: the linguistic 'codex' of the standard German of the Federal Republic consists mainly of the *Duden* volumes (published by Dudenverlag in Mannheim), and since this is continuously revised, it contains a large portion of what have come to be the standard forms. The newest editions of the *Duden* volumes can therefore be used fairly safely as a checklist.

Our method of measuring the DS level of an utterance is not, of course, completely flawless; nevertheless, whilst acknowledging that a number of objections can be made to its use, we do not know of any practicable alternative. It seems better than the crude shortcuts that have been used to distinguish between dialect speakers and standard speakers in previous research in West Germany. For instance, Hasselberg (1976) let the teacher classify his/her pupils into dialect speakers and standard speakers, on the basis of his own intuition. In our own research in Swabia, we attempted to classify pupils into dialect speakers and standard speakers by observing their linguistic behaviour in both informal and formal situations. It is well-known that observing informal language poses methodological difficulties, often known as the 'Observer's Paradox' (see Labov, 1972); our experience, however, was that it was even more difficult to set up a situation outside the classroom that was sufficiently formal to elicit standard speech (for details, see Ammon, 1978). Eventually we distinguished three groups of speakers, on the basis of their linguistic behaviour in two different situations:

A) *broad dialect speakers*: pupils whose DS level in the informal situation was below the median.

B) *moderate dialect speakers*: pupils whose DS level in the informal situation was above the median, but who spoke with at least a slight regional accent.

These two groups had lived in the area for most of their lives. We term these the dialect-speaking pupils, in contrast with group C:

C) *standard-speaking pupils*: pupils who had no regional accent in the informal speech sample.

In the investigations which are reported below, we mainly compared the educational abilities of broad dialect speakers (group A) with moderate dialect speakers (group B); and of dialect-speaking pupils (groups A and B) with standard-speaking pupils (group C). Clearly this division is far from ideal, given our earlier remarks. With the benefit of hindsight it now seems a pity that we treated broad and moderate dialect speakers as dichotomous groups, rather than using the method of DS levels to make finer differentiations amongst dialect speakers. Presumably this could be one reason for the relatively low correlation coefficients that we obtained in our research.

Social characteristics of dialect speakers

In a society as complex as the Federal Republic of Germany it is possible to distinguish many different social characteristics of dialect speakers. When investigating educational problems, and also different types of basic social conflict, it is particularly important to analyse social class differences. Differences in sex, age and type of community (urban versus rural) have also been analysed (Ammon, 1972b, 1973a; Mattheier, 1980); however, these do not appear to be so relevant to educational problems.

As far as social class is concerned, we have often stated our hypothesis that the upper social classes have a greater competence in the standard variety, and that they use it more frequently than the lower classes. In some societies this hypothesis would be trivial in the extreme; it is usually agreed that the standard variety has developed from the speech of the 'power élite', the 'intellectual élite', the Royal Courts and the like, and that these sections of society provided the models for the standard. It is agreed, similarly, that the upper classes are able to educate their children in a way that ensures access to the standard variety, which is not the case for the lower social classes. For societies such as these it would be unnecessary, therefore, to give detailed arguments in support of the above hypothesis. This is not the case, however, in the Federal Republic of Germany, where suggestions along these lines have been vigorously contested. It would be interesting to analyse this dispute and to investigate its ideological background; this, however, would be a separate topic.

For a society such as the Federal Republic of Germany, the hypothesis that the upper classes have greater competence in the standard variety and that they use it more frequently than the lower classes can be supported in many different ways. One line of argument is the following. Members of those professions which can be classed as upper class professions according to the criteria used by sociologists, are more likely to use language in public life: managers, priests, Members of Parliament or university professors, for example, would find it difficult to avoid public speaking in their professional life. In public situations standard (or near-standard) usage is the norm; this, in fact, is one reason why standard varieties develop — to make communication possible beyond the boundaries of any given dialect area. In contrast, the members of the lower classes (manual workers or small farmers, for example) rarely use language in a public situation and rarely, therefore, find themselves in conflict with norms of speech requiring the use of the standard.

Once a relatively clear social differentiation in the use of the standard variety has become established, dialect and standard varieties of the language become stabilised, as social-psychological symbols of the different social classes who use them. In other words, the use of these varieties becomes an integral part of a speaker's social identity. As a result, members of the lower social classes may tend to avoid the use of standard forms, even in situations where the norms of speech require them; and, equally, members of the upper social classes tend to avoid dialect forms even when norms of speech do not require the use of the standard. This is particularly likely to come about where there are extreme linguistic differences between the dialect and the standard variety. Even in private, personal situations, therefore, members of the upper classes tend not to speak broad dialect, often speaking a variety approximating closely to the standard.

There is, of course, variation between the use of dialect and standard in different social situations in the speech of all sections of society; but this variation extends over different parts of the dialect–standard continuum for — speakers of different social classes. It is closer to the standard for members of the upper classes, and closer to the dialect for members of the lower classes.

It can be seen that if there are dialect-related problems in West German schools, these are more likely to affect children from the lower social classes. These children are more likely to identify with the local dialect, whilst children from the upper social classes are more likely to use the standard variety, and to identify with that. The fact that there are more dialect speakers amongst members of the lower social classes and that the lower social classes speak broader dialect has been confirmed by several studies, in various different ways (see, for example, Ammon, 1973a; Hasselberg, 1976; Reitmajer, 1979). This is in contrast with some other German-speaking countries; in Switzerland, for example, all the social classes use broad dialect in private situations, so that dialect-related problems in school are not class-specific. Figure 1 illustrates the difference between the Federal Republic of Germany and Switzerland.

Further research is needed in the Federal Republic of Germany to investigate social class differences in everyday language use, in a range of situations, as well as social class differences in active and passive competence in standard German. The way in which these vary with sex, age and regional

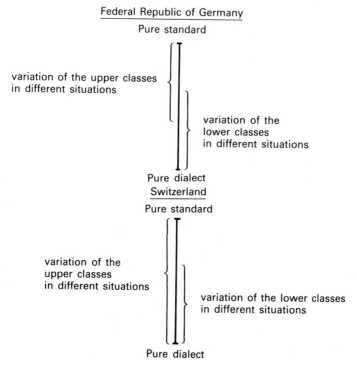

FIGURE 1 *Dialect usage in the Federal Republic of Germany and Switzerland*

background also needs to be investigated. In the meantime, however, it was decided to control for the social class membership of speakers in the study that forms the main basis of the following report (Ammon, 1978).

The Educational Problems of Dialect Speakers: Hypotheses and Results

Preliminaries

When one tries to investigate empirically the school problems that may be encountered by dialect speakers, one faces a very complex set of factors, which include the following.

Distinguishing types of speaker

Different types of dialect speakers need to be distinguished. In our main research project, described by Ammon (1978), we divided speakers into standard-speaking pupils (pupils who had not been born and brought up in the region) and dialect speakers (pupils who were indigenous to the region); the latter group was then further subdivided into moderate dialect speakers and broad dialect speakers (speakers whose DS-level in everyday speech was above the median or below it). This was discussed on pp. 118–19.

Intervening variables

It is necessary to decide which of the potential intervening variables to control for. It is well known that there are many factors other than dialect that can cause difficulties at school. In our main study we controlled for four factors: social class (first dividing the pupils into two distinct classes, then into three), sex, IQ (using Raven's Progressive Matrices test), and residence in the town as opposed to residence in the country. Partial correlations were calculated, which showed, without interference from any of these four factors, the effects of speaking a broad dialect or a moderate dialect on different types of school achievement, and of having been born and brought up in the region (our 'dialect-speaking pupils') or having been born outside the region (our 'standard-speaking pupils'). After controlling for the effects of the four intervening variables, the correlational coefficients remained, in most cases, relatively low, though they were often statistically significant ($p < 0.05$ in two-tailed tests).

Age groups

A decision has to be made about which age groups to study, from a population which ranges in age from 3 (in kindergarten) to 16. Ideally one would monitor a representative sample of children throughout their school career, but it is rarely possible for a research project to do this. For our main study we chose the fourth grade of primary school (age 10–11), since it is at the end of this school year that streaming begins in the West German school system. Streaming is an extremely important factor in determining the subsequent educational 'fate' of school children.

Educational problems

One has to decide which potential school problems to investigate. In our main study we chose to investigate spelling; written composition; reading ability; oral participation in class; marks awarded for German and mathematics; and streaming. In addition, we investigated pupils' attitudes towards dialect speakers and standard speakers, and the extent to which teachers were aware of the educational problems of dialect speakers.

The sample for our analysis of different types of educational achievement consisted of 501 pupils, from 14 school classes, of which 7 were from villages and 7 from cities. For classroom observation a further sample of 13 primary school classes was used. In addition, 106 primary school teachers took part in our investigation of teachers' awareness of potential problems. For some of the analyses the first sample was reduced to 460, as a result of illness or various other problems. Only some of the findings can be reported here; for full details see Ammon (1978).

Spelling

The potential difficulties that dialect speakers have with spelling were investigated by means of a dictation test, which is the main type of spelling test used in German schools. Each error that occurred was listed and individually classified. Five types of error were distinguished (see Ammon, 1978: 58–64).

1. Direct transfer from the dialect, e.g. *Kerper* instead of standard German *Körper*. The dialect pronunciation is ['keʀbəʀ], whereas the standard German pronunciation is ['kœʀpəʀ]; standard [e] is represented in German spelling by *e*, not *ö*, in practically all cases.

2. Hypercorrections, e.g. *heuter* instead of standard *heiter* ('bright'). The diphthong [ɔʏ], which in German spelling is represented by *eu*, does not exist in the Swabian dialect. Instead one finds [aɪ], or sometimes [əi]. There is also a diphthong [aɪ] in standard German, which is represented in spelling by *ei*, or sometimes *ai*. Dialect speakers have to learn to write *eu*, not *ei*, for their [aɪ] in many, but not all, words in which the sound occurs. *Heiter* is one of the words where they do not need to do so, since this is one of the cases where the dialect and the standard pronunciations are identical.

3. Errors possibly related to dialect. These are errors which can be attributed to either archaic or subphonemic dialect features, e.g. *Aarbeit* for standard *Arbeit* ('work'). This could be due to the now rather archaic dialect pronunciation [ˈaːʀbəd], where the standard pronunciation is [ˈaʀbaɪt].

4. Errors unrelated to dialect.

5. Incorrect use of capital letters for the first letter of a noun. This group of errors was analysed separately because at the time when the research was carried out it seemed likely that this would be shortlived as an 'error', as there was an impending spelling reform in the Federal Republic of Germany. It now seems unlikely, however, that this reform will in fact take place.

After controlling for all the intervening variables, there were two results of particular interest. Firstly, the complete group of dialect-speaking pupils (i.e. including both broad and moderate dialect speakers) did not make more spelling errors than the standard-speaking pupils. In fact, the standard-speaking pupils made a slightly higher number of errors, though the difference between the two groups was not statistically significant. The standard speakers made more errors of the types described in 2, 4 and 5, above; the dialect-speaking pupils, on the other hand, made more errors of types 1 and 3. Secondly, the broad dialect speakers made significantly more errors of types 3 and 4 than the moderate dialect speakers, as well as in some subcategories of type 1 and, above all, in the total number of errors (r=0.21).

Some tentative conclusions can be drawn from these results. Firstly, it is mainly broad dialect speakers who have difficulties with spelling; moderate dialect speakers experience few, if any, difficulties. Secondly, spelling errors that can be attributed to speaking a dialect cannot be reliably identified on the basis of a contrastive analysis between the dialect and the standard, since the relationship between spelling and speaking a dialect is a complex one. Finally, monolingual speakers of standard German who live in a dialect area are not immune from spelling problems that appear to be caused by dialect transfer, i.e. errors in spelling that would be identified as dialect transfer on the basis of a contrastive analysis.

The last two results cast doubt on the validity of investigations that attempt to study the spelling difficulties of dialect speakers on the basis of a contrastive analysis alone, without controlling for whether the errors are made by speakers of standard German or by speakers of a dialect (for example, Löffler, 1974; Henn, 1977). They also hint at the shortcomings of the contrastive teaching materials that have been developed for schools in different dialect areas of West Germany (see Ammon, this volume, chapter 14). The results do, however, confirm that dialect speakers — particularly broad dialect speakers — have more difficulties with spelling than standard-speaking pupils.

Written composition

All the participants wrote an essay, for which they had a time limit of 55 minutes, on the topic *Mit Erwachsenen hat man es manchmal nicht leicht* ('It is sometimes difficult to deal with adults'). The compositions were analysed as follows:

1. Number of deviations from the standard norm relative to the length of the text. These were divided into (a) direct dialect transfer, (b) hypercorrection, (c) possible dialect transfer and (d) errors unrelated to dialect.

It should be pointed out that deviations from the standard norm, which include spelling errors as well as other kinds of errors (such as errors in vocabulary or syntax), result in a substantial reduction in the marks awarded for composition in German schools. The explicit recommendation in some cases is that this aspect of writing should represent 20% of the total mark.

2. Length of text in number of words (i.e. word tokens).

3. Use of vocabulary: $\dfrac{\text{number of word types}}{\text{number of word tokens}}$

This last ratio caused some difficulties. Since German is an inflectional language, one has to decide which word tokens to consider as different types, and which to consider as the same type. In addition, the ratio favours writers of short texts, since in general the longer the text, the fewer the number of new words. We assumed that dialect speakers would write shorter texts, on average, which made it more difficult to confirm our hypothesis that they would use a less differentiated vocabulary. Needless to say, length of text and use of vocabulary, as we have defined it, are extremely crude indices of the quality of a written essay.

Some of the more interesting results of this analysis were as follows. When the intervening variables (social class etc.) were not controlled, our first analysis — number of deviations from the standard norms relative to length of text — did reveal the expected differences between the various groups of speakers. As Table 2 shows, broad dialect speakers made more errors on average (relative to the length of the text) than moderate dialect speakers in direct dialect transfers, possible dialect transfers, errors unrelated to dialect, and also in the total number of errors. They did not, however, make more hypercorrections.

TABLE 2   *Errors (Number Relative to Length of Text)*

	direct dialect transfer	hyper- corrections	possible dialect transfer	errors unrelated to dialect	total number of errors
broad dialect speakers	1.83	0.22	1.50	9.17	12.72
moderate dialect speakers	1.00	0.25	1.16	7.91	10.32

Table 3 shows that dialect-speaking pupils also made slightly more errors in all categories than non-dialect speakers.

TABLE 3   *Errors (Number Relative to Length of Text)*

	direct dialect transfer	hyper- corrections	possible dialect transfer	errors unrelated to dialect	total number of errors
dialect speakers	1.43	0.24	1.35	8.54	11.56
standard speakers	0.78	0.17	1.26	8.03	10.24

When the intervening variables were controlled, however, the differences between the groups became less clear cut. Although the broad dialect speakers made slightly more errors than the moderate dialect speakers in all categories except hypercorrections, the differences between the number of errors made by broad and moderate dialect speakers was not statistically significant for any single category of errors, nor for the total number of errors. The dialect-speaking pupils made more errors than the standard-speaking pupils in all categories, but the difference was statistically significant only for category (a) — direct dialect transfer — ($r=0.14$).

The second analysis yielded the following results of note. Broad dialect speakers produced shorter texts than moderate dialect speakers, and the difference was statistically significant when all the intervening variables were controlled ($r=0.18$). However, the texts of the dialect speakers as a whole were not shorter than the texts of the standard speakers, due to the fact that the moderate dialect speakers produced slightly longer texts.

No statistically significant results were obtained for the third analysis. However, when only the number of lexical types was counted, without dividing this by the number of tokens, the results for the broad dialect speakers were significantly lower than those for the moderate dialect speakers ($r=0.18$ when all intervening variables were controlled; $r=0.27$ when they were not controlled). This confirms that broad dialect speakers do, in fact, produce fewer word types in their compositions, though not in proportion to the length of their texts. There was no obvious difference between the vocabulary used by the dialect speakers and the standard German speakers.

The results for the last two analyses, when compared with those for the first, suggest that broad dialect speakers may try to avoid errors by writing shorter compositions with fewer different words. Alternatively, one could say that they appear to know fewer words of standard German and that they have learned not to use dialect words in written composition.

Reading aloud

The main reading test that was administered measured (1) the number of errors in intonation, pausing (within words and between words), accent and pitch, and the number of morphological and lexical errors (such as incorrect prefixes or misread words); (2) the tempo of reading and (3) the overall quality of the reading performances as judged by two independent experts.

The results were as follows:

1. Broad dialect speakers made more errors than moderate dialect speakers, though the difference was not statistically significant. There was practically no difference between the number of errors made by the dialect-speaking pupils and the number made by the standard-speaking pupils.
2. Broad dialect speakers read significantly more slowly than moderate dialect speakers (r=0.16); dialect speakers as a whole, again, did not differ from the standard-speaking pupils.
3. The reading performance of broad dialect speakers was judged as significantly poorer than that of moderate dialect speakers (r=0.17). Dialect speakers as a whole were judged as performing slightly better than the standard-speaking pupils, but the differences were not statistically significant.

We also tested the hypothesis that dialect speakers would be better able to decipher unfamiliar sequences of letters. This seemed a plausible hypothesis, since they are likely to have had more experience at reading unfamiliar texts and, perhaps, to have learned to look at the graphic representation of words more closely, in order to avoid making mistakes whilst reading aloud. We tested the hypothesis by asking pupils to read aloud a short Latin text. The results partly confirmed our hypothesis. Standard-speaking pupils corrected themselves significantly more frequently as they read (r=0.18) and they read significantly more slowly than the dialect speakers (r=0.13). They also made more uncorrected errors, though in this case the difference was not statistically significant. The difference in performance between the broad and the moderate dialect speakers, however, was not as expected. The former performed more poorly than the latter in all respects, though none of the differences was statistically significant. Results for the different groups of pupils follow the same pattern as before, though the extent of the difference here is such that our hypothesis is only partially confirmed: as a group, the dialect-speaking pupils did better than the standard-speaking pupils, but the relatively poor performance of the broad dialect speakers was less extreme than before. This would seem to support the position of Goodman & Buck (1973) that dialect does not, in fact, pose serious difficulties in the acquisition of reading skills as such, though reading texts in the standard variety is more difficult for dialect speakers (cf. also Ammon, 1973b).

Oral participation in class

Our general hypotheses here were (1) that dialect speakers would participate less frequently in class and (2) that they would be reprimanded by the teacher more frequently than standard-speaking pupils. These hypotheses were empirically investigated using three different methods: (A) monitoring group discussions with each class as a whole, (B) asking teachers to evaluate the pupils' overall participation in class and (C) by means of classroom observation. The results were as follows:

(A) Monitoring group discussions

The group discussions followed a short film, which had been independently evaluated as successful in encouraging discussion amongst pupils of that age. I led the discussions myself, using a teacher's speech style and DS-level, and following a set of guidelines that allowed some flexibility. They were observed by an assistant (Uwe Loewer), together with the class teacher.

Only three categories of participation were counted: raising the hand, as an indication of readiness to participate; utterances that were three words in length, or less; and longer utterances, of more than three words. The last two categories were obviously dependent on the choices that were made by the leader of the discussion, who had to choose one pupil from all those whose hand was raised; efforts were made to avoid choosing the same student over and over again.

The dialect-speaking pupils, on average, obtained higher scores than the standard-speaking pupils for all three categories. This difference was not significant, except for raising the hand ($r=0.16$); this, however, is perhaps the most valid category. Within the group of dialect speakers there was a relatively greater difference between the scores of the broad dialect speakers and the moderate dialect speakers; the moderate dialect speakers scored higher than the broad dialect speakers, and these differences were statistically significant for raising the hand ($r=0.23$) and for utterances of three words or less ($r=0.20$).

(B) Evaluating participation

The dialect-speaking pupils were evaluated slightly more favourably by their teacher in terms of their overall participation in class, though the differences were not statistically significant. The broad dialect speakers were evaluated significantly less favourably than the moderate dialect speakers ($r=0.21$).

(C) Classroom observation

Classroom observation took place with a new sample of 13 school classes, since it was not possible to carry out the observations before the classes that formed the main sample dispersed at the end of the fourth year. This new sample was drawn from the same area, but it covered more age groups — from primary class one to primary class four (ages 7–11). Again, it proved possible to distinguish only between the behaviour of dialect-speaking pupils and standard-speaking pupils; it was not possible to further distinguish broad dialect speakers from moderate dialect speakers. The results showed slightly more participation in class from the standard-speaking pupils, but the differences between the groups were not statistically significant (on the basis of the Mann-Whitney U-test). Dialect speakers were reprimanded more frequently, though again the differences within any single class were not significant. A more interesting outcome of the classroom observations was that we were able to describe the different reactions that teachers had towards the use of dialect, both in terms of the strategies of correction that they used and in terms of the general comments that they made (see Ammon, 1978: 139–42). We strongly recommend that further classroom observations should be carried out in the future, using varied methods and different categories of analysis.

Marks in German and mathematics, and streaming

In the tests that took place at the end of the school year the standard-speaking pupils obtained lower marks, on average, in German and mathematics, though only the latter difference was significant ($r=0.15$). This result may indicate that the standard-speaking pupils had fewer difficulties with language than other subjects, being a sample of relatively low achievers in all subjects; on average, however, they were placed in higher streams than the dialect speakers, though here the difference was not significant. Broad dialect speakers obtained significantly lower marks than moderate dialect speakers both in German ($r=0.23$) and in mathematics ($r=0.24$). They were also allotted to lower streams, though the difference was not statistically significant.

Summary of results on school achievement

Figure 2 shows the overall pattern in all the skills that were investigated, and the marks that were obtained by the different groups of speakers (see Ammon, 1978: 241–45). It can be seen that the broad dialect speakers rank below all the other groups. We can assume that this is a result of their linguistic behaviour — or rather, a result of the linguistic situation that broad dialect speakers have to face in the school.

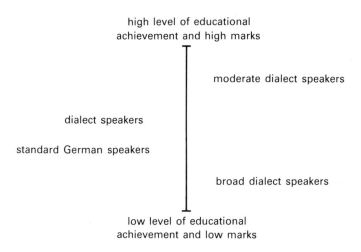

FIGURE 2 *Overall pattern of results*

Somewhat surprisingly, standard-speaking pupils seem to have more difficulties than the group of moderate dialect speakers, despite the fact that their linguistic behaviour conforms more closely to the standard. Perhaps this reflects the educational problems that arise from changing schools and from failing to integrate satisfactorily into a new residential area. The pupils with the fewest difficulties were those moderate dialect speakers who had a regional accent only, and those pupils who were bilingual in dialect and standard German. The overall extent of differences between the groups, however, is relatively small (i.e. the correlation coefficient was low). Various reasons can be suggested for this, the most reassuring of which, of course, would be that the educational difficulties of dialect speakers are in fact relatively slight. However, we are more inclined to see the reasons for our results as stemming from some of the methods that were used (such as the definition of dialect speaker; see p. 119).

Pupils' attitudes towards dialect speakers and standard speakers

A matched-guise test was given to all the pupils in the main sample. The test consisted of two tape recorded passages spoken by the same person, discussing the same topic and using equally elaborate syntax each time. They differed only in that one was in broad dialect whilst the other was in standard German, with a slight regional accent — the usual standard German speech of the local residents. The participants in the test did not realise that the tests were spoken by a single person, presumably because of the shift from dialect speech to standard speech. Pupils were asked to fill in a simple questionnaire containing 13 questions, of which 11 required a decision to be made concerning the 'two' speakers: for example,

Which of the two speakers is more intelligent? The first □ /the second □ ?

Two open-ended questions asked pupils about the occupations of each of the 'two' speakers on the recording.

This simple format seemed to be acceptable to participants of that age group. The results were unsurprising. The broad dialect speaker was judged less knowledgeable about the subject he was talking about — though he said no less than the standard speaker; to be less intelligent; to deserve a lower mark, if his talk had been given in class; to be less influential in society and of lower social status; to be less wealthy; likely to be a farmer (in that area farmers almost all had small farms); and less likely to be a teacher.

The occupations that were assigned to the speaker in this guise were typical manual, lower-class occupations (such as bricklayer, labourer, farmer, or gardener). In the standard guise the speaker was assigned middle-class professions, such as manager, scientist, professor. All results showed extremely clear-cut differences between the two guises (the lowest difference in scores was 70% agreement versus 30%; and some differences were as high as 98% versus 2%).

Results were less clearcut, however, when participants were asked to make judgements about the character of the speakers, or when their personal sympathies were involved. A small majority of the participants said that they would prefer to entrust a secret to the standard speaker rather than to the dialect speaker, and that they considered the standard speaker to be more honest, but a larger majority felt greater sympathy for the dialect speaker (*'konnte ihn besser leiden'*), and a still larger majority of participants judged the dialect speaker as more friendly and good-natured (*'gutmütiger und freundlicher'*). These results have some interesting sociopolitical implications: for instance, the 'people' in this area may, on the whole, trust the upper class members, or the ruling class, whilst not feeling any personal liking for them.

A further result of interest is that judges who were dialect speakers appeared to have more or less the same attitudes towards the speaker in the two different guises as did judges who were speakers of standard German. In other words, it appears that dialect speakers may consider themselves to be less intelligent than standard speakers, and to have the other attributes listed above (see Giles & Powesland, 1975, for similar findings in a British context; and Cheshire & Trudgill, this volume, chapter 6). It would be worth investigating the full implications of this result, including its effects on the personality traits of both dialect speakers and standard speakers (such as, for example, the motivation for studying).

The teachers' attitudes

In order to learn more about teachers' attitudes towards dialect speakers than could be gathered from classroom observations, we interviewed 106 primary school teachers from the local area. They were asked a total of 108 questions, which covered several different areas of enquiry, in particular: whether they were aware of social class differences between dialect speakers and standard speakers; to what extent they were aware of the educational difficulties faced by dialect speakers; how they thought they behaved in class towards dialect speakers; and their opinions on what would be an adequate education for dialect speakers. The questions were standardised and mostly open-ended, leaving ample opportunity for personal comments and for additions to be made. The interview was tape recorded.

For the analysis the teachers were divided into groups on the basis of sex, geographical background (whether they were indigenous or non-indigenous to the region) and age (two age groups were used). Each of the 8 subgroups contained 15 teachers, with the exception of the non-indigenous male group, which contained 7 teachers from the younger age group and 9 from the older age group.

Only a few of the many results obtained from the questionnaire can be outlined here. A large proportion of the teachers were aware of the predominant social status of dialect speakers. 67% gave working-class occupations as typical occupations of the parents of broad dialect speakers, and 71.7% gave upper-class occupations as typical of the parents of pupils who had a good command of standard German. When asked to list all the causes of school difficulties that they could think of, 15.1% mentioned dialect (at the time, of course, the teachers did not know the object of our research). When asked about difficulties caused by speech habits or linguistic behaviour (*'sprachliche Schwierigkeiten'*), 39.6% mentioned dialect.

Teachers were also asked to rank the extent of the educational problems faced by dialect speakers, on a rough scale between the two extremes *'there are no problems'* and *'the problems are very great'*. 9.4% of the teachers claimed that there were no problems for dialect speakers in school, whilst 28.3% claimed that there were difficulties, but that these were only small (these figures altered, however, during the course of the interview). Teachers frequently explained these opinions by saying that the pupils who were intelligent had few if any difficulties as a result of their dialect. If this statement is taken as a general proposition, as often seems to be the case, it can serve as a premise (i.e. a basic assumption) for the conclusion that a dialect speaker who does have difficulties at school is unintelligent. In other words, there is a danger that those teachers who gave opinions of this kind will assume that dialect speakers who have educational problems are less intelligent, rather than that they have dialect-related problems. It is possible, therefore, that they will not try to help them overcome their problems.

Teachers were also asked to specify the kinds of problems that dialect speakers encountered at school. 16% of the teachers mentioned only spelling; 6.6% mentioned writing generally, or written composition; 10.4% saw difficulties as arising only in oral participation in class; 28.3% mentioned two or three different kinds of problems; and a further 28.3% were unable to give any details. Teachers were then asked to be more precise, if possible, about the difficulties that occurred in dictation (spelling), written composition and oral participation. The overwhelming majority of the answers were very vague, clearly showing that the teachers had little linguistic knowledge about the dialect spoken in the region. This was not surprising, since previous investigations have shown that teacher training gives virtually no attention to dialect. This was confirmed by the teachers who took part in our interviews: only 26.4% remembered hearing anything during their training about the educational problems of dialect speakers — and nothing of any detail — while 62.3% of the teachers were firmly convinced that they had never heard anything about dialect and educational problems during the course of their training.

As for the teachers' views about their own classroom language, it is worth mentioning that 45.3% maintained that they spoke only standard German, or standard German with a regional accent, whilst 51.9% maintained that they spoke standard German most of the time. 24.5% of this latter group pointed out that this depended upon the situation. Teachers' expectations concerning the language behaviour of their pupils showed a similar distribution, with 45.5% expecting standard speech from their pupils, and 23.6% expecting standard speech only in the later years of school. 28.3% expected their pupils to use standard speech only in certain situations. Significantly more teachers in the younger age group pointed out that both their pupils' speech and their own speech was likely to vary in different situations — perhaps because nowadays teacher training includes some sociolinguistic content. However, when we framed our questions in a more specific way, giving examples of utterances in dialect, it became clear that the teachers' tolerance of dialect was not as great as we had assumed from their answers to our previous questions. Only 19.8%, in fact, said they would have accepted the utterance that we gave them as an example (which was in broad dialect), without either correcting it themselves or asking the other pupils to correct it.

The methods that teachers said they used when correcting their pupils' work were very varied and cannot be reported on in any detail here. As part of this aspect of the investigation, they were given a written composition containing features resulting from dialect transfer, and asked to correct it according to the standard that they considered appropriate for the fourth year of primary school. The number of errors that they marked on the compositions varied from 0 to 28; and the nature of the corrections varied a great deal (for example, sometimes the errors were specifically indicated, sometimes not; sometimes the correct form was added, sometimes not. See Cheshire, 1982, and Williams, this volume, chapter 11, for accounts of a similar situation in the United Kingdom). All the teachers said that they would give a lower mark for a composition containing features of dialect transfer of that type, although the actual mark that they said they would give varied; on a scale of 0–6, 10.4% of teachers would have taken off half a mark, 44.3% would have taken off 1 mark and 28.4% would have taken off 2 or more marks (7.6% of these would have taken off as many as 3 marks). Again, younger teachers were significantly more tolerant than older teachers, in that they made fewer corrections and they marked the composition less severely.

The teachers' views on the best methods of education for dialect speakers were very varied and, again, cannot be reported here in detail. May it suffice to say that half of the teachers (49.9%) felt that for a variety of reasons they were unable to provide adequate teaching for dialect speakers. 83% considered it important for dialect speakers to acquire full competence in standard German in school; 16.1% were less sure, and 5.7% of these flatly denied the importance of acquiring full competence in standard German at school. The vast majority of this 5.7% (83% of them) were young teachers, as were the majority of the 16.1% who were less sure. Most of these teachers gave as their reason their view that speaking a dialect did not impair thought or general cognitive processes. We assume that this insight had been gained from studying linguistics or sociolinguistics. However, these teachers had apparently forgotten the deplorable fact that dialect speakers are socially disadvantaged if they have not acquired competence in the standard variety. Sociolinguistics would serve dialect speakers badly if it convinced their teachers that learning the standard variety was no longer of importance.

The interviews that took place with teachers had some further objectives. We hoped to increase their awareness of the educational problems faced by dialect speakers, to increase their tolerance of dialect speech and also to encourage them in their efforts to teach dialect speakers the standard variety. We tried to achieve these objectives mainly during conversations that took place after the interviews, and also by distributing copies of recent publications on the topic. There were several indications, however, that the teachers had already begun to appreciate more fully the nature of the problems during the course of the interviews. As an example, we can consider the answers given to the question mentioned above, which asked teachers to rank the extent of the educational difficulties faced by dialect speakers, on a scale from 'there are no difficulties' to 'the difficulties are very great'. During the interview 9.4% were of the opinion that there were no difficulties; at the end of the interview, however, there were no teachers who held that opinion.

Conclusion

The research reported here addressed a wide range of issues. It represents an attempt to determine in which specific areas of the school curriculum dialect-speaking children find themselves at a disadvantage. It also explores another extremely important dimension which is likely to exert considerable influence on the achievement of dialect-speaking children, namely the question of attitudes towards the standard and the dialect.

With the benefit of hindsight, various disadvantages can now be seen in the way in which these issues were investigated. Some of these have been briefly mentioned. Nevertheless, by attempting to investigate the relationship between dialect and educational achievement in a rigorous way, the general awareness of dialect and standard as an educational issue has been increased; and solutions to the problems that exist are being sought.

Notes to Chapter 7

1. The author is grateful to Ellen Reith for typing the manuscript and to Charles Cull for stylistic corrections (they are, respectively, secretary and lecturer in the Department of Modern European Languages (Germanic Section), Australian National University). This paper lingers somewhat immodestly on the author's own research into the topic; this, however, has been explicitly requested by the editors.
2. The term *Umgangssprache* is used differently here and in Rosenberg's chapter from the way in which it is used by Van de Craen & Humblet, in Chapter 2 of this volume.

References

AMMON, U. 1972a Dialekt als sprachliche Barriere. *Muttersprache* 82, 224–37.
——1972b *Dialekt, soziale Ungleichheit und Schule.* Weinheim/Basel: Beltz. 2nd edition, 1973.
——1973a *Dialekt und Einheitssprache in ihrer sozialen Verflechtung.* Weinheim/ Basel: Beltz.
—— 1973b Die Schwierigkeiten der Dialektsprecher im Leseunterricht. In H. BAUSINGER (ed.), *Dialekt als Sprachbarriere?* Tübingen: Gesellschaft für Volkskunde. pp. 111–32.
——1978 *Schulschwierigkeiten von Dialektsprechern.* Weinheim/Basel: Beltz.
——1985 Möglichkeiten der Messung von Dialektalität. In W. BESCH & K. MATTHEIER (eds), *Beiträge zur Ortssprachenforschung.* Berlin: Erich Schmidt. pp. 259–82.
——1986 Explikation der Begriffe 'Standardvarietät' und 'Standardsprache' auf normtheoretischer Grundlage. In G. HOLTUS & E. RADTKE (eds), *Sprachlicher Substandard.* Tübingen: Niemeyer. pp. 1–63.
BERNSTEIN, B. (1971–75) *Class, Codes and Control.* London: Routledge.
BROWELEIT, V. 1978 Dialektologie und Sprachdidaktik. In U. AMMON, U. KNOOP & I. RADTKE (eds), *Grundlagen einer dialektorientierten Sprachdidaktik.* Weinheim/Basel: Beltz. pp. 175–96.
CHESHIRE, J. 1982 Dialect features and linguistic conflict in schools. *Educational Review* 34. (1), 53–67.
GILES, H. and POWESLAND, P. F. 1975 *Speech Style and Social Evaluation.* London: Academic Press.
GOODMAN, K. and BUCK, C. 1973 Dialect barriers to reading comprehension revisited. *The Reading Teacher* 27, 6–12.
GRASSI, C. 1987 Dialektsoziologie. In U. AMMON, N. DITTMAR & K. MATTHEIER (eds), *Sociolinguistics/Soziolinguistik*, Vol. 1. Berlin and New York: de Gruyter. pp. 679–90.
HASSELBERG, J. 1972 Die Abhängigkeit des Schulerfolgs vom Einfluss des Dialekts. *Muttersprache* 82, 201–23.
——1976 *Dialekt und Bildungschancen.* Weinheim/Basel: Beltz.
HELMERS, H. 1973 Die hessischen 'Rahmenrichtlinien Sekundarstufe 1 Deutsch' von 1972. *Die deutsche Schule* 65, 608–24.

HENN, B. 1977 *Mundartinterferenzen. Am Beispiel des Nordwestpfälzischen.* Wiesbaden: Steiner.

DER HESSISCHE KULTUSMINISTER (ed.) 1972 *Rahmenrichtlinien Sekundarstufe 1 Deutsch.* Frankfurt a.M: Diesterweg.

HILDEBRAND, R. 1869 *Vom deutschen Sprachunterricht in der Schule and von deutscher Erziehung und Bildung überhaupt.* Leipzig: Julius Klinkhardt.

JÄGER, S. 1971 Sprachnorm und Schülersprache. In H. MOSER (ed.) *Beiträge zur soziolinguistischen Beschreibung der deutschen Gegenwartssprache.* Düsseldorf: Schwann. pp. 166–233.

KARSTÄDT, O. 1908 *Mundart und Schule.* Langensalza: Beltz.

KLOSS, H. 1978 *Die Entwicklung neuerer germanischer Kultursprachen seit 1800.* 2nd edition. Düsseldorf: Schwann.

LABOV, W. 1972 *Sociolinguistic Patterns.* Philadelphia: University of Pennsylvania Press.

LÖFFLER, H. 1972 Mundart als Sprachbarriere, *Wirkendes Wort* 22 (1), 23–39.

——1974 Deutsch fur Dialektsprecher: Ein Sonderfall des Fremdsprachenunterrichts? *Deutsche Sprache* 2, 105–22.

MATTHEIER, K. J. 1980 *Pragmatik und Soziologie der Dialekte.* Heidelberg: Quelle & Meyer.

MERKELBACH, V. 1973 Materialistische Kritik oder Wasser auf die Mühlen der Konservativen? Hermann Helmers Beitrag zur Diskussion der Rahmenrichtlinien Deutsch, *Die deutsche Sprache* 65, 625–32.

MÖHN, D. 1981 Niederdeutsch in der Schule. In G. CORDES & D. MÖHN (eds), *Handbuch zur niederdeutschen Sprach- und Literaturwissenschaft.* Berlin: Erich Schmidt. pp. 631–59.

REITMAJER, V. 1979 *Der Einfluss des Dialekts auf die standardsprachlichen Leistungen von bayrischen Schülern in Vorschule, Grundschule und Gymnasium.* Marburg: Elwerth.

WIENBARG, L. 1834 *Soll die plattdeutsche Sprache gepflegt oder ausgerottet werden? Gegen Ersteres und für Letzteres.* Hamburg: Hoffman und Campe.

8 The Kerkrade project: Background, main findings and an evaluation

SJEF STIJNEN and TON VALLEN

Introduction

Between 1973 and 1982 a group of researchers at the Nijmegen Institute for Educational Research and the University of Nijmegen Department of Dialectology studied the linguistic situation in the Dutch town of Kerkrade, with the aim of making a helpful contribution to education in the primary schools. This research project — referred to as 'the Kerkrade project' — was financed by the Foundation for Educational Research in The Hague.

The Kerkrade project was set up in response to the findings of an educational survey carried out in 1971 at the request of the Kerkrade Catholic School Council. The survey showed that the headteachers of the Kerkrade primary schools felt there was a possible relationship between the relatively low levels of educational achievement reached by the majority of their pupils, and their use of dialect. The headteachers also emphasised other, more general problems in the schools, which in their view also resulted from the linguistic situation in the area. Their emphasis on the importance of dialect as an educational problem led to a recommendation that it should be investigated further (Claeys, 1971).

Two important factors were taken into consideration when planning the Kerkrade project. First, it was considered essential that both linguists and educational researchers should co-operate in an effort to break away from the 'linguistic deficit' hypothesis (see the introduction to this volume), which during the 1970s had been very influential in Dutch educational research (see also pp. 141–42). Secondly, the research was designed in such a way that it would have a number of practical applications. As far as this second point is concerned, it should be pointed out that the Kerkrade Catholic School Council was involved in the project, as was the Centre for School Service in the south-eastern part of the province of Limburg. During the third stage of the project two sections of the Foundation for Curriculum Development co-operated in the development of new teaching materials and curriculum innovations (the 'Innovations' and 'Mother tongue teaching' sections of the Foundation).

The main aim of the project was, therefore, to carry out sociolinguistic and educational research, directed towards alleviating those school problems that were caused by the use of dialect outside the school. There were three stages to the project:

1. *The preliminary stage* (1973–75), where we explored the situation under study and decided on the most appropriate research methods to be used.
2. *The executive stage* (1975–79), during which we analysed the educational achievement (this was interpreted in the broadest possible sense) of children from a range of social backgrounds and of different ages, and who spoke either the Kerkrade dialect or standard Dutch. We paid particular attention to the children's linguistic background and to the nature of the teaching and learning process at school, including verbal interaction in the classroom.
3. *The innovative stage* (1979–82), during which new school tasks and teaching methods were developed, based on the results of the first two stages. These innovations were intended to improve the educational situation of those children who come to school speaking the Kerkrade dialect.

As can be seen from this brief outline of the project, the linguistic and educational activities that took place as part of the Kerkrade project can be described as exploratory and applied research. For determining the potential innovations in education a 'Research–Development–Diffusion (RDD) model' was used. Within this model the process of innovation is considered as a rational sequence of stages: first, research is carried out to gain some insight into the topics under investigation; subsequently, innovative strategies are developed and put to use, first on a small scale and then on a larger scale.

After brief further discussion of the theoretical background to the Kerkrade project, this chapter will present some of the main findings of the first two stages of research. Full details concerning both these stages can be found in Stijnen & Vallen (1981). We describe the objectives of the first stage, and the activities that were carried out. The results of this first stage will be discussed in conjunction with the main findings of the second, executive, stage. Finally, after a short evaluation of the project, we comment on current research in the Netherlands into the question of dialect and standard language in education, on its future and on the relationship between research of this kind and research into the educational problems faced by ethnic minorities.

Theoretical Background

The Kerkrade project was the first large-scale sociolinguistic and educational project in the Dutch language area to choose the language-difference hypothesis as the point of departure.

In Kerkrade the dialect and the standard language function side by side, in complementary distribution, differing from each other in function and in prestige. From a linguistic point of view, the two varieties are of equal value; but they differ in that the dialect has lower prestige and a smaller range of functions, and this can cause problems for speakers of the dialect, particularly in those situations where the high-prestige variety is required.

Within the terms of the Kerkrade project, therefore, the linguistic difference hypothesis was interpreted as meaning that varieties that were linguistically equal were not necessarily functionally equal. Of course, the Kerkrade dialect is not inferior to standard Dutch either linguistically or functionally, in those contexts where it is appropriate to use it; instead, it can be seen as having the standard language as an indispensable complement for certain functions and for use in certain domains. The distribution of the two varieties can be thought of in the sociologist Tönnies' terms: the dialect belongs to the *Gemeinschaft* and the standard to the *Gesellschaft*. Roughly speaking, the distribution corresponds to Geerts *et al.*'s (1978) domain configurations for dialect and standard language in Flanders, though the Kerkrade project certainly did not assume that in the domain of education only the standard language should be spoken. On the other hand, it did not dispute the assumption that it is the task of education to encourage all pupils, including dialect speakers, to become fluent in the standard language.

Once we accept that the standard language is indispensable as a medium of education and as a goal in education, we are forced to accept a version of the difference hypothesis which recognises that language difference is a source of considerable problems in education. A logical next step is to pay particular attention to these educational problems.

Our interpretation of the difference hypothesis failed to find general acceptance in the Netherlands for some years. For instance, one Dutch sociolinguistic handbook suggested that the essence of the difference hypothesis was the refusal to recognise any language problems in education or in the general upbringing of children (Appel *et al.*, 1979:154). Moreover, a number of Dutch authors (for example, Van Calcar & Van Calcar, 1975) and German authors (such as Dittmar, 1973) surrounded the difference hypothesis with an aura of irresponsibility; other authors (for example, Trudgill, 1975) adopted an unrealistic view of the generally accepted objectives of education. However, if one traces the source of the hypothesis (reading the publications of authors such as Baratz, Shuy or Labov) it becomes apparent that from the beginning it necessitated a political choice concerning language policy, as well as an attempt to institute a bidialectal approach to the education of dialect speaking children. In our view Hudson (1980:219) is correct in his assessment of the educational problems connected with dialect:

1. How can teachers learn to take more seriously, in terms of both quantity and quality, the language of children from a so-called disadvantaged social or linguistic background?
2. If it is necessary for the standard language to be taught and used at school, how can the child's home language be used as a basis upon which to build, without rejecting the child's language and the home culture in the process?

It is often claimed that acceptance of the difference hypothesis leads directly to the adoption of so-called 'middle-class norms' (see, for example, Wesselingh, 1979) and to the reproduction of social inequality. It can be seen from the above discussion, however, that a correctly interpreted difference hypothesis, such as the hypothesis that formed the basis of the Kerkrade project, emphasises only too clearly the need for tolerant attitudes towards linguistic variation, insisting that teachers treat seriously, and with respect, the linguistic knowledge with which children enter school.

Thus the difference hypothesis, as it was formulated during the Kerkrade project, leads neither to a conformist standpoint, where nothing in the relationship between dialect usage and social background is changed, nor to a pseudo-emancipatory standpoint, in which group identity is preserved and cultivated in an unrealistic way. Only a stance which avoids both these extremes is capable of contributing to the reduction of inequality in education (see also Vallen *et al.*, 1984).

In addition, we should point out that we see the acquisition of the standard language by children whose first language variety is a dialect as a specific form of second language acquisition. There is a crucial difference between the acquisition of the standard by dialect speakers and by, say, immigrants, in that the cultural and linguistic differences are much smaller. L1 (the dialect) can be seen as part of a diasystem to which L2 (the standard language) also belongs. This means that similarities in language structure as well as partial differences in language structure will play an important role in the acquisition process.

Methodology

A basic model was used in which three clusters of variables were assumed to influence educational achievement:

— *characteristics of the pupils*, including age, intelligence, motivation, sex and — particularly relevant to the present research — social background and the pupils' first language;
— *characteristics of the school*, including the nature of the teaching and learning process, educational methods, size of school, and — again, particularly important in this case — the teacher's language use and attitudes towards dialect and standard, and the linguistic 'climate' in the classroom;
— *extra-curricular factors*, including language use in the family, social stratification of the community, degree of urbanisation of the area.

The project focused mainly on the first two clusters of variables; it was felt that the third type of variables could be influenced only over a very long period of time.

The Preliminary Stage

It is beyond the scope of this chapter to give a full description of the research design, the activities that were carried out and the results of this preliminary stage of the project. We therefore restrict ourselves to a description of the aims of this stage of the research and a short overview of the main research activities.

The aim of the preliminary stage was to carry out exploratory research in order to obtain information on the linguistic and educational situation in Kerkrade and to prepare the main part of the research, which took place during the executive stage. There were two main objectives for this stage:

to investigate in detail Claeys' (1971) conclusion that dialect speaking children in primary schools in Kerkrade are disadvantaged relative to their standard Dutch-speaking classmates; and to design and evaluate a number of research methods and tests designed to collect language data from pre-school and primary school children in the area.

During the preliminary stage the following four activities were completed:

A survey of relevant literature

This was very necessary for both the linguists and the educational researchers taking part in the project, since a project of this kind had never previously been carried out in the Netherlands and since researchers from these two different disciplinary backgrounds were to work together on several stages of the project.

A pilot study

Thirty children of pre-school age (4–5-year-olds) and first-year primary school age (6-year-olds) took part in a pilot study which tested the usefulness of a number of new tests and other assessment procedures: a reading test in standard Dutch, a bidialectal vocabulary test, a bidialectal story recall test, a linguistic insecurity test in standard Dutch, 'individual' conversations in dialect and in standard Dutch, and group conversations in dialect and standard Dutch.

A teacher study

In this study we examined the way that teachers perceived the relationship between education and dialect, social background and other relevant characteristics. This was done by means of questionnaires and interviews with 242 teachers at infant school and primary schools. The study attempted to estimate the importance of the dialect problem, the extent to which teachers were aware of the potential influence of dialect in various areas of education, and the ways in which teachers tried to minimise any dialect-related difficulties in their teaching methods.

A re-analysis of school tests

400 school tests that had taken place at the beginning of primary school (at age 6) and 1000 tests that had taken place at the end of primary school (at age 11–12) were re-analysed to determine the influence of the pupils' linguistic background and social background on the results of their

tests. In addition, an attempt was made to include some extra-curricular factors in the research, by comparing the effects of language and social background on the national tests that took place at the end of primary school in some additional areas of the Netherlands.

The Executive Stage

During the executive stage we analysed the educational achievement of children who spoke the dialect as their first language and of children who spoke standard Dutch as their first language. As mentioned before, these children came from varying social backgrounds and were of varying ages.

Educational achievement was considered a dependent variable with respect to the central independent variable of 'linguistic background'. Social background and intelligence were the most important control variables. Data were also collected on verbal interaction in the classroom, and these served as a framework for interpreting the results of our analysis.

309 pupils took part in this stage of the research. They were divided into 16 groups: 4 pre-school groups (aged 4–5 years), 4 groups of first-form pupils (aged 6 years), 4 groups of third-form pupils (aged 8 years), and 4 groups of sixth-form pupils (aged 11–12 years). Dialect speakers (D) and standard Dutch speakers (S) were represented within each group; as were children from a lower social class background (L) and children from a higher social class background (H); this meant that the subgroups DL, DH, SL and SH were all represented in the sample.

In this section we will focus mainly on the 'educational achievement' aspect of the analysis. The data consisted of standardised tests, and assessment procedures developed by other Dutch research projects (such as the Friesland project; see Wijnstra, 1976), as well as assessment procedures developed specifically within the Kerkrade project. The battery of tests can be classified as follows:

A. *language tests*
– direct methods: productive spoken language assessment
                               productive written language assessment

– indirect methods: semi-objective intralingual tetss
                               semi-objective interlingual tests
                               objective intralingual tests
                               objective interlingual tests

B. *Other tests*

                        simple numerical problems
                        verbal reasoning tests
                        general knowledge tests
                        geography tests

C. *Other procedures*

                        pupils' questionnaire on attitude to reading
                        pupils' questionnaire on 'speaking anxiety'
                        teachers' questionnaire on evaluation
                        pupils' achievement/motivation assessment
                        teachers' assessment and other evaluative
                        measures

Again, it is not possible in this chapter to discuss in detail this battery of tests (for full details, see Stijnen & Vallen, 1981:165–67). Here we will confine our remarks to the tests listed under A, above.

Examples of oral language in standard Dutch were collected from all the 309 pupils who took part in the research, during group conversations. Samples of four different types of written language were collected, ranging from narrowly circumscribed writing tasks (retelling a story) to 'free' writing (writing a letter to any person of their choice). Obviously only third-form and sixth-form pupils took part in this aspect of the research.

The terms 'semi-objective' and 'objective' listed under 'indirect methods' of language testing above refer to the nature of the assessment procedure (see Wesdorp, 1974). In intralingual tests the focus is on grammatical rules in standard Dutch and on violation of these rules (for instance, in correction tests). In interlingual tests 'errors' are introduced in the standard language that have their origin in the Kerkrade dialect ('interference' phenomena). It was thought that analysis of the results of the tests would reveal exactly where, and to what extent, dialect-speaking pupils underperform relative to standard speakers who are comparable in social background, intelligence and age. Where possible, explanations for the results were sought in the linguistic background of the pupils and in the educational process.

Main Results

We restrict ourselves to a short presentation of the results of the tests and other assessment procedures mentioned under A, B and C above.

A. Language tests

Dialect-speaking pre-school and primary school pupils in the Kerkrade area have greater problems with their grammatical command of the Dutch received standard language than their non-dialect speaking counterparts, as far as oral and written language production is concerned. For oral language production the average percentage of deviations from standard grammar is approximately 5% (of the total number of words produced) for dialect speakers, compared to approximately 2% for standard speakers. For written language production the percentages are approximately 9% and 7% respectively.

In Kerkrade, problems with oral and written language production are chiefly due to the influence of the highly resistant dialect on the use of the standard (i.e. to interference). Although dialect interference tends to decrease in the speech of both groups of speakers during the course of their school careers, it continues to be an important source of errors for dialect speakers right up to the highest form in primary school. In their written standard Dutch, furthermore, dialect interference did not decrease, for either of the language groups. In addition, it was found that standard-speaking pupils made errors that could be attributed to interference from the dialect, albeit to a lesser extent than the dialect speakers. Table 1 illustrates these points.

The influence of the dialect was seen not only in interference but also in the frequency of code switching. Dialect speakers were more likely to switch from standard Dutch to the local Kerkrade dialect. Code switching became less frequent during the course of primary school education, as did the number of interference errors when speaking standard Dutch, as we saw above. This tendency can also be seen in the decrease in the number of grammatical errors that occurred in both oral and the written production of the received standard.

Dialect speakers had greater difficulties with specific areas of Dutch grammar, during oral communication in standard Dutch, and their performance was often 'communicatively inadequate'. There was, admittedly, a slight drop in the percentage of errors that were 'unacceptable' during the course of their education, but after the third year there was evidence of stabilisation. There was no difference in the written standard language of the two groups; nor was there any difference between the written language produced by third form primary school pupils and sixth form pupils.

Dialect speakers were less able to detect interference phenomena in written standard Dutch than were standard Dutch speakers. As with

TABLE 1   *Average Percentage of Interference Mistakes in Relation to the Total Number of Mistakes made by Dialect Speakers and Standard Language Speakers in Their Productive Oral and Written Standard Language Use[1]*

	DL	SL	t-test[2]	DH	SH	t-test[2]
preschool av. oral:	71.01	33.58	t = 3.478	70.44	44.55	t = 1.855
sd:	28.29	35.15	p < 0.01	36.21	30.29	p < 0.05
n :	22	15	df 35	10	15	df 23
1st form av. oral:	76.61	46.22	t = 3.228	73.22	42.29	t = 3.653
sd:	23.50	11.02	p < 0.01	17.30	22.77	p < 0.01
n :	27	7	df 32	12	13	df 23
3rd form av. oral:	66.21	39.77	t = 2.200	65.44	36.98	t = 1.857
sd:	31.23	30.47	p < 0.05	27.74	32.96	p < 0.05
n :	32	9	df 39	11	7	df 16
av. letter to friend:	25.02	15.50	t = 2.187	23	13.33	t = 1.715
sd:	14.64	11.89	p < 0.05	12.91	10.61	p < 0.05
n :	47	14	df 59	14	8	df 20
av. letter to Hilversum:	18.47	10.52	t = 2.004	20.89	8.90	t = 2.126
sd:	12.57	11.97	p < 0.05	12.38	11.97	p < 0.05
n :	47	13	df 58	13	8	df 19
6th form av. oral:	60.36	21.51	t = 4.584	54.10	23.09	t = 3.448
sd:	34.58	18.69	p < 0.01	23.27	17.77	p < 0.01
n :	29	13	df 40	11	12	df 21
av. letter to friend:	33.04	12.72	t = 2.839	33.85	12.56	t = 2.624
sd:	22.96	17.84	p < 0.01	26.34	13.97	p < 0.01
n :	37	13	df 48	15	13	df 26
av. letter to Hilversum:	40.82	25.31	t = 2.032	51.94	25.32	t = 3.151
sd:	23.88	19.74	p < 0.05	20.64	20.74	p < 0.01
n :	33	13	df 44	13	13	df 24

[1] Represented in this table are only those of the 309 participating pupils who took part in *all* the oral and written language procedures (incl. story retelling and story finishing).
[2] t-test (one-tailed) for uncorrelated samples.

the differences that were found in their production of standard language, this can presumably be attributed to a less proficient command of standard Dutch, accompanied by a higher degree of linguistic insecurity. This is shown in Table 2, which gives the results of a linguistic insecurity test and an interlinear correction test at sixth form level.

B and C *Other tests and assessment procedures*

Research results from the executive stage showed no differences between the educational achievement of dialect speakers and that of non-

TABLE 2   *Average Correct Scores for Dialect Speakers and Standard Language Speakers on the Interlingual Linguistic-insecurity-test (L.I.T.) and the Interlingual Interlinear Test (I.I.T.)*

		DL	SL	t-test[1]	DH	SH	t-test[1]
6th form L.I.T.	av.:	17.87	22.85	t = 5.294	20.13	23.38	t = 3.20
	sd:	2.97	2.92	p < 0.01	2.49	2.68	p < 0.01
	n :	38	14	df 50	15	13	df 26
6th form I.I.T.	av.:	27.39	31.38	t = 1.806	32.80	35.38	t = 1.170
				p < 0.05			p < 0.13
	sd:	6.96	6.05		5.26	7.67	(NS!)
	n :	38	13	df 49	15	12	df 25

[1] t-test (one-tailed) for uncorrelated samples

dialect speakers in subjects other than Dutch. Perhaps this indicates that there are no serious problems with receptive language skills. Furthermore, dialect-speaking children show no signs of being more restricted than non-dialect-speaking children in their choice of reading matter; nor do they appear to have lower motivation, nor a greater fear of contributing, in Dutch, in class.

However, teacher assessed dialect speakers in Kerkrade less favourably than standard Dutch speakers on a number of factors related to their expected level of achievement at school and to their fluency in Dutch. Teachers also said that dialect-speaking children were more reluctant to speak in the classroom, particularly those dialect-speaking children who were from a lower social class background. Dialect speakers received lower marks than standard speakers in some subjects (for language, practical tasks, and music, in the third form; for language and reading, in the sixth form); furthermore, a higher percentage of dialect-speaking pupils were made to stay down rather than being allowed to go on to the next form.

There is reason to believe that the teachers' assessments were influenced by their attitudes to language. The evidence comes from a multiple 'global-judgement' assessment of written standard Dutch by a group of six teachers from Kerkrade (third form and sixth form teachers). The written work had been produced by two groups of children — one dialect-speaking, the other standard Dutch speaking — but teachers were not told whether the pupils who had produced the work were speakers of the dialect or of standard Dutch. There were no differences in the assessment that teachers made of the work of the two groups of children.

As mentioned earlier, verbal interaction in the classroom was also studied; and this included an analysis of the use of dialect in the classroom.

It emerged that dialect was rarely used in class by either teachers or pupils. For example, the average frequency of use of dialect by teachers in the four groups that were studied was 1.8 times per 100 minutes. For pupils the average frequency was slightly higher: 3.9 times per 100 minutes. There are very few differences in the frequency with which dialect is used by pre-school teachers and by teachers of the different forms in primary school; there were, however, a few differences for pupils: the highest use of dialect occurred in the speech of pre-school children (5.5 times per 100 minutes), and the lowest frequency of use occurred with third form children (1.1 times per 100 minutes).

The average frequency of dialect usage by teachers was highest during Dutch language lessons; for pupils it was highest in Dutch language and also in arithmetic.

These observations reveal a considerable discrepancy between the extent to which teachers claim to use dialect and their actual use of dialect when teaching. Although during the first stage of the project 75% of teachers said they regularly used dialect in teaching (see Stijnen, 1975), this was not the case in those classes that were observed (see Vallen, 1980).

Final Remarks

From the research that was carried out during the first two stages of the Kerkrade project the conclusion can be drawn that the language spoken at home influences to an important extent the educational achievement of the children in the Kerkrade area, as well as their participation in verbal interaction in the classroom, and the way in which they are assessed by their teachers.

In Kerkrade the results from the educational achievement tests were comparable for dialect speakers and standard speakers from both lower and higher social class backgrounds. Moreover, analyses of variance showed that the social factor and the language factor each have an independent effect on educational achievement. This implies that dialect speakers from low social class backgrounds are doubly handicapped: both by their social background and their linguistic background.

These results were taken as sufficient justification for launching the third stage of the project (the stage of innovation). This stage aimed to improve the educational situation of those children whose first language is the Kerkrade dialect. The results of this stage of the project and an account of the teaching methods that were used are given in Van den Hoogen & Kuijper (this volume, Chapter 13) and also in Hos *et al.* (1982), Swachten & Vaessen (1982) and Kuijper *et al.* (1983).

Some related, smaller studies were carried out at about the same time as the Kerkrade project. Since the completion of the Kerkrade project and these other studies, however, there has been no substantial sociolinguistic-educational research into the problems of dialect speakers at school in the Netherlands. There are several reasons for this. Here we discuss three of the reasons.

1. Despite the fact that language is one of the most important characteristics of the human race — and one of the more directly observable characteristics — little attention is given to language behaviour within most Dutch socio-educational research. For many social scientists, it seems that language is still taken to be a self-evident phenomenon, requiring little investigation. One of the most important factors that has led to this prejudice is the historical separation within various university departments of linguistics and the social sciences. Apart from a few notable exceptions, this has led to artificial boundaries in research.

   The lack of interest on the part of the social sciences makes it very difficult to carry out multi-disciplinary, comprehensive research projects. Most current sociolinguistic research projects in the Netherlands are monodisciplinary, short-term projects carried out by an individual researcher with a predominantly linguistic orientation.

2. Just as sociolinguistics was coming into its own in the Netherlands (at the end of the 1970s), budgetary considerations made it necessary for the central government to enforce a restrictive policy with regard to the establishment of academic institutions. During the 1960s and the 1970s nearly all the academic positions available through direct government grants were filled by grammarians. Consequently there are currently no government-appointed professors in sociolinguistics in the Netherlands, despite the fact that the importance of the discipline is recognised by the central authorities, as evidenced by a number of ministerial reports (see also Van Hout & Vallen, 1985).

3. The study of the educational problems of dialect-speaking children in the Netherlands has been given less attention since the great influx during the 1970s of immigrant groups from Mediterranean countries and from former Dutch colonies. And rightly so: the educational problems of these groups are greater, as is the urgency

of finding a solution. However, it is becoming more and more apparent that there are many similarities between the educational problems of indigenous groups and the educational problems of immigrant groups in Dutch society. It therefore seems reasonable for researchers who have worked with both these groups to carefully study each others' research findings as well as the practical educational innovations that result from their research, simply in order to prevent us from re-inventing the wheel.

With respect to both types of groups it is also very important to study carefully the general mechanisms of dominance which are responsible for the shift of some groups into a subordinate social position and other groups into a superior social position. Too little attention has been paid to the study of these processes both in the Netherlands and in other countries. All too often immigrant groups and indigenous groups are defined on the basis of group-specific characteristics, when in fact these characteristics should be seen as consequences of the processes of dominance, and therefore, in this sense, as second order characteristics. In all the Dutch sociolinguistic and educational research projects with which we are familiar, they have been treated as independent, first order variables.

Whilst recognising some of the reasons for the present lack of research into the problems of dialect speakers, it also needs, more than ever, to be recognised that dialect speakers continue to face educational problems at school, and that these problems will not disappear unless some action is taken to alleviate them. It is to be hoped that recognition of the urgency of these as yet unresolved problems will enable some progress to be made in overcoming the barriers to effective research that we have outlined above, and that progress will thereby be made in overcoming the educational problems that are now faced, with the influx into Dutch society of ethnic minority groups, by more children than ever before.

References

APPEL, R., HUBERS, G. and MEIJER, G. 1979 *Sociolinguistiek*. Utrecht/Antwerpen: Het Spectrum (3rd edn).
CLAEYS, P. 1971 *Onderzoek naar de onderwijssituatie in Kerkrade*. Kerkrade: Vereniging Katholieke Schoolraad.
DITTMAR, N. 1973 *Soziolinguistik*. Frankfurt a.M.: Athenäum-Fischer.
GEERTS, G., NOOTENS, J. and VAN DE BROECK, J. 1978 Attitudes towards dialects

and standard language in Belgium. *International Journal of the Sociology of Language* 15, 33–46.

Hos, H., Kuijper, H. and Van Tuijl, H. 1982 *Dialect op de basisschool. Het Kerkrade project: van theorie naar onderwijspraktijk.* The Hague/Enschede: SLO/SVO (Foundation for Educational Research/Foundation for Curriculum Development).

Hudson, R. 1980 *Sociolinguistics.* Cambridge: Cambridge University Press.

Kuijper, H., Stijnen, S. and van den Hoogen, J. 1983 *Onderwijs tussen dialect en standaardtaal.* Nijmegen: NCDN (Dept. of Dialectology, Univ. of Nijmegen).

Stijnen, S. 1975 *Leerkrachten over het spreken van dialect in verband met onderwijs in Kerkrade.* Nijmegen: NIVOR (Nijmegen Inst. for Educational Research).

Stijnen, S. and Vallen, T. 1981 *Dialect als onderwijsprobleem.* The Hague: SVO/Staatsuitgeverij.

Swachten, L. and Vaessen, M. 1982 *Werken met dialect in de klas. Het Kerkraads voorbeeldenboek.* Nijmegen: NIVOR/NCDN.

Trudgill, P. 1975 *Accent, Dialect and the School.* London: Edward Arnold.

Vallen, T. 1980 Dialectgebruik door leerkrachten en leerlingen in taalgebruikssituaties in het onderwijs. In J. Kruijsen (ed.), *Liber Amicorum Weijnen.* Assen: Van Gorcum, pp. 88–100.

Vallen, T., Stijnen, S. and Hagen, T. 1984 The difference hypothesis in the Kerkrade project: measurement of verbal abilities and intelligence. In K. Deprez (ed.), *Sociolinguistics in the Low Countries.* Amsterdam: John Benjamins, pp. 169–91.

Van Calcar, C. and Van Calcar, W. 1975 *Onderwijs aan (hand)arbeiderskinderen. School, buurt en maatschappij.* Groningen: Wolters/Noordhoff.

van Hout, R. and Vallen, T. 1985 Sociolinguistics: Janus or Aunt Sally? *Sociolinguistics* XV (2), 20–27.

Wesdorp, H. 1974 *Het meten van de produktief-schriftelijke taalvaardigheid.* Purmerend: Muusses.

Wesselingh, A. (ed.) 1979 *School en ongelijkheid.* Nijmegen: LINK.

Wijnstra, J. 1976 *Het onderwijs aan van huis uit friestalige kinderen. Verslag van een evaluatie-onderzoek in een meertalige regio.* The Hague: SVO/Staatsuitgeverij.

9 Dialect and standard Dutch in the first year of secondary school

BERT WELTENS and JOS SONDEREN

Introduction

The research reported in this chapter was carried out in 1979–80.[1] We investigated the language situation in the first year of secondary school in Maastricht, a Dutch city that is traditionally renowned for the strong position of its dialect. The investigation was — and still is — unique in the sense that it addressed the problem of the school language versus the home language in the context of *secondary education*. In 1978 the Advisory Committee for Mother-tongue Curriculum Development (ACLO-M) noted that

> the problem of the home versus the school language increases and becomes more complex as education advances. This means that it is not sufficient to leave it at curriculum development for infants. The work should have a sequel in primary and secondary education (ACLO-M, 1978:63, our translation).

Nevertheless, several more recent publications have complained about the lack of (Dutch) sociolinguistic research in secondary education (see, for example, Hagen & Sturm, 1982; Kroon & Liebrand, 1983). In other language areas this complaint has also been expressed (see, for example, Edwards *et al.*, 1984).

The particular area in which the investigation was carried out, the most southern tip of the Netherlands, is traditionally a very strong dialect area. Within the region, at least, the dialect has not suffered from stigmatisation as much as many other dialects have; it has retained much of its (local/regional) prestige. Münstermann & Hagen (1986), for example, only very recently concluded 'that the dialect still holds a very firm position. Some loss has been shown for the instrumental function, but in general the speakers of the dialect in Maastricht tend to use their dialect for all purposes' (pp. 94–95). The general tendency for dialect to be stronger in rural areas as opposed to towns also applies to this region, but Maastricht is exceptional in that the proportion of dialect speakers is very high for a town of this size (c. 110,000 inhabitants). This situation existed two decades ago, when Weijnen (1967) found that 83.7% of the Maastricht school children spoke dialect whereas much lower percentages were obtained for smaller towns like Venlo (71.5), Weert (60.0), and Heerlen (26.8); and it still exists today, as is witnessed by our own data (cf. pp. 160–163 below), and Münstermann & Hagen's recent investigation mentioned above.

Linguistically, the dialect is a very interesting one in that it had a strong influx from the neighbouring cultural centres in (French-speaking) Belgium and Germany, i.e. Liège and Aachen.

Design of the Investigation

Subjects

The subjects were drawn from the population of one school, the Jeanne d'Arc Lyceum, a school for general higher secondary education with about 1200 students at the time. From the 255 students in the first year we selected 83 by means of the information in their school records. We distinguished between dialect (D) speakers and standard Dutch (S) speakers, and between a 'lower-class' (L) and a 'higher-class' (H) background. The first categorisation was based on the parents' indication of the 'Language spoken in the home' and the 'Language used by the student outside the home'. We allowed the following subjects in our sample:

1. dialect speakers: language spoken in the home: D; outside the home: D, or D and S;
2. standard speakers: language spoken in the home: S; outside the home: S, or S and D.

The distinction between the two social backgrounds was based on the profession of the student's father. For this purpose we used the so-called *Beroepenklapper* developed by the Institute of Applied Social Sciences of the University of Nijmegen (Van Westerlaak *et al.*, 1975), which relates people's professions to one of six social classes. Because we did not need such fine-grained distinctions — whose reality is questionable anyway — we decided to reduce the six-class system to a dichotomy: classes (1), unskilled labourers, and (2), skilled labourers, were labelled 'lower-class', and the others (3 to 6) 'higher-class'. In other words, we did in fact draw a line between working class and non-working class. Defined in this way the total population of first-year students was distributed as indicated in Table 1. From this population we selected 83 students: 27 higher-class S speakers, 24 higher-class D speakers, 5 lower-class S speakers, and 27 lower-class D speakers. We had planned to select about 25 students from each of the four groups, but there were only 5 S speakers of a lower social background in the entire population (see Table 1).

We checked whether there were differences between the four groups in terms of intelligence or age (both items of information were — again — contained in the school records) by comparing the group means by means of a series of t-tests: there were no significant differences; in other words, the variables intelligence and age were controlled.

We would like to make clear at this stage that this investigation was confined to the possible effects of the children's *language background*. In this study, we obviously had to control their *social* background. That is why we have defined two language groups within two social backgrounds, but not analysed the influence of the latter, which we might have done, of course.

It was also part of our investigation to administer a questionnaire to the teachers of the school from which we drew our subjects (cf. p. 158 below). This questionnaire was mailed to all teachers of the school in question (N = 96), together with a letter of introduction from the assistant-director of the school. The response was 48%, i.e. 47 teachers returned the completed questionnaire. The group that responded was representative of the whole group of teachers in terms of age, sex, level of training, and subject area. A factor that cannot be ruled out, however, is that the teachers

TABLE 1   *The First-year Students (N = 255): Social Background and Language Background in Percentages (n)*

	Higher-class	Lower-class	Unclear	Total
Standard	23% (58)	2% (5)	5% (13)	30% (76)
Dialect	41% (105)	18% (47)	4% (10)	63% (162)
Unclear	6% (15)	1% (2)	–% (—)	7% (17)
Total	70% (178)	21% (54)	9% (23)	100% (255)

who did respond may be the ones most consciously aware of the problem of dialect in education. This means we may have to be careful with generalising the findings of the teacher questionnaire. On the other hand, the response rate of 48% provided us with a relatively large sample.

Method

For our methodology we heavily relied on the Kerkrade project (see the contributions by Stijnen & Vallen and Van den Hoogen & Kuijper, this volume, chapters 8 and 13). We used the following in our investigation:

— language tests;
— a teacher questionnaire;
— a student questionnaire.

In the actual project we administered five different language tests (cf. Sonderen & Weltens, 1981; Weltens *et al.*, 1981), but we will limit ourselves to a discussion of two of these in this chapter: an error-detection-and-correction test, and a guided letter writing task. The former we developed ourselves, following the 'interlinear correction test' used in the Kerkrade project. It consisted of a running text of 950 words in which 100 interference phenomena had been incorporated. They had been selected on the basis of Shepherd's (1946) contrastive description of the Maastricht dialect and standard Dutch. Features were used as items in the test only when the most commonly used Dutch dictionary (*Van Dale's Groot Woordenboek der Nederlandse Taal*, 1976) did not list them at all, or marked them as 'regionally confined'. The phenomena that were incorporated in the final version of the test were lexical, morphological and syntactical contrasts between the two varieties in question. The subjects were instructed to read the story first, and then read it carefully once more trying to find as many errors as they could and correct them. No indication was given of the total number of errors contained in the text. The subjects were allowed a maximum of 50 minutes (one lesson) to complete the test.

We explicitly instructed the subjects to consider all kinds of corrective actions: replacing words by others, deleting words, adding words, and changing the order of words. Examples from the test are the following excerpts (targets italicised):

't Was mooi weer *voor te* gaan fietsen . . .
(It was a nice day *for to* go cycling . . .)
Zo, doe *je* je jas maar uit en *zet je*.
(Right, take *you* off your coat and *sit you down*.)

The second test that we will discuss is a so-called guided letter writing task. The students were asked to write a letter to the people in Hilversum who make TV programmes; it was guided in the sense that a number of suggestions were given as to the points that might be raised. For this test they were also allowed one lesson, i.e. 50 minutes.

The teacher questionnaire was developed to elicit the relevant background information from the teachers (age, sex, subject area, teaching experience in general, teaching experience in the area under investigation, etc.), and to gain an insight into their perception of the relation between dialect and the school, their reactions to the use of dialect in the classroom (if it occurred at all), potential problem areas for dialect speakers, and the didactic adaptations required to avoid or alleviate them.

The student questionnaire was, of course, intended to elicit students' opinions on the position of the dialect in the school, and their opinions on (speakers of) the two language varieties in question. We also included a number of questions on the subject of what has been called 'speaking anxiety' or 'linguistic insecurity', i.e. feelings of uncertainty among D speakers in situations where the S variety is required — the school being an example *par excellence*. The questionnaire was prepared in two different versions, one for D speakers and one for S speakers. The difference between the two was that the D speakers had more questions to answer, questions that could not be put to S speakers, e.g. 'Do you think you would say more in the classroom if you were allowed to speak dialect?'. There were six of these 'extra' questions for D speakers, and 16 to be answered by both language groups.

Results

Language data

Error-detection-and-correction test

Since the subjects had been instructed to detect *and* correct the errors in the text, we can look at the scores for (1) detection plus adequate correction, and (2) detection only. The scores for the former are presented in Table 2.

We found a significantly higher score for S speakers of a higher social background, but no significant difference between the two groups of a lower social background. Note, however, that the difference is in the same direction.

TABLE 2 *Mean Scores for the Error-detection-and-correction Test: Detection plus Adequate Correction*

Group	n	Mean	S.D.	t	df	Sign.
SH	26	65.0	12.6	2.32	48	p < 0.05
DH	24	56.6	13.0			
SL	5	57.4	13.2	1.15	29	NS
DL	26	49.8	13.7			

When we look at the second score, i.e. the number of undetected errors, the same picture emerges, but in a more pronounced way (see Table 3). The difference between the S and D speakers of a higher social background was highly significant now; the difference between the two groups of a lower social background was now marginally significant. These results suggest that the main difference between the two language groups lies in the S speakers' superior ability to *detect* dialect interference.

Probably the most remarkable finding is that both groups of S speakers also have considerable problems — although to a much lesser extent than D speakers — when it comes to detecting dialect interference: on average, about 25% of the interference phenomena were not detected by them.

Letter writing task

For technical reasons this test was only taken by 62 of the 83 subjects. As we had set a time limit (50 minutes), the first measure we could look at was production *per se*. Although there was enormous individual variation — the number of words produced ranged from 65 to 300 — there were no significant differences between the language groups in either of the social classes: they produced, on average, 121 to 157 words.

The letters were analysed for grammatical correctness; we will report two aspects of that analysis here: (1) the relative number of errors, and (2)

TABLE 3 *Mean Scores for the Error-detection-and-correction Test: Number of Undetected Errors*

Group	n	Mean	S.D.	t	df	Sign.
SH	26	23.6	12.7	3.42	48	p < 0.01
DH	24	35.9	12.7			
SL	5	31.0	9.5	1.61	29	p < 0.10
DL	26	40.6	12.6			

the proportion of interlingual errors, i.e. errors that could (probably) be ascribed to dialect interference. The first aspect produced the results presented in Table 4. In both social classes the S speakers made less errors than the D speakers, but this difference only reached statistical significance in the higher-class group.

The second aspect, the proportion of interlingual errors in the total number of errors, is shown in Table 5. Again, we found that the S speakers were at an advantage compared to their D-speaking class-mates. This advantage was only significant, however, in the lower-class group.

TABLE 4   Mean Percentage of Errors in the Letter Writing Task

Group	n	Mean	S.D.	t	df	Sign.
SH	16	5.0	3.5	1.93	33	p < 0.05
DH	19	7.7	4.8			
SL	5	5.6	4.0	0.85	25	NS
DL	22	6.9	2.9			

TABLE 5   Proportion of Interlingual Errors in the Letter Writing Task

Group	n	Mean	S.D.	t	df	Sign.
SH	16	21.1	18.6	0.94	33	NS
DH	19	26.4	14.8			
SL	5	8.4	11.6	2.72	25	p < 0.05
DL	22	28.5	15.5			

Questionnaire data

Teacher questionnaire

A large proportion of the teaching staff was born in Maastricht or its immediate surroundings (40%); the second largest group is formed by those who come from other parts of the province of Limburg (34%). The rest (26%) come from outside the province.

Most teachers had spoken a dialect at home (72%), and continue to do so with colleagues and close friends, but only a small majority (53%) still use their dialect at home. So, a large majority of the teachers are familiar with the phenomenon of dialect from personal experience, most of them even with the particular problems that go with being a speaker of a Limburg dialect.

The teachers are unanimous in expressing the need for D speakers to learn standard Dutch, and a large majority (78%) give some kind of a 'communicative' reason to support this view, i.e. reasons like 'In order to be able to communicate with people from other regions', and 'Because Dutch is the official means of communication'. Nevertheless, 22% of the teachers chose (what we labelled) a 'deficiency' reason; they included arguments like 'Because Dutch is richer in its expression than dialects', 'Because Dutch is more prestigious than dialects', and 'Because Dutch is more logical and therefore allows you to think more clearly'.

A small majority of the teachers (51%) believe that the mastery of standard Dutch poses specific problems for D-speaking students. It depends on the teacher's subject area, however, to what degree these problems are recognised. While science teachers rarely acknowledge them (20%), half of the foreign-language teachers believe they exist, and all but one teachers of Dutch recognise these problems.

When the teachers who believe that there are specific problems (n = 24) are asked to further specify the problems, oral fluency (70%) and, to a lesser degree, writing proficiency (44%) are mentioned very often. A third of these teachers (33%) suspect that the problems also influence the students' results in school subjects other than Dutch.

Only a small number of teachers (22%) believe that D-speaking students experience 'speaking anxiety' (cf. p. 158 above). It is remarkable that D-speaking teachers reject this idea more often than S-speaking teachers (74% vs. 50%). When the problem is approached from the opposite angle — in that case we might talk about 'dominance' of S-speaking students — then a considerable number of D-speaking teachers agree (41%), but only very few S-speaking teachers (17%). So, it seems that in general D-speaking teachers reject the idea of speaking fear among D speakers, but more or less confirm the idea of dominance on the part of S speakers in situations where standard Dutch is required.

This explains perhaps why only a very small minority of the teachers (11%) think that if students were allowed to use dialect in the formal classroom situation, D speakers would participate more actively. This being the case, it is understandable that again only a very small minority (16%) believe that students would actually choose to use dialect in the classroom if the choice were theirs.

About half of the teachers think that more attention should be paid to the dialect in the classroom (S: 39%, D: 55%). The actual suggestions provided by those favouring the idea sound very much like the teaching of language variation as it was defined in the contribution by Giesbers *et al.* (this volume, Chapter 15). On the other hand, only a small part of the body of teachers (20%) think that in a school with many D-speaking students dialect should be used in teaching. Nevertheless, 40% say they sometimes use the dialect in the teaching process. Most of these use it for some kind of linguistic purpose: 'for teaching foreign languages', 'for comparing dialect and Dutch', 'for teaching metalinguistic awareness'; a few teachers say they use dialect 'in small groups', 'for an individual approach', and 'for keeping order'.

When students take the initiative to use dialect in class, almost half the teachers (44%) say they *always* correct them in those cases, while another 25% say they do so *sometimes*. D-speaking teachers correct more often than their S-speaking colleagues. Outside the classroom, teachers and students converse in dialect very often: a majority say they 'sometimes' use the dialect in those cases (65%); some even do so 'always' (17%).

Student questionnaire

The results of the questionnaire again confirm the strong position of the dialect in Maastricht (cf. pp. 154–55). While most students have already learned a dialect at home and continue to use it (62%), S-speaking students increasingly start speaking the dialect outside the home: only 30% of originally S-speaking students remain speakers of standard Dutch exclusively.

In line with the well-known distinction between 'covert' and 'overt' prestige, more than half of the students find dialect 'nicer' (54%), but standard Dutch 'more polite' (56%).

A number of questions dealt with speaking anxiety. Both direct and indirect questions showed that D speakers feel more insecure than S speakers in situations where standard Dutch is required. On the other hand, only very few students (15%) find S speakers 'bolder' than D speakers. In other words, the students' responses confirm the existence of speaking anxiety with D speakers, but deny the dominance of S speakers.

Although most dialect speakers (96%) do not mind being recognised as such in a situation where only standard Dutch is used and understood, a majority of them (58%) prefer a dialect situation to talk in. A considerable number say they are 'less talkative' in standard-Dutch situations (32%), and would respond 'quicker and more often' if dialect were permitted in class

(29%). Our investigation on this point confirms the findings reported by Kuijper *et al.* (1979:74): '(. . .) about 1/3 of the dialect speakers would respond quicker and say more if language factors, either personal or situational, were more advantageous for them' (our translation). Contrary to what most teachers think (cf. p. 161 above), the great majority of D-speaking students (80%) would actually choose to use dialect in the formal classroom situation if the choice *were* theirs.

Conclusions

The analyses of the language tests clearly show that D speakers are at a disadvantage in comparison to their S-speaking classmates. Although not all the differences reached statistical significance, it is important to note that they all pointed in the same direction, namely a disadvantage for D speakers. Moreover, some of the relatively large differences did not reach an acceptable level of significance because of the small groups employed in this investigation — remember that the SL group consisted of five subjects only. On the other hand, it should be noted that S-speaking students also exhibit a serious degree of dialect interference. In other words, tackling this problem would be advantageous not only for D speakers, but for all students.

There are indications of the existence of speaking anxiety on the part of the D-speaking students, or, alternatively, dominance on the part of their S-speaking peers. These indications not only derive from the two questionnaires, but also from an interactional analysis of 25 lessons we observed. (The latter results are not discussed in any detail here, but see Sonderen & Weltens, 1981:45–52.) The teachers tend not to believe that allowing the use of dialect in the classroom would result in a more active participation by D-speaking students, but these students themselves have quite a strong preference for the use of dialect. Interestingly enough, this would probably meet with very little opposition from the S-speaking students, in view of the fact that they generally seem to be quite tolerant towards the dialect, and in view of the fact that two-thirds of them can speak the dialect anyway.

A majority of the teachers, except for those who teach a science, recognise that D speakers have specific problems in mastering standard Dutch. Consequently, about half of the teachers think that more attention should be paid to this specific language background in the context of the classroom, for example in the form of a subject like 'dialectology' in a functional, sociolinguistic sense. About the same proportion of the teachers profess to use the dialect sometimes, but in the observation of

25 lessons no indication whatsoever was found that this was indeed the case, neither in terms of actual use, nor in terms of use as a teaching resource.

To sum up, most of our results indicate a certain tension between the dialect and the standard variety in the school. The results, and also our informal experiences during the project, indicate that the Maastricht dialect is the dominant variety for most of the students. Teaching, on the other hand, is exclusively carried out in and aimed at the standard variety. That this discrepancy may result in problems for at least a number of children seems obvious.

Note to Chapter 9

1. The research was carried out as the M.A. project of the two authors, under the supervision of Ton Vallen, who at the time was a research associate at the Institute of General Linguistics of the University of Nijmegen, and Sjef Stijnen, who at the time was head of the Nijmegen Institute for Educational Research. A complete account of the investigation is to be found in Sonderen & Weltens (1981).

References

ACLO-M 1978 *Schooltaal thuistaal*. The Hague: Staatsuitgeverij.
EDWARDS, V., TRUDGILL, P. and WELTENS, B. 1984 *The Grammar of English Dialect. A Survey of Research*. London: Economic and Social Science Research Council.
HAGEN, A. and STURM, J. 1982 *Dialect en onderwijs*. Groningen: Wolters-Noordhoff (DCN brochure 12). Economic and Social Science Research Council.
KROON, S. and LIEBRAND, R. 1983 Middelbare scholieren, dialect en school. *Levende Talen* no. 383, 362–69.
KUIJPER, H., STIJNEN, P. and VALLEN, A. 1979 Spreekangst en linguistische onzekerheid bij dialectsprekers in vergelijking met standaardtaalsprekers. In M. MOMMERS & B. SMITS (eds), *Lees-taalonderwijs in de basisschool*. The Hague: Staatsuitgeverij (SVO reeks 24).
MÜNSTERMANN, H. AND HAGEN, A. 1986 Functional and structural aspects of dialect loss: A research plan and some first results. In B. WELTENS, K. DE BOT & T. VAN ELS (eds), *Language Attrition in Progress*. Dordrecht: Foris, 75–96.
SHEPHERD, P. 1946 *Van taol naar taal. Nederlands voor Maastricht en omstreken*. Maastricht: Goffin.
SONDEREN, J. AND WELTENS, B. 1981 Taalvariatie en schoolsucces in een brugklas. M.A. thesis University of Nijmegen.
Van Dale's Groot Woordenboek der Nederlandse Taal 1976 The Hague: Martinus Nijhoff (10th edition, ed. C. Kruyskamp).
WEIJNEN, A. 1967 Sociodialectologische onderzoekingen in Limburg. In J. DAAN

& A. WEIJNEN, *Taalsociologie*. Amsterdam: Noord-Hollandsche Uitge-versmaatschappij. pp. 16–31.

WELTENS, B., SONDEREN, J., STIJNEN, P. and VALLEN, A. 1981 Taalvariatie en schoolsucces in een brugklas. *Tijdschrift voor Taalbeheersing* 3, 314–21.

WESTERLAAK, J. VAN, KROPMAN, J. and COLLARIS, J. 1975 *Beroepenklapper*. Nijmegen: Institute of Applied Social Sciences.

10 Language attitudes in education

HENK MÜNSTERMANN

Introduction

Almost every study on the problems of dialect and education (in the Netherlands) emphasises the importance of teachers' attitudes towards dialect. The reason for this is the optimistic thought that positive attitudes will automatically lead to positive behaviour towards dialect-speaking pupils, and that recognition of this is a necessary precondition for any approach to the problem.

Some researchers state that there would be no problem at all if it were not for the negative attitudes of teachers (cf. Trudgill, 1975). Illustrative of this view is a statement by Goodman & Goodman (1981), who studied the reading and writing skills of dialect-speaking children and found no significant differences with the results of their standard-speaking peers. They conclude: '. . . that the only disadvantage was rejection of these dialects by the school and the pervasive attitude that speakers of low status dialects have difficulty in learning to read'. But also those who argue for a more explicitly didactic approach, such as the researchers in the Kerkrade project (cf. Van den Hoogen & Kuijper, this volume, Chapter 13), take a great interest in language attitudes and in ways of changing them.

If we accept that attitude change could contribute to a solution of dialect–standard problems in education, then it is necessary to know more about the nature and structure of attitudes to language in this particular setting and about the factors influencing them. For this reason, a research project was carried out between 1980 and 1983 on the attitudes of prospective teachers towards dialect and standard language and, more specifically, towards the use of dialect in the school. The possibilities of attitude change were also investigated. The project was financed by research funding from the University of Nijmegen.

Subjects

The subjects of the study — 548 students from seven teacher training colleges in different regions of the Netherlands — were training to become teachers in primary schools. By taking students as our subjects, we were able to build up a fairly large sample enabling us to investigate the effects of the course, or rather elements in the course, on the attitudes. The sample contained similar proportions of male and female students, the majority aged between 18 and 21 years. The data were gathered from seven regions: Roermond, Breda, Doetinchem, Hengelo, Rotterdam, Amsterdam and Middelburg, differing in terms of degree of urbanisation, regional function and dialect-situation. The degree of urbanisation and the position of the dialect are related phenomena. In the larger cities the use of dialect is mostly limited to lower socio-economic groups, in other words speaking in dialect is socially marked. This belief often causes negative evaluations of city dialects, particularly when it comes to status or social prestige (cf. Trudgill & Giles, 1976, also in Trudgill, 1983). The degree of urbanisation, however, is certainly not the only factor determining the position of the dialect.

Method

Three attitude measurement techniques were used in the project. The first was an adapted version of the well-known matched-guise technique (Lambert *et al.*, 1960; Giles, 1971). In this test five male speakers, reading the same text, were evaluated. The subjects unknowingly heard one of the speakers twice, once in the dialect of their region and once in standard Dutch, with a slight regional accent. A different tape was used for each of the regions. For the evaluation, 16 bipolar scales were used with personality traits as used in other matched-guise experiments, for example intelligence, cheerfulness, trustworthiness, and so on.

The second instrument used was the 'dialect attitude scale', a Likert-type scaling instrument, containing 28 statements on dialect and the use of dialect in school. Some of the items were adopted from the Language Attitude Scale developed by Taylor (1973), and some from a study by Diederen *et al.* (1984), of which the present study was an extended replication.

The third instrument was a domain questionnaire in which the subjects were asked to indicate how suitable they considered dialect for use in a range of situations. In this questionnaire the domain 'school' was divided into six situations, namely: during speech training; in mathematics lessons; in history and geography lessons; in individual conversation between teacher and pupil; in general classroom conversation; and in school, off record. Of course, one may wonder if this questionnaire actually is an attitude questionnaire, but the answers to it do, at least, incorporate attitudes towards the usability of dialect and towards situations in which the dialect is used.

Analysis

In order to reduce the enormous number of variables in the test and, more importantly, to detect underlying patterns in the attitude scores, a factor analysis was carried out for all three tests.

For the matched-guise test this resulted in a clear three-factor solution that explained about 60% of the variance. The pattern which emerged was the same for both dialect and standard versions, as well as for the difference scores. These difference scores were calculated by subtraction of the dialect version scores from those for the standard version on the same item. The factors found could be labelled as 'prestige', 'social attractiveness' and 'personal integrity' (cf. a.o. Giles, 1971; Giles & Powesland, 1975). The first factor had strong loadings for items like 'intelligence', 'ambition' and 'leadership'. Perhaps a more up-to-date label, 'dynamism', would fit even better (cf. Zahn & Hopper, 1985). Social attractiveness is built up from items such as 'cheerfulness' or 'sense of humour'. Integrity, finally, contains items such as 'honesty' and 'trustworthiness'.

Although a Likert-scale, in a classical sense, is meant to be a uni-dimensional scale, our dialect attitude scale was treated as a multi-dimensional scale. Factor analysis extracted three factors: first, a group of items concerning social and pedagogical reasons for the use of dialect in school; second, expectations concerning the learning (cognitive) capacities of dialect speakers; and third, aesthetic judgements on dialects. The factors contained 12, 9 and 6 items respectively.

The solution for the domain questionnaire was somewhat more complicated. The reason being that domain configurations are mostly treated as being uni-dimensional, that is, all domains are ordered on one dimension running from formal to informal. For reasons discussed in a paper by Van Hout and Münstermann (1988), such a solution is considered to be overly simple and inadequate. (If, for example, parent–child communication should gradually become a more exclusive standard domain, this would probably not mean that this domain was then becoming more formal). Better solutions can be found in multi-dimensional models with dimensions such as 'instrumentalism' and 'solidarity'.

In this solution a clear solidarity factor emerged with the domains of 'home' and 'friends' as the variables with the highest factor loadings. The second factor contained all the school situations except 'in school, off record'. The third factor was a little difficult to label, for it contained three situations that did not group well together (adults–children, in school off-record, and at the teacher training college). For want of a better term, it was finally called 'other educational situations'.

For all the factors found, total scores were calculated. These total scores were then divided by the number of terms in the summation. The result is a score between 1 and 5 (or between −4 and +4 for the difference scores). For all the remaining variables, except the difference scores, a higher score indicates a more favourable attitude to dialect. In the difference scores a negative score is in favour of dialect.

A list of the remaining attitude variables (together with abbreviations used throughout the Tables) is presented in Table 1.

TABLE 1   *A List of the Attitudinal Variables in the Study*

Abbrev.	Label	Range
L1	Social/pedagogical considerations for use of dialect in the school	1–5
L2	Expectations of learning capacities of dialect speaking pupils	1–5
L3	(evaluative) Aesthetic judgements of dialects	1–5
PS	Prestige Standard	1–5
PD	Prestige Dialect	1–5
DP	Difference Prestige	−4 to +4
AS	Attractiveness Standard	1–5
AD	Attractiveness Dialect	1–5
DA	Difference Attractiveness	−4 to +4
IS	Integrity Standard	1–5
ID	Integrity Dialect	1–5
DI	Difference Integrity	−4 to +4
DO1	Solidarity	1–5
DO2	School	1–5
DO3	Other educational situations	1–5

Results

As previously pointed out, seven regions were involved in the investigation. These regions differ with respect to degree of urbanisation and dialect situation (which are closely related). As in other western European countries, urban dialects in most towns in the Netherlands are low prestige varieties. The dialects that are more regional (or rural) have differing levels of prestige, which are generally higher than those of urban dialects. Of course, the prestige of a dialect depends on the number of speakers and the status of the speakers.

In Table 2, the results for the attitude variables are broken down by region.

Examination of the first three variables, the factors of the dialect attitude scale, shows that the attitudes measured here are quite positive. For the first factor, social and pedagogical considerations, the students from Doetinchem and Middelburg hold the most favourable attitudes. The lowest scores for the first factor are found in Amsterdam and Breda, and Amsterdam and Roermond for the second factor. It is not particularly surprising that the scores in Amsterdam are rather low, as here, more than in any of the other regions, dialect has become a social dialect. What is surprising, however, is that the lowest score on the second factor was found in Roermond, where the position of the dialect is very strong. One possible explanation could be that the students in Roermond have been confronted with negative attitudes themselves, more so than students in the other regions. As might have been expected, the score on the aesthetic judgements factor is highest in Roermond and lowest, again, in Amsterdam, followed by the other major city, Rotterdam. For the matched-guise variables we will inspect only the difference scores. The scores in the other two columns of Table 2 should be treated with care because they originate from the evaluation of different speakers in each of the regions. In the difference scores speaker-specific characteristics such as voice quality and pitch are ruled out and only the variety used is variable (at least that is the philosophy underlying the matched-guise technique). What we can conclude from the difference score for prestige is that in all but one of the regions the standard has more prestige than the dialect. This is, of course, exactly what could be expected. The one region where the dialect has more prestige is Roermond, and the difference here is, in fact, considerable. Dialects having equal prestige as standard language are rare but certainly conceivable, if we accept the idea of linguistic equality that is expressed in the difference approach (see the Introduction to this volume). But dialects with higher social prestige than the standard language are almost unimaginable. Of course this finding does not fit the real situation in Roermond, however

TABLE 2 *Effects of REGION on the Attitudinal Variables*

	n	Roer (71)	Bred (92)	Doet (49)	Region Heng (118)	Rott (85)	Amst (62)	Midd (71)	F.	Sign.
L1	m	3.71	3.31	3.93	3.59	3.48	3.44	3.76	5.53	0.00
	s	0.72	0.80	0.74	0.75	0.62	0.62	0.70		
L2	m	3.79	4.06	4.07	3.86	4.02	3.82	4.18	3.60	0.00
	s	0.77	0.55	0.75	0.69	0.59	0.67	0.63		
L3	m	3.92	3.37	3.77	3.78	3.36	3.18	3.79	8.50	0.00
	s	0.92	0.87	0.83	0.77	0.66	0.78	0.82		
PS	m	2.76	3.26	3.15	3.82	3.61	3.60	3.65	26.41	0.00
	s	0.57	0.73	0.65	0.63	0.55	0.45	0.71		
PD	m	3.19	2.91	2.98	3.07	3.23	2.99	3.00	2.40	0.03
	s	0.86	0.66	0.54	0.61	0.56	0.57	0.85		
DP	m	−0.43	0.34	0.19	0.75	0.38	0.61	0.62	13.80	0.00
	s	1.01	0.83	0.80	0.87	0.76	0.82	1.21		
AS	m	3.47	2.79	3.19	3.10	3.13	3.58	2.89	8.67	0.00
	s	0.75	0.69	0.74	0.69	0.69	0.69	0.76		
AD	m	4.09	3.52	3.91	3.79	4.08	4.01	3.66	9.26	0.00
	s	0.88	0.79	0.69	0.63	0.56	0.71	0.70		
DA	m	−0.63	−0.56	−0.71	−0.68	−0.96	−0.42	−0.77	2.30	0.03
	s	1.02	1.06	1.00	0.84	0.87	0.74	1.13		
IS	m	3.77	3.52	3.63	4.16	3.74	3.69	3.79	12.63	0.00
	s	0.58	0.67	0.57	0.46	0.49	0.58	0.65		
ID	m	3.96	3.19	3.74	3.80	3.26	3.11	3.72	25.04	0.00
	s	0.72	0.65	0.53	0.52	0.50	0.62	0.62		
DI	m	−0.18	0.32	−0.09	0.35	0.48	0.57	0.06	10.20	0.00
	s	0.71	0.78	0.65	0.65	0.74	0.73	0.82		
DO1	m	4.72	4.18	4.46	4.27	4.38	4.50	4.65	7.07	0.00
	s	0.43	0.89	0.72	0.67	0.59	0.56	0.52		
DO2	m	2.79	2.60	2.85	2.30	2.90	2.91	2.76	3.91	0.00
	s	1.23	1.01	1.05	0.90	1.11	1.08	1.14		
DO3	m	4.05	2.80	3.44	2.98	3.08	3.33	3.35	11.66	0.00
	s	0.90	1.07	1.04	1.07	1.05	1.00	1.06		

m = mean ($\bar{x}$); s = standard deviation

strong the position of the dialect may be. The negative difference score is probably caused by denigration of the standard language. Spoken by a large number of speakers and supported by a strong social position, the dialect becomes a community symbol. The standard language may be felt to be an outgroup symbol or even a threat. Many people in the province of Limburg, in which Roermond is situated, have strong minority feelings and are not very fond of what comes from the western part of the country. So what we found here may very well be a sign of a defensive identity (cf. Persoons, 1986).

What dialects lose in comparison with standard language on social prestige is usually compensated for in the scores for social attractiveness or solidarity (cf. Ryan, 1982). This is what we found here. In all the regions dialect speakers are considered to be more socially attractive. One may wonder if this repeated finding is as favourable as it seems. The cliché of the cheerful, amusing dialect speaker with the great sense of humour is as much prejudice as that of the dialect speaker with less ambition and intelligence! (The media in the Netherlands as well as in many other countries contribute strongly to this image of dialect-speakers whenever possible.)

For integrity, only the scores in Roermond and Doetinchem show preference for dialect. The scores most in favour of standard Dutch are found in the two major cities, Amsterdam and Rotterdam. The domain results show that dialect is considered perfectly suitable for the solidarity situations. For use in school, however, the scores are very low. Remarkably, the highest scores can be found in Amsterdam and Rotterdam. This finding can be easily explained by the smaller linguistic distance between the dialects in these cities and standard Dutch. In fact, these dialects are often regarded as lower-status styles of standard Dutch (regional standard), as became clear from interviews with some of the subjects. (Interestingly enough the subjects in Rotterdam stated that the problems of dialect-speaking children were practically negligible in comparison to the problems the numerous immigrant children in Rotterdam had to cope with.) Nevertheless it seems rather odd that, although the attitudes as measured in the Likert-scale seem moderately positive, the scores in the school domain are not.

There are considerable differences between the regions in their scores for the third domain variable. Roermond has the highest score again. The lowest score is for Breda. Since (informal) educational settings are essential to this factor, these differences are quite meaningful with respect to the vitality of the dialects.

The next independent variable, sex, causes significant effects for most of the attitudinal variables. It is clear that the female informants have more positive attitudes towards standard than the male informants. The evaluation of dialect speakers does not significantly differ for male and female informants. The Likert-scale results show that males are more in favour of the use of dialect in school and that their aesthetic judgements on dialects are more positive. There is no significant difference in the expectations of the school performance of dialect-speaking children. Similarly, for the domain variables, the male informants' scores are significantly more positive.

TABLE 3 *Effects of SEX on the Attitudinal Variables*

		Sex Fem.	Male	F	Sign.
L1	m	3.50	3.73	11.60	0.00
	s	0.75	0.65		
L2	m	3.96	4.00	0.37	n.s.
	s	0.67	0.65		
L3	m	3.55	3.70	3.89	0.04
	s	0.82	0.85		
PS	m	3.53	3.33	9.24	0.00
	s	0.70	0.70		
PD	m	3.06	3.07	0.02	n.s.
	s	0.65	0.74		
DP	m	0.46	0.27	4.70	0.03
	s	0.93	1.02		
AS	m	3.23	3.06	6.22	0.01
	s	0.70	0.81		
AD	m	3.88	3.79	1.75	n.s.
	s	0.70	0.80		
DA	m	−0.65	−0.73	0.85	n.s.
	s	0.88	1.10		
IS	m	3.86	3.66	14.15	0.00
	s	0.61	0.57		
ID	m	3.55	3.51	0.46	n.s.
	s	0.71	0.64		
DI	m	0.29	0.15	4.38	0.04
	s	0.73	0.82		
DO1	m	4.36	4.54	8.10	0.00
	s	0.70	0.61		
DO2	m	2.57	2.89	10.00	0.00
	s	1.04	1.09		
DO3	m	3.15	3.41	6.62	0.01
	s	1.11	1.03		

m = mean ($\bar{x}$); s = standard deviation

There has been much speculation about why female informants should show more preference for standard language than males. The explanation that women derive prestige from using standard while men would derive it from their work (cf. Trudgill, 1974) is not likely to account for the differences found here, for male and female informants are in exactly the same position. However, it is conceivable that women are brought up with the idea that they will need to derive prestige or an appearance of culture from the standard language in later life. In that case, the differences are the result of role-specific education rather than the results of active, conscious strategies in the present.

Of course, these role patterns are quite traditional. They also incorporate, for instance, the preparation of girls for their role as educator, for which standard language is generally considered essential.

For the third variable, socio-economic background, few significant effects were found, but for those that were found the pattern is that the lower the socio-economic background of the informant the more positive his or her attitude to the dialect will be. The correlation between dialect and social class, that holds for many dialect-speaking areas, can make dialect a marker of social class membership. The involvement of the lower socio-economic groups in matters regarding dialect will therefore result in more pronounced attitudes.

TABLE 4   *Effects of Socio-economic Group (SEG) on the Attitudinal Variables*

		SEG1	SEG SEG2	SEG3	Sign.	
L1	m	3.77	3.66	3.47	4.48	0.01
	s	0.78	0.70	0.73		
L2	m	4.05	4.05	3.91	1.96	n.s.
	s	0.63	0.65	0.69		
L3	m	3.81	3.78	3.44	8.32	0.00
	s	0.85	0.80	0.84		
PS	m	3.46	3.48	3.50	0.07	n.s.
	s	0.75	0.69	0.71		
PD	m	3.16	3.12	3.00	1.77	n.s.
	s	0.71	0.60	0.69		
DP	m	0.32	0.35	0.49	1.18	n.s.
	s	1.03	0.94	0.94		
AS	m	3.21	3.13	3.22	0.54	n.s.
	s	0.78	0.78	0.68		
AD	m	3.87	3.93	3.82	0.99	n.s.
	s	0.70	0.67	0.78		
DA	m	−0.66	−0.81	−0.59	2.13	n.s.
	s	1.11	0.95	0.90		
IS	m	3.96	3.79	3.82	1.58	n.s.
	s	0.58	0.60	0.60		
ID	m	3.71	3.61	3.47	3.77	0.02
	s	0.74	0.66	0.63		
DI	m	0.24	0.18	0.35	2.05	n.s.
	s	0.75	0.76	0.74		
DO1	m	4.50	4.50	4.34	2.72	n.s.
	s	0.70	0.57	0.73		
DO2	m	2.61	2.75	2.58	1.05	n.s.
	s	1.00	1.05	1.06		
DO3	m	3.54	3.24	3.06	4.08	0.02
	s	1.10	0.95	1.15		

m = mean ($\bar{x}$); s = standard deviation

Dialect speakers, finally, have significantly more positive attitudes towards dialect than standard-language speakers. This is true for all the variables except for the evaluations of the standard language in the matched-guise test and for views on the appropriateness of the use of dialect in school. Of course, ego-involvement and ingroup-favouring are the important mechanisms behind this finding.

However, a small proportion of the informants who claim to be dialect users, are not mother tongue speakers of the dialect, but second language learners of the dialect. This was discovered from a small domain questionnaire

TABLE 5   *Effects of LANGUAGE BACKGROUND on the Attitudinal Variables*

| | | Dialect | | | |
		No	Yes	F	Sign.
L1	m	3.38	3.86	19.48	0.00
	s	0.77	0.69		
L2	m	3.86	4.01	5.83	0.02
	s	0.70	0.65		
L3	m	3.27	3.77	43.21	0.00
	s	0.82	0.80		
PS	m	3.51	3.42	2.05	n.s.
	s	0.67	0.73		
PD	m	2.88	3.15	18.23	0.00
	s	0.63	0.69		
DP	m	0.62	0.28	15.31	0.00
	s	0.91	0.98		
AS	m	3.15	3.17	0.09	n.s.
	s	0.74	0.74		
AD	m	3.71	3.92	10.16	0.00
	s	0.73	0.73		
DA	m	−0.54	−0.76	5.69	0.02
	s	0.89	0.99		
IS	m	3.79	3.78	0.04	n.s.
	s	0.63	0.59		
ID	m	3.32	3.65	29.09	0.00
	s	0.60	0.68		
DI	m	0.46	0.13	23.04	0.00
	s	0.70	0.77		
DO1	m	4.23	4.52	21.58	0.00
	s	0.78	0.60		
DO2	m	2.56	2.74	3.41	n.s.
	s	1.09	1.06		
DO3	m	2.96	3.37	16.57	0.00
	s	1.11	1.03		

m = mean ($\bar{x}$); s = standard deviation

in which the informants were asked to indicate their use of the dialect in a number of situations. Nevertheless, their attitudes did not differ from the attitudes held by first language dialect speakers. This can be interpreted in at least two ways. First, second language learners of the dialect are looking for integration with first language speakers of the dialect and they do so not only by trying to master the dialect, but also by adopting the corresponding set of attitudes. In communities where the dialect has a strong function as identifier of community membership, the social pressure for non-dialect speakers to adopt the dialect can be considerable. Second, it could be the case that, once non-dialect speakers have managed to speak the dialect, they discover that their previous beliefs on, for instance, the logic and usability of the dialect, turn out to be impossible to hold.

What can we learn from these first findings? First, that attitudes are both regionally and socially bound. For the larger part this can be accounted for by the social connotations hypothesis of Trudgill & Giles (1976, also in Trudgill, 1983), in which it is stated that it is not the language variety itself that is evaluated but the group of speakers associated with it. It is evident from the findings discussed above that there is no such thing as a language attitude in a strict sense, i.e. an attitude towards (a) language.

Second, that traditional patterns play an important role in the establishment of attitudes. This seems to be particularly true for the sex-specific role patterns in primary education.

Third, that attitudes may be used as a self-defence mechanism. The more informants are involved in matters of dialect, in other words the more dialect is part of their identity, the more central dialect as an attitude object will be to them and the more salient their attitudes will be. (As the opposite of self-defence, the self-denigration phenomenon has also been noted (cf. Giles & Powesland, 1975), which can be a sign of a negative identity.)

A curriculum or language awareness programme should include information on at least these aspects. This means that language attitudes cannot be seen as separate attitudes, concerning only language, but as representatives of a whole set of social attitudes. Approaches that seek to eliminate language prejudice cannot be successful if they are not embedded in attempts to eliminate social prejudice in a very broad sense (including racism, sexism, and so on).

What we would need to know next is whether it is possible to change language attitudes, in other words if teacher training courses and language awareness programmes set themselves realistic goals in trying to work on attitude change. Attitude change has been one of the most frequently discussed topics in social psychology since the introduction of the notion of attitude. There is little agreement on the possibilities of attitude change, however, nor on the strategies that should be followed to achieve it.

Fishbein & Ajzen (1975) mention two strategies for attitude change that seem to be commonly accepted, namely active participation and persuasive communication. Active participation in situations relevant to the attitude object may change experiences with that object and therefore change the belief structure. Since attitude is defined by Fishbein & Ajzen as the sum of the evaluated beliefs, it is clear that a change in the belief structure eventually affects the attitude. Perhaps this is a bit of a roundabout, for it could also be assumed that active participation often calls for a change in behaviour or a change in the evaluation. Attitude change may result from this, since people tend to bring their attitudes and their behaviour into line, if possible. Persuasive communication, again, is directed towards a change in belief structure which, in turn, is likely to change attitudes.

These two strategies, in a simple form, are present in this study: active participation in the form of training practice in schools with many dialect-speaking pupils, and persuasive communication in the form of information received during the course on the problems of dialect and school. The effects of these two variables on the attitudinal variables are shown in Tables 6 and 7.

Evidently both strategies of attitude change prove to be successful to some extent. For the variables of the dialect attitude scale (L1, L2, L3), the effects of information are stronger than those of experience. For the matched-guise variables the reverse appears to be the case. The domain variables also show stronger effects for experience. Although both strategies caused significant effects for most of the attitude variables, these effects turned out to be independent. A combination of both strategies, therefore, shows even stronger effects. So, there seems to be reason enough to be optimistic when it comes to the question of the results of courses and programmes that aim to bring about a change in attitudes.

However, some important things should be kept in mind. First, the results presented here are results from tests and questionnaires. Although they were confirmed by observations in educational practice (Kuijper & Münstermann, 1983), they must be treated with some care. The desire to please and give the 'right' (socially desirable) answers may have biased the results to a certain degree. The variables that measure attitudes on

TABLE 6   *Effects of INFORMATION on the Attitudinal Variables*

		Information			
		No	Yes	F	Sign.
L1	m	3.40	3.74	24.84	0.00
	s	0.75	0.71		
L2	m	3.88	4.03	6.03	0.01
	s	0.67	0.66		
L3	m	3.46	3.73	11.98	0.00
	s	0.87	0.81		
PS	m	3.46	3.43	0.19	n.s.
	s	0.75	0.69		
PD	m	2.99	3.14	5.46	0.02
	s	0.66	0.69		
DP	m	0.46	0.29	3.48	n.s.
	s	0.97	0.98		
AS	m	3.20	3.15	0.62	n.s.
	s	0.72	0.77		
AD	m	3.82	3.87	0.61	n.s.
	s	0.79	0.70		
DA	m	−0.62	−0.72	1.38	n.s.
	s	0.99	0.98		
IS	m	3.76	3.79	0.42	n.s.
	s	0.62	0.60		
ID	m	3.46	3.62	6.94	0.01
	s	0.71	0.64		
DI	m	0.28	0.18	2.13	n.s.
	s	0.79	0.76		
DO1	m	4.34	4.49	5.67	0.02
	s	0.69	0.67		
DO2	m	2.59	2.79	3.64	0.05
	s	1.06	1.11		
DO3	m	3.09	3.38	8.28	0.00
	s	1.09	1.09		

m = mean ($\bar{x}$); s = standard deviation

a very conscious level, as in the dialect attitude scale, are particularly susceptible to this effect. Likert-scale items reflecting, for instance, the effects of the use of dialect in a social or educational context, may very well receive answers that express what the informant has learned, rather than what he or she feels. The matched-guise test measures language attitudes on a much less conscious level, and the results will be less affected by 'socially acceptable' answering. Information as a strategy of attitude change showed the strongest effects for the more conscious of the attitude variables, while experience showed the stronger effects on a more subconscious level. The effect of information could be a change in

TABLE 7. *Effects of EXPERIENCE on the Attitudinal Variables*

		Experience No	Yes	F	Sign.
L1	m	3.44	3.66	10.20	0.00
	s	0.75	0.72		
L2	m	3.93	3.99	0.81	n.s.
	s	0.67	0.67		
L3	m	3.46	3.71	10.61	0.00
	s	0.82	0.85		
PS	m	3.61	3.33	19.59	0.00
	s	0.68	0.71		
PD	m	2.96	3.12	7.28	0.01
	s	0.66	0.69		
DP	m	0.65	0.21	24.54	0.00
	s	0.94	0.96		
AS	m	3.15	3.18	0.21	n.s.
	s	0.77	0.74		
AD	m	3.79	3.88	1.91	n.s.
	s	0.75	0.74		
DA	m	−0.63	−0.70	0.70	n.s.
	s	0.97	0.98		
IS	m	3.80	3.77	0.38	n.s.
	s	0.62	0.60		
ID	m	3.41	3.63	12.78	0.00
	s	0.61	0.72		
DI	m	0.39	0.14	11.95	0.00
	s	0.79	0.76		
DO1	m	4.36	4.49	4.11	0.04
	s	0.69	0.65		
DO2	m	2.52	2.80	7.44	0.01
	s	1.13	1.03		
DO3	m	3.01	3.42	16.22	0.00
	s	1.08	1.09		

m = mean ($\bar{x}$); s = standard deviation

ideas about answers that are socially acceptable, just as much as a real change of attitude. This risk is less evident for the effects of experience, and therefore experience should be considered the more reliable of the two strategies.

Second, although attitude change has proved to be an achievable goal, this does not necessarily imply actual tolerance towards non-standard varieties. Tolerance is observable (which attitudes are not), and can directly be derived from behaviour. We may even go one step further and say that tolerance is nothing but a behavioural strategy.

The relation between attitudes and behaviour is known to be a very problematic one. Correlations between measures of attitude and measures of behaviour are rarely high and, according to Wicker (1969), are often near zero. On the basis of the results of this study and results from two comparable studies, the relation between attitudes towards dialect and the reported use of dialect were investigated (Münstermann & Van Hout, 1986, 1988). The multiple correlations of the attitudinal variables on the one hand, and reported use variables on the other, reached a maximum of about 0.50, which means that only 25% of the reported use could be explained by attitudes.

In summary, if attitude change is an aim in teacher training programmes, this can be achieved by giving relevant information, bearing in mind the effects of the social and demographic variables in this study and in comparable investigations. Also, participants in a programme should be enabled to have new experiences with non-standard varieties, preferably in educational contexts with non-standard-speaking pupils. Apart from trying to bring about a change in behaviour through a change of attitudes, behaviour should be addressed directly by the proposal of concrete relevant behavioural strategies. Of course, these last remarks may give the impression that attitude is not such a valuable notion as researchers in the field of language and education have felt it to be. This impression is right, if negative attitudes are considered the one and only cause of problems in the field of language and education. On the other hand, it has been shown that some positive effects can be expected from attitude change. Since every minor improvement in this field is of major importance, these effects, however small they seem to be, may turn out to play an invaluable role in the long run.

References

DIEDEREN, F., HOS, H., MÜNSTERMANN, H. and WEISTRA, G. 1984 Language attitudes of future teachers. In K. DEPREZ (ed.), *Sociolinguistics in the Low Countries*. Amsterdam/Philadelphia: Benjamins. pp. 213–36.

FISHBEIN, J. and AJZEN, I. 1975 *Belief, Attitude, Intention and Behaviour*. Reading, Mass.: Addison-Wesley.

GILES, H. 1971 Patterns of evaluation in reactions to R.P., South Welsh and Somerset accented speech. *British Journal of Social and Clinical Psychology* 10, 280–81.

GILES, H. and POWESLAND, P.F. 1975 *Speech Style and Social Evaluation*. London: Academic Press.

GOODMAN, Y. and GOODMAN, K. 1981 Twenty questions about teaching language. *Educational Leadership*, 38, 6, 437–43.

KUIJPER, H. and MÜNSTERMANN, H. 1983 Verandering van taalattitudes in het onderwijs; enkele observaties in onderzoek en praktijk, *Toegepaste Taalwetenschap in Artikelen* 16A, 126–47.

LAMBERT, W.E., HODGSON, R.C., GARDNER, R.C. and FILLENBAUM, S. 1960 Evaluational reactions to spoken languages. *Journal of Abnormal and Social Psychology* 60, 44–51.

MÜNSTERMANN, H. and R. VAN HOUT 1986 Taalattitudes contra geschiktheid en Gebruik. In J. CRETEN, G. GEERTS & K. JASPAERT (eds), *Werk in uitvoering. Momentopname van de sociolinguistiek in Belgie en Nederland.* Leuven/Amersfoort: Acco. 235–49. (Also to appear in translation in U.KNOPS *et al.* (eds) (1988), *Language Attitudes in the Netherlands.* Dordrecht, Providence: Foris.

PERSOONS, Y. 1986 *De identiteit van de minderheid. Een verkennend sociaal psychologisch onderzoek bij jonge Vlamingen in Brussel.* (Dissertation) Universitaire Instelling Antwerpen. Brussel.

RYAN, E.B. 1982 Why do low-prestige language varieties persist? In H. GILES & R. ST CLAIR (eds), *Language and Social Psychology.* Oxford: Blackwell. pp. 145–57.

TAYLOR, O. 1973 Teachers' attitudes toward Black and Nonstandard English as measured by the Language Attitude Scale. In R.W. SHUY & R.W. FASOLD (eds), *Language Attitudes: Current Trends and Prospects.* Washington, D.C.: Georgetown University Press. pp. 174–201.

TRUDGILL, P. 1974 *The Social Differentiation of English in Norwich.* Cambridge: Cambridge University Press.

——1975 *Accent, Dialect and the School.* London: Edward Arnold.

——1983 *On Dialect: Social and Regional Perspectives.* Oxford: Blackwell.

TRUDGILL, P. and GILES, H. 1976 *Sociolinguistics and Language Value Judgments: Correctness, Adequacy and Aesthetics.* Paper reproduced by the Linguistic Agency of the University of Trier.

VAN HOUT, R. and MÜNSTERMANN, H. 1988 The multidimensionality of domain configurations. *International Journal of the Sociology of Language,* 84.

WICKER, A.W. 1969 Attitudes vs. actions: the relationship of verbal and overt behavioral responses to attitude objects. *Journal of Social Issues* 4, 41–78.

ZAHN, C.J. and HOPPER, R. 1985 Measuring language attitudes: the speech evaluation instrument. *Journal of Language and Social Psychology* 4 (2), 113–23.

11 Dialect in school written work

ANN WILLIAMS

Introduction

During the past three decades, sociolinguistic research has focussed mainly on the speech of urban communities. The written language of such groups is difficult to study since so few adults engage in what Kress (1982) calls 'productive' writing (that is, the creation of new texts) and those who do, generally form part of an educated élite. The causes of the unequal distribution of active writers across social groups lie in the social and economic structure of society but may have their origins in our schools.

In school, all children are obliged to be active writers, although the audience is usually restricted to one — the teacher. Writing is accorded high prestige and a large proportion of school time is spent on it. In a recent survey (Bennett, 1980), it was found that in infant schools an average of 36% of total school time was allocated to language work, a large proportion of which was writing. In junior schools the figure was 31%. Children's progress is largely measured through writing, and their futures depend on the results of written examinations. As Gannon (1985) states: 'Writing is and for a long time will be the chief skill by which children will achieve success or not within the school system.' In spite of its critical role in a child's school career, however, writing has not received the attention given by researchers to children's reading or even speaking.

The research that has been done points to the close relationship between writing and speech in the early stages of learning to write (see, for example, Britton et al., 1975; Kress, 1982; Perera, 1986). Educationists appear to agree on the crucial role played by spoken language in early writing. Tough (1977:7) states: 'Reading and writing both have their basis in talk and ways of using language for writing and reading must be established through talk.' Britton *et al.*, in their influential study (1975:11), propose that 'the writing of young children is very like written down speech,' and is 'fully comprehensible only to one who knows the speaker and shares his context.' Rubin (1975:219) comments that by the age of six 'children are quite set in their pattern of speech and their writing is a close reflection of this.'

It is to be expected, therefore, that all children's early writing will contain grammatical items and grammatical structures that in adult speakers are more typical of speech than of writing. It is, similarly, to be expected that children who use non-standard grammatical features in speech will use them in their writing. Sociolinguists estimate that the majority of the population of the United Kingdom use some indigenous non-standard grammatical features in their speech (see, for example, Hughes & Trudgill, 1987). This would suggest that for large numbers of children the language of the home is not necessarily the language of the school.

Standard English has traditionally been the variety that is expected and rewarded in schools in Britain, and although attitudes to non-standard accents have become more tolerant in recent years, non-standard syntax is still widely stigmatised (see Cheshire & Trudgill, this volume, Chapter 6). While, in the wake of the Bullock Report (1975), a more tolerant attitude to spoken varieties now prevails in schools, there is no evidence to suggest that this tolerance extends to writing, where the only acceptable variety so far is standard English. For those children whose home language is standard English, learning to write will pose fewer problems than for those who natively speak a non-standard dialect. Learning the written code is a difficult task for all children and has been compared to learning a second language (Allen, 1966; Kress, 1982) but the 'standard speakers will start with a knowledge that others have yet to acquire' (Kress, 1982). Teachers may attribute differences in performance in the early stages to differences in ability rather than to lack of familiarity with standard forms. As Kress (1982:33) states: 'there exists therefore an unnoticed hurdle in the learning of writing on which many children stumble and never recover.'

Given the close alliance that is claimed between speech and writing, at least in the early stages, and the fact that the majority of speakers use some non-standard forms in their speech, one would expect to find non-standard dialect forms in the school writing of young children. The research described in this chapter is part of a larger study that was set up in the town of Reading, in Berkshire, to ascertain which, if any, features of spoken English occurred in children's school writing; to what extent these included the syntactic features of the Reading dialect; and how teachers dealt with the dialect and oral features that occurred.

Data

Twenty children (10 boys and 10 girls) aged nine and ten, whose written work contained non-standard dialect features, were selected from the third year classes of Plane Street School, a primary school situated on a large council estate near the centre of Reading. They were matched for sex, age and ability with 20 children who attend Westlands, a primary school situated in the affluent suburbs of the same town (the names of the schools have been changed in the interest of anonymity). In order to control as far as possible for teaching methods and materials, only state schools were used.

The data set consisted of all the extended pieces of writing produced in the children's English exercise books and creative writing books over a period of two terms, autumn 1986 and spring 1987.

In addition, the children were recorded in small informal groups of two or three in order to ascertain whether the non-standard grammatical features that occurred in writing were also present in their informal speech. The recordings showed that all the pupils who attended Plane Street School used some non-standard features in their speech, whereas fewer than 10% of the children from Westlands, the high-status suburban school, used non-standard features in the recorded discussions. The total number of words in the written texts produced by each group can be seen in Table 1. While it was initially felt that it was desirable to control for text genre, this proved to be unnecessary since the majority of texts fell into the category of narrative or personal account.

TABLE 1   *Total Number of Words in the Written Texts*

	boys	girls
Westlands	18,445	18,078
Plane Street	11,463	15,473

The data were analysed for syntactic features of the Reading dialect and features of informal speech occurring in the written texts. Teachers' corrections and comments were monitored.

Syntactic Features of the Reading Dialect

The texts were analysed for the following features of the Reading dialect as listed in Cheshire (1982a). (All examples are taken from the written texts or the recordings of the children's speech: the children's spelling has not been altered.)

1. Present tense verb forms: I *goes* to find food.
2. Past tense of BE: my two mates *was* out before me.
3. Irregular preterites: This is where the smell *come* from.
4. *Ain't* as
   a) negative present of BE: We're making a model *ain't* we.
   b) negative present of HAVE: I *ain't* always been at this school.
5. *Never* as negative preterite: I asked her if she took the money but she *never*.
6. Negative concord: I did*n't* think *nothing* of it.
7. Relative pronouns: I got the present *what* I wanted.
8. Demonstrative adjective: Who dun *them* holes in your pyjamas.
9. Adverbs: Chris was playing *good*.
10. Nouns of measurement: I lost two *pound*.
11. Prepositions: Me and my sister went *down* my nan's.

Results

All the dialect features listed above, with the exception of *ain't*, occurred in the written texts of the dialect-speaking group from Plane Street School. In the writing of the standard-speaking group from Westlands School only items 2, 3, 7, 9 and 11 occurred. The incidence of non-standard features for the Plane Street children was considerably higher than for Westlands, as Table 2 shows.

Figure 1 shows the total number of occurrences of the dialect features that were used by the children from Plane Street School and Westlands School. It can be seen that non-standard past tense forms (of BE and various lexical verbs) formed the largest group of non-standard features in both sets of texts.

TABLE 2 *Number of Non-standard Features per 100 Words*

	Plane Street	Westlands
Boys	1.64	0.30
Girls	1.60	0.28

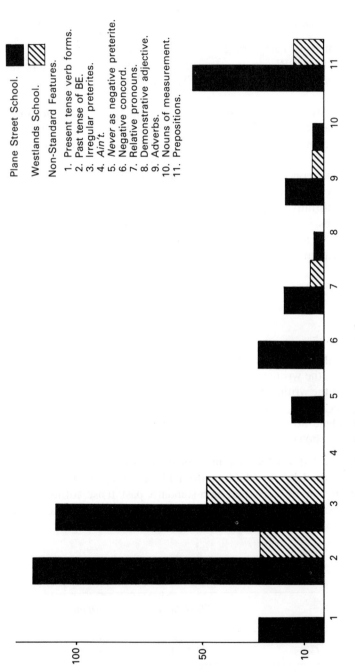

Plane Street School. ■

Westlands School. ▨

Non-Standard Features.

1. Present tense verb forms.
2. Past tense of BE.
3. Irregular preterites.
4. *Ain't.*
5. *Never* as negative preterite.
6. Negative concord.
7. Relative pronouns.
8. Demonstrative adjective.
9. Adverbs.
10. Nouns of measurement.
11. Prepositions.

FIGURE 1   *Total numbers of non-standard features in written texts*

There is an interesting difference, however, between the non-standard past tense forms used by the Plane Street children and those used by the Westlands pupils. In the case of the Westlands children, the non-standard forms that occurred most frequently were 'regularised' –ed forms of verbs that in adult standard English form their past tense by means of a vowel change (verbs that are traditionally known as the strong verbs) e.g. *I drawed* for *I drew*. Other examples were *shined, throwed, hided, standed, teached* and *braked*. These comprised 86% of all non-standard past tense forms. Although such forms are said to occur in Reading English (Cheshire, 1982a) and in many other non-standard English dialects (Edwards *et al.*, 1984) they are also characteristic of a transitional stage in the language acquisition of all English speaking children (see, for example, Perera, 1984:113). Verbs that form their past tense with the –ed suffix (the weak verbs) are of course more numerous in standard English than verbs that form their past tense with a vowel change (Baugh & Cable, 1978), and it is usually considered that the tendency of young children to prefer this pattern reflects their over-generalisation of the more frequent weak verb pattern.

While such verbs did occur in the work of the Plane Street children, they constituted only 28% of irregular preterites. The remaining 72% was made up of non-standard forms of four verbs: COME, DO, GIVE and SEE. In Reading English the following past tense forms of these verbs occur: *come, done, give,* and *see* or *seen.* The examples below illustrate these forms:

> The tarantula *come* out.
> My nan *done* her knitting.
> Mrs. C. *give* us some jars.
> Our class went to a farm and we *see* some sheep.
> On the way we *seen* a dinosaur.

Although the two past tense forms *see* and *seen* both occurred in the data, they did not co-occur in the work of any one child. In the work of two children, Dean and Gavin, *done* for standard English *did* and *seen* for standard English *saw* occurred in 100% of all possible cases respectively. Table 3 indicates that there was a considerable amount of individual variation.

Non-standard *was* with a plural subject occurred frequently in the data. In the texts of the Plane Street children it occurred throughout the paradigm, i.e. with *they, we* and *you* as subject, as well as in sentences with existential *there* and a following plural 'notional' subject (see Quirk *et al.*, 1972, 1985.) The following examples are taken from the Plane Street children's written texts:

TABLE 3 Individual Scores for Standard and Non-standard Features, for Plane Street School Children

	Total no. of words	Past Tense Forms								NEG. CONCORD		NEVER as PRETERITE		RELATIVES	
		BE		SEE		COME		DO							
		S	NS	S	NS	S	NS	S	NS	S	NS	S	NS	S	NS
Girls															
Mandy	3730	15	5	9	0	1	1	0	0	0	3	0	0	3	2
Susan	810	0	7	2	0	0	4	0	0	0	1	0	0	0	0
Judy	1339	2	3	3	1	4	3	4	0	2	0	3	0	0	1
Kathy	1995	6	13	4	0	3	1	1	0	1	0	0	0	0	1
Marylin	1209	3	5	2	1	2	3	0	1	0	2	0	1	3	0
Kelly	932	4	4	2	0	1	0	0	1	0	0	0	1	1	1
Charlotte	1500	1	11	3	0	1	2	0	3	0	1	0	1	0	1
Jackie	1760	4	3	4	0	4	0	0	3	0	0	0	0	0	0
Linda	1240	6	0	2	0	0	1	0	0	7	4	0	0	3	1
Diane	958	2	13	2	0	2	2	0	0	0	3	0	0	1	0
Total		43	64	33	2	18	17	5	8	10	14	3	3	11	7
Boys															
Sean	1342	6	0	3	0	1	1	0	0	0	0	0	0	0	0
Dean	1460	3	7	2	0	2	0	0	8	0	0	0	0	0	0
Ronnie	300	0	3	0	0	0	0	0	0	0	0	0	0	0	0
Gareth	800	2	5	3	1	0	0	0	0	0	3	0	1	0	0
Michael	588	1	5	0	0	0	0	0	0	0	0	0	0	0	1
Craig	1770	11	2	0	1	0	1	0	2	0	2	0	2	2	1
Justin	1408	1	8	0	0	3	1	1	0	1	2	0	0	1	1
Adam	2200	0	15	3	0	2	11	1	0	0	3	1	1	1	6
Gavin	540	2	2	0	8	1	0	0	0	0	0	0	0	0	0
Scott	1055	1	1	4	0	7	1	0	2	2	1	0	5	2	0

All the children *was* at school.
We *was* digging for some bones.
Where *was* you.
There *was* six people.

As Table 3 shows, this feature occurred 112 times in the writing of the Plane Street children. On 72 occasions it was used with a plural subject or with *you*, and in the remaining 40 cases it was used with existential *there*. In the Westlands texts, it occurred only 24 times, and in 20 of those cases it was used with existential *there* followed by a plural notional subject. Although this form has been analysed here as a dialect form, and is considered as such by Edwards *et al.* (1984), it is worth noting that Quirk *et al.* (1972, 1985) include this as a feature of informal 'educated' English. It is arguable, therefore, that this constitutes a feature of spoken language rather than a feature of the Reading dialect.

Two features that did not occur at all in the writing of the Westlands group, but that occurred in the work of 14 of the Plane Street children, were *never* used as a negative preterite and negative concord. The latter feature occurred in a variety of forms:

1. no ≡ any   I wouldn't have no friends.
2. nothing ≡ anything   I didn't win nothing.
3. no more ≡ any more   We was not aloud on there no more.
4. no one ≡ any one   He doesn't want no one to see him.
5. nowhere ≡ anywhere   There was no sound nowhere.

Discussion

Previous studies carried out in the United States have recorded the occurrence of non-standard forms in written composition (Wolfram & Whiteman, 1971; Whiteman, 1981.) Other researchers working with college students who were speakers of B.E.V. (Black English Vernacular) concluded that there were few if any 'errors' solely attributable to dialect influence (see Hartwell, 1980). Kirschner & Poteet (1973) found that 'there were no significant differences between the black, white and Hispanic students in the distribution of non-standard usage categories and their relative frequencies.' Whiteman (1981) analysed written texts of 32 working class black and white eighth graders (i.e. aged between 13 and 14) and found that the omission of the suffixes –s (verbal), –s (plural), –s (possessive) and 'consonant cluster

–ed', was due to the combined effects of dialect influence and acquisitional tendencies, but that there was little or no occurrence of grammatical features that did not involve suffixes (e.g. *ain't* and negative concord). She also found that non-standard phonological features rarely affected spelling. She states, 'Noticeably absent in my data are most non-standard phonological features (e.g. /f/ for /θ/ as in *wif* for *with* or postvocalic *r* absence as in *motha* for *mother*).'

It is perhaps not surprising, therefore, that the present study found that non-standard grammatical features occurred in the written texts of speakers of both standard and non-standard English. The majority of the non-standard features occurring in the work of the Westlands children, however, could be seen either as features of colloquial spoken English (*was* with existential *there*), or as forms which occur as part of a developmental process in the language acquisition of all children (*–ed* past tense forms of verbs that are strong in standard English). The fact that these latter forms occurred in the written work of both groups of children lends support to the view that dialect influence and acquisitional tendencies have a combined effect, but it is noteworthy that although both groups in the present study used past tense forms that could be attributed to developmental tendencies, the Plane Street children used fewer of these non-standard *–ed* forms than the Westlands children. The Plane Street children, on the other hand, used past tense forms that could only be attributed to the influence of dialect. It might be argued, therefore, that on the evidence of their written work at least, the Plane Street children are more advanced in their language development than the Westlands children, since the past tense forms they use in writing more closely reflect the forms used by the adult members of their local community.

It is worth noting, in addition, that *ain't* did not occur in the written texts analysed in the present study, as was the case for Whiteman's data, but that negative concord did occur, together with other grammatical dialect forms that do not involve suffixes (relative pronoun forms, demonstrative *them*, *never* as a negative preterite form and non-standard prepositional usage). The present study does not, therefore, confirm Whiteman's findings that there were few or no occurrences of forms that did not involve suffixes, although it remains to be seen whether the written texts of older children, which have still to be analysed as part of the larger study, will reveal that they use fewer or different dialect features in their writing.

Features of Speech Occurring in School Written Work

The data were also analysed for a second set of variables — features which normally occur only in speech in adults, but which, given the close alliance between speech and writing, might be expected to occur in the writing of young children.

The differences between speech and writing have been widely documented and it is not possible in this chapter to examine the children's writing for all the syntactic and morphological features characteristic of speech. Certain constructions, therefore, that have been identified in the literature as features of informal, unplanned spoken language have been selected for analysis (see Perera, 1986; Chafe, 1982; Ochs, 1979; Brown, 1982). The examples are all taken from the children's written texts.

1.	Sentence Initiator *Well*	*Well* Vanilla and Vanessa . . .
2.	Left Dislocation	*My dog*, it was just about to come down.
3.	Indefinite *this*	They showed us *this* antler.
4.	Amplificatory Noun Tags	There was this frog sitting on a pond, *a china frog*.
5.	Vague Completers	We were checked *and stuff*.
6.	*Sort of/kind of*	I went up to get my *sort of* ribbon thing.
7.	Tags	It was quite a thing *it was*.
8.	Emphatic features	He woke up *ever so* suddenly.

Results

Table 4 shows that examples of all the features 1 to 8 occurred in the Westlands texts. Only features 1, 2, 3, 6, 7 and 8 occurred in the Plane Street School sample.

Table 5 shows the features of spoken English per 100 words in the written texts of the two groups of children. Although scores were not high, at least one example of each oral feature occurred in the data. There appeared to be no correlation between the use of non-standard dialect features and oral features in the children's writing. This would suggest that the use of oral features in writing is not connected with any social group, but may be due to other factors; the individual child's relationship with the teacher, for example, or the ease and fluency with which the child writes. The Westlands girls whose work contained the highest number of oral features appeared to have close and friendly relations with their readers, i.e. their teachers. One girl included messages such as 'continued in a minute' and explanations in parenthesis such as 'Woody (short for Woodruff)' in her writing. The boy with the highest score, a Plane Street pupil, also adopted a confiding and informative tone: 'if they are racing pigeons there

TABLE 4   *Numbers of Features of Speech Occurring in Written Texts*

	Westlands		Plane Street	
	Boys	*Girls*	*Boys*	*Girls*
1. *Well*	-	11	2	1
2. Left Dislocation	2	4	4	1
3. Indefinite *this*	6	8	10	11
4. Amplificatory Noun Tag	-	1	-	-
5. Vague Completer	-	3	-	-
6. *Sort of/kind of*	3	10	2	1
7. Tags	-	1	1	-
8. Emphatic Particles	3	9	3	3
	14	47	22	17
Total:	61		39	

TABLE 5.   *Features of Spoken English per 100 Words*

	Westlands	Plane Street
Boys	0.04	0.17
Girls	0.20	0.14

will be a ring on them — well they have to because if they don't . . .' Such parentheses and asides suggest that far from being unskilled writers, these children are in fact very aware of their audience and are writing fluently. They appear to have passed through the preparation stage of learning to write, during which the mechanics of letter formation, handwriting and spelling inhibit performance, to the consolidation stage (see Kroll & Vann, 1981), when writing catches up with speech and is 'personal, colloquial and text-bound.' It was evident from the data however, that not every child in the sample had reached this stage of development. Children who wrote less fluently and who appeared to have difficulty with the mechanics of writing, such as letter-formation or spelling, tended to include very few features of speech in their written texts. The following text provides an illustration of such a child's work:

> 'I have pigings the same has Alan anb i hev brawn eyes im going to hev a skinhead hoefully to i am small.'

Responding to Dialect Features in Children's Writing

The aims of English teaching have undergone several changes since the abolition of the eleven plus examination in the early 1960s and the subsequent movement away from prescriptivism and concentration on form. English teachers today are seen as responsible for teaching and assessing a wide range of skills which include not only spoken and written language, but in some cases 'the development of self-awareness and the ability to cope with personal relationships' (Gannon & Czerniewska, 1980). Such a wide ranging brief, however, poses problems for teachers when marking written compositions. Expert advice is varied. The Bullock Report (1975) suggests: 'Only after responding to what has been said, is it reasonable to turn attention to how.'

Stewart Frome in his note of dissent to the Report takes the opposite view: 'There is not the rigorous critical marking of spelling, punctuation and grammatical error which there needs to be.'

Stibbs (1979) stresses the need for teachers to attempt to 'assess the qualities of the thought processes' rather than placing emphasis on 'accuracy in speech, writing and reading.'

In the event, many teachers appear to try to compromise between rigorous critical marking of surface features and attempting to assess the thought qualities, adopting the technique of a teacher quoted in Gannon (1985:16): 'I look for the important mistakes and make a general comment.'

The occurrence of non-standard dialect features in children's scripts poses further problems. Advice once again is varied. Gannon states that condoning the use of dialect features 'in the belief that one is freeing the child from the constraints of standard English and doing something to dismantle the power structures of society' is as wrong as inferring that the use of dialect leads to disintegration of moral standards (Gannon, 1985: 27).

He proposes that dialect features in the child's writing should not be crossed out in red, but 'some pointers to social and situational contexts should be given.'

Thornton (1980) also stresses the need for teachers to understand the social and linguistic nature of the problem and urges teachers to encourage children to make the right choices when writing since, 'all children have well-developed intuitions about language choice.'

Edwards (1979) argues that standard English should be used for all school writing and that consistency of approach in the early school years would make 'the ability to produce standard written English where it is required more easily acquired.'

Perera (1984), Edwards (1983) and Richmond (1979), however, advise teachers to ignore dialect features until children are able to discuss them with their teachers. In Perera's view, this would take place once the consolidation stage (see Kroll, 1981) is complete and children are becoming aware of the differences between speech and writing (on average about the age of nine or ten). Edwards recommends that 'in the majority of cases it would seem more prudent to concentrate on the technical aspects of writing, leaving dialect features alone, at least until the last few years of school.' Richmond believes that discussion of dialect features can be left until the fourth year of secondary school when dialect users should be encouraged to use standard forms, lest they are penalised in public examinations.

Trudgill (1975) takes the view that, while standard English should be used in certain kinds of texts, such as business letters or official correspondence, there are occasions, in the writing of personal letters, for instance, when children should be free to employ the grammatical forms that come most naturally to them.

The assumption made by the above writers is that teachers themselves are acquainted with the features of the local dialect and are able to distinguish between such features and genuine mistakes. Teachers interviewed in the course of the present research, however, indicated that they were not sure what constituted local dialect in Reading, and they did not appear to have a consistent policy for dealing with non-standard features that occurred in the children's work. While there were considerable differences between teachers in the number of corrections they made, individual teachers also appeared to be somewhat inconsistent in their own marking and dialect features were corrected in some instances and not in others. Figure 2 shows the percentages of dialect features that were corrected in the written texts of the two groups.

The efficacy of such corrections, however, cannot be guaranteed. The work of one of the Plane Street children, Jackie, provides an illustration of the dilemma that some children face when their non-standard variety encompasses the use of two variable forms — in this case *done* and *did* as past tense forms of DO — whereas standard English has only one. The following sentences occurred in Jackie's work in the course of the two terms:

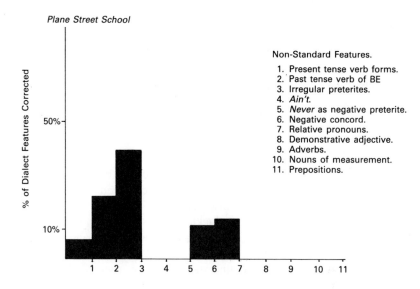

Non-Standard Features.

1. Present tense verb forms.
2. Past tense verb of BE
3. Irregular preterites.
4. *Ain't*.
5. *Never* as negative preterite.
6. Negative concord.
7. Relative pronouns.
8. Demonstrative adjective.
9. Adverbs.
10. Nouns of measurement.
11. Prepositions.

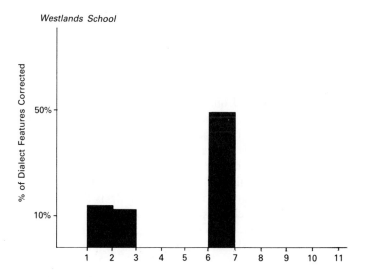

FIGURE 2   *Teachers' corrections of non-standard dialect features*

We down the housework.

we don don done are homework.

My brother dond (i) done *did* (ii) a jigsaw.   (i.   Jackie's correction)

                                                      (ii. Teacher's correction)

We done did a bit more dancing   (Jackie's correction)

When we had done did some housework   (Jackie's correction)

A further illustration is found in the work of another Plane Street child, Susan:

We was were was in the park.   (Susan's correction)

Such examples reveal the underlying uncertainty felt by some children of this age who speak a non-standard dialect, when faced with the need to write standard English. They also call into question the efficacy of teacher's corrections, which in Jackie's case led to hypercorrection. Shaughnessy (1977) identifies this uncertainty when she suggests that

> when learners move into uncertain territory, they tend to play by the rules, even when the rules lead them to produce forms that sound completely wrong. Their intuitions have proved them wrong in so many instances that they may even conclude that sounding wrong is a sign of being right (Shaugnessy, 1977: 99).

Conclusion

The present data indicate that 10-year-old primary school children in the two schools investigated use features of spoken English in their school writing, though, as we saw, the extent to which they do so appears to depend on a number of different factors. The data also indicate that children who use non-standard dialect forms in speech are likely to use some of these dialectal forms in their writing. Certain features such as non-standard past tense verb forms occurred more frequently than others, but this might be attributed to the nature of the writing task, which usually took the form of a narrative or a personal account. Although all the non-standard speaking children used some dialect forms, there was considerable individual variation, which possibly reflects the many factors that come into play when a child is learning to write: individual verbal skills; ability to control the mechanics of writing; the ability to style shift; the nature of the writing task; the relationship with the audience; the influence of reading; etc.

Children who spoke standard English used some dialect features, but not as many as those who spoke non-standard English, and with a much lower frequency. Furthermore, some of the features that were considered as 'non-standard' may be more appropriately considered as developmental features or as features of spoken English. Since children's early writing bears a close relationship to their speech, it is hardly surprising that these three types of features occur in their writing, although it is problematic for the analyst — and presumably for the teachers — when they share the same form.

The multiplicity of variables to consider when assessing a piece of writing is reflected in the variety of correcting strategies used by the teachers in the sample. Whereas some teachers simply made a global assessment in the form of a general comment at the end of the text, others corrected individual features, although in both schools only a relatively small percentage of dialect features were corrected. No features of spoken language occurring in sample texts were corrected or commented on.

Government educational policy, examining boards, and employers still expect children to be able to produce standard written English when required. An alternative approach to attempting to eliminate dialect errors in children's writing might be to offer standard written English as a separate variety and to increase the input of written models. A suitable time to broach this would be in secondary school, when most children have fully mastered the mechanics of writing and are sophisticated enough to be able to benefit from some discussion of differences between spoken and written language, standard and non-standard varieties, and their appropriate uses. Moreover, there is evidence to suggest that by the time they reach their teens, children are able to style shift and are likely to have access to more than one variety of English (Labov, 1972; Cheshire, 1982a). In order to initiate such discussions, however, teachers themselves must be aware of the differences between varieties and of the specific features that are likely to occur in the speech and writing of the children of the area where they teach (see Edwards & Cheshire, this volume, chapter 12).

Finally, there seems, as yet, to be little in the way of policy for dealing with dialect features that occur in school writing. Teachers appear to deal with such features on an *ad hoc* individual basis. A solution to the problem might be found if, as Richmond (1979) suggests, each school had a coherent and consistent policy for dealing with non-standard dialect features that occur in written work. Guidelines for teachers would acquaint them with the main features of dialects occurring in the school, and with the ages at which children could be expected to style shift or at least to benefit from metalinguistic discussions. Such guidelines would enable

teachers of writing to distinguish between genuine mistakes and features
that form part of their pupils' local dialect, and to encourage writing that
incorporates all varieties in their pupils' repertoires.

References

ALLEN, R.L. 1966 Written English is a 'second language'. *English Journal* 55,
    739–46.
BAUGH, A.C. and CABLE, T. 1978 *A History of the English Language*. London:
    Routledge & Kegan Paul.
BENNETT, N. 1980 *Open Plan Schools*. Windsor: NFER for Schools Council.
BRITTON, J., BURGESS, A., MARTIN, N., MCLEOD, A. and ROSEN, H. 1975 *The
    Development of Writing Abilities 11–18*. London: Macmillan.
BROWN, G. 1982 The spoken language. In R. CARTER (ed.), *Linguistics and the
    Teacher*. London: Routledge & Kegan Paul.
BULLOCK, SIR A. 1975 *A Language for Life*. London: HMSO.
CHAFE, W. 1982 Integration and involvement in speaking, writing and oral
    literature. *Spoken and Written Language 9* Advances in Discourse Processes.
    N. Jersey: Ablex.
CHESHIRE, J. 1982a *Variation in an English Dialect: A Sociolinguistic Study*.
    Cambridge: Cambridge University Press.
—— 1982b Dialect features and linguistic conflict in school. *Educational Review*
    34: 1, 53–56.
EDWARDS, J. 1979 *Language and Disadvantage*. London: Edward Arnold.
EDWARDS, V. 1983 *Language in Multicultural Classrooms*. London: Batsford
    Academic.
EDWARDS, V., TRUDGILL, P. and WELTENS, B. 1984 *The Grammar of English
    Dialect: A Survey of Research*. London: ESRC.
GANNON, P. 1985 *Assessing Writing: Principles and Practice of Marking Written
    English*. London: Edward Arnold.
GANNON, P. and CZERNIEWSKA, P. 1980 *Using Linguistics: An Educational Focus*.
    London: Edward Arnold.
HARTWELL, P. 1980 Dialect influence in writing: a critical view. *Research in the
    Teaching of English* 14: 2, 101–18.
HUGHES, G.A. and TRUDGILL, P. 1987 *English Accents and Dialects: An
    Introduction to Social and Regional Varieties of British English* (2nd edn).
    London: Edward Arnold.
KIRSCHNER, S. and POTEET, G 1973 Non-standard English usage in the writing of
    Black, White and Spanish remedial English students in an urban community
    college. *Research in the Teaching of English* 7, 351–55.
KRESS, G. 1982 *Learning to Write*. London: Routledge & Kegan Paul.
KROLL, B. 1981 Developmental relationships between speaking and writing. In
    B. KROLL and R. VANN (eds), *Exploring Speaking/Writing Relationships
    Connections and Contrasts*. Urbana, Ill.: National Council of Teachers of
    English.
KROLL, B. and VANN, R. (eds) 1981 *Exploring Speaking/Writing Relationships
    Connections and Contrasts*. Urbana, Ill.: National Council of Teachers of
    English.

LABOV, W. 1972 *Language in the Inner City*. Philadelphia: University of Pennsylvania Press.

OCHS, E. 1979 Planned and unplanned discourse. *Syntax and Semantics* 12. New York: Academic Press.

PERERA, K. 1984 *Children's Writing and Reading: Analysing Classroom Language*. Oxford: Blackwell.

—— 1986 Language acquisition and writing. In P. FLETCHER & M. GARMON (eds), *Language Acquisition* (2nd edition). Cambridge: Cambridge University Press.

QUIRK, R., GREENBAUM, S., LEECH, G. and SVARTVIK, J. 1972 *A Grammar of Contemporary English*. London: Longman.

—— 1985 *A Comprehensive Grammar of the English Language*. London: Longman.

RICHMOND, J. 1979 Dialect features in mainstream school writing. *New Approaches to Multiracial Education* 8, 10–15.

RUBIN, D. 1975 *Teaching Elementary Language Arts*. New York: Holt, Rinehart & Winston.

SHAUGHNESSY, M. 1977 *Errors and Expectations. A Guide for the Teacher of Basic Writing*. New York: Oxford University Press.

STIBBS, A. 1979 *Assessing Children's Language*. London: National Association for the Teaching of English.

THORNTON, G. 1980 *Teaching Writing: The Development of Written Language Skills*. London: Edward Arnold.

TOUGH, J. 1977 *Talking and Learning: A Guide to Fostering Communication Skills in Nursery and Infant Schools*. London: Ward Lock Educational.

TRUDGILL, P. 1975 *Accent, Dialect and the School*. London: Edward Arnold.

WHITEMAN, M. 1981 Dialect influence in writing. In M.F. WHITEMAN (ed.) *Writing: The Nature, Development and Teaching of Written Communication*. Vol 1. New Jersey: Lawrence Erlbaum Associates.

WOLFRAM, W. and WHITEMAN, M. 1971 The role of dialect interference in composition. *Florida F.L. Reporter* 9, 34–38.

12 The survey of British dialect grammar

VIV EDWARDS and JENNY CHESHIRE

Background

Our knowledge of the phonology of British dialects is considerably in advance of our knowledge of dialect grammar. This can be illustrated, for instance, by the range of books which overview dialect phonology and lexis (including, most notably, Orton *et al.*, 1978; Hughes & Trudgill, 1979; and Wells, 1982) and the dearth of comparable material on morphology and syntax. It is also confirmed by the findings of *The Grammar of English Dialect: A Survey of Research* (Edwards, Trudgill & Weltens, 1984). This overview of research from the beginning of the present century up to 1982 refers to more than 200 studies and abstracts any information about grammar presented either directly or indirectly in the studies. By far the greatest part of this information is derived from discussions of phonology or lexis, in which grammar plays only a peripheral role.

A number of important conclusions emerge from this report. It is evident, for instance, that research on the grammar of non-standard dialects of English is very unevenly distributed. Certain areas have been fairly well documented, although a good deal more work remains to be done, while others have received little or no attention. It is also clear that dialect description is as central to linguistic theory as standard English, and may even be instrumental in challenging assumptions about certain forms and functions which, up to the present, have been based on the description of the standard. But dialect research also has important educational assumptions. It is the educational rather than the theoretical linguistic dimension which we wish to explore in this chapter.

Dialect and British Education

The British education system is based entirely on the assumption that both teachers and pupils will use standard English. Given that the majority of British children are in fact speakers of a non-standard dialect of English (cf. Hughes & Trudgill, 1979), a number of problems can be anticipated. First, it is possible that linguistic stereotyping will lead teachers to evaluate dialect-speaking children more negatively than their standard English speaking peers (cf. J. Edwards, 1979; V. Edwards, 1979); second, a wide range of pedagogic practices are likely to result from inadequate information as to the nature of dialect difference (V. Edwards, 1983; Cheshire, 1984).

Clearly a major step in avoiding bad pedagogic practice would be for teachers to become more aware of the nature of dialect differences and of their educational implications. As Rosen & Burgess (1980) point out:

> The onus is here placed firmly on the teachers not only to adopt a positive attitude to dialect, but also to make sufficient effort to learn about the features of dialect to avoid confusing the children.

The need to recognise the differences between dialect grammar and standard English grammar has been given considerable emphasis recently in the Department of Education and Science's (1984) Pamphlet which attempts to formulate a consistent language policy for schools. For instance, one of the objectives listed for 16-year-old pupils is that they should be aware of the differences between standard English grammar and dialect forms, and use standard English when it is appropriate to do so. The second edition (1986) modifies this so that they are now expected simply to 'use the grammar and vocabulary of spoken standard English where necessary or appropriate'. In both cases, the burden of coping with the differences between dialect grammar and standard English grammar is given to teachers. However, it is unfair and unrealistic to place the responsibility for remedying the mistreatment of dialect in school with teachers when there is so little material on dialect grammar for them to consult.

A start has been made in this direction by James and Lesley Milroy who have been commissioned by the Economic and Social Research Council to edit a volume on regional variations in British syntax (Milroy & Milroy, in press). The intended audience is teachers, speech therapists and others whose work brings them into direct contact with issues related to dialect. The volume will contain a brief account of relevant sociolinguistic topics and short descriptions of Southern English, Scots English, Hiberno-English and Newcastle English. These are the areas of the British Isles which have been relatively well-documented. However, a great deal more work remains to be done on these areas and on others for which there is little or no suitable material for teachers to consult.

The Survey of British Dialect Grammar

It is against this background that the Survey of British Dialect Grammar was conceived. Recognition of the legitimacy of the language which children bring with them to school has gained considerable momentum in recent years, although a great deal more work remains to be done. A host of government reports and other influential publications have acknowledged the danger that negative attitudes towards non-standard speech may be translated into negative attitudes towards non-standard speakers, and have acknowledged the importance of valuing the language and culture of the child's home (see, for instance, Bullock, 1975; DES, 1984; Swann, 1985).

This theme is mirrored in the mushrooming of 'language awareness' programmes both in primary schools and, as part of the modern languages or English curriculum, in secondary schools (see Hawkins, 1984; Jones, this volume, chapter 17). A central tenet of such programmes is that the children themselves are the experts and that their knowledge of their own language can be used in understanding and explaining a wide range of social issues which are important for us all.

Developments in this direction open up genuine opportunities for teachers and linguists to talk to each other. On the one hand, teachers are interpreting the accumulated knowledge of linguists, and, particularly, the findings of sociolinguists, to their pupils. On the other hand, the rapidly expanding awareness of language in teachers and children raises many new possibilities for linguists.

The acute shortage of funds for research at all levels in the United Kingdom at present means that the prospect of extending our knowledge of dialect syntax is bleak. A full-scale study drawing on the expertise of a team of linguists and based on a corpus of the recorded speech of a representative range of speakers throughout the country is simply not achievable in the current economic climate. However, given the surge of interest in language at primary and secondary levels, schools can now become a starting place for the collection of data on dialect grammar. Our project therefore aims to enlist the help of teachers and their pupils in discovering regional features of English syntax. Given the shortage of funds, the project has the difficult task of making maximum progress with a minimum of resources. The survey will therefore take the form of a questionnaire rather than more direct and intensive methods of data collection.

Working with teachers and their pupils is not, of course, a straightforward process. Because non-standard dialects have low status and are the subject of a great deal of corrective pressure from teachers, it would be optimistic in the extreme to imagine that data on dialect grammar usage collected from unprepared pupils would be reliable. For this reason, our dialect survey was conceived as the end point of an extended period of work on language, which could be viewed as a collaborative effort between teachers and pupils. This approach to learning departs significantly from the traditional model, but is by no means novel or unique, and collaborative learning techniques have attracted a considerable following in the United Kingdom in recent years.

Such techniques are important for a project which centres on non-standard language, for a variety of reasons. First, many teachers will not come from the region in question or will themselves be standard English speakers. They will therefore need to call upon the expertise of their pupils. Raleigh (1981), for instance, prefaces *The Languages Book* thus:

> Everyone who reads this book knows much more about language than can be put in a book. Everyone has managed the amazing job of learning at least one language — and when you think about it, you use even *one* language in so many different ways that even *one* is a lot. So you're the expert; make sure you tell the others what *you* know about language and the way it works.

Second, it is essential that discussions of linguistic diversity are handled with care and sensitivity, in order to avoid alienating speakers of non-standard varieties of English. The material of the ILEA English Centre's (1979) booklet on 'Dialect and Language Variety', for example, has been criticised for adopting an 'us' and 'them' approach which does nothing to help those children who have to choose between in-group loyalty and educational participation (see Mercer & Maybin, 1981). If dialect is investigated as a joint project, with the pupils seen as the experts, this should not only provide an excellent opportunity for collaborative learning, but should also help to ensure that the topic is treated with the necessary respect and tact.

Finally, collaborative techniques are useful for ensuring the reliability of subjects' responses. We ask teachers and pupils to discuss as a group the local occurrence of various linguistic features, and to respond to questions on the basis of community rather than individual usage. It would seem that the normative pressures of the group counteract the tendency of individual speakers to deny non-standard usage (see V. Edwards, 1986, for a review of several studies which have produced very reliable results using this approach).

Progress to date

The project began in January, 1986. Our work over the first two years can be organised into five main areas: designing the lesson suggestions and the questionnaire; carrying out the pilot project; gathering information on dialect resources; setting up the national network of teacher contacts; and the preliminary analysis of the questionnaire data.

The lesson suggestions and the questionnaire

If children were to provide reliable information rather than simply the answers which they assumed their teachers wanted, it was felt essential that a period of work on language awareness should precede the administration of the questionnaire. In order to reinforce this point, a programme of suggested lesson outlines and materials was developed, tried out as part of the pilot project described below, and modified in the light of teacher comment.

The questionnaire (see the Appendix) was based on the main areas of difference in English dialect grammar described in Edwards, Trudgill & Weltens (1984). Care was taken to arrange the 196 items in as clear and graphically acceptable a manner as possible, bearing in mind that the questionnaires would be completed by pupils of a wide range of ages and abilities. The questionnaire is three pages long and risks placing an unreasonable strain on the concentration of younger and less able pupils. If teachers find that this is the case, we suggest that classes working collaboratively should divide into three separate groups, each dealing with one page of the questionnaire. The general design and contents of the questionnaire were revised in the light of comments from teachers taking part in the pilot project.

The pilot project

Industrial action taken by teachers in 1985/6 made it impossible to establish the pilot stage of the project as early as we would have wished. It took place in the closing weeks of the summer term in a comprehensive school in Reading, Berkshire, which has 1,500 pupils from a wide variety of social and ethnic backgrounds. It involved seven teachers and some 200 pupils of all abilities, between the ages of 11 and 15.

Collaboration with teachers and pupils during the course of the pilot project enabled us to identify and remedy a number of practical and organisational difficulties with the administration and the design of the questionnaire. It also allowed us to establish that the use of the questionnaire was feasible with a wide band of ages and abilities.

The results of the questionnaire were pleasing. Children's appraisals of those dialect grammar forms that are to be heard in their town coincided closely with those which we know, on the basis of previous research (see Cheshire, 1982), actually do occur. The pilot exercise reinforced our view that, because we are asking children to report on the speech of others rather than on their own speech, the data which we collect will be sufficiently reliable for a preliminary survey.

Information on dialect resources

One of the consequences of the industrial action and the unavailability of schools and teachers was that there risked being insufficient work for the research officer employed to work on the project. We attempted to retrieve the situation by collecting information on dialect resources. This was an exercise which was of considerable relevance for any study of dialect grammar, and which could take place totally independently of teachers.

Press releases were sent to provincial newspapers and local radio stations, and requests for information were sent to county libraries. A great deal of interest has been generated and the response was far more enthusiastic than we believed possible. We now have in our possession a very wide range of information on books, pamphlets, newspaper columns, records and cassettes, local radio broadcasts, sound archives, details of dialect societies and local events. The Economic and Social Research Council has agreed to fund the compilation of this information into a Directory of Dialect Resources, which will be an invaluable resource for teachers wishing to incorporate work on dialect in language awareness programmes or other kinds of language work.

The teacher network

In order to ensure that the dialect survey covered as much of the British Isles as possible, we attempted to establish a network of schools and individuals who would agree to take part in the survey. The first step in establishing this network was to write articles in the *Times Educational Supplement* and the *Education Guardian*, two widely read and highly influential teacher publications, explaining the aims and methods of the research project and inviting teachers to take part. Teachers have also been located through a wide range of other contacts, including examination boards, colleges and universities.

The final total of completed questionnaires is likely to be around 100, a number far short of what we anticipated. Several different factors explain this disappointing rate of response. All schools in the UK during the period that work on the Survey has taken place have faced serious problems. The effects of the industrial action taken by teachers during 1985–6 were still being felt during 1987; in addition to this, teachers had to prepare for the introduction of the new GCSE public examinations in 1988. These problems have been a major contributing factor to the problems of data collection, but with the benefit of hindsight, we can see that it is not possible to seriously sustain a nationwide network of teachers without considerably greater financial resources than we have had available. Nevertheless, the questionnaires that have been completed cover most of England and some of Wales (though not Scotland or Northern Ireland). We anticipate that we will achieve our aim of producing some guidelines for teachers on the regional distribution of features of British English syntax, though each set of guidelines may have to encompass a wider geographical area than we had originally anticipated.

Preliminary analysis of questionnaire data

It is too early either to make pronouncements on the validity of our methodology or to generalise about the patterns emerging from the data. None the less, it would seem in order to make a few generalisations on the progress of our work to date.

Teachers who return the questionnaires are invited to comment on the usefulness of working on dialect issues in the ways which we suggest in the lesson outlines, and on the practicalities surrounding the completion of the questionnaire. Responses have, without exception, been favourable. The general feeling is that the topics used as a basis for classwork have been very successful and have often generated a great deal of discussion and, indeed, written work. The following examples are typical of the kind of comments we have received–

Many thanks for providing an interesting activity which raised many questions from my classes and was an excellent end of term project.

The children found the work and discussions interesting. What I personally found useful was the development in their minds of the thought that we do use different ways of speaking and writing to different people and in different circumstances. This had an interesting pay-off: if I, the teacher, agreed that it was alright for them to speak in their way, they were more prepared to agree that in talking and writing in more formal situations there was a generally accepted form.

The students seemed to enjoy the work. Most of them took seriously the task of writing about the way they speak and, as you'll see, some of them also wrote about the way they write.

We are, however, very aware of the limitations of data collection using questionnaires, and we have tried to guard against them wherever possible. Each questionnaire is examined on return to see if schools have reported examples of dialect usage which, on the basis of existing knowledge, is unexpected for their area. Although such examples are infrequent, they do occur. Our procedure is then to write to the teacher concerned to query the feature, or features, and to ask for further examples of sentences where it occurs, which will allow us to judge for ourselves whether misreporting has taken place. Wherever possible, we also try to cross-check cases of this kind with linguists working in the area.

The overwhelming majority of responses, however, are uncontroversial and we feel confident that with one important proviso, we will be able to produce the fullest description to date of British dialect syntax. This proviso is as follows: any description based on data collected using questionnaire techniques must be viewed as both provisional and preliminary rather than as a definitive account. The primary purpose of analysis of this data should therefore be to point to areas which merit further in-depth analysis using more reliable data collection techniques.

Conclusions

Awareness of the importance of variation in dialect grammar on the part of both linguists and educationalists is certainly greater today than at any point in the past. There is a general acceptance of the desirability of producing linguistically sound descriptions of dialect grammar and of making these descriptions accessible to teachers. The work of the Survey of British Dialect Grammar is an important initiative in this area. Although it will only be possible to treat its findings as tentative, it will, at the very least, present a broad picture of variation and will point to those areas of the country where future research can be most usefully carried out.

The aims of the survey are, of course, far broader than the purely linguistic considerations of charting dialect variation. We have formed a useful focus for a great deal of work in the area of language awareness in British schools and have been able to establish both the practicality and the usefulness of recognising teachers and school children as experts and researchers in their own right. Finally, we have made a start in documenting the many dialect resources which exist and which should form an extremely valuable teaching resource.

Appendix

Questionnaire for the survey of British dialect grammar

No, no a thousand times no!

1. ☐ **Dinna** run too fast
2. ☐ Count on me, I **won't** do **nothing** silly
3. ☐ You **shouldna** go in there!
4. ☐ You've **no** to go in there!
5. ☐ **Anyone** mustn't go in there
6. ☐ My friend broke that, **I never**
7. ☐ No, I **never** broke that
8. ☐ **Will you not** try to mend it – we need an expert
9. ☐ That **ain't** working
10. ☐ That **in't** working
11. ☐ That **ay** working

Got a sweet tooth?

12. ☐ I **likes** toffees
13. ☐ We **liken** toffees
14. ☐ We **likes** toffees
15. ☐ Thee **likes** toffees
16. ☐ Thee **like** toffees
17. ☐ She **like** toffees

What an idiot!

18. ☐ Billy **be** stupid
19. ☐ Billy **am** stupid
20. ☐ He **in arf** stupid
21. ☐ **He's stupid, him**
22. ☐ **It's stupid he is**
23. ☐ **There's stupid he is**
24. ☐ **He's stupid is Billy**
25. ☐ **It was stupid he was**
26. ☐ He **done** that wrong
27. ☐ You **has** to see it to believe it

Wedding Bells

28. ☐ Mary and John **is** getting married on Saturday.
29. ☐ There's cars outside the Church
30. ☐ The bride's walking into the Church, **is it?**
31. ☐ I'm going to see them now, **isn't it?**
32. ☐ I **done bought** them a wedding present.

Happy Birthday!

33. ☐ We always **has** a big cake on our birthday
34. ☐ I **give** her a birthday present yesterday
35. ☐ I **gived** her a birthday present yesterday
36. ☐ What **have** her mother bought her?

37. ☐ We've **gotten** her a present, too – a car!
38. ☐ Is that the car I **see** last night?
39. ☐ Is that the car I **seed** last night?
40. ☐ Is that the car I **sawed** last night?
41. ☐ Is that the car I **seen** last night?
42. ☐ **Do** it go fast?
43. ☐ **Does** we want to go fast?

44. ☐ Fred **do** motor mechanics at college.
45. ☐ But I **does** it at school
46. ☐ She was **sat** over there looking at her car
47. ☐ And he was **stood** in the corner looking at it
48. ☐ I've **a-found** my keys. Let's go!

Music is the food of love...

49. ☐ You **was** singing
50. ☐ You **wan** singing
51. ☐ We **was** singing
52. ☐ We **wan** singing
53. ☐ They **was** singing
54. ☐ They **wan** singing
55. ☐ I **were** singing, too.
56. ☐ And so **were** John.
57 ☐ But Mary **weren't** singing

58. ☐ There **was** some singers here a minute ago
59. ☐ One of the singers said he'll **not can** stay
60. ☐ But he **might can** do it tomorrow.
61. ☐ The other one said he **won't can't** do it.

62. ☐ You **must** be at your music class by 9 a.m.
63. ☐ You **mun** be at your music class by 9 a.m.
64. ☐ You **maun** be at your music class by 9 a.m.
65. ☐ He's out of tune, he **must** be tone deaf.
66. ☐ He's out of tune, he **mun** be tone deaf
67. ☐ He's out of tune, he **maun** be tone deaf

Do as I tell you!

68. ☐ You **haven't got to** be late, or you'll be in trouble
69. ☐ **Let you be listening to me**, Joanna
70. ☐ **Do ee listen to me**.
71. ☐ **Don't be talking** like that
72. ☐ **Not do that**, John

Running repairs

73. ☐ I've come **for to** mend the window
74. ☐ And I've come **for** mend the door.
75. ☐ We **managed mend** it ourselves.
76. ☐ We'd like to **looken** at the TV you broke
77. ☐ How the dog **do jumpy**! He'll knock it over.
78. ☐ I **know** that builder all my life.
79. ☐ She's been a walking disaster **since she's here**
80. ☐ **Are you waiting** long for the plumber?
81. ☐ **He's after going**.
82. ☐ He **has it mended** twice already

Food Glorious food

83. ☐ **Did** you have your dinner yet?
84. ☐ We're **a-going** to start eating now
85. ☐ **Are you wanting** something to eat?
86. ☐ I like pasta. It cooks really **quick.**
87. ☐ Look! The kettle **boils.**
88. ☐ We**'re gone** shopping.
89. ☐ I **d' eat** chicken every day
90. ☐ I **do be eating** chicken every day
91. ☐ I **be eating** chicken every day
92. ☐ I **did eat** chicken every day when I lived there
93. ☐ And I **did eat** chicken yesterday, too.

Count down

94. ☐ That town is nearly twenty **mile** away
95. ☐ To make a big cake you need two **pound** of flour
96. ☐ This string is three **inch** long
97. ☐ This is a **scissors**

Up and Over

98. ☐ He **ups** and gets at him
99. ☐ He knocks his hat **off of** his head
100. ☐ Stop it! He's my best friend, **like**
101. ☐ Goodbye, I'll **away** now
102. ☐ She goes to church **of** a Sunday
103. ☐ If you **had've** been there you would have seen her
104. ☐ If you **would've** been there, you would have seen her
105. ☐ We live **aside** the cinema.
106. ☐ We're **going** pictures

107. ☐ I'm going **up** my friend's house later
108. ☐ I'm going **down** my friends house later
109. ☐ I'm going **over** my friend's house later

Scared stiff

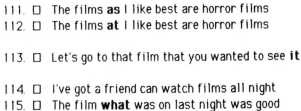

110. ☐ The films **what** I like best are horror films
111. ☐ The films **as** I like best are horror films
112. ☐ The films **at** I like best are horror films

113. ☐ Let's go to that film that you wanted to see **it**

114. ☐ I've got a friend can watch films all night
115. ☐ The film **what** was on last night was good
116. ☐ The film **at** was on last night was good
117. ☐ The film **as** was on last night was good

118. ☐ That's the girl **what's** mum loves horror films
119. ☐ That's the girl **at's her** mum loves horror films
120. ☐ That's the girl **as her** mum loves horror films
121. ☐ That's the girl **what her** mum loves horror films
122. ☐ That's the girl **that her** mum loves horror films

123. ☐ **Himself** gets scared
124. ☐ Did you see **herself** there?
125. ☐ Look at **them** big spiders
126. ☐ Look at **thon** spiders
127. ☐ Look at **they** big spiders
128. ☐ Look at **this** big spiders
129. ☐ And at **yon** big beetle
130. ☐ And at **thon** worm
131. ☐ Look at **thir** spider.
132. ☐ Look at **thick** spider.
133. ☐ Look at **thicky** spider.
134. ☐ Look at **thuck** spider.
135. ☐ Look at **theasum** spider.
136. ☐ And at **this here** worm
137. ☐ And at **that there** creature.

Possession is nine tenths of the law

138. ☐ Look at these coins. I found about **a fifty** of them
139. ☐ That's the father **on** Mary

140. ☐ Don't break the **cup's handle**
141. ☐ That's the **dogs's** dinner
142. ☐ These are my **father boots**
143. ☐ These are my father **boots laces**
144. ☐ Who **is** this book **belonging** to?
145. ☐ This is my book. **Whosen** is that?
146. ☐ **It** cover's got a mark on it.
147. ☐ **O'it** cover's got a mark on it.
148. ☐ **Give it me.** That's my book
149. ☐ **Give me it,** please
150. ☐ Would he do such a thing, **think you**?
151. ☐ I asked him **did he know** who had taken it?

Who's who?

152. ☐ **Her's** got a good appetite
153. ☐ **Him's** got a good appetite
154. ☐ **Them's** got a good appetite
155. ☐ **Me's** got a good appetite
156. ☐ Eat up **thee** cake
157. ☐ Eat up **thy cake**
158. ☐ **Thee's** hungry, I expect
159. ☐ Are **youse** hungry, too, you boys over there?
160. ☐ Give **I** a cup of tea!
161. ☐ Give **he** a cup of tea!
162. ☐ Give **she** a cup of tea!
163. ☐ Give **we** a cup of tea!
164. ☐ Give **they** a cup of tea!

165. ☐ This is **me** cup
166. ☐ This is **o'me** cup
167. ☐ This is **mines** cup
168. ☐ This is **he's** cup

169. ☐ That's my car, where's **yourn?**
170. ☐ That's my car, where's **hisn?**
171. ☐ That's my car, where's **hern?**
172. ☐ This is **us** car
173. ☐ This is **wer** car
174. ☐ This is **wir** car

175. ☐ We service it **usselves**
176. ☐ John likes doing that **hisself,** too
177. ☐ Yes, lots of people do it **theirselves**

Property page

178. ☐ This is the **beautifullest** house I've seen
179. ☐ This is the **most beautifullest** house I've seen
180. ☐ I've never seen a **beautifuller** one
181. ☐ I've never seen a **more beautifuller** one

182. ☐ This is a **more better** one
183. ☐ This is a **more betterer** one
184. ☐ John's got a nice house, but yours is **more nice**
185. ☐ But this is the **worstest** one I've seen
186. ☐ But this is the **baddest** one I've seen
187. ☐ I 've never seen a **worser** one
188. ☐ I 've never seen a **badder** one
189. ☐ We've got **a old** house
190. ☐ We've got **old** house
191. ☐ Your house is **an recent one**
192. ☐ I'd like to buy this house **without** you want it

193. ☐ I'll have **the headache** if I carry on talking
194. ☐ Yes, change the subject, **else** I'll go mad
195. ☐ Look **at time**: you're late for school!
196. ☐ You should **of** left half an hour ago!

References

Bullock, Sir A. 1975 *A Language for Life*. London: HMSO.

Cheshire, J. 1982 *Variation in an English Dialect: A Sociolinguistic Study*. Cambridge: Cambridge University Press.

—— 1984 Indigenous and non-standard English varieties and education. In P. Trudgill (ed.), *Language in the British Isles*. Cambridge: Cambridge University Press. pp. 546–48.

Department of Education and Science (DES) 1984 *English from 5–16. Curriculum Matters I*. London: HMSO.

—— 1986 *English from 5–16. Curriculum Matters I*. London: HMSO 2nd Edition.

Edwards, J. 1979 *Language and Disadvantage*. London: Edward Arnold.

Edwards, V. 1979 *The West Indian Language Issue in British Schools*. London: Routledge & Kegan Paul.

—— 1983 *Language in Multicultural Classrooms*. London: Batsford.

—— 1986 *Language in a Black Community*. Clevedon, Avon: Multilingual

EDWARDS, V., TRUDGILL, P. and WELTENS, B. 1984 *The Grammar of English Dialect: A Survey of Research.* London: Economic and Social Research Council.

ENGLISH CENTRE 1979 *Dialect and Language Variety.* ILEA English Centre, Sutherland Street, London SW1.

HAWKINS, E. 1984 *Awareness of Language.* Cambridge: Cambridge University Press.

HUGHES, A. and TRUDGILL, P. 1979 *English Accents and Dialects. An Introduction to Social and Regional Varieties of British English.* London: Edward Arnold.

MERCER, N. and MAYBIN, J. 1981 Community language and education. In N. MERCER (ed.), *Language in School and Community.* London: Edward Arnold.

MILROY, J. and MILROY, L. in press, *Regional variation in British English syntax.* London: Economic and Social Research Council.

ORTON, H., SANDERSON, S. and WIDDOWSON, J. (eds) 1978 *The Linguistic Atlas of England.* London: Croom Helm.

RALEIGH, M. 1981 *The Languages Book.* ILEA English Centre, Sutherland Street, London SW1.

ROSEN, H. and BURGESS, T. 1980 *Languages and Dialects of London School Children.* London: Ward Lock Educational.

SWANN, LORD 1985 *Education for All.* London: HMSO.

WELLS, J. 1982 *Accents of English.* Volume 3. Cambridge: Cambridge University Press.

Part III
Classroom initiatives

13 The development phase of the Kerkrade project

JOS VAN DEN HOOGEN and HENK KUIJPER

Introduction

The first two stages of the Kerkrade project (see Stijnen & Vallen, this volume, chapter 8) established the nature and degree of linguistic and educational difficulties faced by dialect-speaking children in this part of the Netherlands. The present chapter reports on the next task which was faced by the project team, namely the attempt to find solutions for these difficulties. In the first part of the chapter we will describe the composition of the project team, our aims and how we set about realising these aims. Then we will go on to report on the findings and the main conclusions which emerged from our development work in selected Kerkrade schools.

Participants and Methods

Composition of the project team

The practical nature of the development phase had implications for the composition of a project team which until this point had consisted mainly of linguists and educational researchers. After preliminary meetings with the teaching staff of a number of different primary schools we found three schools willing to participate: a primary school, a primary school with a nursery class and an independent nursery school. In order to establish a good working relationship, we felt it was essential to set up a working group in each school which would oversee the general direction of the project. These working parties consisted of: the teaching staff; a parent representative; a member of the National Council for Curriculum Development (SLO) in Enschede; a school counsellor from the regional Teachers' Resource Centre

(SPC) in Heerlen; a member of the Institute of Dialectology of the University of Nijmegen (NCDN); and a member of the Nijmegen Institute for Educational Research (NIVOR).

The project schools differed both in their teaching methods and in the linguistic and social class backgrounds of the children they worked with. The proportion of dialect-speaking children varied between 38% and 70% and the proportion of standard speakers between 13% and 54%. For the purposes of analysis, we divided the various school populations into four different groups: working class dialect speakers (DL); middle class dialect speakers (DH); working class standard speakers (SL) and middle class standard speakers (SH).

Methodology

The early stages

Initial analysis (see Stijnen & Vallen, this volume, chapter 8) pointed to three major areas of attention for this next stage of research: the oral participation of dialect speakers in class; the attitudes of teachers and pupils towards the use of dialect in school; and writing skills, with particular attention to children's ability to write in the standard language.

At the first meeting with the three working parties we discussed the findings in each of these three areas. The aim was to relate research results to the individual experience of parents and teachers. We also tried to come to an agreement as to which activities we would undertake. The research findings gave an overall picture of the main problems of school children in Kerkrade. Every teacher, however, has his or her own personal experience of these problems because every teacher is coping with different children and different teaching materials and has different ideas about education. On the basis of these early discussions, the working parties decided to concentrate for the first few months on the acceptance of dialect use in the classroom.

Acceptance of dialect in class

A number of priorities emerged in the period which followed, the most important of which were letting the children feel that their 'home language' was no longer taboo at school; accustoming both children and teacher to speaking dialect in the classroom; offering the children more possibilities for expressing themselves in dialect; and gathering information on which situations, areas of the curriculum and techniques promoted dialect usage in the classroom most successfully.

A wide range of activities was developed in order to encourage the use of dialect and to allow us to observe the children's reactions. This part of the research and development programme culminated in a conference at which all participants could exchange and evaluate their experiences. The most significant conclusion to emerge from this conference was that, while the acceptance of dialect is an important aspect of the problem, it was also important to develop a more direct and structured approach to the question of proficiency in the standard language.

A 'themes and skills' approach

It was felt that traditional teaching methods were not compatible with the aims of the project. Traditional teaching materials often display a very middle class and ethnocentric bias and are thus open to the criticism that they are irrelevant for the needs and interests of large sections of the school population (CWMO, 1980:15). In addition, the decontextualised language teaching drills which are often found in school textbooks do not encourage children to integrate and apply subskills learned separately into natural, communicative language use.

Arguments for a shift to a more communicative form of language teaching are based on recent insights into the relation between language and social factors. It is therefore understandable that many writers on this subject emphasise the view that language teaching should start from the children's own language experience. Communicative teaching techniques allow pupils to practise a structure by using it to exchange information or debate a subject. The communicative approach is thus based on the principle of 'learning language by using language'. In a broader sense, there are also more general goals, such as the development of social skills and the child's own personality (cf. CWMO, 1980:1).

A thematic or topic based approach to the curriculum lends itself very readily to the developments of communication skills. Students involved in discovering, processing and passing on information on a particular theme are exposed to a wide range of real communicative situations. This form of language teaching therefore encourages not only the development of oral skills but a communicative framework in which there is a place for both the standard language and the dialect.

It was important that the topic-based approach which we were advocating should be in line with the methods used in the participating schools, as well as with the age of the children and the educational philosophy of the teaching staff. The SLO member of the project team made suggestions to the teachers about ways of choosing a suitable theme on the basis of their existing materials. The guiding principle was that any reading material chosen should be relevant to the experience of children in Kerkrade. Once a topic was chosen, a number of tasks were devised which would allow children to deepen their knowledge of the subject. In this way the exercises in the traditional textbooks were replaced by a wide range of activities around a particular theme. We found that, as teachers gained experience in this approach, they put the textbooks aside and started to choose the themes for themselves.

Topic-based teaching is heavily predicated on communicative aspects of language. This does not mean, however, that attention cannot be paid to the training of subskills in supporting language lessons. Classes such as these can focus on the specific difficulties which stem from the children's linguistic background, especially in relation to using the standard in written language, since the norms for writing are much stricter than those for the spoken language.

In the course of the next few months, increased attention was paid to developing teaching methods to deal with interference from the dialect in the standard language. A great deal of effort was expended in ensuring that this approach would not be at odds with the tolerant attitudes towards children's use of dialect which had been developed in the early stages. The focus on dialect interference was, in any case, limited to work with older pupils who are more aware of the expectations and attitudes of Dutch society about grammatical correctness (cf. Kuijper *et al.*, 1979). It was also agreed that observation of and reflection on the language used by the children should play a central role in the development of these supporting activities.

Developing methods for teaching the standard

Any attempt to teach the standard depends on an understanding of the systematic similarities and differences between the standard and the dialect, and of the language learning problems which result. One of the difficulties which confront teachers of dialect-speaking children is that it is not always possible to discriminate between interlingual (i.e. caused by interference) and intralingual errors. Clear examples of interlingual errors would be dialect words or loan translations of dialect expressions used in the standard language. In many cases, however, it is not too obvious what has caused a particular error. If, to use one of Cheshire's (1982) examples, children in certain parts of England use the past tense form *bringed*, this error could be explained as arising from intralingual overgeneralisation of the conjugation of weak verbs in standard English. However, it may also have resulted from the interlingual transfer of the weak past tense form in the children's dialect. If we are to establish which interpretation is more plausible, we need to test both hypotheses experimentally. But teachers have no time and are not trained to do this.

Even when teachers know that a particular error is due to dialect interference, it is not immediately clear how they should respond. Further information is required: why and under what circumstances do linguistic differences lead to interference errors? Questions such as these clearly concern the psycholinguistic mechanisms underlying the production of an error.

Our practical suggestions to teachers for handling interference errors are based on the language neutral/language-specific hypothesis of Kellerman (1977), which attempts to explain why interference should be so prevalent in language learning situations where the L_1 and the L_2 are closely related. In brief, this hypothesis states that the occurrence of interference depends on the degree to which the second language learner is aware of differences between the first and second languages. If the learner believes that there is no difference between certain features in the first and second languages, these features will be language neutral and will be easily transferred to the second language. If the learner believes that a certain feature does not occur in the second language, then this feature will be language specific and will not easily be transferred to the second language.

We therefore proposed that teachers ask two questions concerning interference errors:

1.   Can pupils detect the errors in the utterances?
2.   If they can detect the errors, can they correct them themselves?

If children cannot detect an error, the item is probably language neutral and consequently they are not aware of having wrongly transferred it to the standard language. They will also be unable to correct the utterance afterwards. In this situation, they need specific teaching on the difference between the standard and the dialect.

By the same token, if children can detect the error in an utterance, but are unable to correct it, they are obviously aware that interference has taken place but, since they cannot correct the utterance, they probably have a gap in their knowledge of the standard language. In this case, too, the teacher should offer instruction on this particular standard language feature.

One promising form of standard language teaching which draws on these distinctions requires the teacher to collect a number of interference errors from children's writing and to incorporate these errors into a story. Children are then asked to underline what they think is wrong with the story and write in the appropriate form above the offending word. In this way it is possible to gather information on children's ability to detect and correct interference from the dialect. On the basis of this information they can decide which pupils need what kind of instruction.

Attitudes of teachers and pupils towards the use of dialect in the classroom

The importance of positive attitudes towards dialect in an educational setting is widely recognised. Trudgill (1975), for instance, argues that positive teacher attitudes are in themselves sufficient to remove educational obstacles. Supporting this view, Goodman & Goodman (1981) conclude that the only disadvantage experienced by non-standard speakers is 'rejection of the dialects by the school and the persuasive attitude that speakers of low status dialects have difficulty in learning to read'.

However, the prevailing feeling in the Kerkrade project was somewhat less optimistic. It was felt that positive teacher attitudes are not enough in themselves to produce changes in either pupil attitudes or teaching methods. For this reason, our activities during the development phase of the project were directed at the kind of changes in approach to teaching which we have outlined above. Moreover, we were convinced that giving information about dialect to teachers can only produce change when that information is related to practical experience. We therefore tried to effect attitude change both by supplying teachers with information and by giving them opportunities for putting the information into practice.

We were, of course, concerned with both teacher and pupil attitudes towards dialect. The 10–13 year olds involved in the project discussed the nature and function of their dialect with their teachers in language awareness lessons. These lessons were based on Kroon & Liebrand's course for the primary school (see Giesbers, Kroon & Liebrand, this volume, chapter 15) which we adapted for use with younger children.

Research Findings

In the following sections we will address three main issues. First we will present some general observations on the possible role of dialect in the classroom and ways of introducing it. Next we will discuss our research findings concerning the effect which dialect use in the classroom has on the oral participation of dialect-speaking children. Finally, we will attempt to compare certain aspects of the language attitudes of teachers and children in project schools and other schools in Kerkrade which acted as a control.

Practical implications of introducing dialect into the classroom

Our own observations and interviews with teachers and children led to a number of conclusions about the introduction of dialect into the classroom. It soon became apparent, for instance, that using a dialect in situations previously reserved for the standard is a complex undertaking. The children's initial response was often to laugh when dialect was spoken and they found it difficult to keep up any kind of sustained usage. Teachers, for their part, felt that speaking dialect was unnatural and artificial. But as they gradually got used to it, teachers regularly made use of dialect both when talking to the class as a whole and also in small group work with dialect-speaking children. Little by little, a number of situations emerged in which it was perfectly normal to use the dialect.

It also became apparent that some situations lent themselves more readily to the use of dialect than others. Some teachers found it easiest to introduce dialect into informal situations, such as the playground, PE lessons, role play and drama, and went on to use dialect in the classroom only after it had been established in these areas. However, not all teachers found it necessary to take this step by step approach.

Another consideration is the competence of both teacher and pupils in dialect. Not surprisingly we found that encouraging the use of dialect increases in difficulty in proportion to the number of children in the class who have no command of the dialect. The linguistic background of the teacher is also important and dialect-speaking teachers obviously had an advantage over teachers who had no command of the dialect. If a teacher actually uses dialect, children are more likely to speak dialect themselves. All the same, standard-speaking teachers are able to encourage the use of dialect in the classroom by creating situations which elicit dialect (a thematic approach generates many situations in which it is perfectly natural to use dialect) and by showing that they have positive attitudes towards dialect variation.

Finally, we found that it was easier to encourage dialect usage with older children than with younger ones, possibly because the older children are more linguistically aware. Attempts to help children change from monolingual to bidialectal conversation proved most effective when there were opportunities for open discussion of language variation in language lessons.

The effect of dialect on oral participation in class

The rate of participation

One of the main reasons for deciding to introduce dialect into the classroom was that we believed this move would encourage dialect-speaking children to participate more fully in classroom discussions. Our classroom observation left no doubt that our assumption was correct. The research phase of the project had shown that dialect-speaking children participated less frequently in classroom interactions than their standard-speaking peers. Our observations of the development phase, however, showed that, with the introduction of dialect into the classroom, this was no longer the case. In fact, working class dialect speakers spoke more often than working class standard speakers in situations where both the dialect and the standard language were used. This finding serves to support our initial hypothesis that the use of dialect in the classroom would increase the rate of participation of dialect-speaking children.

The quality of participation

We also suspected that dialect-speaking children would have less difficulty in expressing themselves when they were allowed to use their

TABLE 1 *Mean Number of Speaking Turns, in Dialect as well as in Standard Language per 60 Minutes in Conversations in which Dialect as well as Standard Language was Spoken*

		DL	SL	p-one sided with t-test	DH	SH	p-two sided with t-test
5–6 yrs &	n	46	5	ns	20	14	ns
6–9 yrs	x̄	14.73	26.1		18.73	17.33	
	s	13.82	15.6		16.31	16.73	
9–12 yrs	n	35	16	< 0.05	10	17	ns
	x̄	13.87	7.09		8.76	7.37	
	s	13.11	8.13		6.77	5.83	

dialect. In other words, we anticipated qualitative as well as quantitative outcomes of this new policy. We should emphasise at this point that the ultimate goal of allowing dialect usage in the classroom was that dialect-speaking children would be able to express themselves as easily in the standard as in the dialect. Because this can only be a long-term goal, we had to satisfy ourselves with the more intermediate goal that dialect-speaking children would express themselves more easily when allowed to speak dialect. To analyse this effect, tape recordings of classroom observation periods were transcribed. In these transcripts the number and length of T-units was assessed.

From about the age of 10, the mean length of T-unit of working class dialect speakers in dialect is greater than in the standard language ($t = 3.54$; p one sided < 0.005; df $= 20$). The length of T-units of working and middle class dialect speakers in the standard is shorter than that of the standard speakers (middle class: $t = 2.07$; p one sided < 0.05; df $= 18$; working class: $t = 3.39$; p one sided < 0.005; df $= 34$). When the mean length of T-units for 10–13 year olds of both language groups in their own language is compared, no differences are found between dialect and standard speakers. The only difference is between the working class groups where the mean length of utterance of the dialect speakers is even

TABLE 2 *Mean Length of T-units of Dialect-speaking Children in Dialect and Standard Language and of Standard-Language-Speaking Children in Standard Language*

		DH	DL	SH	SL
grades 1–3					
T-unit length in dialect	x̄	4.86	4.39		
	s	1.92	1.67		
	n	10	23		
T-unit length in standard	x̄	5.13	4.46	5.04	6.33
language	s	2.83	1.90	2.27	2.43
	n	10	23	13	5
grades 4–6					
T-unit length in dialect	x̄	5.85	7.16		
	s	2.82	2.56		
	n	5	21		
T-unit length in standard	x̄	5.25	4.97	7.20	6.02
language	s	2.43	2.76	2.24	2.58
	n	5	21	15	15

greater than that of the standard speakers (t = 3.56; p two sided < 0.01; df = 34). In younger children there were no differences at all. It would therefore seem to be the case that encouraging the use of dialect in the classroom not only increases the rate of participation of dialect-speaking children but also the confidence with which they express themselves.

The attitudes of teachers and pupils

The attitudes of the teachers

Teachers in the project schools completed attitude questionnaires at three different points during the development phase. The third of these questionnaires was also completed by teachers in other Kerkrade schools which acted as a control. Comparison of general language attitudes of the two groups showed no differences, both groups viewing the dialect positively.

However, there were differences in responses to questions about dialect usage in different teaching situations. Teachers in the project schools, for instance, reported more dialect usage in a wide range of teaching situations than teachers in the control schools. Further, only 20% of the project school teachers found it necessary to correct children when they spoke dialect compared with 76% of teachers in the other schools.

Attitudes of the pupils

Observation of classroom interaction and the attitudes of teachers both confirm the shift which took place in the development phase from a situation where the classroom was an exclusively standard-speaking domain to one where both standard and dialect were felt to have a place. We wondered whether this shift would also affect pupils' attitudes towards dialect in the classroom. To answer this question, we decided to compare the language attitudes of 8–13 year olds in both project and non-participating schools. Like the teachers, both groups showed similar attitudes towards dialect in general. For example, both groups preferred dialect outside as well as inside the classroom and said that they could express themselves better in the dialect. There were also indications of linguistic insecurity on the part of the dialect speakers. In the 10–13 age group approximately 70% of the working class speakers and 60% of the middle class speakers reported that they lacked confidence in speaking

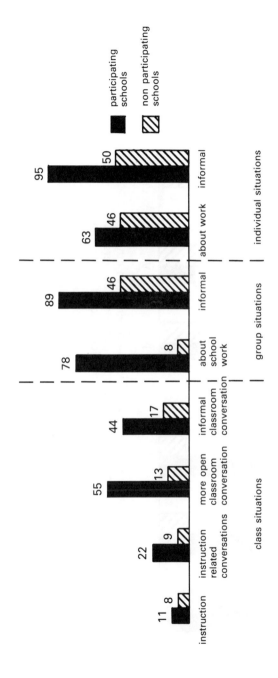

FIGURE 1 *Percentage of dialect-speaking teachers reporting to speak dialect with the children always or often in different teaching situations*

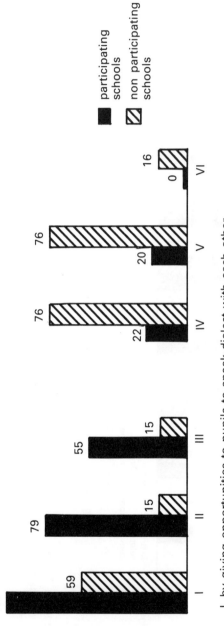

I   by giving opportunities to pupils to speak dialect with each other
II   by stimulating dialect speaking in more open classroom conversations
III by stimulating dialect speaking in instruction related classroom
     conversation

IV   by solely speaking standard language as a model for pupils
V   by correcting errors in spoken standard langage
VI   by forbidding dialect speaking

FIGURE 2 *Percentage of teachers taking the problems of dialect-speaking
children into account in other ways than by speaking dialect*

the standard, though these proportions were lower among younger children.

At the end of the development stage children were asked additional questions relating to dialect usage in the classroom. For example:

— Do children find it strange to speak dialect in the classroom or to hear their teachers doing so?
— Does dialect have a place in the classroom and which variety do teachers prefer?
— Do the children themselves speak dialect with the teachers?

There were no differences in the answers of children in either group to the first question. Most children did not find it strange to speak dialect with their teachers or to speak dialect themselves. However, the second question showed important differences between the two groups. 75% of the 10–13 year old children in the project schools reported that their teacher did not mind which variety they used, whereas 95% of the children in the control schools said that their teachers preferred them to speak the standard.

Differences were also found in responses to the question concerning the children's opinion on the place of dialect in the classroom. Children in the control schools were clear that the standard was the only suitable language for the classroom, while the majority of children in the project schools felt that there was a place for both standard and dialect. These differences are also reflected in the children's rate of reporting of their own dialect usage in the classroom.

TABLE 3 *Answers of Children of Participating and Not Participating Schools to the Question Whether they do Occasionally Talk Dialect with their Teachers*

| | | 8–10 years | | 10–12 years | |
		partici- pating schools	non partici- pating schools	partici- pating schools	non partici- pating schools
	never	22%	63%	13%	48%
dialect speakers	sometimes/often	78%	37%	87%	52%
lower class	n	27	72	37	87
	never	35%	65%	13%	55%
dialect speakers	sometimes/often	65%	35%	87%	45%
middle class	n	17	31	8	38

8–10 years: alternatives = never/sometimes
10–12 years: alternatives = never/sometimes/often

More children in the project schools said that they used dialect with their teachers than children in the control schools. The differences were statistically significant at least at the 5% level.

Dissemination of Findings

In terms of an RDD Model (Research – Development – Diffusion) the work reported in this chapter clearly comes under the heading of Development. We were also concerned with making the findings of our work more widely known. Because of financial constraints, however, dissemination had to be restricted to a small number of publications. Two of these publications, Hos, Kuijper & Van Tuijl (1982) and Swachten and Vaessen (1982), were addressed to practising teachers, student teachers and teacher trainers. The third, Kuijper, Stijnen & Van den Hoogen (1983) takes the form of a research report on the development phase.

Concluding Remarks

The process of co-operation between linguists and teachers allowed us to identify a number of extremely important issues for those interested in the question of dialect and education. It allowed us to generate several important hypotheses and then to test these hypotheses. Because of the small scale nature of the development phase of the Kerkrade project it is not, of course, possible to generalise our findings to other situations. This does not in any way, however, detract from the value of a development project of this kind. Our evaluation of the innovations which have taken place in the project schools leaves us in no doubt as to the educational benefits of encouraging dialect usage in the classroom.

References

CENTRALE WERKGROEP MOEDERTAALONDERWIJS (CWMO) 1980 *Raamplan voor het taalonderwijs van morgen*. Den Bosch.
CHESHIRE, J. 1982 Dialect features and linguistic conflict in school, *Educational Review* 34 (1), 53–67.
GOODMAN, Y. & GOODMAN, K. 1981 Twenty questions about teaching language, *Educational Leadership* 38 (6), 437–43.
HOS, H., KUIJPER, H. and VAN TUIJL, H. 1982 *Dialect op de basisschool*. Enschede: Stichting voor de Leerplanontwikkeling.

KELLERMAN, E. 1977 Towards a characterization of the strategy of transfer in second language learning, *Interlanguage Studies Bulletin* 2, 58–145.

KUIJPER, H., STIJNEN, P. and VALLEN, A. 1979 Spreekangst en linguistische onzekerheid bij dialectsprekers in vergelijking met standaardtaalsprekers. In M. MOMMERS & B. SMITS (eds), *Lees – en taalonderwijs in de basisschool.* Den Haag: Stichting voor Onderzoek van het Onderwijs.

KUIJPER, H., STIJNEN, P. and VAN DEN HOOGEN, J. 1983 *Onderwijs tussen dialect en standaardtaal.* Nijmegen: Nijmeegse Centrale voor dialect – en naamkunde, Katholieke Universiteit Nijmegen.

SWACHTEN, L. and VAESSEN, M.1982 *Werken met dialect in de klas. Het Kerkraads voorbeeldenboek.* Nijmegen: Nijmeegse Centrale voor dialect – en naamkunde, Katholieke Universiteit Nijmegen.

TRUDGILL, P. 1975 *Accent, Dialect and the School.* London: Edward Arnold.

14 Teaching materials for dialect speakers in the Federal Republic of Germany: The contrastive booklets

Teaching materials for dialect speakers are not by any means a recent idea in the German language area. There are several older publications which were mainly intended to inform teachers about the linguistic differences between certain dialects and the standard variety, and the major difficulties which dialect speakers had in acquiring skills in the standard (see, for example, Karstädt, 1908, 1920, 1922; Meyer-Markau, 1908; Kramer & Kürsten, 1935).

These materials are well worth reading, despite the fact that the difficulties of dialect speakers were only guessed at, rather than being based on proper empirical research, and despite the fact that the linguistic descriptions appear a little outmoded today. These older materials, however, were largely ignored by teachers (with the exception of Karstädt's materials, which ran to at least three editions); they had been so thoroughly forgotten that they were hardly mentioned when similar ideas were put forward in the Federal Republic in the early 1970s (see, for example, Ammon, 1972; Löffler, 1972).

In the new publications of the 1970s it was pointed out from the beginning that contrastive grammar should be used as a basis for dialect description. Only Werner Besch and Heinrich Löffler, however, seriously tackled the task. They presented their plans to develop and to publish contrastive booklets (*Kontrastive Hefte*) for dialect speakers at a conference on 'Dialect as a Language Barrier?' at the University of Tübingen in 1972 (see Besch & Löffler, 1973). For each major dialect area of the Federal Republic of Germany a booklet was to be published which would contain the major sources of 'errors' made by dialect speakers, specified on the basis of a contrastive grammar of the dialect and standard German. The booklets were to be available only to teachers, not to their pupils. They were intended to provide teachers with specific information on the difficulties faced by dialect speakers, so that these could be taken into account in their teaching.

The first contrastive booklet was published in 1976 for the Hessian dialect region (Hessisch, by Hasselberg & Wegera). Since then booklets have appeared for Alemannic (Besch & Löffler, 1977), Bavarian (Zehetner, 1977), Swabian (Ammon & Loewer, 1977), Westfalian (Niebaum, 1977), Rhenian (Klein, Mattheier & Mickartz, 1978), Palatian (Henn, 1980) and Lower Saxonian (Stellmacher, 1981) (see Map 1, from Löffler, 1982:531).

All the booklets follow the same schema which was developed by Besch & Löffler with the help of Hans H. Reich, an expert in language teaching, and revised together with the authors at two conferences at the University of Bonn. Each booklet contains at least the following three main parts; these, however differ from booklet to booklet in length and proportion:

(i)   A general introduction
(ii) A description of the dialect area in question
(iii) An overview of the specific linguistic difficulties faced by dialect speakers in the area

In some of the booklets these parts do not form separate chapters; for example, Parts (i) and (ii) may be combined. In each case Part (iii) is by far the longest section in the booklet. The booklets also vary considerably in their style, insofar as some use more scholarly terminology, particularly linguistic concepts. There is a tendency to use more technical vocabulary in the later booklets (particularly Stellmacher, 1981). The effect of this on their reception by teachers is not known. Part (ii) and, particularly, Part (iii), differ in length from booklet to booklet, depending mainly on the extent of internal regional variation within the respective dialect areas, and on the extent to which the dialect diverges from the standard. The dialect regions which were distinguished for the booklets are by no means regionally homogeneous; it would not have been financially viable to publish a separate booklet for (relatively) homogeneous regions. The Low German dialects in the north actually diverge more from Standard German than the High

MAP 1 *Map of the Federal Republic of Germany, showing main dialect areas*

--- State borders within the Fed. Rep. of Germany
——— Underlining indicates that a contrastive booklet has been published.
Niedersächsisch = Lower Saxonian, Westfälisch = Westfalian, Ostfälisch = Ostfalian, Rheinisch = Rhenian, Hessisch = Hessian, Pfälzisch = Palatian, Ostfränkisch = East Franconian, Südfränkisch = South Franconian, Alemannisch = Alemannic, Schwäbisch = Swabian, Bairisch = Bavarian.

German dialects in the south. The dialects in the north, however, are rarely spoken in a pure form nowadays, and the varieties that are spoken there now are closer to standard German than the dialects in the south (see Ammon, this volume, Chapter 7). The extent of the internal regional variation that exists in some of the areas posed serious difficulties for some of the authors of the booklets, as did the distinction between the original broad dialect and the varieties that are spoken today; these difficulties were not always satisfactorily resolved, and some of the booklets, it seems, are more difficult for teachers to read and to use than need have been the case.

The general introduction (Part (i)) which was written by Besch, Löffler & Reich is the same for each booklet. It gives a general overview of the school problems of dialect speakers, sets out the objectives of the booklets and discusses their use in teaching. The main objectives are to teach the standard variety to dialect speakers (a) more efficiently and (b) with less potential trauma for dialect speakers. It is pointed out that (b) presupposes that the dialect is not denigrated, and that it is accepted as a variety which is adequate in private situations, which may even include certain situations at school. The contrastive booklets advocate dialect–standard bilingualism rather than the use only of the standard.

A criticism that could be made, however, is that it is implicit in the booklets that this kind of bilingualism is actually only intended for the dialect speakers; to teach the dialect to monolingual standard speakers is not one of the objectives — an asymmetry which is ultimately not unproblematic. In addition, this is not, of course, the same kind of bilingualism that has been imposed on colonised populations, where it is planned that literacy should be acquired in the dominant national language (for example, Spanish, in Mexico) via literacy in the indigenous language (in Mexico, for example, an Amerindian language — see Heath, 1972:113–22). Instead the bilingualism that is intended is restricted to oral communication. A further criticism is that some teachers may mistake the objective of bilingualism, when seen in conjunction with the positive evaluation of dialect, as a justification for simply accepting the dialect in class; in other words, for not seriously attempting to teach the standard variety.

The authors suggest that teachers use the booklets on the one hand for curriculum planning and class preparation and on the other hand as a guide for corrections and marking. The first kind of use relates mainly to devising efficient and considerate ways of teaching the standard; the second to the diagnosis of specific dialect difficulties and to fair evaluation and marking. Part (i) ends with some general suggestions about teaching methods.

Parts (ii) and (iii) were written by the individual author (or authors) of the booklet, who in each case was a dialectologist knowledgeable about current discussions on dialect and education, and in most cases a native speaker of the dialect. Part (ii) gives an overview of sociolinguistic and social-psychological research findings, including attitudes towards dialect and standard speech, and it points to some specific problems which dialect speakers face in school in the respective dialect areas. In addition, it informs teachers, in most cases, of the official recommended guidelines with respect to dialect speakers for the schools of the Federal State (staatliche Rahmenrichtlinien). There are hardly any private schools in West Germany. In virtually all cases, these recommendations could easily be reconciled with the objectives of the booklets, though the guidelines had been of little value whilst adequate teaching material was unavailable. The booklets could largely be presented as filling this gap; in other words, as instruments for implementing the intentions expressed in the official guidelines.

The specific linguistic difficulties of dialect speakers are set out in Part (iii). They are based on the empirical research that was considered necessary by the individual author. As a minimum, a large number of written compositions were analysed for dialect transferences. The linguistic difficulties found are then presented in the booklets in some 20 to 40 chapters. Each chapter concentrates on a relatively narrow section of grammar; for example, the short vowels of the standard variety which are missing in the dialect, certain differences in consonants, in the forms of the definite article, in the tenses, in the semantics of certain nouns, in word order in subordinate sentences, etc. Each of these chapters follows the same pattern of presentation:

1. A rough linguistic description of the problem area, the rounded front vowels (Alemannian, Swabian), noun gender (in all areas), or the cases governed by prepositions and verbs (Westfalian, Lower Saxonian).
2. A list of attested errors of dialect speakers in their attempts at written or spoken standard German. This list is sub-divided in most cases into direct transferences from dialect and hypercorrections. In Alemannian and Swabian there are, for instance, no rounded front vowels (y, y:, œ, Ø) as in Standard German. Therefore one finds direct transferences in orthography like *Phisik* (instead of *Physik* 'physics'), *zwelf* (instead of *zwölf* 'twelve') or hypercorrections like *vermüssen* (instead of *vermissen* 'to miss') or *mölken* (instead of *melken* 'to milk').
3. A short explanation of how these errors may have been caused, specifying mainly which processes of transference or hypercorrection can be assumed to be responsible.

4. Suggestions of teaching methods for the particular problem area. These suggestions are not very detailed in most cases, since teachers are repeatedly reminded, both here and in Part (i), that they should use their pedagogical expertise to form their own judgements, in different situations. For example, it is suggested that teachers might use minimal pairs (a list of these is provided) where phonemic distinctions in standard German are not made in the dialect (such as /y-ɪ, œ-ɛ, z-s/, etc.), and that they might ask dialect speakers to pronounce aloud these minimal pairs, in order to make them aware of the difference. With respect to spelling mistakes, the teacher may decide to familiarise dialect speakers with certain morphological relationships which might be helpful (again, examples are listed in the booklets, such as *müssen – muss*; *öfter – oft*, etc.). In addition, short cloze tests are offered, where critical letters are omitted, and games are suggested, where rhymes for difficult words have to be found. Most chapters contain suggestions of these kinds, which are specifically related to particular grammatical problems, though the booklets differ in the number of practical suggestions that they make.

5. A more detailed grammatical description than was given at the beginning of the section then follows.

To our knowledge there has been no systematic evaluation of these teaching materials so far. It is known that the booklets have been used by teachers, but it is not known to what extent they have been used, nor what the effect has been. It seems obvious today that the editors and authors made a mistake in not seeking the explicit support of the school administration of the federal states. It was probably not enough simply to show teachers that the booklets were in line with the official guidelines. It was always left to individual teachers to take the initiative in using the booklets; there was no official recommendation or encouragement. In addition, the booklets had to be sold at a relatively high price (approximately 25 DM, which was expensive at that time), because of the small editions that were published (about 2000, or less, depending on the size of the dialect area). Interested teachers normally have to pay this money out of their own pockets. In fact, the publishing company has recently threatened to stop the series altogether, since sales have been sluggish; this, however, was prevented by the protests of the editors and the authors. This threat inspired the editors and the authors to make new efforts to encourage the use of the booklets. Nevertheless, overall sales have remained low. According to the publisher, approximate figures for sales at the end of September, 1987, were: Hessian: 1,300; Alemannic: 1,300; Bavarian: 1,000; Swabian: 1,300; Westfalian: 1,000; Rhenian: 800; Palatial: 400; Lower Saxonian: 400. These figures indicate that the booklets cannot be used very extensively by teachers, especially if one bears in mind the fact that they have undoubtedly been bought not only by teachers but also by interested scholars and the like.

These experiences should certainly be taken into account if similar efforts to make dialect materials accessible to teachers are attempted in other countries. It was intended to carry out an empirically-based evaluation of the contrastive booklets project after a suitable period of time, but no definite plans for this exist so far. In spite of all the criticisms that can certainly be made, however, the contrastive booklets project is, to my knowledge, the most comprehensive attempt in Europe — if not in the world — to develop specific teaching materials for dialect speakers.

A serious attempt at evaluating the booklets on an empirical basis could, in addition, shed light on various aspects of dialect and education which have not yet been researched in any detail. Some of the questions that could be raised concern methodological problems, others could reveal gaps in our empirical knowledge, and this in turn might stimulate further research. In conclusion, I will mention just a few possibilities:

1. It could be asked whether the frustration of dialect speakers in school is really reduced by the use (or a certain aspect of the use) of the contrastive booklets. This raises the question of how this frustration could be empirically assessed, i.e. measured in a more comprehensive and less superficial way than has been the case so far.

2. Another question might be whether dialect speakers actually acquire a more solid mastery in standard speech and writing when the booklets are used. This would raise the question of what 'greater or lesser mastery of the standard' means precisely, or what it could mean. In other words, the question is again raised of how this could be tested and measured. In this context the related question could be asked — what would be an adequate level of skill in the standard variety for an individual who wants to perform certain actions in a given society, such as participating in public political discussions? It is easy to see that such additional questions open an abyss of extremely complex and politically loaded problems which would have to be separated out for proper empirical research to take place. In the pursuit of such questions it might well become evident — as is, for instance, the case in the Federal Republic of Germany — that very inadequate data are available on the actual skills that pupils have in the standard variety, at the end of their schooling.

3. When attempting to evaluate the booklets one would certainly have to compare different ways of using them in teaching. This would raise the complex question of adequate teaching methods.
4. Finally, it would have to be asked whether the most serious linguistic difficulties are really given adequate consideration in the booklets. Here even the contrastive principle itself would have to be questioned.

References

AMMON, U. 1972 *Dialekt, soziale Ungleichheit und Schule.* Weinheim/Basel: Beltz.
AMMON, U. and LOEWER, U. 1977 *Schwäbisch* (= Dialekt/Hochsprache – kontrastiv 4). Düsseldorf: Schwann.
BESCH, W. and LÖFFLER, H. 1973 Sprachhefte: Hochsprache/Mundart – kontrastiv. In H. BAUSINGER (ed.), *Dialekt als Sprachbarriere?* Tübingen: Gesellschaft für Volkskunde. pp. 89–110.
——1977 *Alemannisch* (= Dialekt/Hochsprache – kontrastiv 3). Düsseldorf: Schwann.
HASSELBERG, J. and WEGERA, K.-P. 1976 *Hessisch* (= Dialekt/Hochsprache – kontrastiv 1). Düsseldorf: Schwann.
HEATH, S.B. 1972 *Telling Tongues.* Language Policy in Mexico, Colony to Nation. New York/London: Teachers College Press.
HENN, B. 1980 *Pfälzisch* (= Dialekt/Hochsprache – kontrastiv 7). Düsseldorf: Schwann.
KARSTÄDT, O. 1908, 1920 (2nd edn), 1922 (3rd edn) *Mundart und Schule.* Langensalza: Beltz.
KLEIN, E., MATTHEIER, K.J. and MICKARTZ, H. 1978 *Rheinisch* (= Dialekt/Hochsprache – kontrastiv 6). Düsseldorf: Schwann.
KRAMER, W. and KÜRSTEN, O. 1935 *Von der Mundart zur Hochsprache: Sprechkunde und Sprachlehre für Thüringer und Sachsen.* Erfurt: Stenger.
LÖFFLER, H. 1972 Mundart als Sprachbarriere, *Wirkendes Wort* 22, 1, 23–29.
——1982 Interferenz-Areale Dialekt/Standardsprache: Projekt eines deutschen Fehleratlasses. In W. BESCH, U. KNOOP, W. PUTSCHKE and H.E. WIEGAND (eds), *Dialektologie*, Vol. 1. Berlin/New York: de Gruyter. pp. 528–38.
MEYER-MARKAU, W. 1908 *Sprachliche Heimatkunde.* Minden: Marowsky.
NIEBAUM, H. 1977 *Westfälisch* (= Dialekt/Hochsprache – kontrastiv 5). Düsseldorf: Schwann.
STELLMACHER, D. 1981 *Niedersächsisch (= Dialekt/Hochsprache – kontrastiv 8). Düsseldorf: Schwann.*
ZEHETNER, L.G. 1977 *Bairisch* (= Dialekt/Hochsprache – kontrastiv 2). Düsseldorf: Schwann.

15 Language variation study in the classroom

HERMAN GIESBERS, SJAAK KROON and RUDI
LIEBRAND

Introduction

In the mid-1970s in the Dutch town of Gennep a sociolinguistic research project was set up to explore the relationship between the use of dialect (as a mother tongue) and school achievement in primary education (see Giesbers, Kroon & Liebrand, 1988). This project resulted in some suggestions for improving the educational performance of the dialect-speaking children involved in the study. Although the starting point of the project had been the sociolinguistic difference theory, these suggestions could not escape being 'therapeutic' in one way or another. After all, we intended to 'help' dialect-speaking children to improve their performance in teaching/learning situations where standard Dutch is the 'normal' means of communication.

Taking the difference theory as a starting point in sociolinguistic research implies that dialect and standard language are seen as linguistically equal, highly structured, albeit different, language systems that are perfectly adequate for the communicative needs of those who use them. Research results from various countries (including the Netherlands; cf. e.g. Stijnen & Vallen, this volume, chapter 8, and Giesbers *et al.*, 1988), however, make abundantly clear that this linguistic equivalence does not prevent dialect-speaking pupils from being confronted with specific problems in school and society. As a consequence, the adherents of the sociolinguistic difference theory have been searching for ways to prevent dialect-speaking children from failure (cf. Hagen, 1981).

A critical observer could now point out that the latter position and the practice that emerged from the so-called deficit theory, which we explicitly rejected as a useful starting point in our research on linguistic and pedagogical grounds, are basically the same. They both take the notion of 'something being wrong' as a basis for pedagogical action. Apart from these two approaches (difference and deficit), however, there is still another way in which sociolinguistics and its research findings and insights can contribute to language teaching. Not the idea of 'something being wrong', but of 'something being right' lies at the heart of this contribution. This particular 'something' is the positive image of language variation as a feature of society and as a source for language teaching and learning for all pupils, whether they are pupils in multilingual or monolingual classrooms, whether they are dialect speakers or not.

Objectives and Organisation of Language Variation Study

In the Netherlands, as in many other European countries (cf. Herrlitz *et al.*, 1984), there is an old and ongoing debate about the pros and cons of traditional grammar teaching, and the concept of Language Study has been developed as an alternative for traditional grammar as part of the Dutch lessons (cf. Sturm, 1984). Language Study has been described as all those instances in the teaching/learning process in which the teacher and his/her pupils, in a structured and goal-oriented manner, look at, play with, think, talk and write about language and language use. Not only the language system itself, but also the way in which language is used form the object of investigation (cf. Nijmeegse Werkgroep Taaldidactiek, 1985). Because we think that this description makes it possible not only to pay attention to standard Dutch but also to incorporate other, for example non-standard, varieties in Language Study, we used it as a starting point for Language Variation Study as well.

In the early 1980s, inspired by publications such as *Language in Use* (Doughty *et al.*, 1971) and some predecessors of *The Languages Book* (Raleigh, *et al.*, 1981), we devised two courses of lessons on various aspects of language variation, to be used by teachers of Dutch in secondary education with 12–13 and 16–17-year-old pupils respectively (cf. Kroon & Liebrand, 1982 and 1984). In developing these lessons we tried to make use of language variation in an educational context without addressing ourselves simply and solely to dialect-speaking children and their supposed 'deficiencies'.

The objectives of our Language Variation Study courses are threefold.

1. Language Variation Study aims at providing all pupils with interesting knowledge about a phenomenon (language variation) they all have to deal with in every-day life because the Netherlands is a multilingual country (cf. Kroon & Sturm, 1985). Language Variation Study should reveal to pupils the richness of linguistic variation in classrooms and society and the relation of that variation to the written and spoken standard language (cf. Donmall, 1985). In our opinion, in the context of Dutch as a school subject, giving information about language variation in a broad sense is not less important than, for example, teaching a course on Dutch literature.

2. Language Variation Study aims at making all pupils aware of the negative opinions and prejudices that are often connected with dialect, the use of dialect and the people who speak a dialect. Language Variation Study has to challenge and eliminate linguistic prejudice and parochialism and feelings of antagonism and inferiority associated with language variation (cf. Hawkins, 1984). As a result children will hopefully be willing and able to overcome negative attitudes and behaviour towards language variation. Moreover, if they happen to be dialect speakers, they should know how to handle the consequences of such negative attitudes. In this sense we think Language Variation Study is a useful step towards equality of opportunity for dialect-speaking children.

3. Language Variation Study aims at increasing the pupils' insight into the phenomenon of language in general. According to Miller (1983) this insight into 'the nature of language and its role in human life' (Donmall, 1985: 7), or language awareness, leads to a greater readiness to learn language and, as a consequence, to an improvement of standard language proficiency for all pupils.

As far as the organisation of Language Variation Study is concerned, several approaches are possible. Sturm (1982), for example, has proposed an approach in which the teacher pays attention to aspects of language variation every time the opportunity occurs. If, for example, a pupil makes an error in standard Dutch that is caused by the dialect he or she uses as a mother tongue, the teacher should explain this error to the class, thereby referring to the dialect system in which such a construction is probably perfectly all right. This explanation could then be elaborated in the next lesson or lessons. Such an approach, which totally depends on what happens in the classroom and merely reacts to the 'contributions' of the pupils, has several disadvantages.

First of all we think that the pupils will get confused by the wealth of information that happens to come their way often in an unstructured manner. Secondly, the demand that is made on the flexibility and ready knowledge of the teacher hardly seems realistic to us. The advantage of a course on Language Variation Study, in contrast, is that it can be prepared by the teacher beforehand, and that it has a clear and explicit place in the curriculum.

In order to be able to make informed choices as to the aspects of language variation that could be studied in the classroom, we used Fishman's (1965) well-known description of sociolinguistics as 'The Study of Who Speaks What Language to Whom and When' as a general point of reference. In our lessons we therefore pay attention to speaker characteristics (who speaks), to the different language varieties that exist in the Netherlands (what language), to conversational and situational aspects of using different language varieties (to whom and when). Following Lasswell's claim that communication sciences should deal with the question 'Who says what to whom, how and with what effect', dating, incidentally, from the early 1950s (cf. Lasswell *et al.*, 1952: 12), we paid additional attention to the question why people use different varieties and what are the possible consequences of using different varieties.

On the basis of this description we propose a didactically motivated four-step approach. The stages in this approach are: description (what exactly is being said/is written down), explanation (why is it said/put down as it is), evaluation (what is my opinion on that), and application (what can I learn from it for my future (language) behaviour). Depending on their classroom situation (pupils' age, language and social background, topic, etc.), teachers will, of course, have to decide themselves which of these stages they emphasise.

This brings us to a last remark here, concerning the activity of teachers in Language Variation Study. It will be clear that giving Language Variation Study lessons in the classroom is a very demanding task for the language teacher. He/she has to be well-informed not only about language as a linguistic and social phenomenon, but also about possible ways to convey this scientific knowledge to children, without trying to make them little (socio)linguists. In order to provide the teachers with the knowledge that they need we paid explicit attention to the various aspects of language variation in the presentation of our Language Variation Study course in teacher journals. Furthermore, we suggested a few books for further reading on sociolinguistics in general and language variation in particular that are acceptable in scope and in size for teachers to read after a tiring day of teaching (cf. e.g. for the Netherlands, Hagen, 1982, and Daan *et al.*, 1985).

Some Examples of Language Variation Study

The lessons that will be presented in this section originated from everyday classroom experience; they had all been put into practice before we published them in 1982 and 1984 respectively.

The first course we designed was meant for 12/13-year-old pupils. It consists of ten lessons published in a booklet under the rather prosaic title 'Ten Lessons on Language Variation'. The following is a short description of the course.

In *Lesson 1*, by means of two mapping tasks, it is shown that the Netherlands is a multilingual country. First the pupils have to indicate on a map of the Netherlands where a number of different dialects played to them on a recorder come from. In discussing the results, mention is made of the existence of language variation, the existence of fairly homogeneous dialect areas with certain characteristics, and the existence of differences between (indigenous and non-indigenous) standard language, (regional and urban) dialect, and accent. In the second task the pupils have to indicate on a detailed map of the region in which they live, which neighbouring villages, in their view, speak the same dialect as their own town. The results of this task show that native speakers are able to distinguish a certain number of dialect differences within their own dialect area.

Lesson 2 provides an overview of the linguistic history of the Netherlands (cf. Donaldson, 1983). The pupils have to study this overview as background knowledge for the lessons to come.

Lesson 3 is about the linguistic characteristics of the dialect area under investigation as compared with standard Dutch. The children learn that the dialect has its own system as to phonology, morphology, syntax and lexicon. Part of this system is demonstrated by means of a translation task. Furthermore, as homework, the pupils have to collect dialect texts in, for example, local newspapers and other written material.

In *Lesson 4* a comparison of the dialect texts that the pupils brought to school makes clear that dialects are non-standard languages in the sense that they are not standardised in, for example, orthography. That this does not mean that dialects are illogical, primitive or defective languages is shown by comparing some elements of the dialect morphology with the morphology of standard Dutch. The two systems turn out to be different, but these differences cannot be judged in terms of 'better' or 'worse'.

Lesson 5 makes clear that speaking a dialect as a mother tongue (and living in a dialect area) can cause errors in the production of standard

Dutch. This is done by having the pupils correct a written text containing a fairly large number of errors that stem from interference between standard Dutch and the dialect system. In our case these errors were collected from the writing of pupils we had worked with previously, but they can also be constructed by the teacher. It is very important that the teacher clearly explains afterwards which specific structural differences between the two language systems are responsible for the errors that occurred, in order to enable the pupils to prevent them on future occasions.

Lesson 6 is about functional differences between dialect and standard language. By filling in a questionnaire about the use of dialect and standard language in a number of different domains (writing a letter to be published in a newspaper, talking to your headteacher, to someone in a local shop, in a municipal office, in a radio game, etc.), the pupils find out that dialect is limited to regional/social use in mainly informal situations, whereas the standard language can be used on a national level (or even beyond) on formal and informal occasions.

In *Lesson 7* by means of a limited matched-guise technique with four voices, two of them being from the same speaker, who speaks a dialect and standard Dutch respectively, the pupils explore negative attitudes towards dialect and dialect speakers. Questionnaire responses to the 'different' speakers invariably point to a systematically 'worse' evaluation of the 'dialect speaker' with respect to schooling, intelligence, status etc., as compared with the 'speaker of standard Dutch'. It is hoped that the discovery that they have evaluated the same speaker differently according to the language variety he used, will convince the children of the incorrectness of arriving at conclusions about people only on the basis of the language variety they use.

In *Lesson 8* by means of a role-play, the pupils learn that there are occasions, as, for example, a job interview, in which the use of a dialect, and even an accent, is not accepted and can sometimes have severe consequences. The children learn that the use of dialect or standard should always be a matter of deliberate choice, depending on the situation in which they find themselves and the people with whom they communicate.

In *Lesson 9* a number of viewpoints on dialect, standard language and prejudices are discussed by the pupils in small groups. These viewpoints cover elements from all the previous lessons, and as such form a kind of rehearsal for the task that is presented in Lesson 10.

In *Lesson 10* the pupils have to write a letter to colleagues at another school, preferably in another dialect area, who have also worked with the material. In their letter they have to explain what they did during the last nine lessons, and what they learned from these activities.

The second course, for 16–17-year-old pupils, has been organised in three parts.

In the first part (one lesson) the course is introduced through discussion of various aspects of language variation. Points of attention in this discussion include: which language varieties exist in the Netherlands? What are the differences between dialect and standard Dutch? In which situations are dialect and standard Dutch mainly used? At the end of this lesson, the pupils fill in a short questionnaire about their own and their parents' language background.

In the second part (two or three lessons) some basic information on language variation is provided. All pupils need to be in possession of this information in order to be able to carry out the optional tasks that are presented in part 3. The information in part 2 is arranged on the basis of the Fishman/Lasswell questions that were quoted earlier. It contains a mapping task involving different dialect extracts, a discussion on the basis of research findings about the relationship between speaking a dialect and socio-economic status, reading a text and some figures about situational, functional and attitudinal aspects of dialect use, and an inventory of educational and social problems that can arise as a result of speaking a dialect.

The third part of the course contains a number of assignments from which the pupils have to choose one to work on, alone or in small groups, during some four or five lessons. The results of this work have to be reported on in a written account and have to be presented to the class verbally.

The optional assignments are the following.

1. Making up a page of a dialect dictionary. Points of attention: What do (dialect) dictionaries look like? Which words do you choose? How do you collect them? Which orthography do you use?
2. Writing down a part of a dialect grammar as compared with the grammar of standard Dutch with respect to, for example, morphology. Points of attention: What do grammars look like? Where do you gather the data you need?
3a Drawing a map that contains a limited number of words that differ in different dialect areas in the Netherlands. Points of attention: Which words do you choose? How do you collect them?

3b Drawing a map of dialect boundaries in a limited area on the basis of asking a number of people which dialects in neighbouring villages they think are definitely different or definitely the same as their own dialect.

4a Making up an inventory of the various views people take of the appropriateness of using dialect or standard language in a number of different situations or domains and drawing conclusions from that inventory.

4b Collecting examples of dialect use in every-day life that, in your opinion, is not appropriate, interpreting these examples and asking other people their opinion.

5a Making up an inventory of prejudices towards dialect and speakers of dialect by means of a questionnaire for people you know, and a matched-guise technique in the classroom.

5b Making up an inventory of situations in which dialect speakers are likely to meet negative effects of speaking a dialect.

6. Reading some texts about dialect and primary education, and presenting the main findings to the class.

7. Investigating the thesis 'Speakers of a dialect generally receive lower status secondary education and meet more difficulties there than speakers of standard Dutch' by means of a questionnaire with pupils and interviews with primary and secondary school teachers.

8. Studying the position of the Frisian language on the basis of reading some texts on this subject, thereby paying attention to questions like: What is the difference between Frisian and Dutch dialects? What do you think of Frisian as a compulsory school subject in primary education? Why do you think Frisians are so determined when it comes to their language?

The reading texts that are mentioned in the assignments are taken from books that deal with language variation in a way that is suitable for pupils in the second half of secondary education. These books should be made available in the school library at the very beginning of the course.

Language Variation Study and Multicultural Education

The examples we have presented so far were limited to Dutch dialects. There is, however, no fundamental reason for that. On the contrary: the Netherlands is a multilingual country and it is obvious that this multilingualism is not limited to indigenous varieties. Apart from the Dutch and Frisian standard language and their dialects, there is also a large number of non-indigenous languages and dialects spoken by members of the different ethnic minority groups that choose the Netherlands as their temporary or permanent place of residence, and that make up about 7% of the Dutch population (cf. Extra & Vallen, 1985).

In response to the permanent multi-ethnic character of Dutch society, the present Dutch Primary Education Act says that 'Education starts from the principle that pupils grow up in a multicultural society'. In our opinion, Language Variation Study is an excellent way to put this principle into practice.

The ultimate aim of what we would like to call Multicultural Language Variation Study is to develop the human capacity to communicate and get on with people of different ethnic backgrounds. If it is successful it will influence the pupils' actual behaviour. Linguistic differences and similarities are the starting point. To achieve this aim, a positive attitude towards 'being different' is essential. So, too, is a critical attitude that puts what belongs to one's own culture in the proper perspective as a basis for fighting prejudice, stereotypes, discrimination and racism. As far as language is concerned this means fighting against so-called lingocentrism as a counterpart of ethnocentrism (cf. Molony, 1980). Lingocentrism means that people think their own language and language habits to be superior and, at the same time, disrespect other languages and language habits, thereby consciously or unconsciously transferring these feelings of superiority and disregard to the people who speak other languages. 'That language is different' then quickly becomes 'That language is strange' or even 'The people who speak that language are strange' (cf. Giesbers & Kroon, 1986 and Kroon & Rasenberg, 1987). An anti-lingocentric attitude means that pupils can see their own feelings and values with respect to linguistic differences and similarities in perspective and can accept the feelings and values of people from other ethnic backgrounds. To achieve this end, it is vital that pupils should be informed about linguistic differences and similarities between people from different ethnic and cultural backgrounds.

The intended relevance of Multicultural Language Variation Study for all pupils makes it necessary to link the study of indigenous variation (dialect-standard variation) and non-indigenous variation (ethnic minority languages) to each other (cf. V. Edwards, 1983). In order to reach as many pupils as possible, Multicultural Language Variation Study courses could demonstrate certain language and language use phenomena by comparing these phenomena in standard and non-standard, indigenous and non-indigenous varieties, by applying the four stages of description, explanation, evaluation and application that were mentioned on p. 245.

In order to make these rather theoretical notions on Multicultural Language Variation Study somewhat more concrete, we will give three examples. The first one is on code switching, the second is on the semantics of diminutives, and the third is on foreigner talk. It should be pointed out here that these suggestions have not been tried out so far in a real classroom situation.

A mish-mash: Code switching

Code switching can be described as the alternate use of structures and/or elements from two or more languages or language varieties by the same speaker. Intrasentential code switching, in particular, is often thought of as language degeneration, language decline, language attrition, language loss, proficiency in neither of the two languages, language mish-mash, etc. (cf. J. Edwards, 1985). Only recently, as a result of code-switching research in Hispanics in the United States, has a more positive attitude towards code switching emerged (cf. Poplack, 1980). This position stipulates that code switching is in fact an indication of a very well-developed structural as well as pragmatic language proficiency.

A large number of possible topics for Multicultural Language Variation Study could be derived from this discussion. On the level of description and explanation: To whom and when L1 (home language; mother tongue; dialect) is used, and to whom and when standard Dutch? Which standard Dutch words are used always, even in the L1, and why? Which L1 words are maintained in standard Dutch, and why? What changes occur in L1 as a result of contact with standard Dutch, and what is your opinion about that? Under what conditions are both languages or language varieties mixed?

In the Netherlands, English words and expressions are very popular (more popular than in most other European countries (Donaldson 1983: 76); some people think of that phenomenon as language degeneration too). What about the situation in your class? Why is English so popular? What about German, often used as a kind of made-up language as an object of fun (cf. Peter Sellers' creation of Dr. Strangelove, and, more recently, the cartoon character Dr. Strange Snork)? Attention can also be paid to code switching within one language in terms of style or register shift. Note that children who attend kindergarten when talking to even younger children adapt their language to them.

Furthermore, it seems evident, that Multicultural Language Variation Study offers a good opportunity to pay attention to those negative attitudes towards code switching that are implicitly incorporated in expresssions like 'Spanglish' in the United States and 'Franglais' in France. Obviously, within this topic, Multicultural Language Variation Study enters the area of evaluation and application.

'Mannetjes' versus 'mannekes': Diminutives

Multicultural Language Variation Study can help pupils understand that, while languages express the same meaning, they also differ considerably as to the way in which they do so. This can be very well illustrated by examining diminutives. In Dutch, but also in German, Spanish and Italian, diminutivisation is possible by means of morphological rules. Some Dutch dialects show some variation in these rules, as for example in the occurrence of vowel change in words such as standard Dutch *popje* versus North Limburg dialect *pupke*, both meaning 'little doll' and derived from *pop* (doll). On the other hand, there are languages like English and French that form diminutives by adding adjectives like *small* and *petit* (description). In all these languages, however, diminutives do not only express 'smallness' in terms of objective measurement: they can also be used to express depreciation, modesty, affection or euphemism. Italian, for example, has several ways to form diminutives depending on whether a neutral, positive or negative meaning is intended (e.g. *cavallo* — horse; *cavallino* — little horse; *cavallucio* — measly little horse). In Italian morphological endings are also used to express greatness, robustness (e.g. *una dona* — a woman; *un*(!) *donnone* — a robust woman). Multicultural Language Variation Study could aim at confronting all pupils with various possible ways of diminutivisation in the various languages that are present in the classroom, and acquaint them with different pragmatic aspects of diminutivisation in standard Dutch; pupils who speak languages other than standard Dutch as their mother tongue could do the same for their own languages. Perhaps the pupils themselves could discover that the Italian diversity exists in Dutch as well, albeit in a more limited way. The use of the regional diminutive suffix *-ke* in standard Dutch usually carries a totally different emotional value from the more neutral standard Dutch *-tje* (compare e.g. *moeke* versus *moedertje* (mother), *vrouwke* versus *vrouwtje* (woman), *manneke* versus *mannetje* (man), in which the former, when used in standard Dutch, generally speaking express more affection than the latter). Here the level of description gradually moves over to explanation and judgement.

Double Dutch: Foreigner talk

In a lot of children's books a very strange kind of Dutch is put into the mouth of 'foreigners'. In an issue of *Donald Duck* for example, the little Red Indian Hiawatha says to his little sister: 'Me be the driver of the big iron horse that crawl on steel snakes through the prairie and you be underdeveloped Indian that form an obstacle with your tepee', whereas Witte Veder (White Feather), the Dutch equivalent of Winnetou, in a book entitled *Arendsoog grijpt in (Hawkeye steps in)* says to his white friend: 'Meghalla's not be stupid. They now know Fort Blue Hill be warned. Think and say: soldiers first ride to battlefield. Then come to village. Then they lay ambush. Maybe we fall in ambush. Then they still more prisoners or . . .' (both in a literal translation). A description of this kind of Double Dutch could deal with questions such as: what exactly is wrong with it (strange words; different word order; infinitives; wrong words etc.)? How would you put it in regular Dutch, etc.? A further step would be to explain why Indians talk like that in books and comics and what Double Dutch expresses apart from content. This explanation leads to the conclusion that this Double Dutch does not show great esteem for other languages: apparently they are considered as inferior, ridiculous deviations. People are ridiculed by being made to talk in a very special way. This could be a starting point for fighting lingocentrism and ethnocentrism in the classroom.

Conclusion

While we recognise that categories such as class, sex and race are ultimately a question of political power (cf. for example Ball, 1987 and Banks & Lynch, 1986), we have been trying to show that in everyday classroom practice there are various opportunities for responding in a positive way to the multi-ethnic character of Dutch society. Multicultural Language Variation Study is a case in point. It aims at lingo-relativism as a basis for fighting prejudice, stereotypes, discrimination and racism, especially if we do not restrict ourselves to dealing with standard Dutch, but also incorporate indigenous and non-indigenous minority languages in language teaching.

Multicultural Language Variation Study is of course only part of the story of language education in a multi-ethnic and multilingual society. It is no doubt also very important to deal in a sociolinguistically sound manner with language diversity in language teaching as well as in other school subjects, and to pay attention to both the teaching of Dutch as a second language and to minority language teaching. A central difference, however, between these issues and Multicultural Language Variation Study is, that the latter is principally meant for all pupils, no matter what ethnic or language groups they belong to, whereas the former are addressed to specific groups of pupils. Multicultural Language Variation Study considers language variation and language diversity as a positive starting point for language teaching for all children, and not as a difficult obstacle in teaching children from ethnic minority groups.

References

BALL, S.J. 1987 English teaching, the state and forms of literacy. In S. KROON and J. STURM (eds), *Research in Mother Tongue Education in an International Perspective*. Enschede: VALO-M (Advisory Committee for Curriculum Development: Mother Tongue Section). pp. 19–35.

BANKS, J.A. and LYNCH, J (eds), 1986 *Multicultural Education in Western Societies*. London: Holt, Rinehart & Winston.

DAAN, J., DEPREZ, K., VAN HOUT, R. and STROOP, J. 1985 *Onze veranderende taal*. Utrecht/Antwerpen: Het Spectrum.

DONALDSON, B.C. 1983 *Dutch. A Linguistic History of Holland and Belgium*. Leiden: Martinus Nijhoff.

DONMALL, B.G. (ed.), 1985 *Language Awareness*. NCLE Papers and Reports 6. London: Centre for Information on Language Teaching and Research.

DOUGHTY, P., PEARCE, J. and THORNTON, G. 1971 *Language in Use*. London: Edward Arnold.

EDWARDS, J. 1985 *Language, Society and Identity*. Oxford: Basil Blackwell/André Deutsch.

EDWARDS, V. 1983 *Language in Multicultural Classrooms*. London: Batsford.

EXTRA, G. and VALLEN, T. 1985 Language and ethnic minorities in the Netherlands: Current issues and research areas. In G. EXTRA and T. VALLEN (eds), *Ethnic Minorities and Dutch as a Second Language*. Dordrecht: Foris. pp. 1–14.

FISHMAN, J.A. 1965 Who speaks what language to whom and when? In *La Linguistique*, 2, 67–88.

GIESBERS, H. and KROON, S. 1986 Intercultureel onderwijs, moedertalen anders dan standaard-Nederlands en taalbeschouwing. In *Moer*, 1/2, 116–24.

GIESBERS, H., KROON, S. and LIEBRAND, R. 1988 Bidialectalism and primary school achievement in a Dutch dialect area. *Language and Education 2*, 77–93.

HAGEN, A. 1981 *Standaardtaal en dialectsprekende kinderen. Een studie over monitoring van taalgebruik*. Muiderberg: Coutinho.

——1982 Dialect. In A. HAGEN and J. STURM, *Dialect en school*. Groningen: Wolters-Noordhoff. pp. 13–117.

HAWKINS, E. 1984 *Awareness of Language: An Introduction*. Cambridge: Cambridge University Press.

HERRLITZ, W., KAMER, A., KROON, S., PETERSE, H., and STURM, J. (eds), 1984 *Mother Tongue Education in Europe. A Survey of Standard Language*

Teaching in Nine European Countries. Enschede: SLO (Institute for Curriculum Development).

KROON, S. and LIEBRAND, R. 1982 Tien lessen over taalvariatie. In *Moer*, 3, 22–34.

——1984 Taalvariatie en dialectbeschouwing. In W. VAN PAASSEN, G. RIJLAARSDAM and F. ZWITSERLOOD (eds), *Taalbeschouwing voor gevorderden. Een bundel artikelen over enkele aspecten van de taalbeschouwing in de bovenbouw.* Den Bosch: Malmberg. pp. 63–85.

KROON, S. and STURM, J. 1985 Implications of Defining Literacy as a Major Goal of Teaching the Mother Tongue in a Multicultural Society; the Dutch Situation. Presentation at the Conference on Plurilingual Education, Venice, April 1985. TILL Paper 83. Tilburg: Tilburg University.

KROON, S. and RASENBERG, A. 1987 Interculturele taalbeschouwing. In *Handboek Intercultureel Onderwijs*. Alphen aan den Rijn: Samsom, 2705/1-2705/16.

LASSWELL, H.D., LERNER, D. and DE SOLA POOL, I. 1952 *The Comparative Study of Symbols: An Introduction.* Stanford: Stanford University Press.

MILLER, J. 1983 *Many Voices. Bilingualism, Culture and Education.* London: Routledge & Kegan Paul.

MOLONY, C. 1980 Choosing bicultural programs for Moluccan pupils: an argument for a sociolinguistic approach. *Toegepaste Taalwetenschap in Artikelen*, 8, 7–38.

NIJMEEGSE WERKGROEP TAALDIDACTIEK 1985 *Taaldidactiek aan de basis.* Groningen: Wolters-Noordhoff.

POPLACK, S. 1980 Sometimes I'll start a sentence in English Y TERMINO EN ESPAÑOL: toward a typology of code-switching. *Linguistics*, 18, 581–618.

RALEIGH, M., MILLER, J. and SIMONS, M. 1981, *The Languages Book.* London: ILEA English Centre.

STURM, J. 1982 Onderwijs in dialectbeschouwing. In A. HAGEN and J. STURM, *Dialect en school.* Groningen: Wolters-Noordhoff. pp. 119–44.

——1984 Report on the development of mother tongue education in the Netherlands since 1969. In W. HERRLITZ *et al.* (eds), *Mother Tongue Education in Europe: A Survey of Standard Language Teaching in Nine European Countries.* Enschede: SLO. pp. 238–76.

16 Language in the classroom: The Amsterdam and Groningen projects

CO VAN CALCAR, WIM VAN CALCAR
and COEN DE JONGE

Inequality of Opportunity in Education and Society

There has been a growing interest in the post-war period, both in the Netherlands and abroad, in whether the opportunities available to children from so-called disadvantaged backgrounds can be improved by any kind of social or educational intervention. This question has not merely been a matter of academic interest. In the Netherlands, for instance, a series of local projects were set up with the aim of informing educational policy.

Interest in this general area gained much of its force from a series of empirical studies in the 1960s and 1970s. Empirical study, moreover, preceded, accompanied and followed a great many projects for change. These studies showed clearly that children from disadvantaged backgrounds — the children of uneducated manual workers or the increasing number of children from ethnic minorities — are poorly equipped to do well in school or society, even when they are of normal or above normal intelligence. These children run a considerable risk of becoming cultural and social outsiders through social circumstances for which they are not responsible.

Emphasis on Language in Two Educational Projects

Major emphasis was placed on new approaches to language teaching in the various local and national educational research projects. This was seen as necessary not only because of underachievement in the traditional 'language' domain but also because of underperformance in other parts of the curriculum which was considered to be language related. At the primary level, for instance, it became apparent that simple mathematical calculations were proving difficult because of children's lack of familiarity with the language of mathematics.

Two projects in particular attached a great deal of importance both to language study and 'language across the curriculum'. The first was the 'Innovatieproject Amsterdam' (Amsterdam Innovation Project), a local initiative supported by the Ministry of Education and the Ministry of Welfare and Culture as well as by the Bernard van Leer Foundation between 1970 and 1979 (van Calcar, 1976; 1980a). The second was the A-2 Project in Groningen. This formed part of a national research project started in 1974 designed to promote educational innovation on a national level (de Jonge, 1986).

In both projects, the new approach to language teaching was just one aspect of a whole range of new developments, including efforts to change the content of — and approaches to — teaching. The basic assumption was that the 'new style' school would try to ensure that all children would have equality of opportunity in education. In order to achieve this end, inequalities in all aspects of the children's lives would need to be addressed: the widespread belief that change could be affected by the school alone was beginning to be questioned. Three priorities for change emerged — educational policy and practice within the school; the recognition of the educational potential of family and community; the creation of neighbourhood facilities which would lead to an improvement in living conditions.

Developments within langage teaching which form the focus for the present chapter need to be seen within the context of broader educational developments. For instance, there was a move from the traditional highly competitive 'chalk and talk' style lessons towards more collaborative teaching methods. It was felt that the pupil's independence should be fostered by paying attention to the processes of learning and discovery: there was no longer any room for the notion of the omniscient teacher as dispenser of knowledge and the pupil as an empty vessel absorbing knowledge. The curriculum became more child-centred and started to incorporate topic work. Possibly of greatest significance, however, was the growth on the part of the teacher of acceptance and appreciation of the social identity of the pupils.

The culture hypothesis

Both the Amsterdam and the Groningen projects recognised the need to improve both home–school relations and facilities in the wider community and therefore worked in co-operation with neighbourhood centres, libraries and community groups. The aim was to improve out-of-school opportunities for personal development and thus broaden experience.

The basic assumption of the projects was that the children's own experience was valid in itself and could serve as a valuable starting point for extending children's knowledge still further. In the context of the Groningen project, the children's own experience was used as a starting point for the teaching of reading and arithmetic (Bollen & de Jonge, 1985; Meijnen, 1982). The Amsterdam project developed this approach still further on the basis of what they formulated as 'the culture hypothesis' (Mens & van Calcar, 1981). The basic assumption of this thesis can be stated in the following terms: language acquisition increases and the acquisition of knowledge improves when the learner has access to a greater range of socio-cultural experience.

In this view of learning, language acquisition is a function of the different activities in which we are involved. In an educational setting we therefore need to multiply the number of situations in which language can be used both actively and passively. Children need to be given more responsibility for organisation, control and decision making. And all of this must take place in an atmosphere where children's non-standard language use is accepted as a reflection of their personality and social identity.

The culture hypothesis can thus be seen as having a great deal in common with the functional approach and arguably represents a breakthrough in the long-standing impasse in the different–deficit debate. In an educational context, the functional approach to language implies that while the uniqueness of children from disadvantaged backgrounds is acknowledged and respected, the emphasis is, none the less, on helping children to acquire the higher status standard language. The culture hypothesis goes a step further by suggesting that the acquisition of the standard language should be mediated through the social and linguistic experience of the child and need not in any way detract from the value of the non-standard speaker's language and culture.

A Theory of Language in Education

Language deals with reality. Since it is not within the school's power to singlehandedly transform the present social reality, it makes sense to formulate a theory of language which will enable the school to work within the limits of what it can achieve. Such a theory needs to take into consideration the three main functions of language: language in action; language in knowledge; and language in communication.

Language in action

Since language leads to action, educators generally have no difficulty with the notion that the language production of children from disadvantaged backgrounds is adequate and effective, at least in certain situations. This emerged very clearly from interviews with teachers on the Groningen project (van Calcar, 1980b). Dialect' is recognised as the language spoken by everyone in rural areas and is only problematic when transfer takes place from the dialect to the standard language. This would be the case with a sentence like 'My mother is out camping' spoken by a native of the north-west English town of Blackburn. The speaker is not implying that mother is engaging in an activity involving tents but rather is chatting to someone, since the dialect word 'camping' means just that. The same would apply to a dialect construction such as 'I be tired' used in the south-west of England in preference to the standard 'I am tired'. In point of fact, many of the Groningen teachers expressed great admiration for the communicative skills of their dialect-speaking children in certain circumstances. As one of the teachers remarked,

> The children often use graphic language. When they were describing one of the women teachers taking part in a sponsored walk they described her as a 'walking powder compact'. They can express themselves very well, especially when they are allowed to be spontaneous' (van Calcar, 1980b: 52)

Teachers' appreciation of dialect speakers' communicative abilities in more formal situations, however, is a great deal more grudging. The following remarks are typical of the Groningen sample:

> Their vocabulary is pretty limited. The number of words they have at their disposal is not very great. If I compare the way that a child here talks with the way my son talks, I see a world of difference . . . They have very little experience of things outside their own neighbourhood. At one stage I was sitting with some parents in a meeting to discuss a merger between two schools. Parents and teachers were hardly out of the door when the parents said to me: 'My God! What a load of rubbish they were talking! They led us up the garden path, the lousy lot!' And I said, 'Good grief! Why couldn't you have said that before now? Let's go back and you can tell them what you've just told me.'

But you have to ask yourself how this can happen. There seems to be some kind of blocking mechanism.

Teachers thus tend to judge dialect-speaking children's language as inadequate for school or the wider society. In their terms, language does not lead to action in these situations. This has implications for the two other functions of language: language for acquiring knowledge and language for communication.

Language and knowledge

Knowledge transmitted through language is not only descriptive in its nature but also establishes values and norms (Klaus, 1971). Take the word 'school'. The Concise Oxford Dictionary offers the following description:

–institution for educating children or giving instruction
–buildings of such institution.

Yet words are not purely descriptive. Values and norms are not vague notions, but are inextricably linked with language. School is important or unimportant, useful or useless, pleasant or unpleasant. There are strong indications that the values and the assumptions of educators are not shared equally by all the children in their care, and the starting point of many children from disadvantaged backgrounds may be very far removed from that of their middle class teachers. This has important implications for the performance of children from different social backgrounds. If the teacher fails to start from where the child is, there is a serious risk that they will be working at cross-purposes. The transmission of knowledge can only be successful when teachers accept the norms and values of their pupils.

Language and communication

Speakers of a language know not only the grammatical rules but how to use language appropriately for different purposes and in different situations. There are rules for dialogue, statement, reasoning, propaganda, informal conversations, idle chatter, interviews, policy statements. In many kinds of formal communication, for instance, there is an assumption that the speaker does not refer to personal values and norms. As a result, speakers can be caught off balance if they are unfamiliar with the rules for a particular situation, and operate in a different way. This, of course, is precisely what happened with the parents mentioned in the interview above who reported that they felt 'led up the garden path'. They had failed to understand that you can find yourself at a serious disadvantage if you do not observe the communicative norms for a given situation.

Knowledge of the language user

There are two other areas of language use in which dialect speakers find themselves at a disadvantage in a school system which is predicated on the use of the standard language and middle class values. The first relates to the knowledge of language structures; the second to the knowledge of social relations.

When they speak proper Dutch they dry up completely. They pronounce the words incorrectly. The syntax is unacceptable. It gets all mixed up or you get unfinished sentences. And of course this is even more so in the case of immigrant children. The children are not at all reticent when speaking dialect at 'News Time', but don't bother telling them: 'Now try it in proper Dutch'.

Teachers can thus be seen to be critical of non-standard speakers in all four areas of knowledge which play a role in the use of language. Children are seen as lacking knowledge of meanings and combinations of meanings and, as a result, knowledge of the reality that language is dealing with. They are seen as lacking in their knowledge of syntax and pragmatics. Finally, they are seen as lacking knowledge of social and personal relationships and their consequences.

Skills in this area can be seen as relevant not only to talking and listening, the subject dealt with in the interviews quoted above. They are arguably even more important for reading and writing.

A closer look at reading

Reading is not simply a matter of deciphering words or stringing them together to make a sentence. It is a complex activity bound by rules and it must be learned. One example of these rules is that reading must be meaningful. In a story about a girl running away from home, for instance, the reader might expect to find information on questions such as Why? Where to? Alone or with others? What are the consequences? Fluent reading is active reading: predicting what comes next and possibly modifying the prediction in the light of what follows (Bol, 1982; Westhoff, 1981).

'Meaning' depends not only on the written words but on the reader's knowledge of the world. For instance, anyone who reads, 'After queuing up for hours at the theatre, they went home empty handed', needs to know about booking seats and picking up tickets if they are to understand the text. Good readers are also familiar with the cultural protocol to which texts are subjected: they know that an essay makes different demands from a review or a newspaper editorial. When they read they do so in the light of this knowledge. They will also know that, while there is a general expectation that language users speak the truth or, at least, do not deliberately mislead their audience, there are some occasions on which this rule is deliberately transgressed.

If the school wishes to encourage children to become good readers, it has to familiarise them with the rules of the game. This means that teachers need to extend children's knowledge of the language, the use of language and their conception of reality. They need to teach them to identify the base lines and teach children to be able to use them to their own advantage.

Language awareness

Children learn language not only by doing — talking and listening — but also by reflecting on content and form. They listen to themselves, try out sounds, explore the boundaries between meaning and sound with the help of word games or jokes, by asking questions and being critical (Britton, 1970; van der Geest, 1975; Levelt, Sinclair & Jarvella, 1978). This process continues well beyond the first stages of language acquisition and is a necessary part of any language teaching which takes place in school.

Teachers as well as pupils need to develop an awareness of language. The teacher needs to have an insight into both language and language use. Children need to be exposed to a wide range of different language situations that will enable them to develop a broad linguistic repertoire. The teacher will also need to have a well-thought out policy on language matters as diverse as spelling mistakes, dialect features and slang.

A basic programme of language awareness would encompass:

a) *Sociolinguistics.* Children need to develop an understanding of the appropriateness of different linguistic varieties for different situations. We do not speak in the same way to someone younger than us as we do to someone who is older; we write differently from the way we speak, etc.

b) *Pragmatics*. Children need to understand that, for example, a text is constructed in a particular way and that its parts have various functions. They need to know what to expect when they are reading and that they must follow the same conventions when they write.

c) *Semantics*. Children must know that words are not simply descriptive but also have an evaluative dimension.

d) *Syntax*. Children need, for instance, an awareness of the rules concerning word order, sentence length and explicitness of relationships.

e) *Phonology*. In the area of spelling or pronunciation, children need to know the areas which require their particular attention.

We are, of course, talking in terms of developing an awareness of these areas rather than imparting factual knowledge. The main aim of work in this area is to encourage children to look objectively at the language which they use themselves and which is used all around them.

Children are faced with the challenge of mastering two quite different skills: the one executive (reading, writing, listening, talking), the other supervisory (evaluating, checking) (Wagoner, 1983: Fischer & Mandl, 1984). They have to become their own consciences, building their own monitoring systems. We need to remember, of course, the broader social context and the power structures in the world beyond the school. In the final analysis language is worth what the user is worth (Bourdieu, 1982). But the school can certainly help to improve children's life chances through good language education, as the renewal projects which drew their inspiration from these insights have been able to show (van Calcar, 1980a; Meijnen, 1981; Soutendijk, 1986). The ways in which theory has been translated into practice in these projects are described in the paragraphs which follow.

Consequences for Language Teaching

Our analysis of language use as a kind of action influenced the form of the language teaching in the two projects. The language teaching techniques led ultimately to various modifications of our initial hypothesis (reported in *Moer*, 1974: 3; 1975: 3; 1979: 4; van Calcar & van Calcar, 1975; Koster, 1980). This mutual interaction between theory and practice was the cornerstone of policy in both projects. Some of the ways in which this happened are outlined below.

Reading readiness

Children gain an understanding of the reading process through their own experience of the written word. By communicating their own thoughts and wishes in writing and drawing they can learn that real people are concealed within a text. Hence it was thought important to pay attention to the way in which children communicate their own experiences. The following example shows how this can be done.

Children were asked to make drawings of things they had experienced, imagined or learned from their teachers. Subsequently the teacher — or an adult auxiliary, usually a parent — was told the story behind the drawing and wrote out the story. Drawings and texts were then bound together to form a simple book. This meant that part of the children's experience was recorded. The children could refer to it whenever they wished and it soon became clear that they made frequent use of their own books. There is evidence that the knowledge of letters in children who used this approach was considerably in advance of that of children from similar backgrounds at the start of formal teaching of reading and writing (van Calcar, 1976: 184).

There are many other examples of ways of recording children's experience. It is possible, for instance to make holiday diaries; birthday calendars, possibly in the form of self-portraits, or graphs recording characteristics such as the number of girls and boys or the number of people with blue eyes in the class (Noot & van Schaik, 1976; Hülsenbeck, 1979). The direct and personal experience of the children finds expression in a written form. Children's own need to develop is thus channelled via reading and writing, as can be seen in the following example:

> He got me to go over to a corner of the classroom where he was busy with two other boys. They were working on an old bill that one of them had found: a little scrap of headed paper with an advert for beer printed on it. They wanted to make this 'official' piece of paper into a ticket for the teacher. After some confusion I realised they meant a parking ticket that they wanted to put on the windscreen of her car. They asked me if I would help them write it. I asked them what they wanted to put on the ticket. First of all 'Bureau' [police station] had to be on it because the teacher had to go to the police. They already had a 'B'. This was from Bennie (one of the three boys). They were also able to copy the letter out of a book they had in the cupboard. But they wanted to know how to go on from there. There was a flannelgraph in the class with separate stick-on letters. I walked over

to it and got the 'u', the 'r' and the 'o'. I put these down in front of them. Now they could write 'buro'. Later one of the boys drew a star on the paper and explained: 'Now it says *police* station'. When I asked him to explain, he said that it was what you saw on police cars (which is right: the white police cars in Amsterdam have a kind of star for a badge). Then the boys wanted to make clear that the ticket was for driving under the influence of too much alcohol. Another of the boys drew a bottle of brandy. Finally, happy with their efforts, they agreed to put the ticket on the windscreen after school.

In a child centred approach to learning of this kind, the teacher starts with the pupils' own experience and extends from this base to an exploration of the outside world, even at a very young age. This can be

FIGURE 1 *Example of work done in 'writing corners' in the Oost-Indische Kers Infant School in Amsterdam*

illustrated by an example from the Groningen project. One of the 5–7-year-olds brought a stick insect into school. The whole group talked about it together. The teacher drew a stick insect on the board and wrote the words underneath. After a thorough discussion of the subject, the children recorded the event with a collage. The children's collages were hung from a string in a prominent position for some time so that parents would see them when they brought their children into the classroom. Later the collages were put in the children's personal record books.

In the meantime the school had begun with the help of parents to set up a 'documentation corner'. Pictures were cut out of various magazines and sorted out into various headings. Shoeboxes labelled with the different headings were placed on a shelf in the corridor and teachers, parents and children added new pictures to the boxes. Then the pictures were mounted on to white paper and placed in a file to make a whole series of books on subjects which ranged from pets to festivals and toys to food.

In Groningen, reading readiness activities led to the setting up of what came to be known as scribble corners, which in later years developed into writing and composing corners. Here the children were able to work independently with the minimum of guidance.

Initial reading and writing

Personal experience is also an important starting point in the formal teaching of reading and writing. In a 'language experience' approach children dictate stories to the teacher about their own activities and experience. They then read back what the teacher has written down so that their own stories can supplement published reading material.

Spelling, composition and more advanced reading

Most children dislike traditional exercises on grammar, spelling and style. Equally important there is no evidence of successful transfer from these exercises to the children's own writing. By drawing on the children's own experience, however, it is often possible to find more interesting and acceptable ways of discussing areas such as these.

A class of 9–10-year-olds had decided to write a book. One of the children had made up the story and this was duly tape recorded. This method was chosen because the children were having difficulty in actually transcribing the story. The recorded story was later typed out, duplicated and distributed to every child during a language lesson. Discussion centred on whether the story, revised or not, was suitable for inclusion in the class book. Points of discussion included whether the story was too long, too dull, too happy or too sad.

One story told of a stupid duck who wanted to leave duck land because everybody treated him as though he were stupid. The class liked the story well enough but they found it dull because it was full of sentences beginning 'and then, and then . . .' This led to the class looking at the parts of the textbook which dealt with conjunctions and adverbs (van Calcar, 1976: 254).

Various aspects of the traditional teaching of reading need also to be carefully scrutinised. Teachers tend to overemphasise the decoding of the text at the expense of reading with understanding. Reading aloud in turn is used as a means of maintaining classroom order. A great deal of attention is paid to testing reading achievement and not enough to the spontaneous enjoyment of books. In both projects, reading was promoted as an enjoyable and meaningful experience: children were encouraged to discuss the books they were reading and exchange experiences with other children.

Conclusion

We have given here some examples of the ways in which the Groningen and Amsterdam projects developed a language experience approach, the main thrust of which was to build on, rather than to criticise and reject, the social and linguistic skills of non-standard Dutch speakers. The projects tackled many other language related issues, too. Most notable was the development of materials for topic work at both primary and secondary level which allowed the children to draw on their own experience and make both reading and writing more relevant.

Such developments give rise to all sorts of problems and obstacles. They require, for instance, that teachers completely rethink their approach to both literacy and the curriculum. They can also generate a great deal more work, especially when it comes to monitoring individual children's progress. However, the advantages are plain to see. An approach which makes learning more enjoyable, more relevant and more meaningful produces children who are eager to read, happy to write and motivated to learn.

References

BOL, E. 1982 *Leespsychologie, Leerpsychologie en onderwijs*. Groningen: Wolters-Noordhoff.

BOLLEN, N. and DE JONGE, C. 1985 Gezellig achterblijven of energiek inhalen? *Onderwijs en Opvoeding* 36(8).

BOURDIEU, P. 1982 *Ce que parler veut dire*. Paris: Fayard.

BRITTON, J. 1970 *Language and Learning*. London: Allen Lane, The Penguin Press.

FISCHER, P.M. and MANDL, H. 1984 Learner, text variables and the control of text comprehension and recall. In H. MANDL, N.L. STEIN & T. TRABASSO (eds), *Learning and Comprehension of Texts*. Hillsdale, N.J.: Erlbaum Associates.

GEEST, T. VAN DER 1975 *Some Aspects of Communicative Competence and their Applications for Language Acquisition*. Assen: Van Gorcum.

HÜLSENBECK, C. 1979 *Van krastekening tot zelfgeschreven kinderboek*. Amsterdam: ABC.

JONGE, C. DE 1986 *A-2 Project Groningen, Eindverslag 1975–1983*. OVB-reeks 143, Groningen/Hoevelaken.

KLAUS, G. 1971 *Sprache der Politik*. Berlin: Ost.

KOSTER, K. 1980 *Haalbaar projectonderwijs*. IPB-reeks 42. Amsterdam: APS.

LEVELT, W.J.M., SINCLAIR, A. and JARVELLA, R.J. 1978 Causes and functions of linguistic awareness in language acquisition. Some introductory remarks. In A. SINCLAIR, R.J. JARVELLA & W.J.M. LEVELT (eds), *The Child's Conception of Language*. Berlin: Springer.

MEIJNEN, G.W. 1982 *Schoolloopbanen in het lager onderwijs*. Groningen: Sociologisch Instituut.

MENS, A. and VAN CALCAR, C. 1981 *Onderwijsstimulering op weg. Samenvatting van ITS en SCO-onderzoeken uit 1978–80*. Nijmegen/Amsterdam: ITS/SCO.

MOER, A. 1979 *Tijdschrift voor het Onderwijs in het Nederlands*. Alkmaar: Vereniging voor Onderwijs in het Nederlands (VON).

NOOT, A. and VAN SCHAIK, S. 1976 *Engelse brieven: een bezoek aan Engelse Infant scholen*. Amsterdam: RITP/ABC.

SOUTENDIJK, S. 1986 *Striptease van een valse boodschap*. Amsterdam: ABC.

VAN CALCAR, C. 1976 *Innovatieproject Amsterdam, deel 11: Tussenstand*. Amsterdam: Van Gennep (English translation (1977): *Innovation Project Amsterdam, Volume 11: A Summary*. Amsterdam: RITP).

——1980a *Innovatieproject Amsterdam, Eindverslag: een Opening*. Amsterdam: Van Gennep.

——1980b *Stimuleringservaringen onder woorden gebracht*. Interviews uit Groningen en Helmond. Deelverslag 5 - Evaluatie Onderwijsstimulering. Amsterdam: RITP.

VAN CALCAR, C. and VAN CALCAR, W. 1975 *Onderwijs aan (arbeiders) kinderen. School, buurt en maatschappij*. Didactische Analyse 3b, no. 18. Groningen: Wolters-Noordhoff.

WAGONER, S.A. 1983 Comprehension monitoring: what it is and what we know about it. *Reading Research Quarterly* 18, 328–46.

WESTHOFF, G.J. 1981 *Voorspellend lezen*. Een didactische benadering van de leesvaardigheidstraining in het moderne vreemde talenonderwijs. Groningen: Wolters-Noordhoff.

17 Language awareness in British schools

ANN PIERCE JONES

Introduction

Over the past few years a new phenomenon has made itself known on the curriculum of some British schools. It is concerned with the study of language in various forms, and generally given the name 'Language Awareness'. For most of this period, language awareness (LA) has existed only in a few schools, and has had a transitory, temporary status: however, it appears to be growing, with more schools either initiating their own courses or requesting permission to teach those developed in other schools. One significant feature of LA is the tendency for schools to produce their own courses and materials instead of using commercially produced ones. This suggests that LA enjoys a strong sympathy in the staffroom, backed up by practical commitment. The role of Local Education Authority advisers, although noticeable in some areas, is generally secondary. It seems fair to say that LA has considerable grass roots support among teachers. However, one commercial course has had a deep influence on thinking in LA, and continues to be widely used. This is Hawkins' (1984) 'Awareness of Language', which is both a general discussion of LA and an LA course.

Despite the proliferation of LA courses, it is not a straightforward matter to define what language awareness is. The National Congress on Languages in Education (NCLE) says that LA 'refers to a person's sensitivity and conscious awareness of the nature of language and its role in human life.' (Donmall, 1985) This could embrace the toddler's liking for the sound of a particular word, an older child or adult's musing on the origins of a word, and the linguist's hypotheses about stages in Second Language Acquisition. What distinguishes LA from the simple use of language would seem to be the presence of conscious scrutiny; the making of language into something external to ourselves, unfamiliar, and subject to analysis. This would therefore seem to be the global aim of all LA work. But it does not address the questions of why or how this should be done. Is it worth decontextualising language in this way (intellectual enjoyment apart), and how can it be done?

The discussion which follows looks at how a number of LA courses have tried to answer these questions. Their aims relate to the purpose of LA, while their contents and methodologies represent ways of accomplishing these. The second part of the discussion attempts to situate LA within a historical context. It argues that LA should be seen as the hybrid product of four influences, and that because of this it is almost bound to be a confusing compromise. Finally, the place of assessment of LA is considered.

Aims of Language Awareness Courses

The focus of interest in this section is the aims and methods of LA courses. Seven courses are looked at. These courses were chosen because they cover the period 1980–87 and seem to be representative of the main trends in LA during that time. Courses for a variety of ages are included. To some extent, Hawkins' 'Awareness of Language' is taken as a reference point. Whereas early LA work tended to be more exploratory, courses which appeared after 1984 showed the influence of Hawkins' ideas and his recommended practice.

The first published accounts of LA work in schools appeared in a volume of case studies which formed part of the Open University (1985) In-service pack, *Every Child's Language*. Here, Robins describes an LA course developed in 1980 for 11–12-year-olds in Concord Middle School, Sheffield. The main aims were reducing reluctance to, or increasing motivation for, learning a second language, and the promotion of a more positive attitude to languages other than English. She also stresses a methodology which invites intellectual exploration by the pupils. Redfern (1985), whose 'Class Project on Language' was done with Junior pupils aged 9–10 in 1982, does not specify any aims. However, the report mentions the use of pupils' linguistic skills and parental involvement. Hudson's 'Project on Spoken Language', designed in 1984 for 8–10-year-olds, specifies five aims. They include encouraging children to view their own bilingualism in a positive light, as well as strengthening respect for the child's own mother tongue and that of others. Children were to be familiarised with dialects and helped to value these. The remaining aims concerned body language and biological aspects of talk. The classroom method involved much discussion-based work, with or without a teacher present, and Hudson comments that 'This sharing of experiences and ideas was seen as an extremely important part of the work.'

Hawkins' 'Awareness of Language' was published in 1984. It was a key book because it established a coherent framework for LA, effectively placing it within the educational and conceptual concerns of the period. The range of objectives which Hawkins outlines for LA indicates the breadth of his concerns. Firstly, LA is seen as a bridge between primary and secondary work, a way into the specialised language of secondary school subjects. Secondly, it provides a common ground for various aspects of language education (Modern and Classical Languages; English as a Second Language or ESL; Mother Tongue Teaching, including English). It seeks to prompt curiosity about the nature of language in general. Through giving support to language diversity, LA aims to challenge linguistic prejudice. Two further aims relate to language learning: giving insight into pattern in language, and practice in learning to listen. The course aims to promote a new approach to the process of matching spoken and written language. The final aim has to do with teaching methods. This is seen as centred around pupil-based activities, such as pair work; however, a degree of teacher-initiated information-giving is also envisaged.

Perhaps one of the most surprising things about these objectives is the absence of any emphasis on compensatory-education, given the importance that language deprivation is given in Hawkins' overall position. However, elsewhere Hawkins stresses that the 'fundamental need' is to restore adult time to young children who are deprived of it (Chapter 5, 97–98). From this perspective Hawkins would presumably see LA as only complementary to an adult-time provision programme throughout schooling. In fact, though, no special provision is outlined for those whose adult-time provision might be considered unsatisfactory in the LA Topic Books which accompany 'Awareness of Language' (viz. Astley, 1983; Hawkins, 1983; B. Jones, 1984; Astley & Hawkins, 1984; Dunlea, 1985; Pomphrey, 1985; McGurn, 1986). This would lead one to believe that the language deprivation element is not an essential part of Hawkins' LA programme. This issue is revisited in pp. 275–76 of this chapter.

The aims of three London secondary schools which have initiated LA courses will now be considered. The courses are typical of developments all over the United Kingdom, and were chosen because they exemplify three different approaches within one metropolitan education authority.

Quintin Kynaston School, North London, started LA work in 1983, and has been reviewing and redesigning it since. The short introductory language course run for first year pupils has three aims. Firstly, to combat linguistic narrow-mindedness by presenting samples of world languages; secondly, to acknowledge the language skills of bilingual pupils, and thirdly to make all pupils feel that they have the ability to master another language. The course draws in part on the Hawkins Topic books. It also uses pupil discussion and language resources, but in a fairly limited way.

In Crofton School (South East London) the LA course was initiated by the Head of Languages, Tony Roberts, in 1984–85. It lasts one year and is aimed at first years. Roberts shares Hawkins' view that a large proportion of working class children are linguistically deprived and sees the course as partly designed to alleviate language deficit. The course is intended to prepare students for foreign language learning, through experiencing 'tasters' of four languages. (A taster course is a short language course which aims mainly to teach simple social exchanges, and usually draws on all four language skills.) One of the language tasters offered at Crofton is Turkish, the school's most widely spoken minority language, which is offered as a language option in the fourth year. An additional aim of the course is to enhance positive perception of community languages. The course methodology is mainly teacher-centred.

The final LA course to be looked at is the one developed by Geoffrey Frith, the Head of Languages at Plashet School in East Ham. This was piloted in 1986–87. No less than 13 aims were put forward for it. However, they may be grouped into four categories. Five pertain to stimulating a positive attitude towards language diversity (including dialects as well as other languages) and bilingualism. Four aims relate to language study, in particular etymology. There are two very open-ended aims: one, bridging the gap between primary and secondary schooling, echoes Hawkins. The other claims to give insight into the role of language at home and at school, and probably concerns the range of linguistic skills possessed by pupils. Finally, LA is seen as promoting study skills. The course methodology aims to draw on pupils' language proficiency, the intention being to create an environment in which 'pupils can feel free to share their knowledge with others.'

This rapid survey of seven LA courses has highlighted some recurring concerns. First, predictably, there is a desire to excite interest in language for its own sake, which matches up with the global aim described earlier. This is especially noticeable in the early programmes, such as those of Redfern and Robins. Another common aim is the challenging of linguistic prejudice towards minority languages and non-standard dialects, mentioned in all but one course and implicit in the exception (Redfern, 1985). This is frequently accompanied by a desire to improve the status of bilingualism. Yet another prominent aim is the fostering of positive attitudes towards language learning, mentioned by all but two courses. Hawkins and Roberts are alone in subscribing to language compensatory aims. Hawkins' specification of awareness of language across the curriculum is not taken up in any of the courses. What is very interesting is that in addition to these stated aims, virtually every course propounds a methodology which stresses child-centredness. But there are varying degrees of commitment to this educational principle, from Hudson's 'the main resource for the project was the children themselves' (1985: 19) to Hawkins' more cautious 'a classroom method relying chiefly on pupils' activities' (1984: 5).

Influences on Language Awareness

LA courses, then, are definitely hybrids. But why are the hybrids made up of these particular strains? The second part of my discussion deals with four influences which appear to have helped to parent LA. They are: child-centred education; the impact of Commonwealth immigration into Britain on the education system; the effects of the Bullock report, and the gestation of a new approach to modern languages teaching.

A child-centred approach to education

The child-centred perspective on education which developed in the 1960s saw the child both as the starting point of the educational experience and as an actor, rather than recipient, in that experience. The latter view led to greater involvement of children in finding things out in the classroom, and to the use of group talk as an educational tool. We have seen that these teaching methods are characteristic of LA work. But child-centred education involved more than the decentralisation of teaching methods; it also meant the decentralisation of knowledge. The knowledge brought to school by the child was given validity and recognition.

The 'Language in Use' materials developed by Doughty, Pearce & Thornton (1971) illustrate this. Thornton (1986: 53) reports a teacher who had introduced these materials into the classroom as saying 'It was as if those kids were being listened to for the first time in their lives.' One of the aims of 'Language in Use' was to show that all individuals have a wide range of language registers, which can be used on different occasions. The movement towards greater acceptance of dialect has been an issue since 1911 at least, when a writer named MacBride vigorously contested a report on teaching English in London elementary schools which called the Cockney dialect 'a modern corruption without legitimate credentials' (Thornton, 1986). Linguistic opinion fed into the debate in the 1970s, with Trudgill (1975) arguing that dialects are linguistically well-formed and that verbal and written forms of dialect should be looked on favourably in school. More recent work on the rule-governed nature of British Black English or Patois, which is just beginning to be known in schools, bears out this view (Sutcliffe, 1982; Edwards, 1986).

The contribution to LA of the child-centred approach to education is found in the aim of lessening linguistic parochialism, especially where dialect is concerned. It is also found in the predominating view of pupils as linguistically resourceful, with a large and varied stock of language strategies. Thus it affects LA on many levels, not least the very concept of education as starting with the child. In fact another movement, which we shall consider now, culminated in a similar type of input into education in general and into LA in particular.

The educational impact of New Commonwealth immigration

The arrival in the UK of substantial numbers of Afro-Caribbean and Asian children, who were bidialectal and bilingual, has had important long-term repercussions on the curriculum. The first provision made for bilingual pupils was the teaching of English as a second language (ESL) in withdrawal groups. This separatist policy, criticised in Swann (1985) and in a report by the Commission for Racial Equality (1986), is being replaced by English language development in the classroom, together with support of bilingualism. The bilingualism support programmes are still tentative and exploratory. Support can take the form of having teachers working alongside mainstream teachers whose brief it is to foster the overall language development of bilingual students (that is, in both English and their mother tongue). Alternatively, it can consist of providing resources for bilingual students' use in classrooms. A major initiative in the second category is the ILEA's 'World in a City' bilingual pack (1985), which was designed to be an optional resource in mainstream classrooms. Houlton (1985) documents ways in which both types of bilingual support can be made available in primary classrooms.

In a general sense as well as the specifically linguistic one, a gradual awareness of the need to replace an anglocentric curriculum with a multicultural one has made itself felt. The Department of Education and Science has set up courses; books have been written, and the concept has been sanctioned by the Swann Report. Increasingly, however, the emphasis is passing from multicultural education to anti-racism. Whereas multicultural education proposes the replacement of an ethnocentric educational framework with a pluralist one, anti-racism identifies racism in society as the root cause of under-achievement and emphasises strategies for combatting racism.

The multicultural and anti-racist impetus has contributed to the emphasis in LA on perceiving linguistic diversity as positive. This works on a number of levels; it attempts to put the English language into a relativist perspective as one of many world and community languages; whilst at the same time it brings community and world languages into focus in the classroom. The 'taster' approach has similarities with bilingual education in the latter respect, but also represents a half-way measure because of its limited scope and duration. In the same way as multicultural education, LA is intended to work for the benefit of cultural majority and minority alike.

The effects of the Bullock Report

The Bullock Report (1975) with its title 'A Language for Life', addressed itself to the role of language in all areas of the curriculum. It reinforced the child-centred view of education, with its famous axiom that the child should not be expected to cast off the language of the home as (s)he crosses the school threshold. Three aspects of the Report concern us in particular: language across the curriculum, teacher training about language, and language deprivation.

The main thrust of the notion of 'language across the curriculum' was to make teachers aware of the part played by language in all specialised subject work. It stressed above all the need to build on pupil talk as a way of exploring new concepts. There is also an emphasis on widening the scope of writing tasks and the utility of study skills. Follow-up books and projects (such as Robertson, 1981) bring out the mediating role of talk as a means to learning. Hawkins sees LA as an opportunity to put into effect what Bullock preached. Firstly, it offers a coherent start to the child's secondary school language experience. It also provides an opportunity for teaching staff from different departments to come together to plan and implement the LA work. As we have seen, many LA courses offer study skills practice as well as organising work around talk.

The Bullock Report gave renewed vigour to the language deprivation debate. The Report claims that:

There is an indisputable gap between the language experiences that some families provide, and the linguistic demands of school education. (5.9)

It lists several types of talk which are said to be in short supply in working class homes (economic classes IV and V); for example, projecting into the future and creating experiences through the imagination (Tough, 1974, cited by Bullock). This is linked with the failure to give children adequate adult talk. The language deprivation issue is lent some validity by the scholastic underachievement of working class pupils. However, the picture is more complex than Bullock or Hawkins assume. More recent research undertaken with young children and mothers from working class backgrounds shows the types of talk that Tough claims to be lacking in these environments in fact being used (Tizard & Hughes, 1984). The authors are critical of Tough's conclusions, and point to a disparity between the relative richness and breadth of learning and talking experiences at home and the more restricted possibilities for intellectually stimulating talk offered at nursery school. The work of Wells (1981; 1984) on language development in pre-school children also supports this position. The whole issue of the gap between the demands of school and what the child brings to school requires a multi-dimensional approach which encompasses language attitudes, teacher expectations and teacher interaction style. In J. Edwards' (1979) study, children from 'disadvantaged' homes tended to be perceived as potentially low achievers by teachers, while V. Edwards' (1978, 1979) work with trainee teachers suggests disquietingly stereotypical assumptions triggered by working class and West Indian accents. Research has therefore helped to shift the spotlight away from children's home backgrounds and to focus it, instead, on the preconceptions of the school and educators. The language deprivation issue has thereby lost energy, although it continues to linger on in the work of Hawkins. There is clearly tension between the emphasis on the child's linguistic resourcefulness, which is embodied in most LA courses, and the tenets of language deprivation. Not surprisingly, the courses which give credence to language deprivation (Hawkins, Roberts) tend to be less oriented towards independent pupil activity.

Developments in modern languages teaching

The final contribution to LA to be discussed is that of modern languages teaching. During the 1970s dissatisfaction grew with the highly routinised audiolingual approach to language teaching. At the same time the take-up rate for language options dropped. This led to a renewed interest in a more cognitive approach. Work on aptitude testing indicated that the ability to perceive patterns or rules correlated highly with success in learning a foreign language (Carroll, 1983; Green, 1975). Similarly, research on short term memory points to the usefulness of pattern recognition in facilitating memorisation. This suggested that practice in spotting and making patterns would be a fruitful way of preparing for foreign language learning. In the Hawkins Topic books, this finds expression in a book on language structure and organisation which culls examples from a variety of languages. Other courses have chosen to represent it in the form of language taster courses. This trend was accompanied by a growing impatience with the dominance of French in Modern language teaching (Mobbs, 1984; 1985), which caused community languages and world languages to become candidates for the LA taster courses.

Language awareness: an autonomous development?

The argument followed here has been that LA is the offspring of several strains of thought which have different roots. It could also be described as the delta where various streams join. But how successfully do they mingle? Let us review each contribution briefly to see how LA tries to fulfil its demands.

The first, global aim of LA is to make language a focus of interest in its own right. This is reflected in the aim of LA courses to stimulate curiosity about language, and should be seen as the cumulative effect of doing a course. There is an overlap here with the concept of Language across the Curriculum (LAC), especially insofar as the latter sought to make the language of school subjects visible and not taken for granted. However, LA differs from LAC in not being curriculum-related (languages excepted). Thus, while LAC permeated into departmental work (Robertson, 1981), LA forms a mini 'subject' apart. In this sense LA is the inverted image of LAC: the same preoccupation is embodied in a diametrically different form.

Another major goal of LA concerns the shaping, or re-shaping, of attitudes towards minority (often non-European) languages and non-standard dialects of English. The assumption made is that the acquisition of linguistic knowledge will dispel linguistic prejudice. The extent to which attitudes can be affected by new information is a moot point. While it could be said that the possibility of changing attitudes in this way must be assumed in an educational context, it would be wrong to forget that language attitudes are predominantly influenced by socio-political factors such as the social status and institutional support enjoyed by the languages concerned (Giles, Bourhis

& Taylor, 1977). Even if LA itself is seen as helping to increase the institutional support factor by bringing a minority language into the classroom, this contribution to the overall status of a language contribution is a small and temporary one. Language attitudes are a complex and subtle field, and LA practitioners do not appear to have thought through the ways in which LA can and cannot be expected to change attitudes.

LA also sets out to provide a preparatory training in learning a foreign language, through focussing on grammatical pattern-formation or etymology. It may be queried whether LA courses, or the language skills component in them, last long enough for this to take place successfully, even if it can be done. This difficulty is exacerbated on courses which are very wide-ranging in content. It is important to note that in this respect the aims of LA highlight *linguistic skills*, in contrast with the emphasis elsewhere on *linguistic attitudes*.

Finally, a few LA proponents see it as a way of developing the general language skills of the less able (Hawkins, 1984; Roberts, p. 272). Apart from being vague and difficult to assess, this aim seems to be in conflict with the trend towards child-centredness in a positive sense (viewing children as linguistically proficient contributors to the learning process) noted in many courses. However, the language-deprivation theorists do tend to favour a more teacher-centred approach, and the apparent contradiction may be explained by the diversity of approaches in LA.

Future Developments in Language Awareness

A major drawback of most LA courses is their all-inclusiveness, which leads them to try to cover many language-related themes and to have multiple aims. As a corrective to this it might be possible to systematise LA courses under the auspices of a body such as the National Congress on Languages in Education (NCLE) or the Centre for Information on Language Teaching. CILT already collects LA materials. LA courses specialising in language diversity, language skills and Varieties of English, to give some examples, could be categorised, and materials for each could be built up. This would have several benefits. Firstly, materials would not be replicated. Secondly, teachers' evaluations of courses could be collected, thus monitoring successes and failures. Thirdly, it would have the considerable advantage of enabling schools to reflect on the type of course which would best meet their needs (instead of, as sometimes happens now, 'buying in' another school's LA course, which may not be appropriate for them).

A different point of departure for reforming LA courses might be the pupils themselves. Although LA methodology claims to be child-centred, its concepts are far from being so. The term 'Language Awareness' means nothing to most pupils. It is a teacher's concept, and often courses are book-based and do not draw on the school or the community's own resources. An alternative approach would be to anchor the LA course firmly to the nearest minority language communities. (This would mean taking minority languages as the principal focus.) A very specific course suited to a particular community and culture would therefore be produced, with its own title (e.g. 'Turkish Life and Language in Lewisham'). Before designing the course care should be taken to research the potential of the area in terms of language resources and language attitudes, as well as researching language attitudes within the school. In this way, course conveners would have a clearer idea at the outset of the levels of awareness their students had, and could take this into account. An attempt along these lines to generate understanding of a way of life as well as a language offers more hope for influencing language attitudes than purely language-based courses.

A survey of the present situation suggests that LA courses will be with us for some time to come. Since LA course organisers and writers tend to formulate fairly ambitious aims, such as fostering positive attitudes towards the bilingualism of oneself or others, claims are implicitly being made for the effectiveness of LA. It therefore makes sense to monitor the effects of LA courses or to set up some form of assessment. It is less easy to see what form such assessment should take. Traditional methods of measuring attitudes, derived from Social Psychology, do not seem appropriate. For example, the scale-rating technique, where subjects are asked to rate their responses to a given statement on a 1–5 scale, fails to register subtle changes in attitude.

Alternative and more flexible methods of assessment are, however, being pioneered. One recent study into LA courses (Biggs, 1987) initiated diary-keeping for the duration of the course. This meant that students could comment freely on what they did and how it affected them. Another evaluation procedure which seems promising entails the assessment by students of pieces of writing in Standard English and in dialect (A. Jones, 1987). This allows a comparison to be made between students' attitudes towards non-standard English at the beginning and at the end of the LA course. Similarly imaginative means of assessment need to be developed in relation to other aspects of LA; to monitor, for example, student willingness to work with bilingual material.

Conclusion

To conclude: Language Awareness is a concept which needs to be approached with caution. Superficially very attractive, it promises to act as a panacea to all problems and dilemmas concerned with language. But how we influence attitudes to minority languages and non-standard English, and how we promote language learning skills, are very real and perplexing questions which current LA courses do not really get to grips with. The one indisputable virtue of Language Awareness is that it has set us looking for better answers.

References

ASTLEY, H. 1983 *Get the Message*. Cambridge: CUP.
ASTLEY, H. and HAWKINS, E. 1984 *Using Language*. Cambridge: CUP.
BIGGS, A. 1987 Teacher and Pupil Perceptions of a Language Awareness Programme. Unpublished MA dissertation, Birkbeck College.
BULLOCK, A. Sir 1975 *A Language for Life*. London: HMSO.
CARROLL, J.B. 1983 The prediction of success in intensive foreign language training. In R. GLASER (ed.), *Training, Research and Education*. New York: Wiley.
COMMISSION FOR RACIAL EQUALITY (CRE) 1986 *Teaching English as a Second Language. Report of a Formal Investigation in Calderdale Local Education Authority*. London: HMSO.
DONMALL, G. (ed.) (1985) *Language Awareness*. London: Centre for Information on Language Teaching and Research.
DOUGHTY, P., PEARCE, J. and THORNTON, G. 1971 *Language in Use*. London: Edward Arnold for the Schools Council.
DUNLEA, A. 1985 *How Do We Learn Languages?* Cambridge: CUP.
EDWARDS, J. 1979 Judgements and confidence reactions to disadvantaged speech. In H. GILES & R. ST. CLAIR (eds), *Language and Social Psychology*. Oxford: Blackwell.
EDWARDS, V. 1978 Language attitudes and underperformance in West Indian children. *Educational Review* 30(1), 51–8.
——1979 *The West Indian Language Issue in British Schools*. London: Routledge & Kegan Paul.
——1986 *Language in a Black Community*. Clevedon, Avon: Multilingual Matters.
GILES, H., BOURHIS, R. and TAYLOR, D. 1977 Towards a theory of language in inter-group relations. In H. GILES (ed.), *Language, Ethnicity and Intergroup Relations*. London: Academic Press. pp. 307–48.
GREEN, P.S. 1975 *The Language Laboratory in School: The York Study*. Edinburgh: Oliver & Boyd.
HAWKINS, E. 1983 *Spoken and Written Language*. Cambridge: CUP.
——1984 *Awareness of Language: An Introduction*. Cambridge: CUP.
HOULTON, D. 1985 *All Our Languages: A Guide for the Multilingual Classroom*. London: Edward Arnold.

HUDSON, M. 1985 A project on spoken language for 8-10 year olds. In OPEN UNIVERSITY, *Every Child's Language*. Clevedon, Avon: Multilingual Matters for Open University. pp. 17–21.

ILEA 1985 *World in a City*. London: ILEA Learning Resources.

JONES, A.P. 1987 Assessing the Effectiveness of Language Awareness Courses. Unpublished MA dissertation, Birkbeck College.

JONES, B. 1984 *How Language Works*. Cambridge: CUP.

McGURN, J. 1986 *Comparing Languages*. Cambridge: CUP.

MOBBS, M. 1984 Time to come in from the cold: community languages are modern too. *Times Educational Supplement*, 26 October: 39.

——1985 Towards the evolution of linguate primate (Angliensis). *Times Educational Supplement*, 4 November.

OPEN UNIVERSITY 1985 *Every Child's Language*. Clevedon, Avon: Multilingual Matters for the Open University.

POMPHREY, C. 1985 *Language Varieties and Change*. Cambridge: CUP.

REDFERN, A. 1985 Class Project on Language. In OPEN UNIVERSITY, *Every Child's Language*. Clevedon, Avon: Multilingual Matters for Open University pp. 22–25.

ROBERTSON, I. 1981 *Language Across the Curriculum: Four Case Studies*. London: Schools Council Publications.

ROBINS, M. 1985 Language Awareness. In OPEN UNIVERSITY, *Every Child's Language*. Clevedon, Avon: Multilingual Matters for the Open University. pp. 26–30.

SUTCLIFFE, D. 1982 *British Black English*. Oxford: Blackwell.

SWANN, Lord 1985 *Education For All*. London: HMSO.

THORNTON, G. 1986 *Language, Education and Ignorance*. London: Edward Arnold.

TIZARD, B. and HUGHES, M. 1984 *Young Children Learning*. London: Fontana.

TOUGH, J. 1974 *Focus on Meaning: Talking to Some Purpose with Young Children*. London: Allen & Unwin.

TRUDGILL, P. 1975 *Accent, Dialect and the School*. London: Edward Arnold.

WELLS, G. (ed.) 1981 *Learning Through Interaction: The Study of Language Development*. Cambridge: CUP.

——1984 *Language Development in the Pre-School Years*. Cambridge: CUP.

Part IV
Language planning and policy

18 Frisian in schools: Problems in planning

OMMO WILTS

The Present State of North Frisian

North Frisian is a collective term for the nine Frisian dialects now spoken in the northernmost part of Germany, south of the Dano-German border. The region encompasses a small strip of the coastal mainland and several islands including the island of Heligoland. Perhaps the most surprising thing about North Frisian in school is that it found its way into school at all, as the odds were dramatically against it. Differences between the dialects are so great that the formation of a standardised North Frisian is impossible. Even up to the present day it has been a matter of debate, whether the Frisian dialects of the mainland and those of the islands could be traced back to one and the same root. Each dialect which is to be taught at school must thus be treated as a separate language requiring its own grammar, dictionary and schoolbooks. Even if there are only four dialects at the moment being taught in school, costs for the development of teaching materials are enormous as the market is so limited. It is generally thought that there are about 8,000 native speakers, most of them between 60 and 80 years of age, with very few children still speaking Frisian. Even this small number must, however, be further divided among the different dialects so that the number of speakers for each dialect varies between 20 and 2,000.

Although North Frisian is diminutive in size, it is the only dialect or, to be more precise, language with dialect status in Western Germany to be officially promoted in school and be treated as a language in its own right, i.e. its role is not limited to singing a Frisian song or telling a Frisian tale as is the case with Low German in school, but means regular Frisian lessons

285

comparable to English or French lessons in German schools. Frisian is taught in practically every primary school in North Frisia proper with two lessons a week for 8 to 10-year-olds. Frisian tuition is also to be found in several schools at the secondary level. At the moment there is a total of 20 teachers teaching 143 lessons at 28 schools. The number of pupils in the school-year 1986/87 is 819. Frisian tuition could even be expanded, if it was not for a shortage of qualified teachers. Only recently the position of Frisian in school was strengthened by the appointment of a Frisian native speaker as schools inspector. Qualifications for the teaching of Frisian can be acquired at the regional university of Kiel and at the teacher training college in Flensburg. In addition to the Frisian professorship in Kiel a second full professorship for Frisian will shortly be instituted in Flensburg.

The History of North Frisian in School

Attempts to teach Frisian were first made on the island of Sylt shortly after 1900. Lacking support from the general public, however, these attempts were not very successful. Things changed when in 1924 the then Prussian Government gave instructions that, to ensure the preservation of Frisian, there should be a weekly lesson in every school with a predominantly Frisian background. As there were not teachers able to teach Frisian at every village school, peripatetic teachers went from village to village. This period, which lasted for about ten years, was probably the heyday of North Frisian tuition. The didactic model it was based upon was that of tuition in the mother tongue, concentrating upon vocabulary building, compositions, storytelling and local history. New teaching methods were also tried by using Frisian as the medium in physical education, and by setting up Frisian youth camps for interested pupils.

During the period of the Third Reich Frisian tuition came practically to a standstill. The centralistic national-socialist government was not very eager to support a language which claimed to be of non-German origin and which, because of its singular character, was difficult to control.

After World War II Frisian tuition was taken up again, but there was a steady decrease in Frisian lessons as interest in Frisian was limited and conditions had changed radically for the worse for Frisian in general. As a result of the great shifts of population Frisians became a minority even in their strongholds. A further factor which had devastating consequences for the Frisian language of the school-children was the decision of the Ministry of Education in Schleswig-Holstein to give up the small village schools and to build large central schools instead. Confronted with German or Low

German speaking children, or Frisian children with a different local dialect, Frisian children would soon give up Frisian and change over to German. The only positive sign during that period was the founding of a Danish-Frisian minority school on the Frisian mainland where at least at the beginning an attempt was made to use Frisian as the general medium of education.

The turn of the tide came by surprise. Intended solely as an experiment, Frisian was introduced into the schools in the eastern part of the island of Sylt in 1976/77. This found the backing of the local schools inspector and surprisingly enough an overwhelming majority of parents also decided that regular Frisian lessons should be taken up again. As these lessons proved successful, Frisian tuition was extended to other parts of North Frisia — even to parts of the country that had never had a Frisian speaking population but were Low German. The present state, which was reached within a period of about ten years, is due to a combination of several factors.

Distribution of Frisian

Although a linguistic map of North Frisian with a realistic presentation of prevailing conditions should consist of dots rather than of shadings, each dot representing a Frisian speaking family, the obvious reduction in quantity has not automatically lessened the prestige Frisian is enjoying among speakers and non-speakers alike. The tenacity with which people are clinging to Frisian is no longer motivated by the desire for social integration into a linguistically homogeneous community, but has become part of a family tradition. 'I speak Frisian because I like to speak Frisian with my grandparents', is a common answer among Frisian-speaking children. In each of the various dialect areas of Frisian, a handful of 'kernel'-families can be distinguished as dominating most of the Frisian activities in this area, and exerting a certain stimulating influence upon linguistically less committed Frisians and non-Frisians. By using Frisian, the Frisian speaker is not stigmatised as speaking a non-standard variety, as is often the case with speakers of the neighbouring dialect, i.e. Low German and Jutish. In certain domains, though in a very limited number, e.g. local festivities, public speeches addressing local audiences, the use of Frisian is more appropriate even than that of the standard language, so that speakers of standard German have to find excuses for not being able to speak Frisian.

Attitudes

Another important factor is the weakness of Frisian itself. Reduced as it is to almost diminutive size, Frisian no longer poses any threat whatsoever to the official state language. Being merely nice and exotic and part of the cultural heritage, Frisian in official eyes deserves support and subsidising. With the waning importance of Frisian in every-day life, the anxieties of parents that Frisian could be disadvantageous to their children also lessened. The shift of attitudes among parents towards Frisian tuition is significant, but one has to differentiate between the various groups. In the beginning of the 1950s the Frisian-speaking parents in the then completely Frisian area of Westerland-Föhr voted against the setting up of a Frisian primary school because of the apparently secure position of Frisian in this region. The decision of the non-Frisian-speaking parents of the island of Sylt to allow the introduction of Frisian in school owed less to linguistic but more to social motives. These well-to-do parents, mostly businessmen and academics in their new 'old Frisian' homes, could afford the luxury of letting their offspring learn an additional language that was chic and nostalgic, as the future of their child was secure anyway. Characteristically, the introduction of Frisian was much more problematical on the Frisian mainland, which is economically less developed. Here the parents were afraid that Frisian lessons would mean fewer lessons in German and arithmetic. They could only be won over by guaranteeing that Frisian tuition would not interfere with German spelling lessons.

Support

Support for Frisian in school is not without political implications, as the question whether the Frisians should be considered a minority or not is still part of the borderline strife between the German side and the Danish side, with both sides having 'their' minority the other side of the border. Whereas the Danish side would prefer minority status for the Frisians as a factor strengthening the position of their own Danish minority on German soil, the German side is very reluctant to grant this on the grounds that there is neither a cultural nor political Frisian identity to be found. However, since supporting the rights of the Frisians is incorporated in the political programme of the Danish minority party which has one seat in the regional parliament, German politicians cannot afford to leave matters to the Danish side, as the North Frisians still command sufficient votes to be possibly decisive in elections. The present rather favourable state of Frisian in school must thus also be seen in the light of endeavours to win over a small but nevertheless not unimportant constituency.

Expansion

At the same time, expansion of Frisian in school is rather welcome to the school administration as the need for additional teachers which it generates is greatly welcomed by the many teachers looking for jobs today. Practical measures such as giving Frisian a certain preference in school are facilitated by the fact that the federal constitution of Western Germany gives complete autonomy in educational and cultural matters to the regional governments. Support for Frisian is part of a general school policy typical of Northern Germany, which tries to strengthen dialect, though admittedly never going as far as in the case of Frisian. However, this policy stands in sharp contrast to that adopted in Southern Germany where, as a result of a completely different linguistic situation, the school aims rather at the eradication of the dialect which is seen as an obstacle to social advance.

Parental approval

Frisian tuition also finds the general approval of the parents. By taking up such themes as local history, local traditions and local geography it is filling a sorely felt gap created by the emphasis of the modern German primary school on more 'scientific' models in geography etc.

The Need for Language Planning

Considering the rapid and unexpected development of North Frisian tuition in recent years, it should not come as a surprise that its prevailing features are goodwill and improvisation rather than expertise and planning. This is all the more regrettable as the present phase of North Frisian tuition is confronted with a situation radically different from that of 40 years ago, and the old recipes will simply not do any more. Whereas formerly the teacher could rely upon a majority of Frisian-speaking pupils in class, the Frisian teacher now is lucky if there is at least one Frisian child in class, or two with a Frisian-speaking grandfather. For the majority of children, however, Frisian must be considered a foreign language. If it is one of the positive aspects of North Frisian tuition that the Frisian teacher as a rule is a native speaker, this qualification in most cases is also the only qualification he or she has to teach the language. The normal Frisian teacher neither has had any academic tuition in Frisian, nor is he or she familiar with the principles of foreign language teaching. This situation is worsened by the fact that the North Frisian teacher has very few resources for private study and even less for use in class. Whereas in the 1920s a number of expert teachers were given a sabbatical of one year to prepare the necessary schoolbooks, which they also produced, the teachers of today were simply asked to plunge in, unprepared though they were.

Although the Frisian teachers come together twice a year to visit a colleague teaching in the classroom and to exchange views and ideas, this is hardly sufficient to solve practical and theoretical problems. Thus the quality of North Frisian tuition is solely dependent upon the teaching skills and initiative of the individual teacher. Some advantages though can be seen. The necessity to produce one's own school material, if the teacher is not just content to muddle through, allows a greater identification with the material. Basing teaching on themes such as 'Our Village' and 'Plants and Animals around us', concentrating upon projects such as producing a Frisian play instead of following a systematic language course, which is out of reach for most of the teachers anyway, can be more intriguing for children than the dullness of pattern drills common in modern language teaching.

Part of the totally unsystematic character of Frisian tuition are the many activities outside school. Children here have the chance of using language in its social setting by visiting senior citizens' homes, singing Frisian songs, being present at birthdays of old and well-known people, performing a play during village festivities, etc. Similarly, the children go out on excursions to learn something about their immediate neighbourhood. Not only can Frisian tuition afford this, as there is no grading and there are no fixed goals to be reached, but these pedagogical extras are even a must to keep Frisian tuition attractive, since participation is completely voluntary. Thus numbers of pupils differ considerably from region to region and from school to school. Participation not only depends upon the quality of Frisian tuition, but also upon the support by the parents and the schools, i.e. the headmaster and colleagues. For the pupils it is important whether the lessons are integrated within the normal syllabus, or are extra lessons very early in the morning or late in the afternoon, when the other pupils, not taking part in Frisian tuition, are allowed to go home.

Motivating the pupils, however, seems to be easier than motivating the Frisian teachers themselves. For even the most idealistic of teachers become worn out and disillusioned in the daily fight for survival in the classroom, having to do everything themselves, getting no support from outside, with no prescribed curriculum and an anything-is-better-than-nothing-philosophy rather than a thorough theoretical framework. Instead of planned efforts they merely find a patchwork with a little Frisian in the third grade here and a little Frisian in the fifth grade there, but without the continuity necessary to achieve satisfying results in language acquisition.

The present unsound condition of Frisian tuition is, however, not only the fault of politicians using Frisian tuition as a kind of figleaf to cover up years of neglect and indolence. (And one must remember that figleaves are not a very suitable outfit to keep one warm in the cold and windswept regions of North Frisia.) Part of the fault also must be passed over to Frisian philology and Frisian philologists and their almost complete neglect of structural, morphological and syntactical questions of dialect. Instead of aiming at a systematic assessment of linguistic data, which could serve as a sound basis for the teaching of Frisian, Frisian philology still clings very much to the concept of classical dialectology with the focus upon historical phonology and lexicography, paying attention to grammar only in so far as this grammar can be prefixed with a 'middle-' or 'old-'. This problem would be even more acute if it was not for Frisian laymen compiling small and modest grammars and dictionaries for practical use.

Outlook for the Future

If Frisian tuition, in spite of its state of apparent bloom at the moment, is not to come to a stop as suddenly as it started, methods of language planning must be applied with close co-operation between linguists and educationalists. Decisions have to be made not only as to how to teach Frisian in the most effective way, but also what kind of Frisian is to be taught. Even within the single Frisian dialect, a choice has to be made between the regional varieties and between the different standards of Frisian spoken by grandparents, parents, and children. Since the relationship between Frisian and German seems to be a one-way-road, with Frisian losing steadily those phonetic, phonological, morphological, and syntactic features it does not share with German, it seems, for instance, advisable to use a contrastive approach so as to avoid the very real danger of language death from within. On the other hand one should not overestimate the role of school in language planning, especially if directed towards a language like Frisian, which never has had any official status — and has lived quite comfortably without it. Frisian survived because it was realistic enough to know its domain: Frisian only in the family and with fellow-Frisians, German in school and in church, and Low German with non-Frisians outside the village. The downfall of Frisian began with the toppling of this balance. Thus even if we could see Frisian in school as something like Custer's last stand, we should remember, that Frisian tuition here is actually defending a territory Frisian never possessed.

Bibliography

FALTINGS, V. 1982 Zur besonderen Problematik des muttersprachlichen Unterrichts in Nordfriesland. *Nordfriesische Sprachpflege*, 3, 11–15.
HOFMANN, D. 1979 Die Entwicklung des Nordfriesischen. In A. WALKER & O. WILTS (eds), *Friesisch heute*, Schriftenreihe der Akademie Sankelmark 45/46, pp. 11–28.

MARTINEN, H. 1986 Sprachpflege in Nordfriesland - gestern - heute - morgen. *Zwischen Eider und Wiedau 1986*, pp. 73–79.

PETERSEN, C. 1979 Der Friesischunterricht in Vergangenheit und Gegenwart aus der Sicht des Schulamtes. In A. WALKER & O. WILTS (eds), *Friesisch heute*, Schriftenreihe der Akademie Sankelmark 45/46, pp. 69–77.

PETERSEN, J. 1979 Üt min Årbe as freesche Liirer. In A. WALKER & O. WILTS (eds), *Friesisch heute*, Schriftenreihe der Akademie Sankelmark 45/46, pp. 78–86.

WALKER, A. 1984 Applied sociology of language: vernacular languages and education. In P. TRUDGILL (ed.), *Applied Sociolinguistics*. London: Academic Press. pp. 159–202.

19 Education and the vernacular

BRIAN HOLLINGWORTH

In England and Wales the foundations of a state education system were not laid until 1870, when the Education Act passed during Gladstone's first ministry finally allowed local authorities, as well as the various Christian denominations, to establish elementary schools. Sadly, evidence suggests that this new system of education, intended to ensure that all children received basic schooling, proved strongly antagonistic to local dialects and played a significant part in weakening, or even destroying them.

We can take reports from geographically distant areas of the kingdom as support for this contention. In relation to Scotland H.H. Speitel (1975) records

> Central government and schools . . . have, with few exceptions, seldom shown a tolerant or positive attitude to speech varieties loosely termed 'dialects'.

In the North of England, Provost in the *Northern Counties Magazine* for 1901 remarks on 'the destruction wrought by the up-to-date school teachers who insist on the children speaking 'English' both as regards the words themselves and the grammar'. Twenty years later Partington (1920), another local writer, is even more vehement in his attack.

> Ever since 1870, the Education Board has done its utmost to kill dialect. Up to that eventful year the truest educationists taken in bulk were found in working class circles. They offered no opposition to the passing of the first Education Act. This noble magnanimity has been ill-requited. The reader may have seen Professor Moorman's illuminating statement of how Government Inspectors complimented

teaching staffs on having eliminated all trace of dialect from their scholars' mode of speech.

In Dorset, we have the witness of a more distinguished, though not necessarily less romantic commentator. In his introduction to the *Select Poems of William Barnes*, Thomas Hardy (1908) records

> Since [Barnes] death (1886), education in the west of England as elsewhere has gone on with its silent and inevitable effacements, reducing the speech of this country to uniformity, and obliterating every year many a fine old local word. The process is always the same: the Word is ridiculed by the newly taught; it gets into disgrace; it is heard in holes and corners only; it dies; and, worst of all, it leaves no synonym.

The commentators seem agreed and Inspector's reports or Government Reports do not contradict. The significance of Inspector's Reports between the year of the Education Act and the turn of the century for instance, is how uniformly silent they are about spoken language. References to language are almost invariably to the written code and the assumption is absolute that the written code is coterminous with standard English. If local spoken language is mentioned at all, therefore, it is mentioned as something which is likely to interfere with learning because of its distance from standard written English, and therefore something which constitutes a problem. For example Rev. H. Smith (1870) writes

> I am inclined to think that most schoolmasters would prefer to teach the English language ab initio to a foreigner than to undergo the labour of undoing the Cheshireisms learnt from the mother's knee.

And the Rev. C.F. Johnstone (1872):

> They cannot write English because they do not understand English. They have had no homes, perhaps in which they could associate with educated persons, and no familiarity with educated speech, and the want has never been made good by any training in their schools which could give them the understanding of their language and a facility in the use of it.

Occasionally the language can be stronger. As late as 1921, the Report on *The Teaching of English in England*, (HMSO) inspired by George Sampson, and regarded by many as a high-water mark of enlightened liberal attitudes towards the subject, at one stage (p. 67) argues that children should be bilingual in dialect and standard English, yet this is only eight pages after proclaiming that it is more difficult to teach English in elementary schools because of 'evil habits of speech'. There is a need, the Report argues to give elementary children 'speech', to give them speech training and replace the vernacular.

Moreover, not only was the local language under attack in the classroom, but also the offensive was extended to the playground. Partington (1920) condemns one apparently common practice

> It must be felt by teachers as a degradation to be sent out during 'out to play' to detect lapses in speech among children when amusing themselves outside school buildings.

If one accepts the evidence that formal state education proved to be so antagonistic to dialect, two questions might be raised. Why did this antagonism arise? And do any traces of this antagonism persist today?

The answer to the first question is a complex one, and not entirely a language issue at all. I have argued elsewhere (Hollingworth, 1977) that many teachers in the new state system regarded themselves as involved in a moral crusade to educate the masses. It was easy for them to equate dialect with ignorance and to attack it for educational reasons in the cause of greater equality. Equally there was a social inevitability, as Hardy is acknowledging, that mass education, along with other mass developments of the Victorian age, such as transport and newspapers, by depending upon, and making more familiar standard forms of language, would prove to be an enemy of local forms of speech, however neutral its practitioners might wish to be.

Nevertheless, the virulence of the opposition requires some explanation. And this is particularly so in the light of two considerations which might suggest that there would have been more tolerance of dialect. The first consideration is, as I have suggested elsewhere (Hollingworth, 1977) that in the period after the institution of the Revised Code (1862) there was a lively debate among teachers in elementary schools about the importance of the mother tongue in schools, often with very enlightened viewpoints being expressed. The second is that this attack upon dialect in the schools actually coincides with the time when dialects themselves were achieving prominence as subjects of sympathetic study, and indeed, in areas such as Dorset, Lancashire and the North East, as the subject of a not inconsiderable oral and written literature.

Dialect, after all, gained great prestige as a direct consequence of the English romantic movement. It was Wordsworth (1802) who had spoken of the 'real language of men', the virtue of 'simple and unelaborated expressions' as being 'a more permanent, and far more philosophical language than that which is frequently substituted for it by Poets'. It was Scott who had traced back the old vernacular songs of Scotland in his *Minstrelsy of the Scottish Border* (1802, 1803) and introduced the dialect as a serious vehicle for communication of thought and feeling in the Waverley Novels. The sympathetic interest in dialect had been maintained in the writings of Dickens, Gaskell, Emily Brontë and George Eliot. One might have thought that the status of dialect among the educated might have been higher and that this status might have been reflected in the attitudes of teachers.

Similarly the philological researches of pioneers such as Joseph Wright and Max Müller, might have been expected to make dialects respectable. As they painfully explored the family tree of languages, tracing them to their Indo-European roots, it was obvious that dialects had a key role to play in establishing missing links, and that philologically they shared the status of more socially acceptable forms of language. William Barnes, the Dorset dialect poet and schoolteacher, is indeed a living testament to the close relationship that there was in many a linguist's mind between a passionate interest in theories of language origin and diversity and a belief in the significance of local language for communication and for literature. His publications included, *Elements of English Grammar* (1842) which lists among its aims:

> to keep up the purity of the Saxon English language, to give pupils a comprehension of the principles of the English derivation, and to offer teachers a grammar so scientifically based as to prepare the pupil's mind for further philological studies.

Why, then, the antipathy between mass education and dialect? And why did dialect not put up a more spirited resistance? The reason is, I believe, because throughout the nineteenth century the dominant linguistic theories were essentialist and idealist, and were therefore so unreliable that they provided no sound basis for a reasoned defence of dialect, any more than they provided a basis for attack. In the absence of a more adequate theory of language, prejudice and class snobbery prevailed.

The claims *for* dialect, as so often in language study, were essential on two fronts, and doubtful on both. Firstly dialect was claimed to be nearer to the essence of language. According to the Lancashire dialect writer Tim

Bobbin, it preserved 'the venerable and valuable reliques of the Ancient Anglo-Saxon and Gallic languages' (1820). The search of language study in the nineteenth century was so much a search for origins, for the language of Eden, that inevitably dialect was predominantly seen in the context of this search:

> Much of what is dialectic was once the correct form of our mother tongue. Words formerly used by the best English authors are preserved for centuries by the peasantry – This may serve to show how much the conservative people have retained the well of English undefiled (Wilkinson, 1874).

Such preconceptions had two weaknesses. In the first place they placed the emphasis on dialect not as a living language but as a museum of the past — a familiar romantic attitude which of course stretches well beyond concerns for language. Thus Axon (1870) comments

> The irrational prejudice against dialects is fast dying out, and is being succeeded by a more catholic spirit of criticism. Philology has shown us their value, and many a curious relic of old world belief has been found fossilised in the provincial speech.

In the second they inevitably made claims to 'correctness' and 'purity' which it is plain were matters of opinion. For example one of the commonest adjectives applied to Lancashire dialect by its supporters in the nineteenth century was the word 'doric', as though somehow Lancashire talk had maintained a primitive purity which was lost to the standard English speaker. The Romantic connotations of this attitude will need no elaboration, but it did not provide a very adequate defence for dialect within the educational system.

The second essentialist claim which was made for dialect came in that almost inevitable slide of logic, particularly in a romantic age, from discussing language as form to discussing it as morality. The slide is there in Wordsworth's discussion clearly, when his plea for 'simple and unelaborated expressions' becomes a claim for a 'more permanent language'. It becomes a familiar feature in mid-century defences of dialect, particularly when the claim is made that dialects are 'pure'. Not only is this a claim to primitive origin in a historical sense, it also carries the romantic correlation of prelapsarian innocence, and moral simplicity. It echoes fully romantic notions of the corruption of sophistication, artificiality and ratiocination. Similarly a key word attributed to the use of dialect, particularly in any literary form, is one redolent with meaning to the Victorian bourgeoisie. Dialect is frequently characterised as 'homely': when supporters were seeking a Civil List pension for the dialect writer, Edwin Waugh, typically they reflect on 'the homely virtues and aspirations of the past'; he is devoted 'to the fostering of the domestic affections, and of the best feelings of human nature'. Similarly, Barnes' publication of dialect poems in 1857 was entitled *Hwomely Rhymes*.

The important point about these arguments in support of the vernacular, widely ventured by scholars and antiquarians in the nineteenth century, is that they are no more than the opposite of the accepted wisdom of the time from those experts who unquestioningly assumed that standard English must be the language of education, and that dialect had no part to play in the education of the masses. With equally essentialist, equally idealist assumptions did such educationalists argue on moral as well as linguistic grounds.

Two examples may illustrate this point. I will emphasise the key words in the two statements about language and education, one dating from mid-century, the other from the early 1900s, which display typical essentialist views in favour of standard forms. Tylecote (1957), speaking of the Huddersfield Mechanics Institute in 1847, records:

> The grammar teacher pointed out that 'so firm a hold have the *vulgar* provincialisms on their minds, and so few are the opportunities they have for conversing with people who speak *good* language, that the ridding themselves of our *barbarous* northern dialect is a work of no easy accomplishment — persons become confirmed in the peculiar dialect of their district, and however hearty and honest the dialect may be (as is the case with that of Yorkshire), it very materially militates against those who can speak no other and have to push their fortunes where the English language is more *purely* spoken

At a prize giving in Bury, Lancashire, 60 years later, George Harwood (1910), the local Member of Parliament, is reported, 'speaking plainly as a Yorkshire man', as being afraid that there was

> a wave in favour of what was called Lancashire talking. It was utterly *bad*, it was *ugly*, it was ungrammatical. He had heard people in the streets — he heard someone in Bury as he walked from the station — talking in a way civilized people ought not to talk — the pronouns all wrong, and the whole thing upside down . . . When he was a boy it was thought to be a mark of *misbehaviour* to speak in that way.

To the teacher in Huddersfield and to the Lancashire Member of Parliament, dialect is 'barbarous' and 'uncivilised': to the antiquarians it had been 'doric' and 'primitive'. In the moral realm, the teacher and the MP see standard forms as 'good' and 'pure', the dialect as 'bad' and 'a mark of misbehaviour'; at the other extreme, the antiquarians spoke of the standard as 'adulterated' and 'oversophisticated' and the dialect as 'pure' and 'simple'. Both sides are taking extreme positions and offering diametrically opposite opinions on language, but both are arguing from firmly held, though sometimes unconscious, essentialist and idealist views of language.

Both sides have their absurdities too. On the one hand we find William Barnes searching for linguistic innocence by coining words such as 'wheel-saddle' for bicycle. On the other we find in conjunction with that report from the Huddersfield Mechanics Institute that a candidate for bass singer in a church choir did not get the job because 'Yorkshire dialect — would not harmonize with psalms and sacred tunes'.

The sound and the fury of these idealist arguments from both sides of the controversy lack the one thing needful, the sweetness and light which might have been available through relativistic notions of appropriateness, register or code. These notions were not unknown — indeed they crop up in some unexpected places — but they do not occupy the foreground of the nineteenth century debate. Hence, I believe, since the debate was a matter of assertion set against assertion, with little room for negotiation, compromise or even discussion, it is not too surprising that the vernacular fared so badly in the elementary schools. The folk prejudice of the teachers was faced only by another prejudice, equally fiercely held, but no source for practical action in terms of curriculum and attitudes to language. Harwood's speech is an indication, perhaps, that the pro-dialect lobby had succeeded in raising the issue in educational thinking, but the evidence of observers is that the schools still pursued their familiar policies of attack upon the vernacular.

If, now, we move to the present day, we might ask whether these antagonisms to the vernacular still persist, and whether, learning from the past, there is any chance that we can counter them more effectively. The short answer to the first part of the question must unfortunately be in the affirmative. Despite all the new knowledge about language acquired in the past 50 years, many educationists still persist in essentialist and idealist views of language which are by and large inimical to the vernacular. It remains a popular assumption that the standard is superior, that there is a correct form of language, and that the use of the vernacular is a sign of laziness and sloppiness — the linguistic and the moral censure remain hopelessly confused. Unfortunately this simplistic view may well gain a new impetus through the recently appointed Kingman Committee of Inquiry into the teaching of English, whose membership has been carefully selected to avoid teachers with language expertise and is commissioned to seek, as the *Guardian* reports, 'a standard model of the English language'.

Of course the cynic might argue that after a hundred years of state education, the issue hardly matters any more. English Vernaculars have been so thoroughly dispersed over this time that it can be argued there is no longer any point in defending them. Yet this is hardly the case. During the past 30 years, we have the unfortunate experience of the Black British pupil in our schools to remind us that educational prejudice in language matters is still a potent force for alienation and underachievement. Frequently language prejudice has mixed with racism in the latter half of the twentieth century, just as it mixed with elitism in the latter half of the nineteenth century, to convince us that Black children have some 'barbarous' form of the language, or even no language at all. Indeed the situation of the Black child in state schools of the 1970s in terms of the threat to her vernacular language must be closely analogous, by all accounts, to that of the Lancashire cotton operative's child in board schools a hundred years earlier.

And this unpleasant fact should also remind us that educational theorists have to shoulder some of the blame for the serious failures of the recent past, if only because they have repeated the mistakes of their ancestors. The energy-sapping argument over Bernstein's codes for instance, can be characterised in several of its manifestations as an essentialist, idealistic argument transferred from the 1860s obsession with philology to the 1960s obsession with sociolinguistics.

Despite Bernstein's later protestations, it is difficult to seriously maintain that the nomenclature of these codes as 'restricted' and 'elaborated' was not pejorative and not based on the notion of an 'ideal' language. He could, after all, have named them 'simple' and 'sophisticated' and within the romantic tradition, left them in a more ambiguous position for evaluation.

Nor can his detractors, though they may engage more of our sympathy, escape some censure for failing to avoid just those over-emphases which blighted the pro-dialect arguments a hundred years ago. If we look back on a book like Nell Keddie's *Tinker Tailor: The Myth of Cultural Deprivation* (1971), we notice the tendency to idealise working class culture in a manner reminiscent of the dialect writers of that age. And even Labov's (1971) splendid riposte to Bernstein, 'The Logic of Non-Standard English', as it discusses Black language in Harlem, does not altogether avoid the temptation to indulge in the familiar over-generalisation. In the Open University tape discussing his paper in the context of Bernstein's theories, Labov claims a superior rationality for Black American English as against examples of the elaborated code, which is not altogether self-evident.

The propensity of educators to evaluate, judge and condemn is indeed a great burden, especially where language is concerned. It is a burden which is unfortunately likely to increase in a decade which seems to delight in extremist positions and antagonistic attitudes. But the propensity, the judging tendency, is most burdensome because it may shut our eyes, as it blinded the teachers of the Victorian age, to the possibilities which lie around us. If those teachers a hundred years ago could have shaken off their hierarchies, if they could have ceased their search for universal forms, or the speech of Eden, they might have heard with fascination the wide varieties of English round them in the dialects of Scotland, of Lancashire, or Dorset. They might even have recorded it, fostered it, encouraged it, without opposing it or evaluating it against standard forms.

In the book *The Linguistic Sciences and Language Teaching* (1964) Halliday makes a most valuable analysis of approaches to language teaching. Language teaching, he says, can be seen as descriptive, prescriptive or productive. The elementary school teachers in the early days of state education were certainly schooled in their grammar and in their use of the red pencil. It was as producers of English that they fell down, suppressing the local tongue rather than encouraging it, and successfully playing their part in destroying the vernacular.

It is in this historical context, that the issue of Black English and the status of language in a multi-racial society gains a particular focus and a specific significance, in indicating whether, despite all our hard-gained knowledge about language, we can act any more sensibly than the Victorian schoolmaster. By chance, through the immigration of the 1950s and 1960s, we are faced with an English language situation even more varied and diverse, potentially more rich, than faced then. In theory we are no longer bound by the essentialist views of language which held the Victorians. We should be in a position to celebrate language in its variety rather than grade it and restrict it to its narrow standard form. But will this happen in practice? The pronouncements of the inspectors and the behaviour of the schools do not inspire confidence.

References

AXON, W.E.A. 1870 *Folk Song and Folk Speech of Lancashire*. Manchester: Tubbs & Brook.

BARNES, W. 1842 *The Elements of English Grammar*. Dorchester: Longman & Co.

——1857 *Hwomely Rhymes*. London: John Russell Smith.

BERNSTEIN, B. 1970 *Class, Codes and Control*. Volume 1. London: Routledge & Kegan Paul.

BOBBIN, T. 1820 Dedication to 'Truth in a Mask' in *Miscellaneous Works of Tim Bobbin Esquire*. Manchester: J. Slack.

FAIRHALL, J. 1987 Heads reject idea of 'model' English, The *Guardian*, 13 July: 2.

HALLIDAY, M., McINTOSH, A. and STREVENS, P. 1964 *The Linguistic Sciences and Language Teaching*. London: Longman.

HARDY, T. (ed.) 1908 *Select Poems of William Barnes*. London: Henry Froude.

HARWOOD G. 1910 Speech at Prize Distribution, Bury Technical School and School of Art. Reported in the *Bury Times*, November 5th.

HMSO (1921) *The Teaching of English in England*. The Newbolt Report. London: HMSO.

HOLLINGWORTH, B. 1977 Dialect in School: an Historical Note, *Newcastle and Durham Research Review* 8, 15–20.

JOHNSTONE, Rev. C.F. 1872–73 Report of the Committee of Council of Education, 92–3. London: HMSO.

KEDDIE, N. (ed.) 1971 *Tinker, Tailor: The Myth of Cultural Deprivation*. Harmondsworth: Penguin.

LABOV, W. 1971 The Logic of Non-Standard English. In N. KEDDIE (ed.), *Tinker, Taylor: The Myth of Cultural Deprivation*. Harmondsworth: Penguin. pp. 21–66.

——1972 Tape published in conjunction with A. CASHDAN & E. GRUGEON (eds), *Language and Education: A Source Book*. Milton Keynes: Open University Press.

PARTINGTON, S. 1920 *Romance of Dialect*. Rochdale.

PROVOST, E.M. 1901 The Study of Dialect. *Northern Counties Magazine*, February, 304–9.

SCOTT, W. 1802 *Minstrelsy of the Scottish Border*, Volumes 1 & 2, Kelso: Ballantyne.

——1803 *Minstrelsy of the Scottish Border*, Volume 3. Edinburgh: Ballantyne.

SMITH, Rev. H. 1870–71 Report of the Committee of Council of Education, p. 188. London: HMSO.

SPEITEL, H.H. 1975 Dialect. In A. DAVIES (ed.), *Problems of Language and Learning*. London: Heinemann. pp. 34–53.

TYLECOTE, M. 1957 *The Mechanics Institutions of Lancashire and Yorkshire before 1851*. Manchester: Manchester University Press.

WAUGH, E. (undated) Memorials to Gladstone and Disraeli on behalf of Edwin Waugh. Waugh archives, Manchester Public Library.

WILKINSON, T.T. 1874 Address to the Manchester Literary Club, 'The Dialects of East Lancashire', quoted in 'Local Notes and Queries', *Manchester Guardian*, Note 263.

WORDSWORTH, W. 1802 Preface to the Lyrical Ballads. In D.J. ENRIGHT & E. DE CHICKERA (eds), *English Critical Texts*. London: Oxford University Press. pp. 164–65.

20 Language variation and mother tongue education in the Netherlands: Reflections on some old disputes about language and education

JAN STURM

Introduction

Good reasons for doing research on dialect and education

There are many good reasons for doing research in the field of dialect and education (Walker, 1983), though, on closer examination, they sometimes appear rather pretentious. Take the question, for instance, of the complex process of language variation in the reproduction of inequality in education (cf. Halsey, 1975). Most people would agree on the need to consider the international dimensions of this process. By taking a sociolinguistic perspective on different societies, it might thus be possible to distinguish surface features which are peculiar to a given society from deeper and perhaps more universal features which operate in every society. This might then suggest ways in which society-specific features could be changed so as to ensure greater equality in education and social justice.

While very few people would question the rationale for such a course of action, it would none the less seem reasonable to examine the implications more closely before we can assess just how likely it is to achieve its lofty aims. There is good reason for caution. When sociolinguistics was emerging

as a separate discipline in the 1960s many extravagant predictions were
made about what could be achieved if teachers had access to the same
information and insights as linguists (Sturm, 1984a). Sadly, many of the
promises of this era have never been fulfilled.

It is not my intention to provide a critique in this chapter of all or
even the more important 'good reasons' for doing research on dialect and
education, whether in an international framework or a local one. None the
less, I feel it would be helpful to outline my own personal 'good reasons'
before starting to reflect on the longstanding debate on language variation
and education in the Netherlands.

In pursuit of understanding through research

Generally speaking, the epistemological basis for research is to produce
'knowledge about' in a systematic and disciplined way. Depending on one's
own epistemological position, the 'knowledge about' refers to reality or
'reality', the latter conceived as a symbolic representation of reality that is
supposed to be essentially unknowable in a direct way. 'Reality' may
therefore be defined as a set of social constructions, each of which is based
on interactive interpretation by people. Scholarly knowledge thus consists
of specific — i.e. systematic and disciplined — interpretations of ordinary
prevailing interpretative knowledge: specific reconstructions of existing 'social
constructions of reality'.

For centuries, the dominant knowledge was almost exclusively a
product of research in the *humanities*; its main thrust was to understand the
deep meanings of 'reality', especially as that reality was reflected in the
language of written texts. The predominance of the humanities, however,
gave way over a period of time to the *natural sciences*. This field of study
emphasises the importance of causal explanation and prediction in order to
control and manipulate reality. Although language began as an object of
study within the humanities, the influence of the natural science approach
gradually made itself felt, as is witnessed, for instance, by the rapid
development of phonetics and phonology and their influence on dialectology
around the turn of the century. It is still possible to detect a certain tension,
too, between humanities and science models for research in the study of
language and literature, though the scientific model has remained the
dominant and therefore the more attractive model for 'real' scholarship in
most fields of research, including language and education.

Taking an historical perspective, it is possible to argue that when the
social sciences began to evolve as independent fields of study in the

nineteenth century, the humanities might have proved as valid a model as the physical sciences. As Nisbet (quoted in Plummer, 1983: 5) observes, 'How different things would be' if that had been the case. However, the fact remains that the social sciences, including later educational research, was modelled primarily on the natural sciences. This has led to far-reaching assumptions about the nature of causation in human social relations, especially in positivist social and behavioural sciences. As a result, mechanical, chemical and ecological metaphors have been applied to human society which, then, is often viewed as a machine, an organism or an ecosystem of animate and inanimate entities (cf. Erickson, 1985).

There is, none the less, growing unease with the scientific bias of much educational research. Erickson (1985), for instance, concludes on the basis of a survey of recent educational research on the relationship between language variation and educational achievement, that 'No universal theory . . . provides by itself an adequate explanation for phenomena of school achievement in the United States'. As a result he pleads for

> interpretive research on teaching, asking what are the specific features of social organization and meaning that arise in a given classroom ecosystem, the enacted hidden curriculum of social organization and the enacted manifest curriculum of subject-matter organization, which must be considered together (1985: 66).

According to Erickson, 'the core issues in teacher and student effectiveness concern meaningfulness — the ground for legitimacy and mutual assent — rather than causation in a mechanical sense'.

Erickson would thus seem to be advocating a humanities approach to educational research. Nor is he alone in this position. Hammersley & Atkinson (1983: 7), for instance, argue that

> a wide range of philosophical and sociological ideas cannot be understood in terms of causal relationships or by subsumption of social events under universal laws. This is because human actions are based upon, or infused by, social meanings: intentions, motives, attitudes and beliefs.

Raymond (1982: 781) also subscribes to this view, pointing out that social science

> methodologically excludes questions about values, ethics, aesthetics, meaning, politics, justice, causality involving human motives, and causality involving an indeterminate number of variables.

Interestingly, these are the very topics which have formed the substance of research in the humanities for hundreds of years.

An interpretative versus social sciences approach to educational research

In summing up these introductory remarks, I would like to declare my own personal preference for conducting educational research within a humanities framework. Using this approach, I hope to offer new understanding of an old problem which dates from at least the end of the last century. I would like to go further and suggest that alternative approaches to the same question simply cannot provide satisfactory solutions in practice. I do not wish, however, to suggest that other approaches to research are in any way less valid. My position is simply that, for purely practical reasons, certain research issues in education can be handled just as well with a humanities approach as with the scientific model (which has nevertheless become the norm in much recent educational research). For both 'modes' merely produce knowledge about 'educational reality' and thus, as far as the question of language variation in education is concerned, I can see no clear reasons for preferring a scientific approach. On the contrary, an empirical-interpretative approach of the kind advocated by Erickson and an increasing number of other writers may well greatly deepen teachers' and researchers' understanding of this question.

In the remainder of this chapter, I would like to offer some reflections based on empirical-interpretative research in language and education.[1] The emphasis will be on the debate about mother tongue education in the Netherlands, though a good number of the issues raised will be of relevance for an international audience. In the second part of the chapter I will draw attention to the gap between what we claim to be doing in education and what we actually do. I will argue that a useful first step in trying to understand this gap is through historical case-studies. For it is only when we know and understand the norms and values of a given community at a given time that we can begin to grasp why people behave in a particular way. I will also propose that an empirical-interpretative approach, in the mode of the humanities, has tremendous potential for exploring problems such as this.

In the third part of the chapter, I will go on to argue that, if we develop such a perspective on the current debate on mother tongue education, it will yield rather interesting insights. An exploration of the ways in which we construct social reality suggests that the issue of dialect in education can best be understood as situated in an area of tension between the dominant social needs and educational beliefs of the community.

Deep Meanings of Mother Tongue Education

The committee on curriculum development

In late 1986 I attended a Dutch conference on curriculum development organised by the Advisory Committee on Curriculum Development in Mother Tongue Education, which as been in operation since 1974. Increasing cutbacks have gradually but dramatically reduced the size and influence of the committee. It was established by a Social Democrat Minister of Education and Science as an independent body to advise the Minister and other interested parties on curriculum development in the area of mother tongue education. Now, however, it serves as an advisory body only for the Dutch National Institute for Curriculum Development, a private foundation which is funded by the state and must therefore respond to ministerial pressure. Despite rather radical structural and financial changes, the committee's remit has scarcely changed. Its responsibility is to provide a platform for all those involved in mother tongue education and to articulate their needs for curriculum development.

When the committee was first formed, a major focus of attention was dialect and education. Drawing on sociolinguistic research of the 1960s, it argued for curriculum development which would allow the school to meet the needs of dialect-speaking pupils. During the research and development phases of the Kerkrade project (see Stijnen & Vallen, this volume, chapter 8), for instance, the committee acted as advisor to the funding body. The impact of this research, however, seems to have been minimal and the position of dialect-speaking children in the Netherlands would appear to be unchanged. My point in discussing the committee at this stage is simply to draw attention to what, according to the educational rhetoric of the day, it was expected to do and has actually done. This leads me to focus on the obvious acceptance of a gap between rhetoric and practice by the people involved. As chairperson of the committee, I am a very good example of someone who has accepted that gap.

Returning to the November conference, I would like to make some more concrete observations about this particular event, which will demonstrate the mismatch between rhetoric and reality and, at the same time, illustrate my own position on educational research.

Voices from the past

The conference was held in a building called the King's Court, a name which scarcely disguises its historical origins: a Roman Catholic boarding school run by a religious order. It seemed to me that the change from 'chapel' to 'plenary hall' does very little to mask that history. Superficial changes such as these do not affect deep structures: the building has been used both in the past and at present as a means of influencing people.

A similar superficial change has taken place in schools. Until the early 1950s the greater part of the Dutch education was dominated by the clergy, whereas today you would be hard-pressed to find a cleric teacher. It is not difficult to notice the disappearance of the clergy from schools, nor the change in the use of buildings. But what has happened to the Church's received wisdom on education? What about the underlying structures and meanings?

It should come as no surprise that Roman Catholic educators have been responsible for some (or perhaps the greatest part) of the publications on language teaching, in primary education, at least in the first half of the twentieth century in the Netherlands (see Hagen & Vallen, 1974; 1976 for a review of the early literature on dialect, standard language and education and language teaching methodology). While their publications do not figure in the current debate, we can none the less learn a great deal by looking carefully at their ideas.

Preachers of culture and status quo

It seems reasonable to suggest that writers on dialect belong to various 'paradigmatic communities' (cf. Ball & Lacey, 1980; Tuthill & Ashton, 1983) characterised by their own social construction of educational reality. Indeed, Hagen & Vallen differentiate varying attitudes to the question of dialect in the writers whose work they review. They do not, however, explore why these authors should differ in their opinion. I am well aware that the researcher who asks questions of this nature is engaging in speculation and that there is no received, more or less mechanical procedure for checking the results. To reiterate Raymond's (1982: 781) observation, social science methodology — unlike the humanities — excludes 'questions about human values, ethics, aesthetics, meaning, politics, justice, and causality involving an indeterminate number of variables'. It would therefore seem that a humanities approach can, at least, very usefully complement a social science approach. It is possible to argue that when educational researchers are dealing with questions which the social sciences, by definition, cannot resolve, they have a responsibility to employ the methods of the humanities.

The humanities approach is not, of course, without problems of its own. As the Rockefeller Foundation's specially appointed Commission on the Humanities points out, 'Humanists seem unable to tell each other, and much less other people, how they do what they do and how their methods relate to methods in other fields' (cited by Raymond, 1982: 783). This does not mean that we are doomed to wait for a more explicit methodology to be developed within the humanities before we can proceed: there seems to be no urgent reason to stop the study of Shakespeare, even though, from a social science perspective, this field of study seems to suffer from methodological weaknesses. The only logical conclusion is that it would be both irresponsible and unnecessarily limiting to restrict ourselves to a single methodology in educational research.

It is interesting that in the literature reviewed by Hagen & Vallen, the handbook highlighted as the most sympathetic to dialect in an educational context (Evers & Van Gelder, 1962) was co-authored by a well-known Dutch socialist writer. In contrast, the work felt to be least sympathetic to dialect was written by a Roman Catholic educationalist, Brother Van Nispen (1946). Such an observation, though not formulated explicitly by Hagen & Vallen, seems to me pertinent to any evaluation of the content of these books.

This can be illustrated by some quotations. Van Nispen, for instance, makes an ardent plea for teachers 'to carry the children of the people from the lowlands of the colloquial vernacular [i.e. dialect] into the highlands of the normal daily speech [i.e. standard Dutch]'. This exodus from the lowlands to the highlands 'holds out to our pupils, including the children of the people, prospects of social advancement, and, in particular, gives them a sharper eye on their supermundane destination'. In other words, standard language teaching opens up the Porta Caeli. Conversely, Evers & Van Gelder remark: 'A teacher who has sufficient knowledge of the vernacular should not fail to turn that to advantage by allowing children to talk etc. in their own language occasionally. This will greatly stimulate the pupils' interest in language use'.

To understand any perspective on language education — which does not imply that one agrees with or legitimates it — the researcher needs an in-depth knowledge of the community, its values and norms and how these are legitimated. In other words, one has to reconstruct for a specific period the arena in which the fight takes place in order to arrive at several valid answers — dominant or alternative — to the question: what counts as

mother tongue education for whom? Only within such an arena — an
interpretative framework, to use a less literary metaphor — is it possible to
understand, for instance, why 'democratisation' is a rather pejorative notion
in the eyes of Van Nispen, whereas 'élite' is not. Only within such an
interpretative framework is it possible to understand his rather ambivalent
attitude towards dialect, folklore and the culture of the people.

Historical case-studies in mother tongue education of this kind not
only enlarge our knowledge, but also allow us to gain more experience in
applying research strategies from the humanities in the field of education:
to establish an interpretative educational research tradition. History seems
to me to be an ideal starting point, not unduly overshadowed by research
initiatives in the social sciences. Comparisons of such case studies can
probably contribute to a more general interpretative framework, allowing
us to understand both the received and alternative knowledge on mother
tongue education current in a specific period and the differences and
similarities in this knowledge from one period to another.

My interest in historical case studies is thus intimately tied up with my
interest in methodology. While I do not feel moved to engage here in a
fruitless debate on the relative merits of qualitative versus quantitative
research paradigms, it would none the less seem useful to argue that those
researchers in the field of mother tongue education who have an arts
background might be well-disposed towards developing this expertise in
designing and conducting their research. Yet my own experience, borne out
by many colleagues in educational research with whom I have discussed this
matter, is that anyone who dares to take this course does so on pain of
being excluded from 'the scientific community'. It seems to me that we need
to pursue this course, come what may.

Disguising Society's Problems

The social context of multicultural education

I have something else on my mind, too. Returning for a third time to
the November conference that I started with, I will try to explain what this
is. The conference was devoted to a Dutch curriculum project called LEGIO
(Dutch for *legion*) which presumably is intended to evoke the Bible
quotation: 'Their name was Legion'. LEGIO is actually a Dutch acronym
which stands for 'Curriculum Development for Ethnic Groups in Education'.
For the sake of clarity, this complex task was divided into four different
areas:

— multicultural education
— maternal language/culture instruction as part of the curriculum
— teaching Dutch as a second language
— educational priority policy

Everyone familiar with the recent international debate on multicultural education will be aware of the burning question of the agenda for educational and research priorities in this field. Once more, I do not intend to report on the conference. I shall confine myself instead to two observations.

First, while preparing for the conference, my attention was drawn to a brand new publication which was relevant to the topic — John Edwards' (1986) book on *Language, Society and Identity*. I bought the book immediately but did not have time to read it until I went to King's Court. I leafed through its pages as I travelled on the train and one particular sentence fixed itself in my mind. 'We might want to opt, for present purposes', Edwards writes, 'for a scenario in which the overall social context is perforce larger than any of its constituent parts, language included'. In qualifying this statement, Edwards calls it a 'simple observation'.

Now that I have read most parts of the book thoroughly, I think that simple observation can be interpreted as the thread of the whole. I would like to apply this same observation to my own experience. I started as an optimistic, sociolinguistically inspired teacher trainer and researcher in the 1960s who was pleasantly surprised by the discovery that all languages are equal, at least as a cognitive instrument, and that consequently there must be a logical and scientific way to reform language instruction so as to remove the so-called disadvantage of low-status speakers. It has been a rather long and painful process to admit that our social construction of reality, at least for the time being, merely allows for the slightly different conclusion that 'only for God and the linguist are all languages equal' (Mackey, 1978: 7, quoted in Edwards, 1986: 124). I am afraid that I overlooked for a considerable period of time Bernstein's (1970) admonition that education cannot compensate for society. I am forced now to concede, however, that this observation applies as much to progressive as to traditional education and as much to educational practice based on research as to practice based on common sense.

Plus ça change . . .

Edwards' observation seems simple enough. Perhaps that is why, as a participant in that November conference, I had a strong feeling of *déjà vu*. This is the second of my observations about that conference. As I have already mentioned, the organising committee's first activity in the early 1970s was the organisation of a series of sessions on school and dialect. Although the language of immigrant children formed part of those discussions, the main emphasis was on Dutch dialect-speaking pupils.

In the 1970s the agenda comprised:

— the lore and language of children speaking urban and regional dialects (instead of multicultural education)
— the dialect as a language of instruction (instead of bilingual education)
— teaching the standard language (instead of Dutch as a second language)
— compensatory education (instead of educational priority policy)

I suppose that a naive participant at the 1986 conference might have concluded that the problem of dialect and education has been resolved in the Netherlands and that we now only have to worry about the problems of ethnic groups in education.

Actually, I think the opposite is true. It seems to me that an educational problem which, as Grace (1978), Mathieson (1975) and others have shown, has existed for a considerable period of time, has simply reappeared in another guise. For this reason, I have no alternative but to agree with the rather discouraging conclusion to Hagen's (1981) doctoral thesis: 'The most important benefit of the linguistic contribution to the disadvantage research seems to be alerting people to the nature of dialect and the role of dialect speaking as related to that problem'. But who is alerted? And more importantly, who is not alerted? And why not? If I take a pessimistic view, I have to concede that the only people who are alerted are God and sociolinguists.

Hagen goes on to say that a knowledge of linguistics can help bring about more positive attitudes towards dialect speakers. This also raises intractable problems. Attitudes are not tangible things which can be seen and easily measured. How do we go about comparing those attitudes previously held and those now current? Hagen's benefit depends on the belief, as formulated by Münstermann (this volume, chapter 10), 'that whatever approach one supports in trying to solve the problems regarding dialect and school, a positive attitude towards the home language of the pupils is a necessary condition for success'.

A need for understanding

To be more concrete: throughout its history, language teaching has been constantly influenced, on the one hand, by the needs of the overall social context (e.g. counteracting anarchy by literacy; cancelling technological inferiority by compensatory programmes; preventing social fragmentation by cultural integration) and, on the other hand, by educational beliefs (e.g. personal growth, equality, identity).

In my opinion, educational research and, by implication, research into dialect and school, are situated in the area of tension between social needs and educational beliefs. This is why I am advocating a more interpretative approach in this area. It is extremely difficult to explore educational beliefs using social science research methods alone, and the time is ripe for exploring the possibilities of empirical-interpretative approaches to research, such as are found in the ethnography of schooling (cf. Hammersley & Atkinson, 1983), a discipline which draws on the traditions of the humanities.

I would not wish to suggest that an empirical-interpretative approach will necessarily yield solutions for the problems of language variation and schooling. As far as I can see, its main value lies in providing the teachers and researchers involved with a touchstone or a mirror artfully cut, by means of which they can become aware of their deeply rooted ideas on mother tongue education and the relation between what happens — in the classroom, at universities, in parliaments and in ministries — and those ideas.

Despite a rather extensive body of 'knowledge about' produced in the social sciences tradition and a great many innovations in language curricula based on that 'knowledge about', there seems to be little hope that the socially divisive nature of education can be changed for the benefit of the children who for many years now have been recognised as its victims. Though they are labelled differently in different times, they belong to the same groups: working class children, disadvantaged students, minority students (cf. Hagen, 1981, for a linguistic perspective; Erickson, 1985, for an educational perspective). It is not a question of allocating blame. Rather, we should be asking: what is happening in mother tongue education in real classrooms? How can we, teachers and researchers, come to an understanding of why education does not achieve what we think and expect it should achieve?

Conclusions

In my opinion, the main achievement of sociolinguistic research in the field of language and education has undoubtedly been the development of the linguistic-difference hypothesis. It has had the effect, at least on a rhetorical level, of protecting (mother tongue) education against the damaging influence of the genetic and social deficit hypotheses. The research which allowed us to arrive at this position was undertaken within the mainstream perspective on research in teaching: in other words, it drew on a social science approach. As persuasion is a very important part of scholarly and/ or scientific discussions, it was obviously necessary to fight fire with fire.

Gradually, however, I have come to realise that the dichotomy between deficit and difference appears to be false. It now seems to me that the ideological roots of the deficit and difference positions are identical in their essential parts. Both hypotheses take the dominant norms and values for granted and assume that these norms and values are fixed. The social inequality which results can only be surmounted, in both views, through individual adjustment. The views only differ in the way the problem is tackled in an educational setting (cf. Sturm, 1984a). One can develop as many curricula based on sociolinguistic research as one likes. They will not, however, have any effect at all unless teachers' attitudes change.

My own recent research on teacher interpretations of mother tongue education suggests that our knowledge of this area is very incomplete. For this reason, I have become increasingly pessimistic about prospects for change. As a result, I feel that I have finally arrived at a somewhat less pretentious position. I believe that teachers and researchers must work collaboratively to explore and understand their social construction of reality by examining classroom practice as it relates to language and language teaching. To work in this way, we need to draw on the skills of observation, comparison, contrast and reflection, which we all possess. The researcher's task is to facilitate an awareness of the potential for using these everyday skills in a more systematic and deliberate way. In my opinion, the humanities offer an exciting body of expertise, accessible to researchers and teachers alike (cf., for instance, Groundwater-Smith, 1984; Schostak, 1985). The sociolinguist who comes from an arts background would seem to be an ideal person for working in this way.

Unless teachers and researchers understand their perspectives on language in education, there can be no end to the old debate. Even so, understanding one's own perspectives offers no guarantees of solutions to the problems that underlie that debate.

Acknowledgement

My heartfelt personal thanks go to Viv Edwards for her empathy and unfailing efforts in substantially revising various drafts of this chapter. I think she has made my chapter — originally written in 'Dutch-English' and from a particular epistemological perspective — accessible for an English speaking audience accustomed to another scientific register. Nevertheless, imperfections in grammar and sense are due to my obstinacy in insisting on a wording that, while clear to me, may not be the best. Perhaps Feyerabend's observation holds true in one way or another. In this case: 'Languages and the reaction patterns they involve are not merely instruments for *describing* events (facts, states of affairs) . . . their 'grammar' contains a cosmology, a comprehensive view of the world, of society, of the situation of man, which influences thought, behaviour, perceptions'.

Notes to Chapter 20

1. The research project referred to is reported mainly in Dutch. However, for English papers from the project, see Sturm, 1984b; 1987; and Kroon & Sturm, 1987.

Bibliography

ALATIS, J. (ed.) 1978 *Georgetown University Round Table on Language and Linguistics*. Washington DC: Georgetown University Press.
BALL, S.J. and LACEY, C. 1980 Subject disciplines as the opportunity for group action: a measured critique of subject sub-cultures. In P. WOODS (ed.), *Teachers' Strategies*. London: Croom Helm. pp. 149–77.
BERNSTEIN, B., 1970 Education cannot compensate for society. *New Society* (26/2/1970), no. 8, 64–69. (Also in: COSIN *et al.* 1977).
COSIN, B.R. *et al.* (eds) 1977 *School and Society; A Sociological Reader* (2nd edn). London: Routledge & Kegan Paul.
DEPREZ, K. (ed.) 1984 *Sociolinguistics in the Low Countries*. Amsterdam/Philadelphia: Benjamins.
EDWARDS, J. 1986 *Language, Society and Identity*. Oxford: Blackwell.
ERICKSON, F. 1985 *Qualitative Methods in Research on Teaching*. East Lansing: IRT. (Also in WITTROCK 1986, 119–61).
EVERS, F. and VAN GELDER, L. 1962 *Nederlandse Taal: Didactische aanwijzingen vor het lager onderwijs*. Groningen: Wolters-Noordhoff.
FEYERABEND, P. 1975 *Against Method*. London: New Left Books.
GRACE, G. 1978 *Teachers, Ideology and Control; A Study in Urban Education*. London: Routledge & Kegan Paul.
GROUNDWATER-SMITH, J.S. 1984 The portrayal of schooling and the literature of fact. *Curriculum Perspectives* 4, no. 2, 1–6.
HAGEN, A.M. 1981 *Standaardtaal en dialectsprekende kinderen; een studie over monitoring van taalgebruik*. Muiderberg: Coutinho.
HAGEN, A. and VALLEN, T. 1974 Dialect, standaardtaal en school; de Nederlandse literatuur van heemtaalkunde tot sociolinguïstiek. *Mededelingen NCDN* 13, 14–44.
——1976 Dialect, standaardtaal en school; de Nederlandse literatuur van

heemtaalkunde tot sociolinguïstiek. II (Taal-)didactische literatuur. *Mededelingen NCDN* 15, 41–65.

HALSEY, A. 1975 Sociology and the Equality Debate. *Oxford Review of Education* 1 (1), 19–23.

HAMMERSLEY, M. and ATKINSON, P. 1983 *Ethnography; Principles in Practice.* London/New York: Tavistock.

HERRLITZ, W. *et al.* (eds) 1984 *Mother Tongue Education in Europe; a Survey of Standard Language Teaching in Nine European Countries.* Enschede: SLO.

KROON, S. and STURM, J. 1987 Understanding teaching the mother tongue: explorations in historical and international comparisons. In G. GAGNE *et al.* (eds), *Selected Papers in Mother Tongue Education.* Dordrecht: Foris. pp. 111–24.

MACKEY, W. 1978 The importation of bilingual education models. In J. ALATIS (ed.), *Georgetown University Roundtable on Language and Linguistics.* Washington, DC: Georgetown University Press.

MATHIESON, M. 1975 *The Preachers of Culture: a Study of English and its Teachers.* London: Allen & Unwin.

NISPEN, V. VAN 1946 *Verkenningen op het gebied van taal en taalonderwijs.* Tilburg: R.K. Jongensweeshuis.

PLUMMER, K. 1983 *Documents of Life: An Introduction to the Problems and Literature of a Humanistic Method.* London: Allen & Unwin.

RAYMOND, J.C. 1982 Rhetoric: The methodology of the humanities, *College English* 44, no. 8, 778–83.

SCHOSTAK, J.F. 1985 Creating the narrative case record. *Curriculum Perspectives* 5, no. 1, 7–13.

STURM, J. 1984a Deficit and difference: a false dichotomy in educational perspective. In K. DEPREZ (ed.), *Sociolinguistics in the Low Countries.* Amsterdam/Philadelphia: Benjamins. pp. 193–209.

——1984b Report on the development of mother tongue education in the Netherlands since 1969. In W. HERRLITZ *et al.* (eds), *Mother Tongue Education in Europe.* Enschede: SLO. pp. 238–75.

——1987 The challenge of comparative research in mother tongue education as a school subject: What can be learnt from the debate on methodology? In S. KROON & J. STURM (eds), *Research on Mother Tongue Education in an International Perspective.* Enschede: VALO-M, pp. 111–21.

TUTHILL, D. and ASHTON, P. 1983 Improving educational research through the development of educational paradigms. *Educational Researcher* 12, no. 10, 6–14.

WALKER, R. 1983 Three good reasons for not doing case studies in curriculum research, *Journal of Curriculum Studies* (15) 2, 155–65.

WITTROCK, M.C. (ed.) 1986 *Handbook of Research on Teaching* (3rd ed.). New York: Macmillan.

21 Dialect and education in Europe: A postscript

VIV EDWARDS

A close examination of European initiatives in the sphere of language teaching in the 1970s and 1980s reveals a great deal of activity. Much of this activity was inspired by the 'difference hypothesis' which argued that, while there were clearly *social* differences between language varieties, no one language or dialect was linguistically superior to another. There were, for instance, serious attempts to establish the extent to which language variety was correlated with educational achievement (cf. Stijnen & Vallen; Weltens & Sonderen; and Ammon, this volume). However, whereas previous discussions had centred on the inadequacy of the dialect in educational settings, such assumptions rarely informed this new research tradition. There were also notable efforts to integrate the insights gained from both the ideological stance associated with the difference hypothesis and empirical research into practical courses of action in the classroom (cf. Van de Craen & Humblet, Van den Hoogen & Kuijper; Giesbers *et al.*; Van Calcar *et al.*, this volume).

New Pedagogies

One of the most important conclusions to emerge from this research is the need for information. The co-existence of standard and dialect grammar is now widely recognised as giving rise to problems in education systems which are predicated on the use of the standard language, and the burden of coping with these problems is usually assigned to teachers. However, it is both unfair and unrealistic to expect teachers to develop appropriate strategies and pedagogies in the absence of adequate and accessible descriptions of the dialect. Continental European researchers have made considerably more progress in this sphere than their British counterparts. German teachers, for instance, are able to consult booklets which present the main areas of difference between the standard and the dialect, at least for some areas of their countries (cf. Ammon, this volume).

The question remains, however, as to how we use this information even when it is available. Several trends emerge from the work included in this volume. There has been a marked move throughout Europe from more traditional language teaching pedagogy with its heavy reliance on drills to more communicative teaching techniques: learning language by using language, especially using a thematic approach (see, for example, Van den Hoogen & Kuijper; Van Calcar *et al.*, this volume). Some researchers none the less still feel the need for a more structured approach to language teaching, particularly with older children (cf. Van den Hoogen & Kuijper, this volume). It is noteworthy, however, that teaching of this kind is now far more likely to take place within an overall approach which also emphasises communicative teaching techniques.

There has also been a marked movement towards using dialect in the classroom (Edwards, 1983; Jones; Van den Hoogen & Kuijper; Giesbers *et al.*, this volume). There are various reasons for this development. The move to a child-centred philosophy of education has predisposed teachers to an approach which builds on, rather than rejects, existing knowledge. The use of dialect in the classroom can be seen as a transitional prop in the acquisition of the standard, which remains none the less the primary educational target. The emphasis has therefore changed from exclusive attention on the standard language to viewing the standard as part of a much larger linguistic repertoire (cf. Rampton, 1981).

The observation that children participate more actively in classrooms where the use of dialect is encouraged (Van den Hoogen & Kuijper, this volume) would certainly lend support to the potential of this approach, though the inherent difficulties should not be minimised. The introduction of relatively low status varieties into domains where the standard has previously been the sole medium of instruction is an extremely complex issue. Both teachers and children can feel embarrassed by the use of dialect in school. And, in cases where the teacher does not speak the non-standard variety, there is a need for extreme sensitivity. The use of British Black English or Patois is a case in point. Given that this variety, like many non-standard dialects, is often used as a language of resistance, attempts to introduce it into the classroom may be interpreted as an attempt to defend the 'legitimate' culture of the school against the 'heretical' culture of black people. It has been argued by writers like Carby (1980) and Stone (1981) that such attempts will simply result in the development of new forms of Patois which serve the same functions as the present forms.

There is an urgent need for research into innovations such as these to evaluate their effectiveness. It also remains to be seen whether strategies which appear to be successful in one linguistic situation can be successfully transferred to others.

New Populations

One of the more significant developments across Europe in the last few decades has been the settlement of immigrant or migrant worker populations. It is interesting to note the ways in which it has gradually been acknowledged that, while details of each case are different, the problems faced by the bilingual children of immigrants and dialect-speaking indigenous children are essentially the same (Edwards, 1983; Giesbers et al., Sturm, this volume). One of the more depressing conclusions which faces any researcher in the field of language and education is the lack of progress which has been made. It is certainly not the case that the earlier problems of dialect-speaking children have been resolved and that the solutions can now be applied to the very similar situation confronting bilingual children. On a more optimistic note, however, the renewed attention to this area has had the effect of rejuvenating many of the old debates and focussing attention more keenly on helpful strategies and approaches.

One recent innovation which owes its existence, in part at least, to the presence of ethnic minority children in school is 'Language Awareness' (Doughty et al., 1971; Raleigh, 1980; Hawkins, 1984; Jones; Giesbers et al.; Van den Hoogen & Kuijper; Van Calcar et al., this volume). Exponents of Language Awareness suggest various different aims for work in this area, the most important of which, for the purposes of the present discussion, is to challenge linguistic prejudice towards minority and non-standard speakers. Linguistic diversity is viewed as a resource on which to build, rather than a problem to be overcome. The underlying philosophy is that all children are likely to gain in understanding by exploring — and sharing — their own language use. Many myths and stereotypes about language gain ground, in school and elsewhere, either as a result of overt statements or because of more subtle errors of omission. Language Awareness provides opportunities for exploring and challenging linguistic prejudice. Although it is unlikely to substantially change the racist (and classist) realities of society as a whole, it can be seen as a useful element in attempts to promote anti-racist and intercultural teaching.

Ways Forward

The problems of language and education are now well-known. Solutions to these problems are less clear cut, however, and the need for research would seem to be just as urgent today as it was when attention was first directed to this area in the 1960s and 1970s. Much of the research conducted in Europe and elsewhere during the 1970s and early 1980s drew on the insights of sociolinguistics, but it promised far more than we have been able to achieve. We are forced, therefore, to ask if we have actually been addressing ourselves to the right questions. Dialect speakers were identified as underachievers and their ultimate educational success was framed in terms of helping them to acquire the standard language. Although those who have tried to apply the insights of sociolinguistics have done so within the context of the 'linguistic difference' position, they have none the less accepted the need to teach the standard.

The aims of these researchers have, in one sense, been extremely realistic. The alternative — equality of non-standard and standard dialects within an educational setting (as articulated, for instance, in Trudgill, 1975) — is more properly an item on political agendas rather than pedagogical agendas and has no hope of acceptance in the foreseeable future. However, it can be argued that the various strategies that have been devised for teaching the standard — democratic or élitist — are no more realistic than calls for all language varieties to be given equal status in school. In spite of new sociolinguistically inspired attempts to help children acquire the standard language in Europe and beyond, we still await evidence of the efficacy of these approaches.

Are we to assume that, because of the prevailing power relationships, any attempts to teach the standard to non-standard speakers are doomed to failure? Whereas there is much to criticise in the earlier work of Bernstein, it is difficult to argue with his observation that education cannot compensate for society. But does this mean that linguists and educators of more liberal persuasion should therefore dissociate themselves from the field of language and education and devote their energies to less frustrating and more realistic lines of inquiry? The answer to this is, I hope, a most emphatic, 'No'.

Although it can be argued that the attempts to apply the insights of sociolinguistics to education have in many ways been naïve, we start today from a much firmer knowledge base. We understand the ways in which attitudes towards a language are generalised towards users of that language, and the gulf between the actual and the perceived communication skills of many groups of language users. We are also beginning to appreciate the nature of the linguistic differences between dialect and standard varieties (see Ammon, this volume, chapter 14 and Edwards & Cheshire, this volume, chapter 12), and to disseminate this information in a form accessible to teachers, speech therapists and the general public. We are also beginning to analyse the very considerable amount of stylistic variation that is part of everyday interaction in the classroom, for both teachers and pupils (see Van de Craen & Humblet, this volume, Chapter 2). We are turning our attention to the nature of the relationship between speech and writing and to the implications of this relationship for education (see Milroy & Milroy, 1985), as well as to the way in which dialect fits into this relationship (see Williams, this volume, Chapter 11). Prejudice and stereotypes may still prevail, but it is no longer possible to justify them, for instance, on genetic grounds, as has been the practice in the past.

Sociolinguists have acknowledged their responsibility to disseminate information about linguistic prejudice not only to teachers but, through teachers, to children. Some important developments in this direction have been taking place in the form of Language Awareness work. It is important to remember, however, that attitude change is a highly complex issue (see Münstermann, this volume) and ways must be found of monitoring and evaluating work in this area.

The social responsibility of linguists is as serious a concern today as ever, particularly in the light of recent political events. For instance, the Kingman Committee of Inquiry into the Teaching of English set up in the United Kingdom was chaired by a mathematician and included no linguists. One can be forgiven for fearing that unless the voice of linguists is heeded, the 'folk linguistics' seriously challenged by the last 30 years work in descriptive linguistics and sociolinguistics, will once again hold sway in educational circles. One continuing priority, then, has to be the continued dissemination of sociolinguistic research findings beyond the research community.

A further need is the development of ways of evaluating the effectiveness of different teaching and learning processes, and of the practical classroom initiatives that researchers and others have proposed. Many of the contributors to this volume stress the need to evaluate the results of their research; but as yet there is no effective methodology for doing so. Furthermore, language assessment procedures are often biased against dialect speakers, as Milroy & Milroy (1985) point out.

It would also be useful to extend research into dialect and education beyond a simplistic dialect–standard approach, to give greater emphasis to the nature of the spoken language of different groups in our society. Recent research shows the different types of verbal skills associated with different types of family backgrounds, and reveals sub-cultural differences in the organisation of topics in discourse (see, for example, Heath, 1983; Romaine, 1984; Michaels, 1981). The relationship between these matters and the acquisition of public, formal speech styles needs to be better understood, as well as their relation to the acquisition of literacy, and the extent to which such styles are used by speakers of dialect and standard varieties.

Finally, we need to extend the research paradigms that are used in this area of enquiry. Much of the research presented in this volume uses an experimental research design. There are problems in this approach to classroom research, however, not least of which is the number of variables that are involved. Age, sex, social class, language background, teaching style are just some of the variables which need to be taken into account. Given the relatively small numbers of children in any classroom, there will always be difficulty with experimental research designs.

There is a growing move towards more observational studies, particularly those which build on the insights of both teachers and pupils in a kind of triangulation exercise with the researcher (see, for instance, Erickson, 1986; Sturm, this volume). Such research is inevitably hypothesis generating rather than hypothesis testing. Its promise lies in its potential for making the dimensions of any problem much clearer and better defined. It moves away from the situation in which researchers, often external to the problem being studied, impose their own perception of what the problem may be. Of course, illuminative studies of this kind do not necessarily yield ready solutions, but they none the less have much to recommend them.

The development of more ethnographic or qualitative approaches to classroom research has the advantage of throwing new light on old problems and, even if it is no more successful in producing solutions for the problems of linguistically and socially stratified societies than the other approaches that have been used so far, it may well result in new lines of inquiry. Certainly the greater the number of different approaches that are used, the more likely we are to find solutions to the problems that dialect speakers continue to face in our schools today.

The problem of language and social disadvantage is, of course a general societal problem, not just an educational problem; yet because of the function of education, the problem crystallises in the schools. Society has given schools the responsibility of teaching the language skills that it considers to be necessary; we owe it to those schools and to the children who attend them to find out how best to do this.

References

CARBY, H., 1980 *Multicultural Fictions*. Occasional Stencilled Paper No. 58, Centre for Contemporary Cultural Studies, University of Birmingham.

DOUGHTY, P., PIERCE, J. and THORNTON, G. 1971 *Language in Use*. London: Edward Arnold for the Schools Council.

EDWARDS, V. 1983 *Language in Multicultural Classrooms*. London: Batsford.

ERICKSON, F. 1986 Qualitative Methods in Research on Teaching. In M.C. WITTROCK (ed.), *Handbook of Research on Teaching* (3rd edition). New York: Macmillan. pp. 119–61.

HAWKINS, E. 1984 *Awareness of Language*. Cambridge: Cambridge University Press.

HEATH, S.B. 1983 *Ways with Words*. Cambridge: Cambridge University Press.

MICHAELS, S. 1981 Sharing time: children's narrative styles and differential access to literacy. *Language in Society* 10, 423–43.

MILROY, J. and MILROY, L. 1985 *Authority in Language: Investigating Language Prescription and Standardization*. London: Routledge & Kegan Paul.

RALEIGH, M. 1980 *The Languages Book*. London: ILEA English Centre, Sutherland Street, London SW1.

RAMPTON, A. 1981 *West Indian Children in Our Schools*. (Interim Report of the Committee of Inquiry into the Education of Children from Ethnic Minority Groups). London: HMSO.

ROMAINE, S. 1984 *The Language of Children and Adolescents*. Oxford: Basil Blackwell.

STONE, M. 1981 *The Education of the Black Child in Britain: The Myth of Multiracial Education*. London: Fontana.

TRUDGILL, P. 1975 *Accent, Dialect and the School*. London: Edward Arnold.

List of contributors

ULRICH AMMON, University of Duisburg, Postfach 10 16 29, D-4100 Duisburg 1, Federal Republic of Germany.

JENNY CHESHIRE, Department of Applied Linguistics, Birkbeck College, University of London, 43 Gordon Square, London WC1H 0PD, UK.

COEN DE JONGE, Educational Counselling Centre Groningen, Ubbo Emmiussingel 59, Groningen, The Netherlands.

VIV EDWARDS, Department of Applied Linguistics, Birkbeck College, University of London, 43 Gordon Square, London WC1H 0PD, UK.

HERMAN GIESBERS, Institute for General Linguistics, University of Utrecht, Trans 10, 3512 JK Utrecht, The Netherlands.

ANTON HAGEN, Department of Dialectology, University of Nijmegen, Erasmusplein 1 , Nijemgen, The Netherlands.

BRIAN HOLLINGWORTH, Derby College of Higher Education, Mickleover, Derby DE3 5GX, UK.

ILSE HUMBLET, Department of Germanic Linguistics, Free University of Brussels, Pleinlaan 2, Brussels, Belgium.

NORMANN JØRGENSEN, Department of Danish Language and Literature, Royal Danish School of Educational Studies, Emdrupborg, Copenhagen, Denmark.

SJAAK KROON, Faculty of Letters, University of Brabant, PO Box 90153, 5000 LE Tilburg, The Netherlands.

HENK KUIJPER, National Institute for Educational Measurement (CITO), Nieuwe Oeverstraat 65, Arnhem, The Netherlands.

RUDI LIEBRAND, Kievitshof 94, 6662 ZS Elst, The Netherlands.

HENK MÜNSTERMANN, Department of Social Sciences, Open University, Valkenburgerweg 167, Heerlen, The Netherlands.

ANN PIERCE JONES, Department of Applied Linguistics, Birkbeck College, University of London, 43 Gordon Square, London WC1H 0PD, UK.

KAREN MARGRETHE PEDERSEN, Institute for Regional Studies, Persillegade 6, Aabenra, Denmark.

PETER ROSENBERG, Department of German, Free University of Berlin, Habelschwerdter Allee 45, Berlin, Federal Republic of Germany.

JOS SONDEREN, DUNO Comprehensive School, Cardanuslaan 18, Doorwerth, The Netherlands.

SJEF STIJNEN, Department of Social Sciences, Open University, Valkenburgerweg 167, Heerlen, The Netherlands.

JAN STURM, Department of Dutch, University of Nijmegen, Erasmusplein 1, Nijmegen, The Netherlands.

PETER TRUDGILL, Department of Language and Linguistics, University of Essex, Wivenhoe Park, Colchester CO4 3SQ, UK.

TON VALLEN, Department of Language and Literature, University of Brabant, PO Box 90153, Tilburg, The Netherlands.

WIM VAN CALCAR, Teacher Training College D'Witte Leli, Nieuwe Spiegelstraat 17, Amsterdam, The Netherlands.

PETE VAN DE CRAEN, Department of Germanic Linguistics, Free University of Brussels, Pleinlaan 2, Brussels, Belgium.

JOS VAN DEN HOOGEN, State School of Translation, Keizer Karelplein 19, Maastricht, The Netherlands.

BERT WELTENS, Department of Applied Linguistics and Research Methodology, University of Nijmegen, Erasmusplein 1, The Netherlands.

ANN WILLIAMS, Department of Applied Linguistics, Birkbeck College, University of London, 43 Gordon Square, London WC11 0PD, UK.

OMMO WILTS, Nordfriesische Wörterbuchstelle, Der Universität Kiel, 23 Kiel, Federal Republic of Germany.

Index

Note: Numbers in italics refer to tables and figures.